Your Lie in April

*I met the girl
under full-bloomed cherry blossoms,
and my fate has begun to change.*

8

Naoshi Arakawa

✲ STORY & CHARACTERS ✲

When his mother died in the autumn of his 12th year, piano prodigy Kōsei Arima lost his ability to play. Without a purpose, his days lost all color and continued on in a drab monotone. But the spring he was 14, he met the exceptionally quirky violinist Kaori Miyazono.

As he accompanied Kaori and played solo in a piano competition, Kōsei's days gradually filled with color. Then, Kaori was invited to play at the Tōwa Hall gala concert. Watari and the others rejoiced at the prospect of seeing the invincible duo, Kōsei & Kaori, back in action. But…the day of the concert, Kaori was nowhere to be seen!

Kōsei stepped onto the stage alone and began to play Love's Sorrow. In a world devoid of sound…Kōsei played the piece that was packed with memories of his mother. As he performed, the boy was filled with thoughts of the days when his mother loved him…memories connecting him to her. His mother's ghost was a shadow created by his own weakness…Kōsei accepted this fact and quietly brought his performance to a close.

✲ Kōsei Arima

An ex-piano prodigy who lost his ability to play when his mother died. He and Kaori were supposed to make a comeback together at the gala concert, but he ended up playing alone.

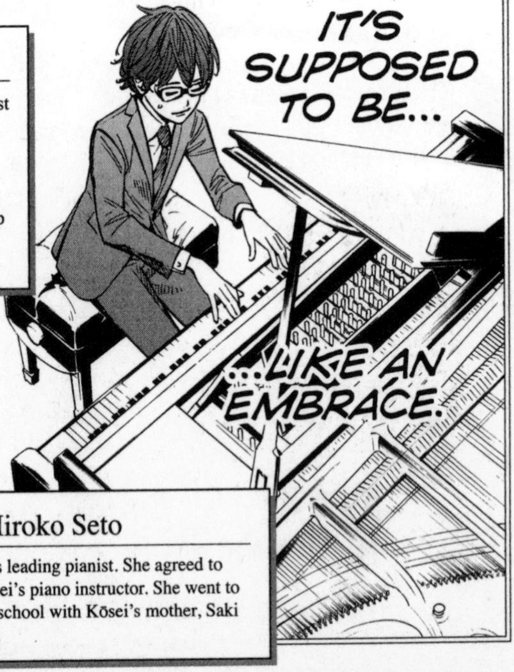
IT'S SUPPOSED TO BE...
...LIKE AN EMBRACE.

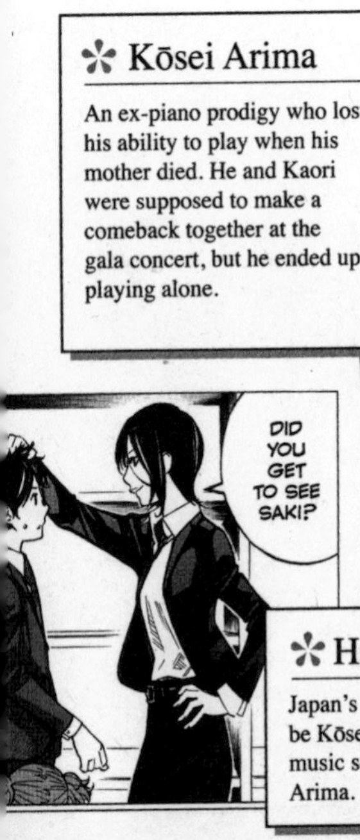
DID YOU GET TO SEE SAKI?

✲ Hiroko Seto

Japan's leading pianist. She agreed to be Kōsei's piano instructor. She went to music school with Kōsei's mother, Saki Arima.

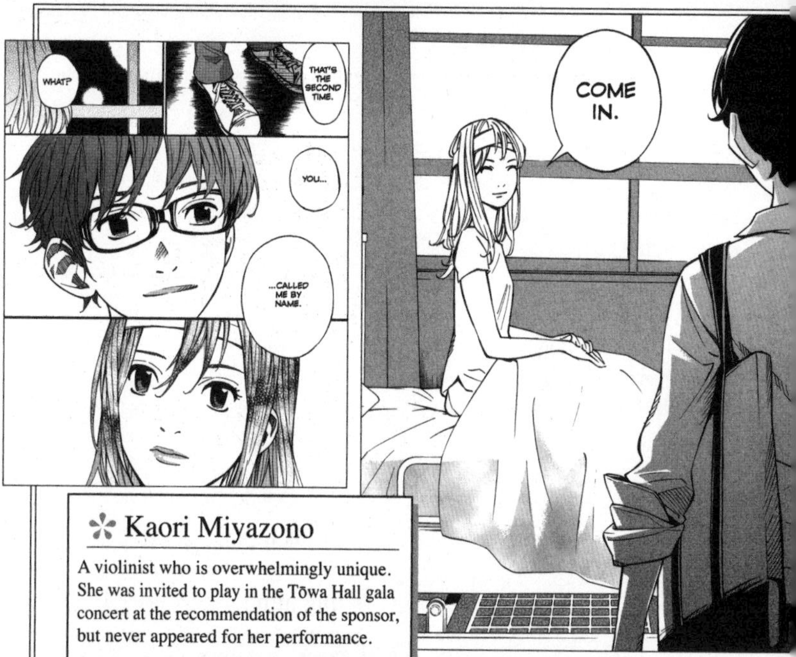
COME IN.
THAT'S THE SECOND TIME.
WHAT?
YOU...
...CALLED ME BY NAME.

Kaori Miyazono

A violinist who is overwhelmingly unique. She was invited to play in the Tōwa Hall gala concert at the recommendation of the sponsor, but never appeared for her performance.

Released from his mother's curse, Kōsei begins on his path as a pianist. Meanwhile, the girl who never appeared at the concert was in a hospital room. Having seen Kaori wrapped in bandages, Kōsei was reminded of his mother…and anxiety and uneasiness spread through his heart. Then…Tsubaki, who had been watching over Kōsei, realized how she truly feels about him.

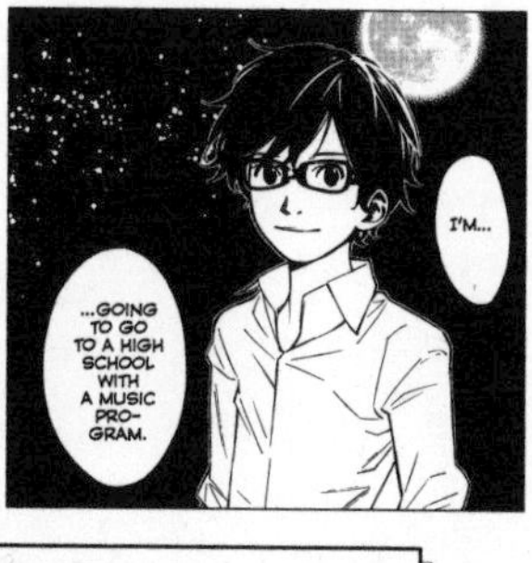
I'M...
...GOING TO GO TO A HIGH SCHOOL WITH A MUSIC PROGRAM.

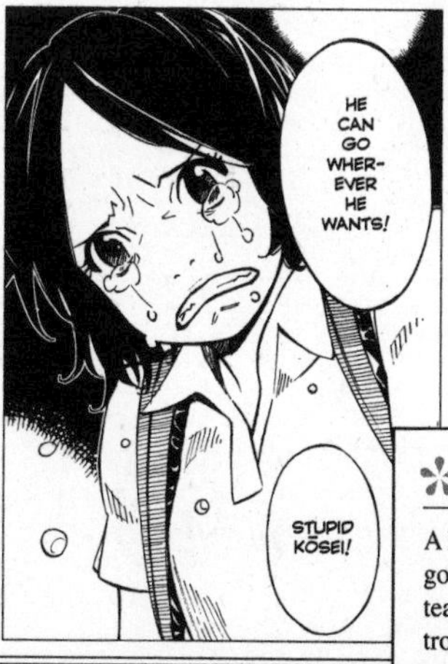
HE CAN GO WHEREVER HE WANTS!
STUPID KŌSEI!

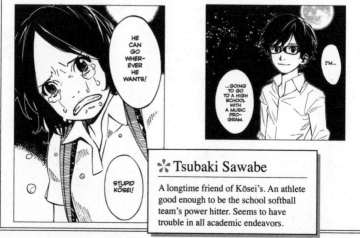

Tsubaki Sawabe

A longtime friend of Kōsei's. An athlete good enough to be the school softball team's power hitter. Seems to have trouble in all academic endeavors.

contents

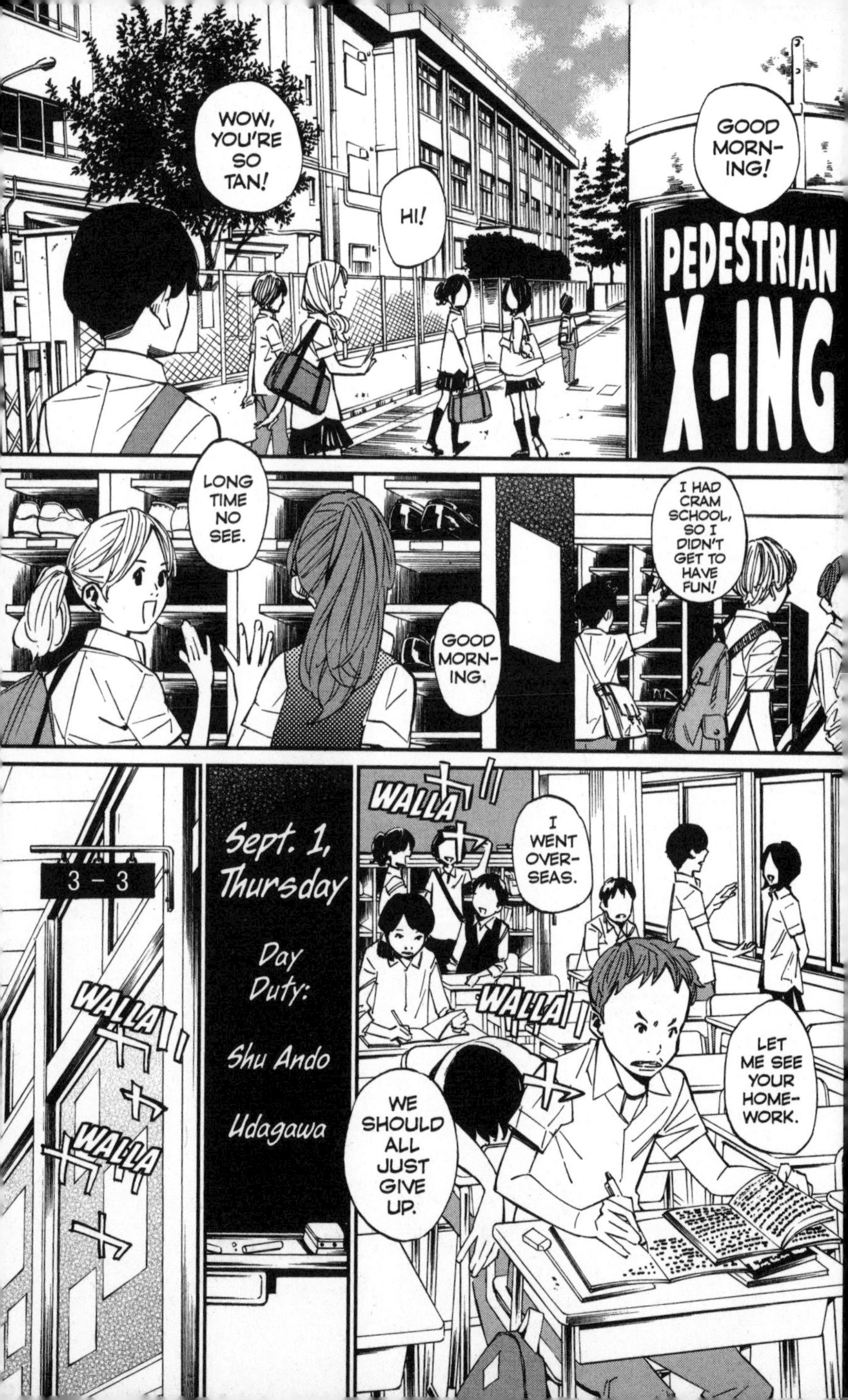
GOOD MORNING!
PEDESTRIAN X-ING
HI!
WOW, YOU'RE SO TAN!
I HAD CRAM SCHOOL, SO I DIDN'T GET TO HAVE FUN!
GOOD MORNING.
LONG TIME NO SEE.
WALLA
I WENT OVERSEAS.
WALLA
LET ME SEE YOUR HOMEWORK.
WE SHOULD ALL JUST GIVE UP.
Sept. 1, Thursday
Day Duty:
Shu Ando
Udagawa
3 - 3
WALLA
WALLA

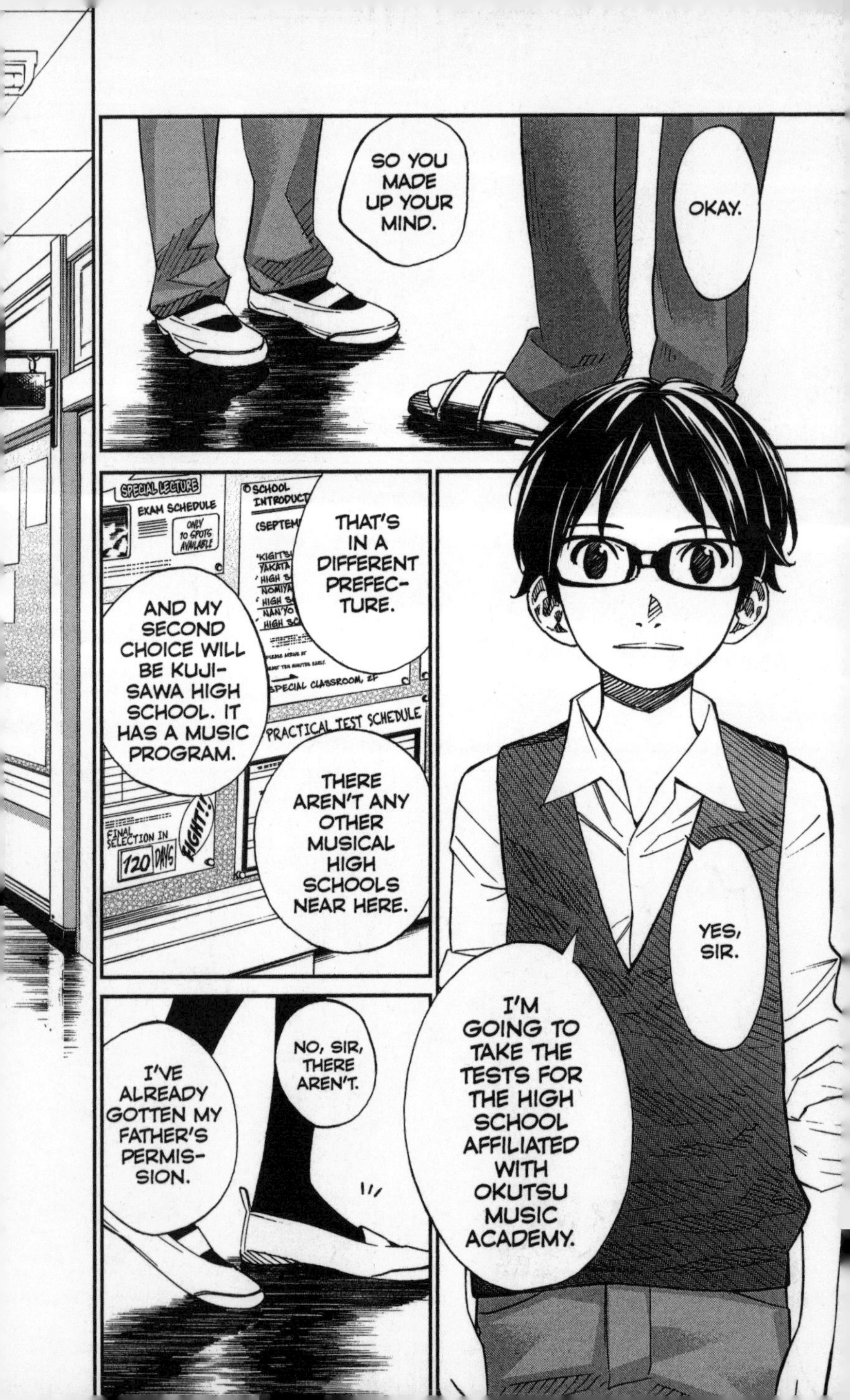
OKAY.
SO YOU MADE UP YOUR MIND.
YES, SIR.
I'M GOING TO TAKE THE TESTS FOR THE HIGH SCHOOL AFFILIATED WITH OKUTSU MUSIC ACADEMY.
SPECIAL LECTURE
EXAM SCHEDULE
ONLY 10 SPOTS AVAILABLE
THAT'S IN A DIFFERENT PREFECTURE.
AND MY SECOND CHOICE WILL BE KUJISAWA HIGH SCHOOL. IT HAS A MUSIC PROGRAM.
SPECIAL CLASSROOM, 2F
PRACTICAL TEST SCHEDULE
THERE AREN'T ANY OTHER MUSICAL HIGH SCHOOLS NEAR HERE.
FINAL SELECTION IN 120 DAYS
FIGHT!!
NO, SIR, THERE AREN'T.
I'VE ALREADY GOTTEN MY FATHER'S PERMISSION.

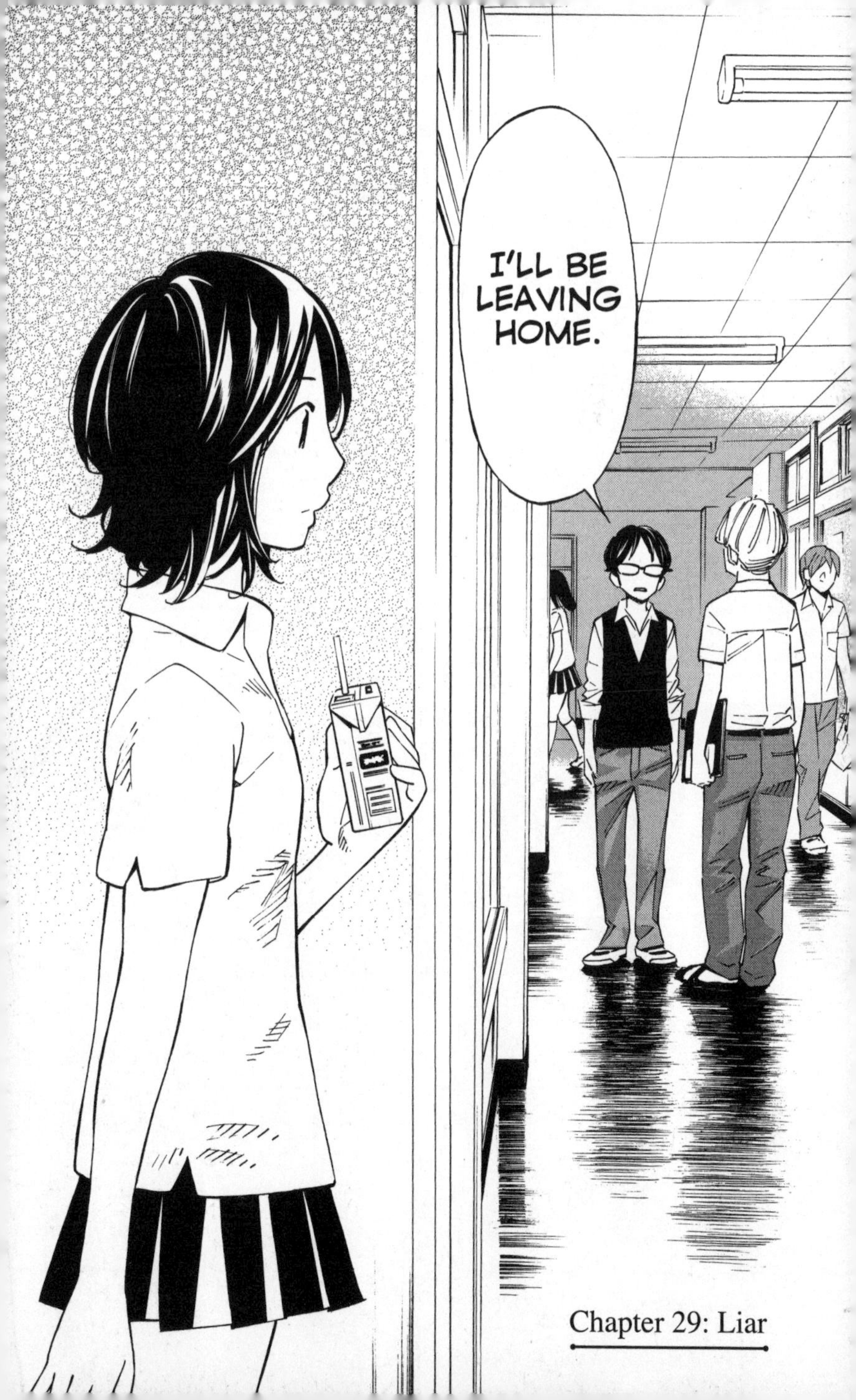
I'LL BE LEAVING HOME.
Chapter 29: Liar

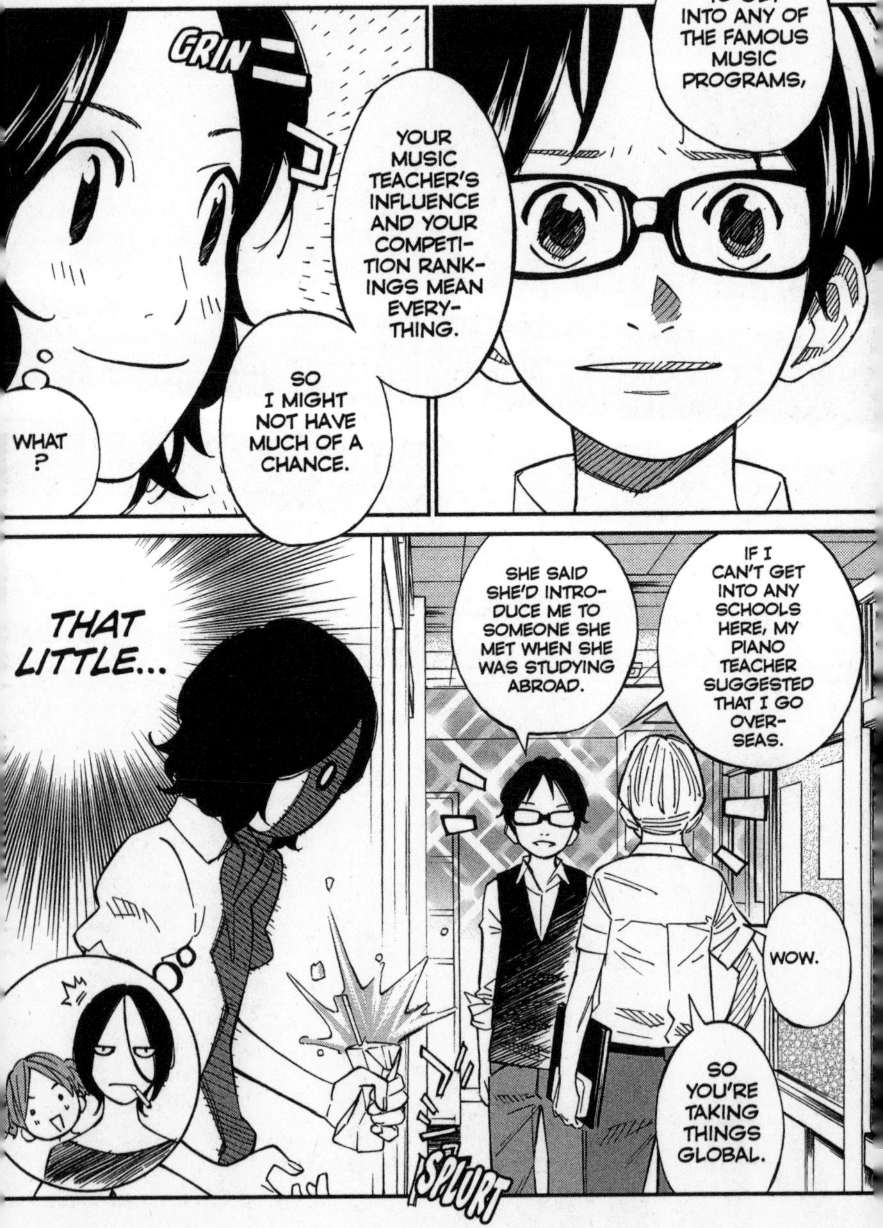
TO GET INTO ANY OF THE FAMOUS MUSIC PROGRAMS,
YOUR MUSIC TEACHER'S INFLUENCE AND YOUR COMPETITION RANKINGS MEAN EVERYTHING.
GRIN
SO I MIGHT NOT HAVE MUCH OF A CHANCE.
WHAT?
IF I CAN'T GET INTO ANY SCHOOLS HERE, MY PIANO TEACHER SUGGESTED THAT I GO OVERSEAS.
SHE SAID SHE'D INTRODUCE ME TO SOMEONE SHE MET WHEN SHE WAS STUDYING ABROAD.
WOW.
SO YOU'RE TAKING THINGS GLOBAL.
THAT LITTLE...
SPLURT

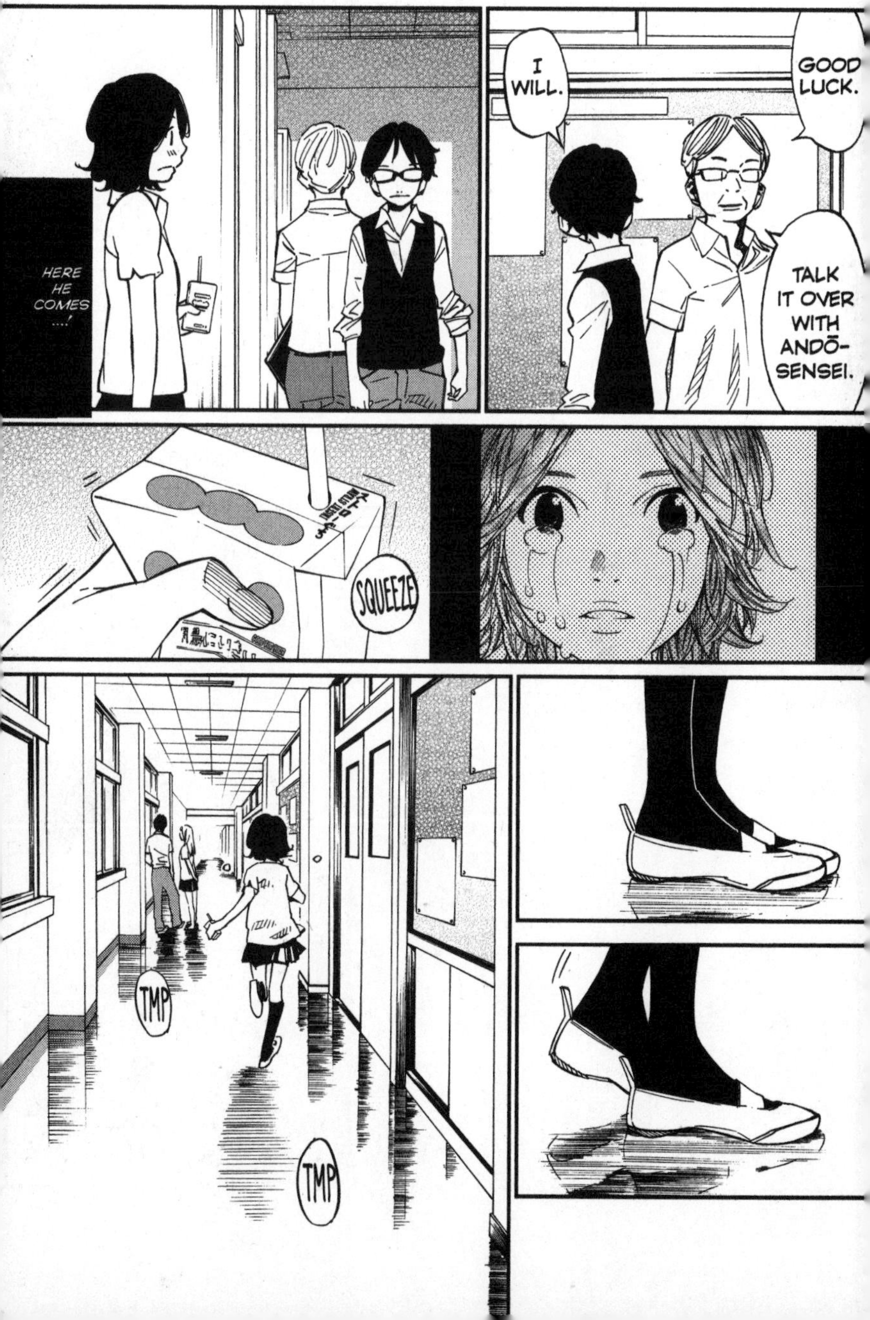
GOOD LUCK.
TALK IT OVER WITH ANDŌ-SENSEI.
I WILL.
HERE HE COMES ...!
SQUEEZE
TMP
TMP

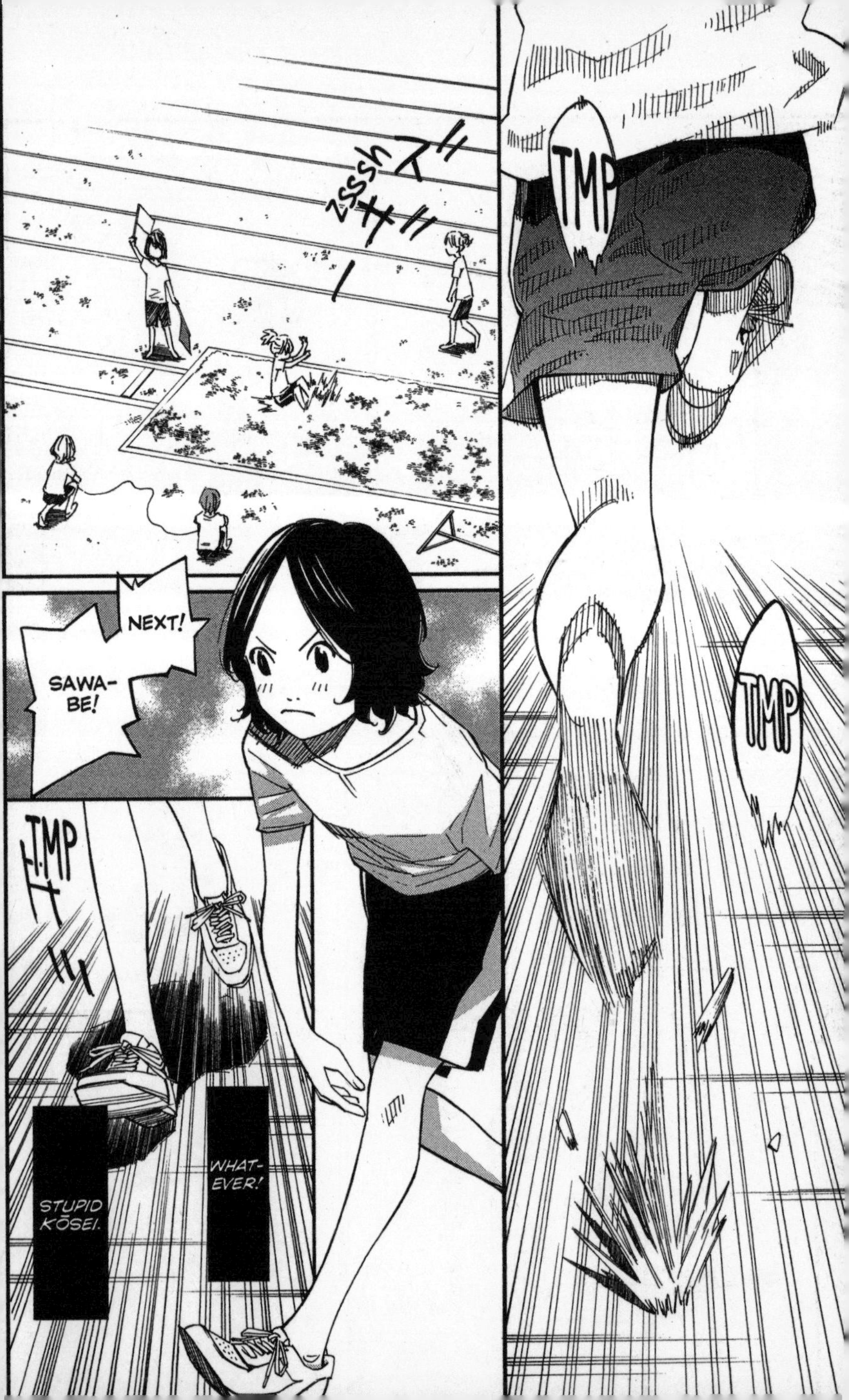
TMP
TMP
zsssh
NEXT!
SAWABE!
TMP
WHAT-EVER!
STUPID KŌSEI.

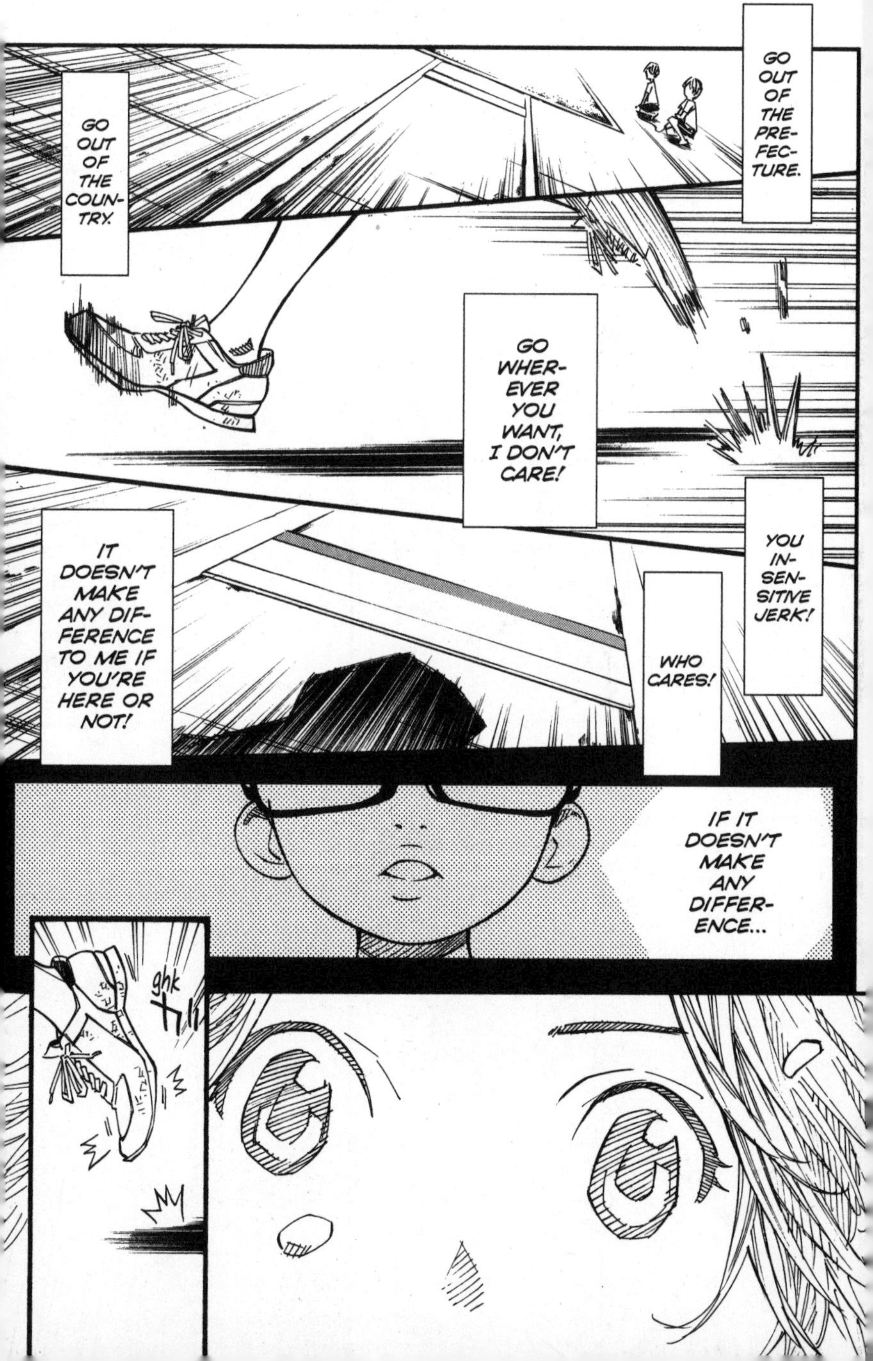
GO OUT OF THE PREFECTURE.
GO OUT OF THE COUNTRY.
GO WHEREVER YOU WANT, I DON'T CARE!
YOU INSENSITIVE JERK!
WHO CARES!
IT DOESN'T MAKE ANY DIFFERENCE TO ME IF YOU'RE HERE OR NOT!
IF IT DOESN'T MAKE ANY DIFFERENCE...
ghk

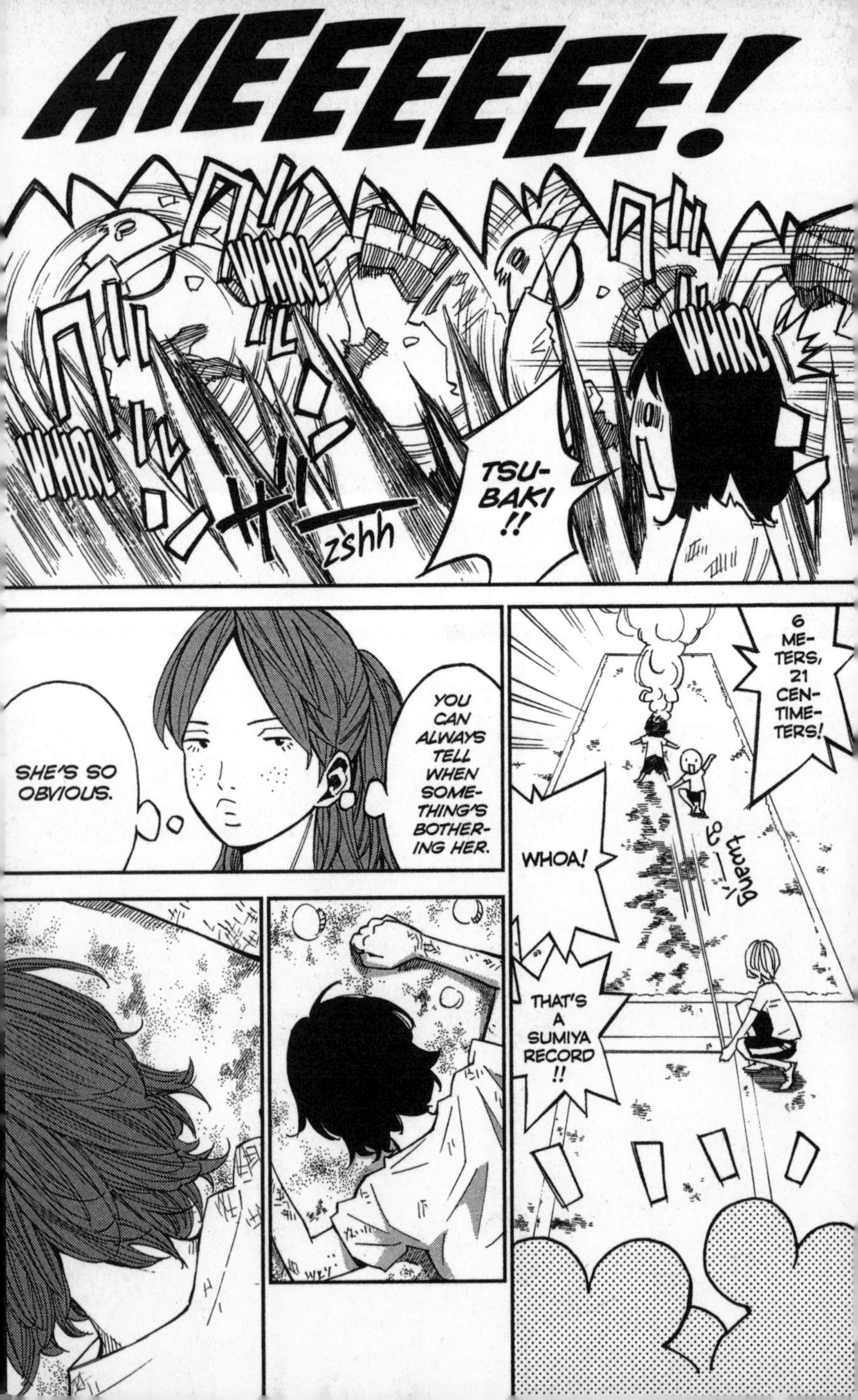
AIEEEEEE!
WHIRL
WHIRL
WHIRL
TSU-BAKI!!
zshh
6 METERS, 21 CENTIMETERS!
WHOA!
twang
THAT'S A SUMIYA RECORD!!
YOU CAN ALWAYS TELL WHEN SOMETHING'S BOTHERING HER.
SHE'S SO OBVIOUS.

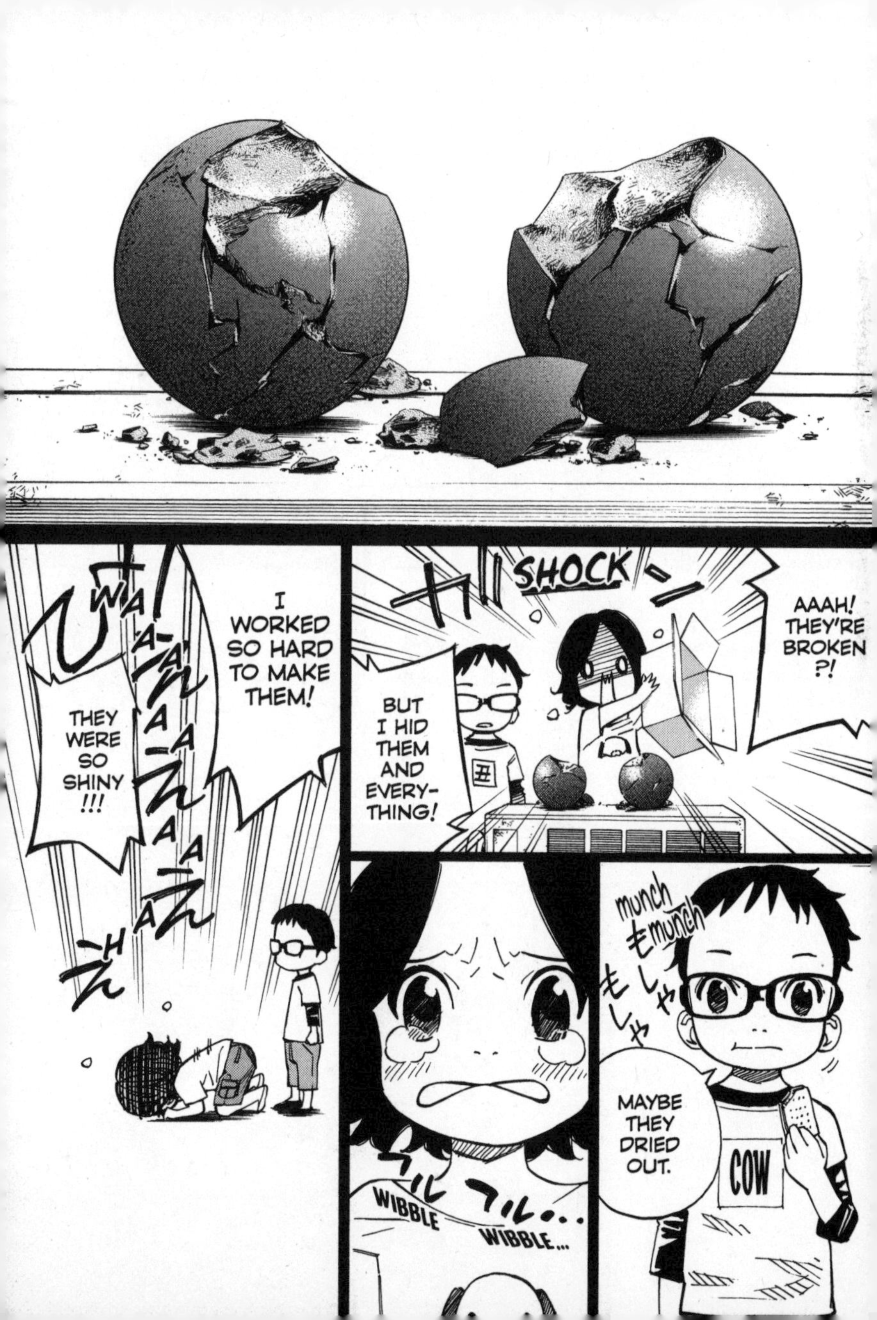
SHOCK
AAAH! THEY'RE BROKEN ?!
BUT I HID THEM AND EVERY-THING!
munch munch
MAYBE THEY DRIED OUT.
COW
WIBBLE WIBBLE...
I WORKED SO HARD TO MAKE THEM!
THEY WERE SO SHINY !!!

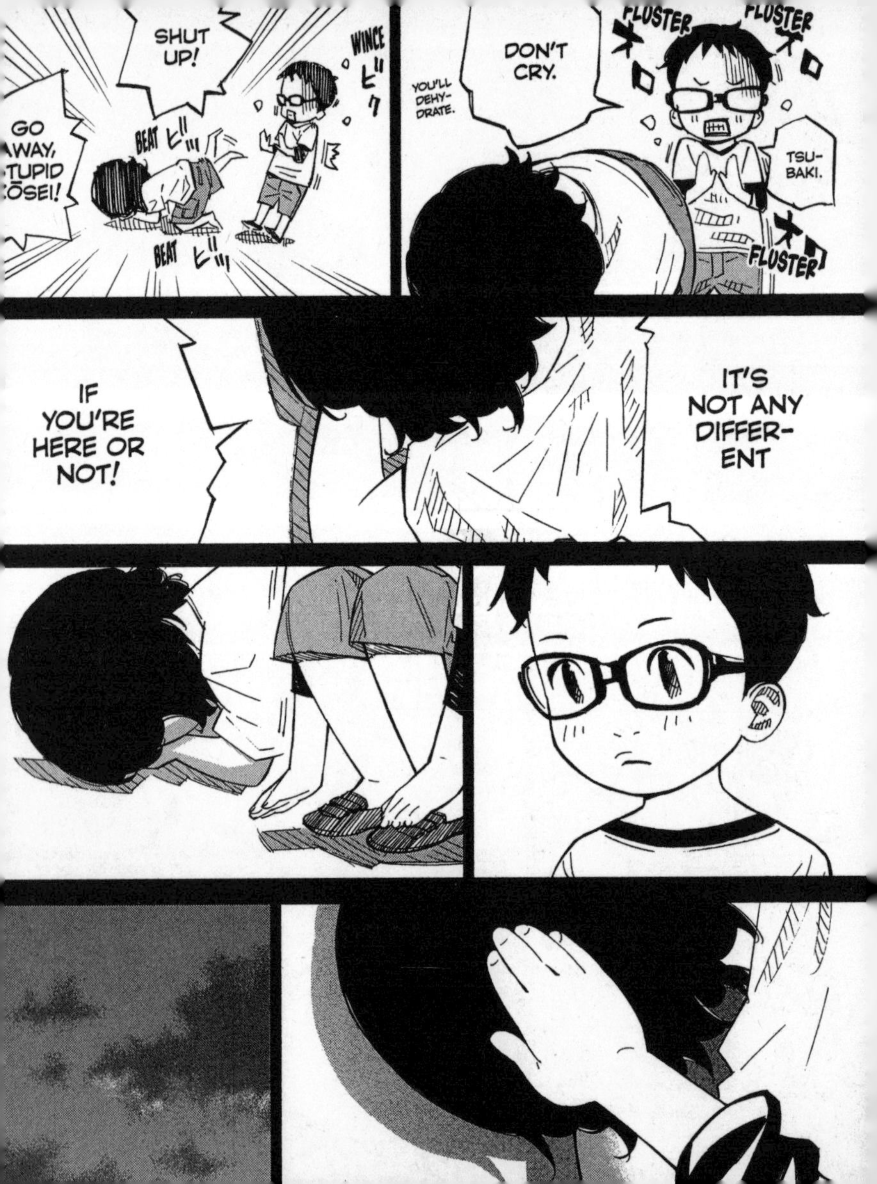
FLUSTER オロ
FLUSTER オロ
DON'T CRY.
YOU'LL DEHY-DRATE.
TSU-BAKI.
オロ FLUSTER
SHUT UP!
WINCE ビク
GO AWAY, TUPID ŌSEI!
BEAT ビッ
BEAT ビッ
IT'S NOT ANY DIFFER-ENT
IF YOU'RE HERE OR NOT!

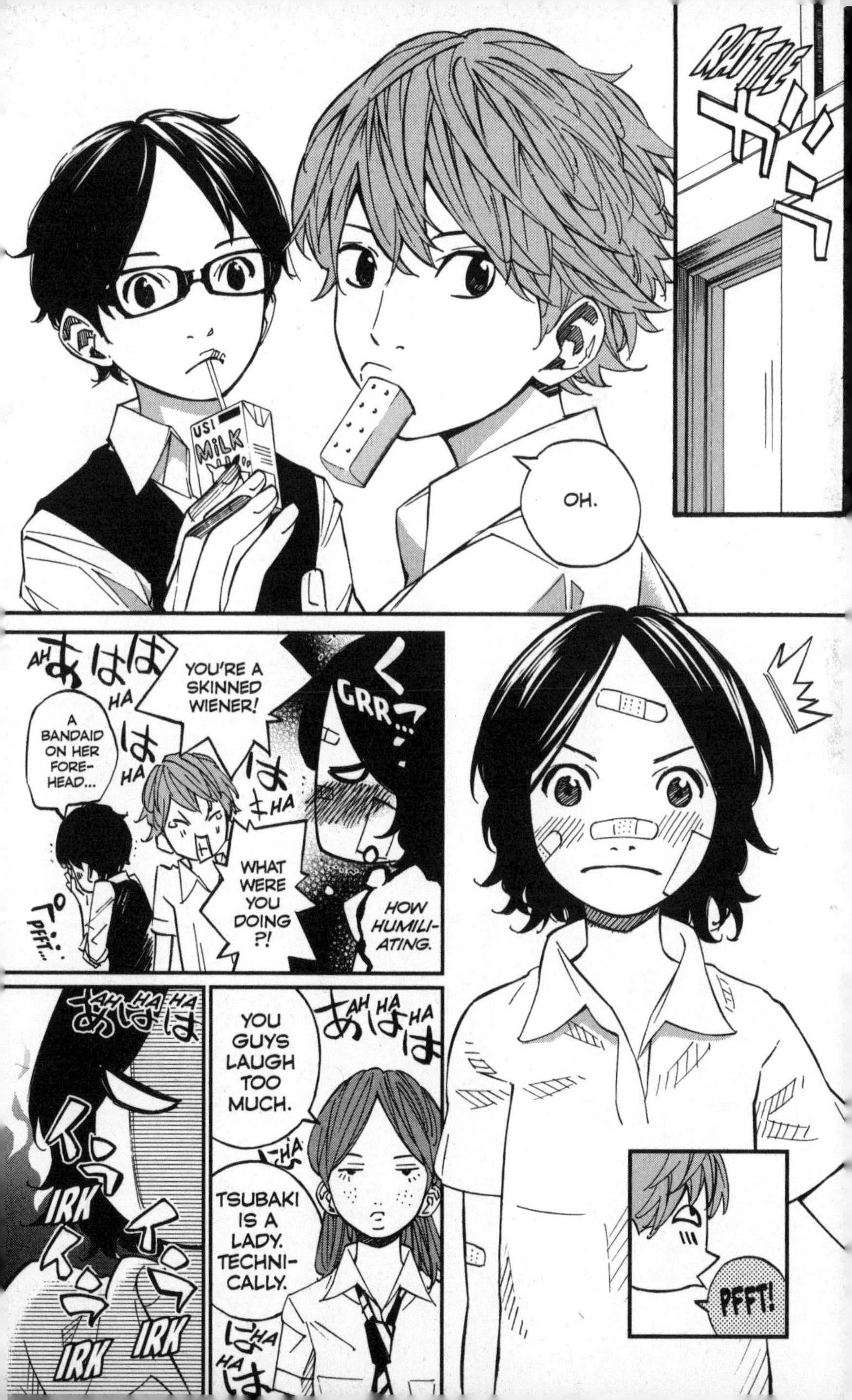
RATTLE
OH.
PFFT!
GRR...
YOU'RE A SKINNED WIENER!
AH HA HA
A BANDAID ON HER FORE-HEAD...
HA
WHAT WERE YOU DOING?!
HOW HUMILI-ATING.
PFFT...
AH HA HA
YOU GUYS LAUGH TOO MUCH.
HA
TSUBAKI IS A LADY. TECHNI-CALLY.
HA HA
AH HA HA
IRK
IRK
IRK

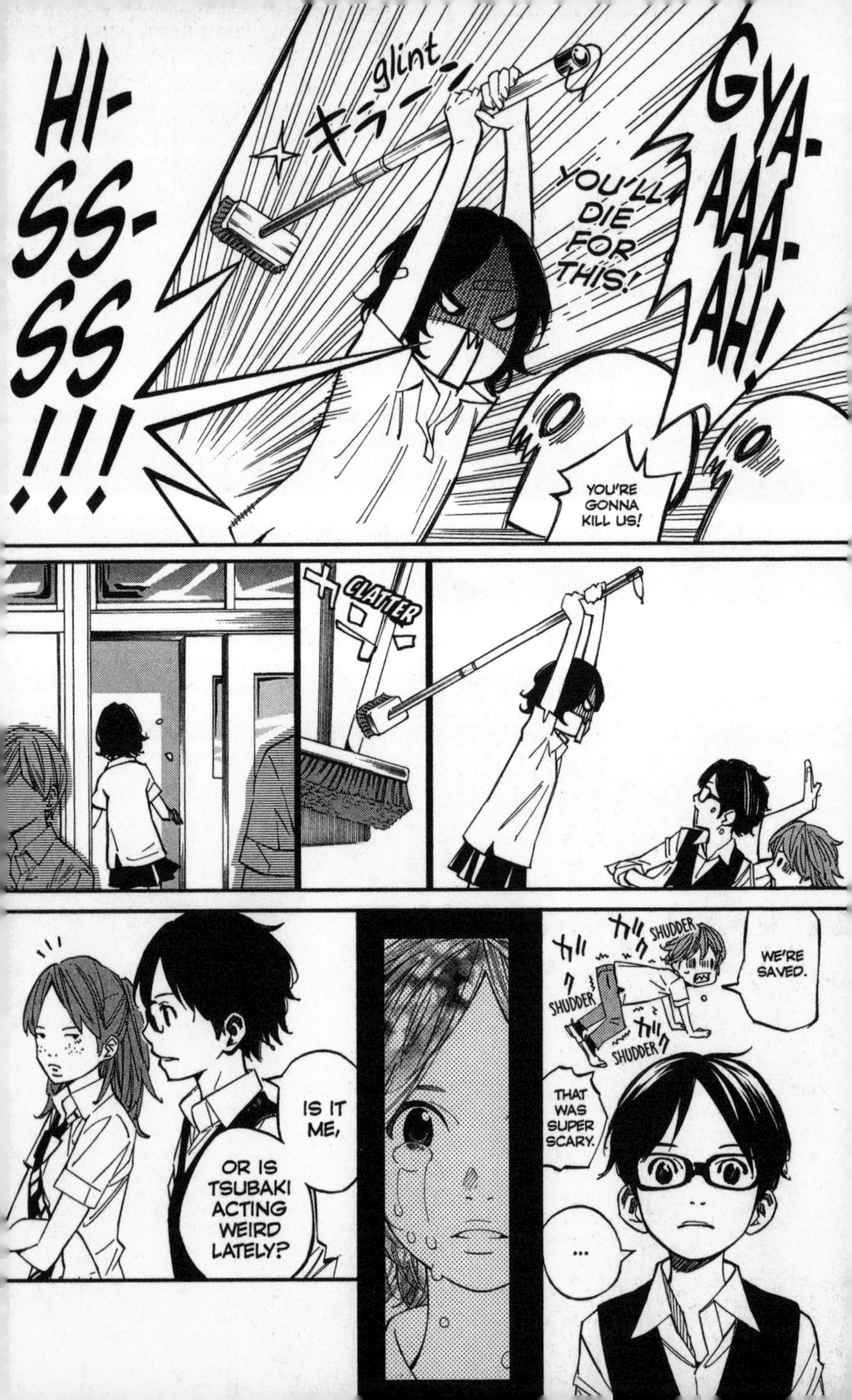
GYA-AAA-AAH!
YOU'LL DIE FOR THIS!
glint
キラー
HI-SS-SS-SS!!!
YOU'RE GONNA KILL US!
CLATTER
SHUDDER
SHUDDER
SHUDDER
WE'RE SAVED.
THAT WAS SUPER SCARY.
...
IS IT ME,
OR IS TSUBAKI ACTING WEIRD LATELY?

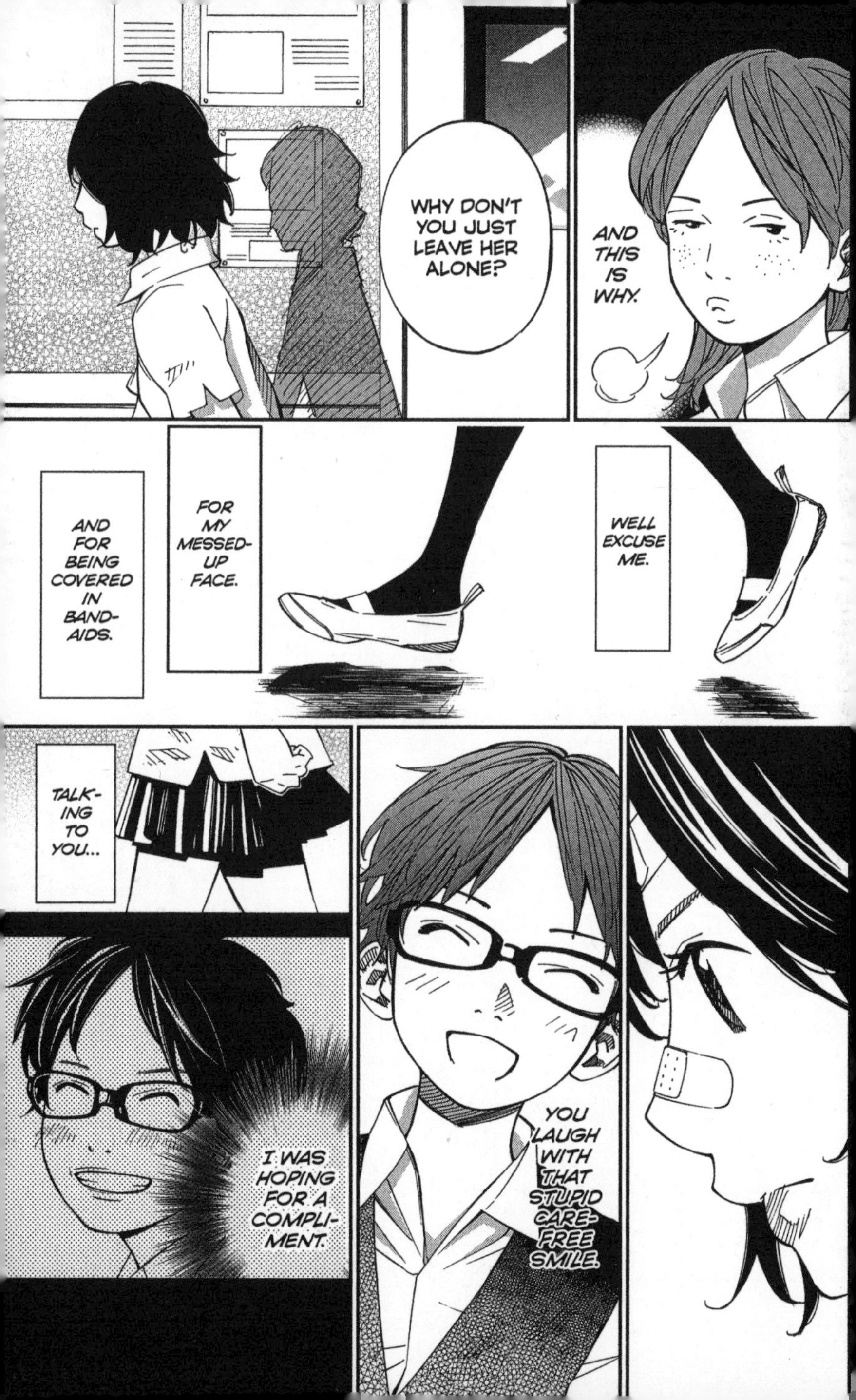
AND THIS IS WHY.
WHY DON'T YOU JUST LEAVE HER ALONE?
WELL EXCUSE ME.
FOR MY MESSED-UP FACE.
AND FOR BEING COVERED IN BAND-AIDS.
YOU LAUGH WITH THAT STUPID CARE-FREE SMILE.
TALKING TO YOU...
I WAS HOPING FOR A COMPLIMENT.

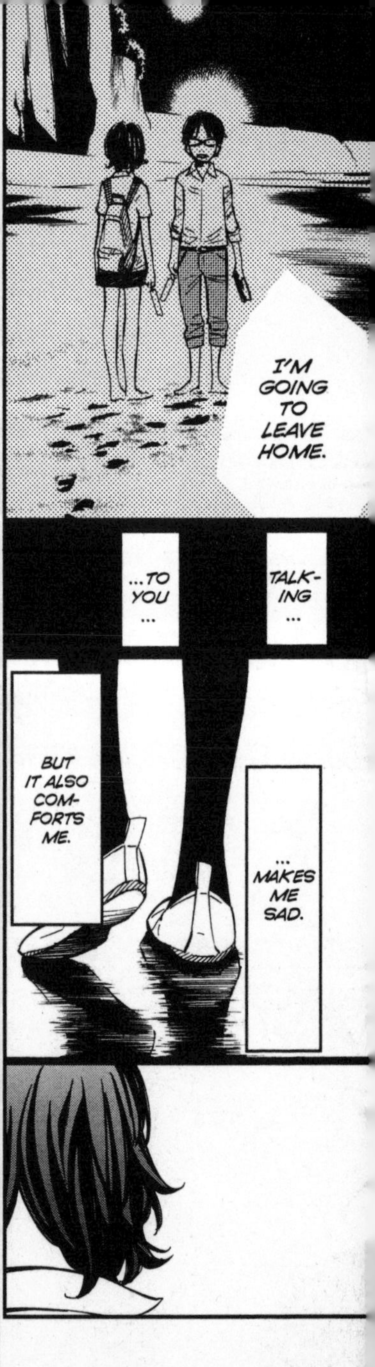
I'M GOING TO LEAVE HOME.
TALKING-ING...
...TO YOU...
...MAKES ME SAD.
BUT IT ALSO COM-FORTS ME.
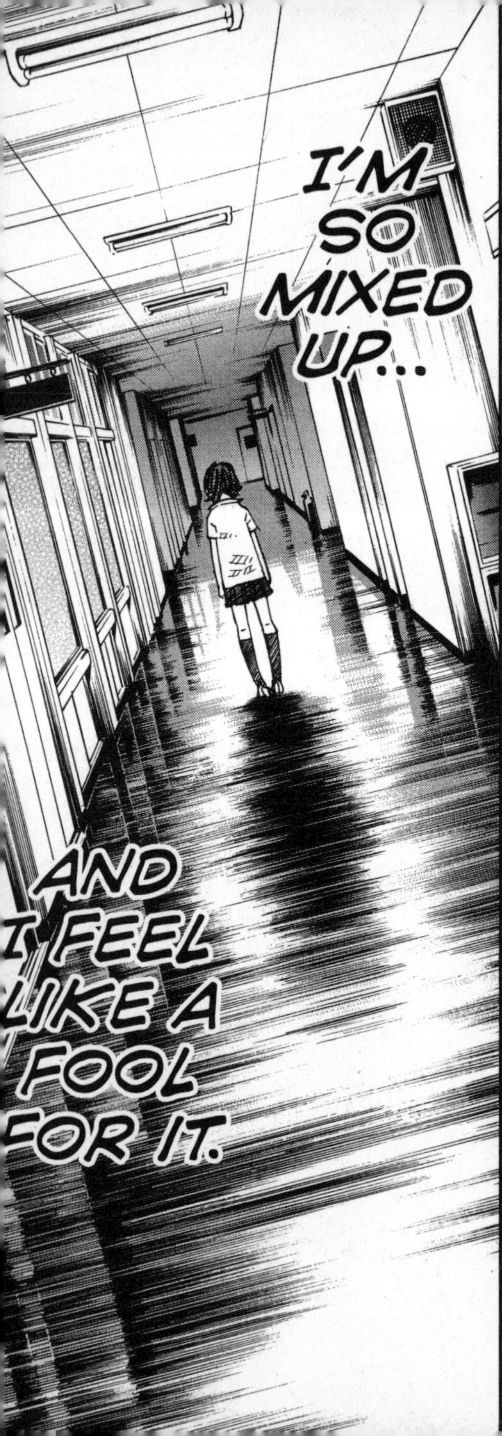
I'M SO MIXED UP...
AND I FEEL LIKE A FOOL FOR IT.

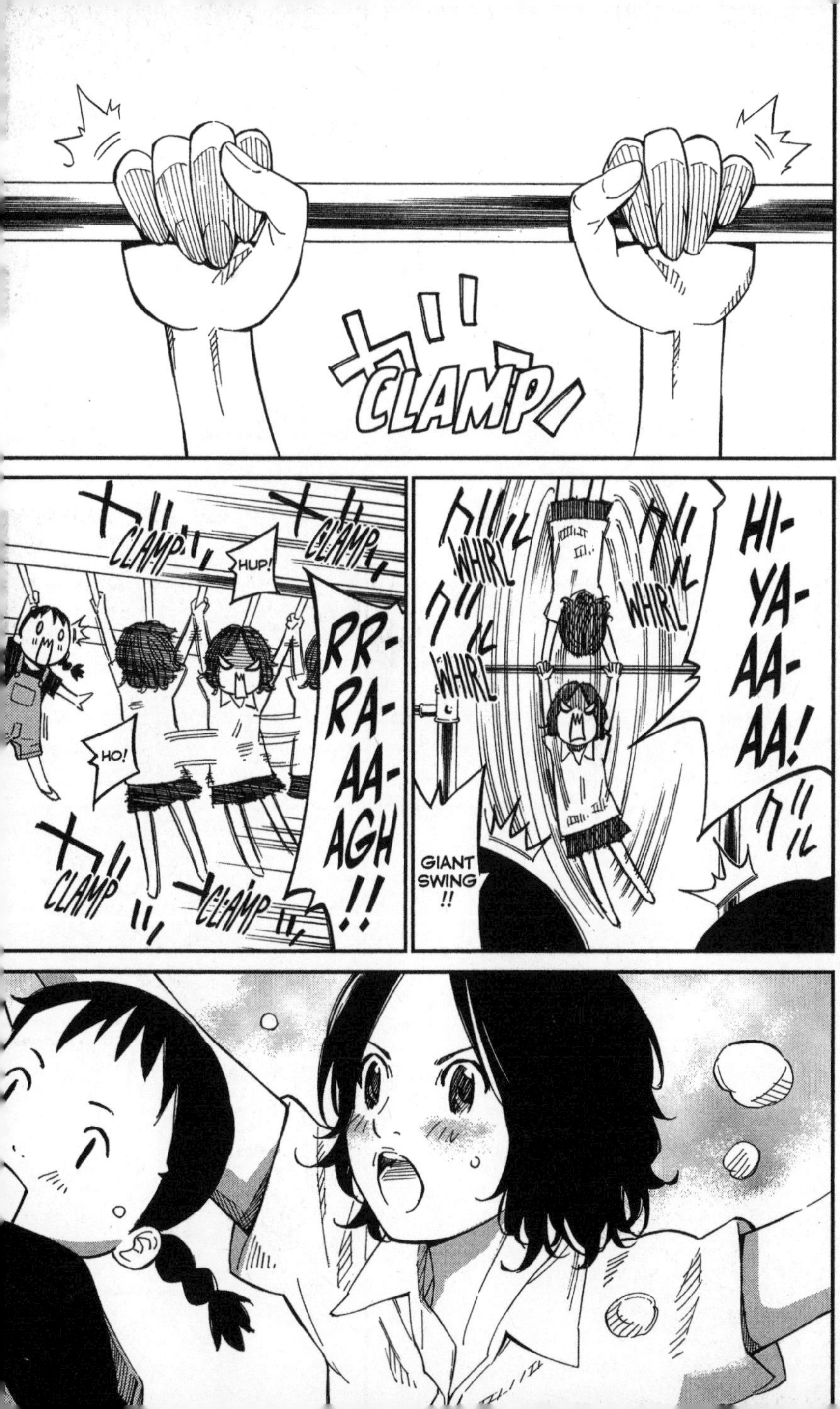
CLAMP!
WHIRL
WHIRL
WHIRL
HI-YA-AA-AA-AA!
GIANT SWING!!
CLAMP!
HUP!
CLAMP
RR-RA-AA-AGH!!
HO!
CLAMP
CLAMP

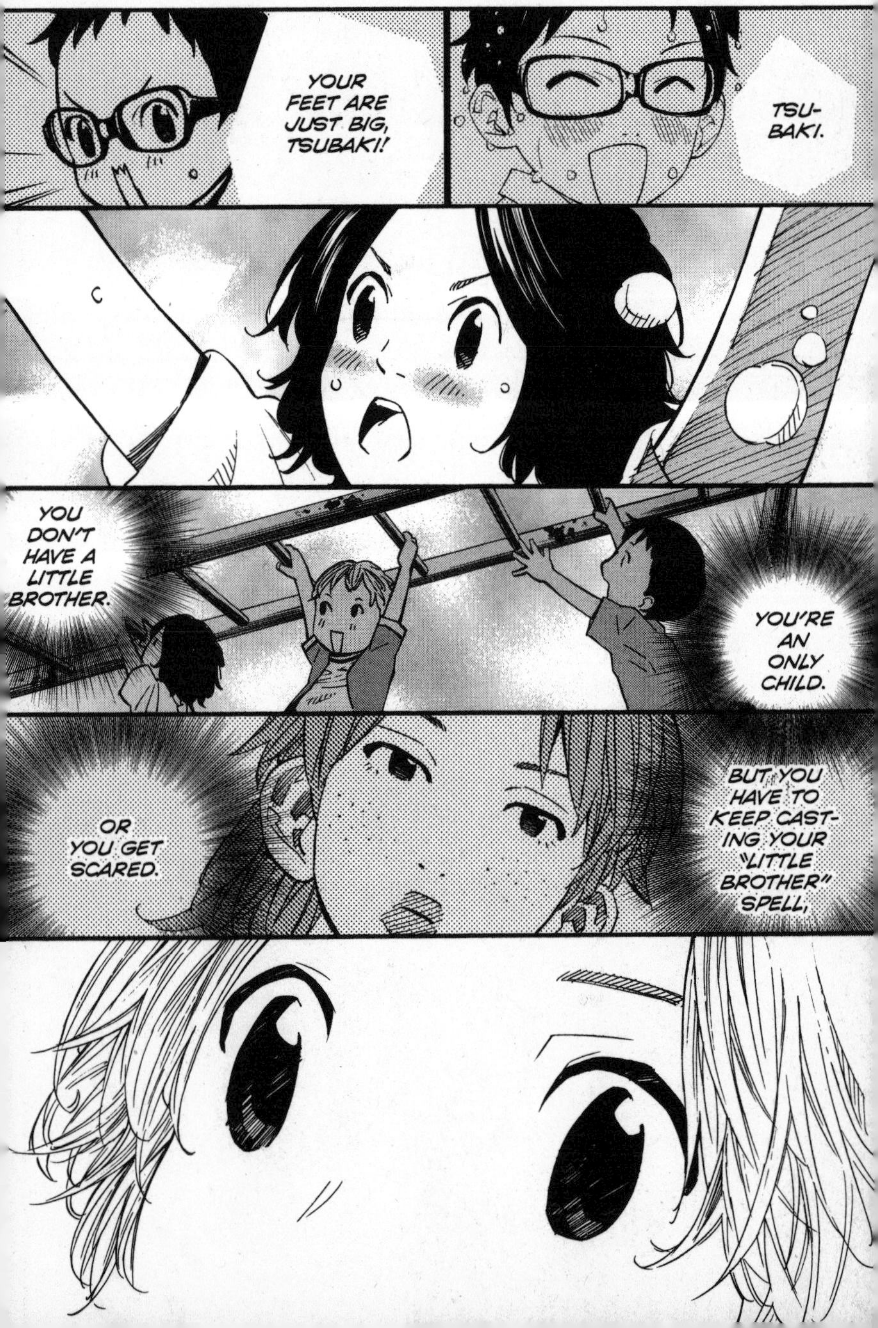
TSU-BAKI.
YOUR FEET ARE JUST BIG, TSUBAKI!
YOU DON'T HAVE A LITTLE BROTHER.
YOU'RE AN ONLY CHILD.
BUT YOU HAVE TO KEEP CAST-ING YOUR "LITTLE BROTHER" SPELL,
OR YOU GET SCARED.

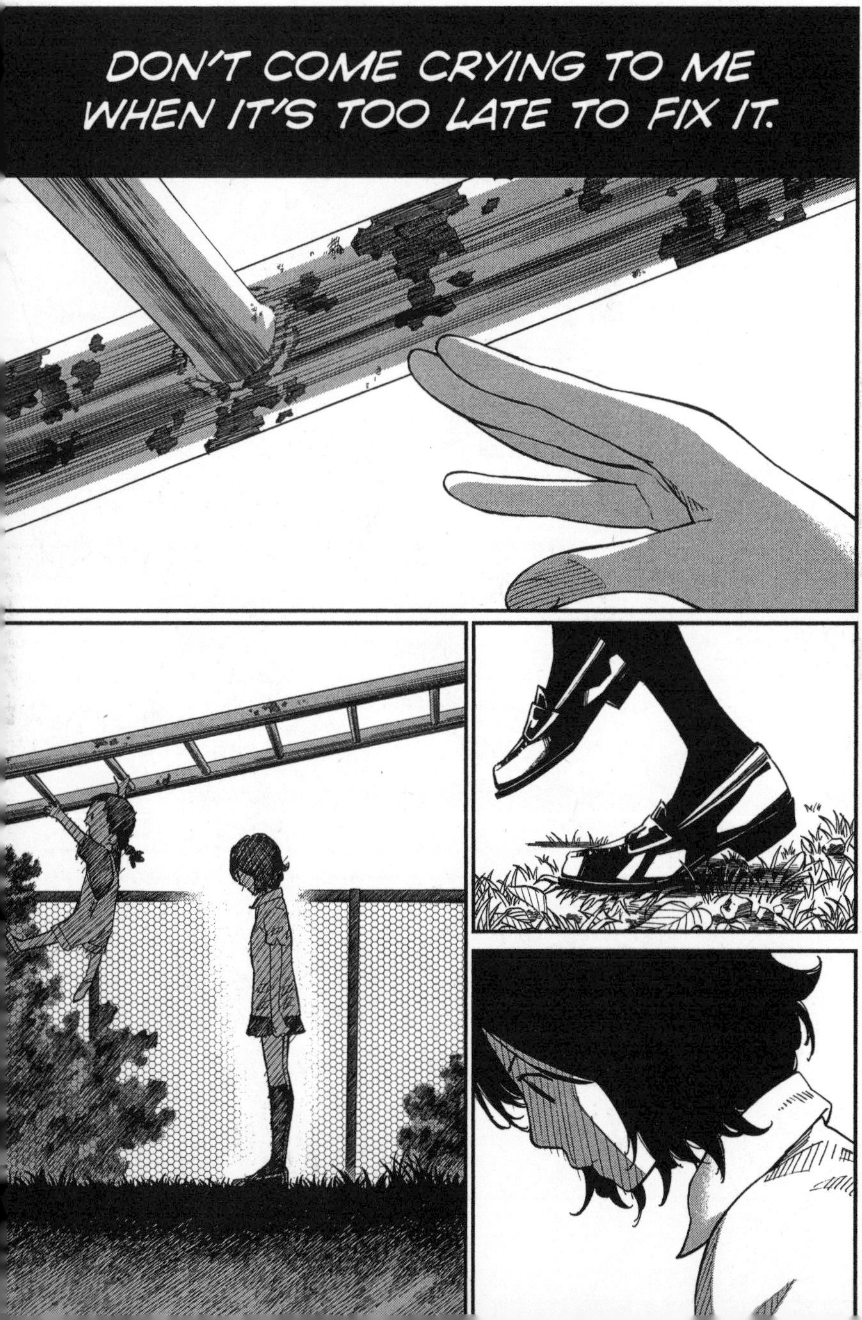
DON'T COME CRYING TO ME WHEN IT'S TOO LATE TO FIX IT.

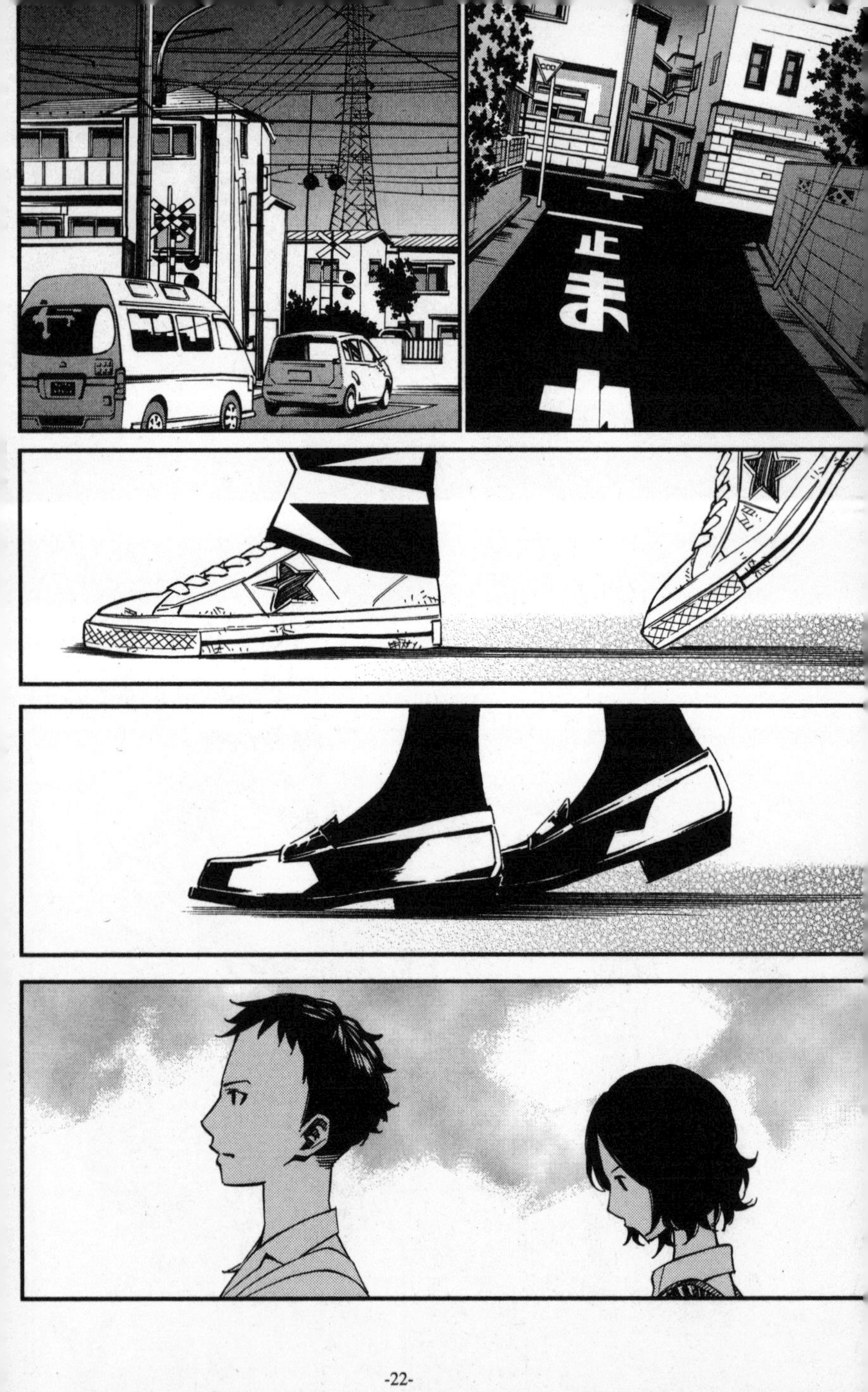

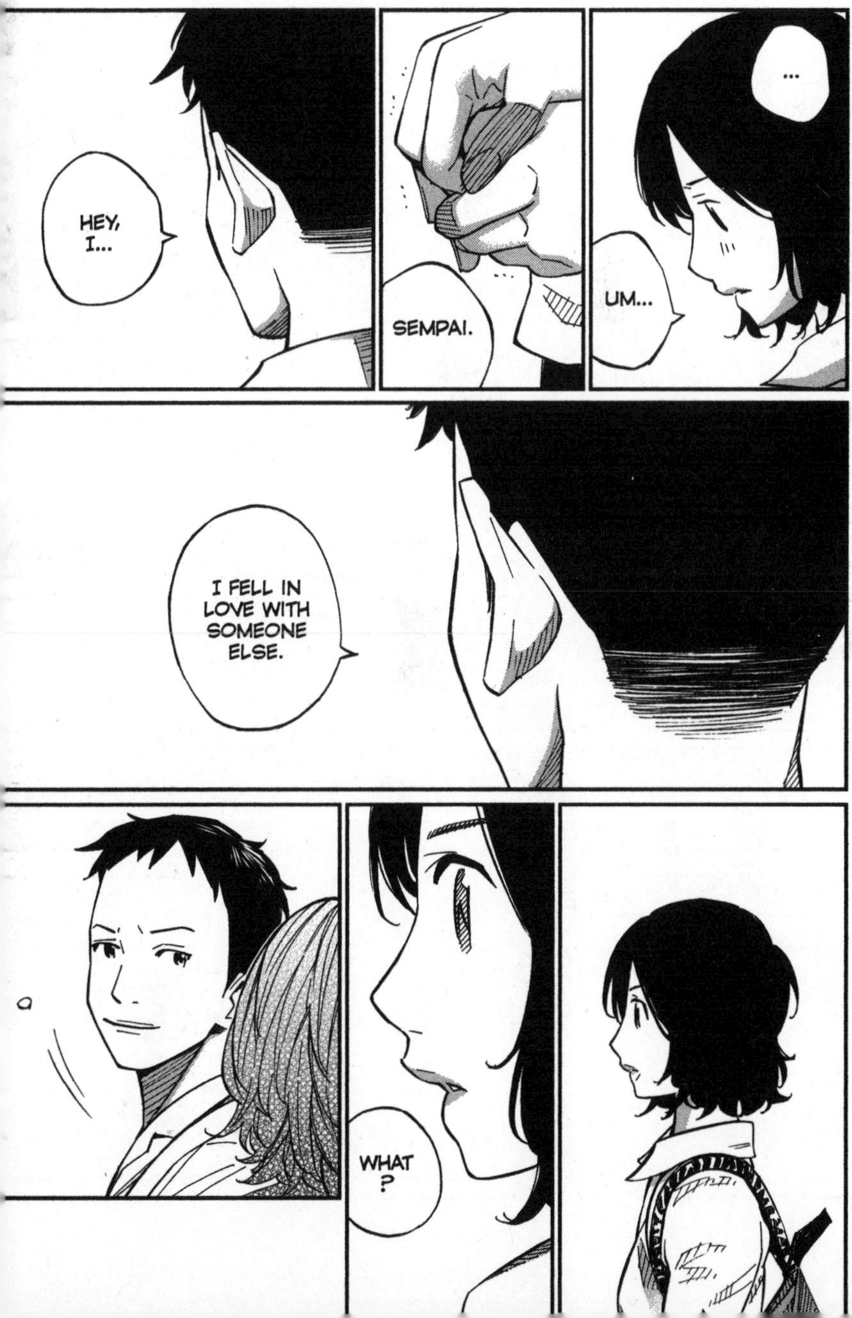
...
UM...
SEMPAI.
HEY, I...
I FELL IN LOVE WITH SOMEONE ELSE.
WHAT ?

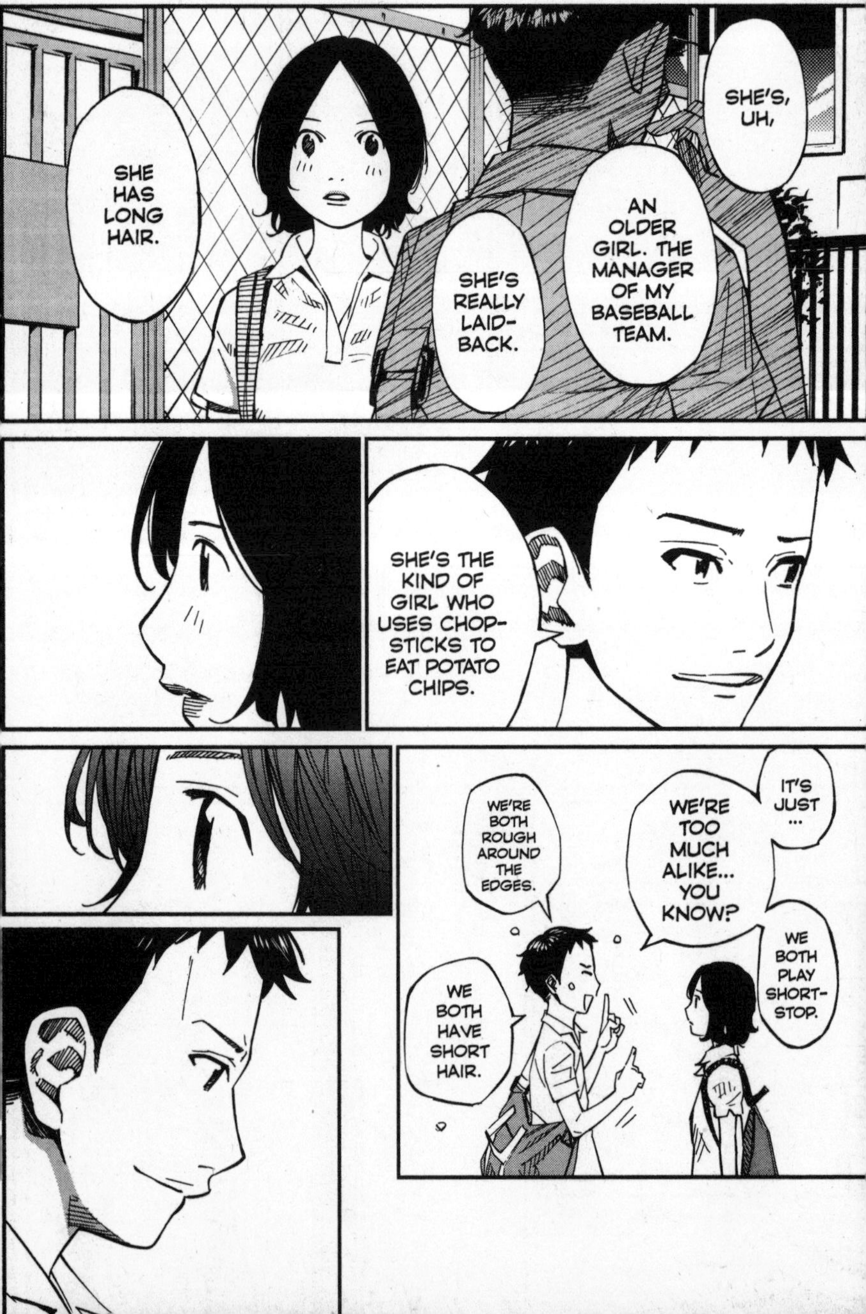
SHE'S, UH,
AN OLDER GIRL. THE MANAGER OF MY BASEBALL TEAM.
SHE'S REALLY LAID-BACK.
SHE HAS LONG HAIR.
SHE'S THE KIND OF GIRL WHO USES CHOPSTICKS TO EAT POTATO CHIPS.
IT'S JUST ...
WE'RE TOO MUCH ALIKE... YOU KNOW?
WE'RE BOTH ROUGH AROUND THE EDGES.
WE BOTH PLAY SHORTSTOP.
WE BOTH HAVE SHORT HAIR.

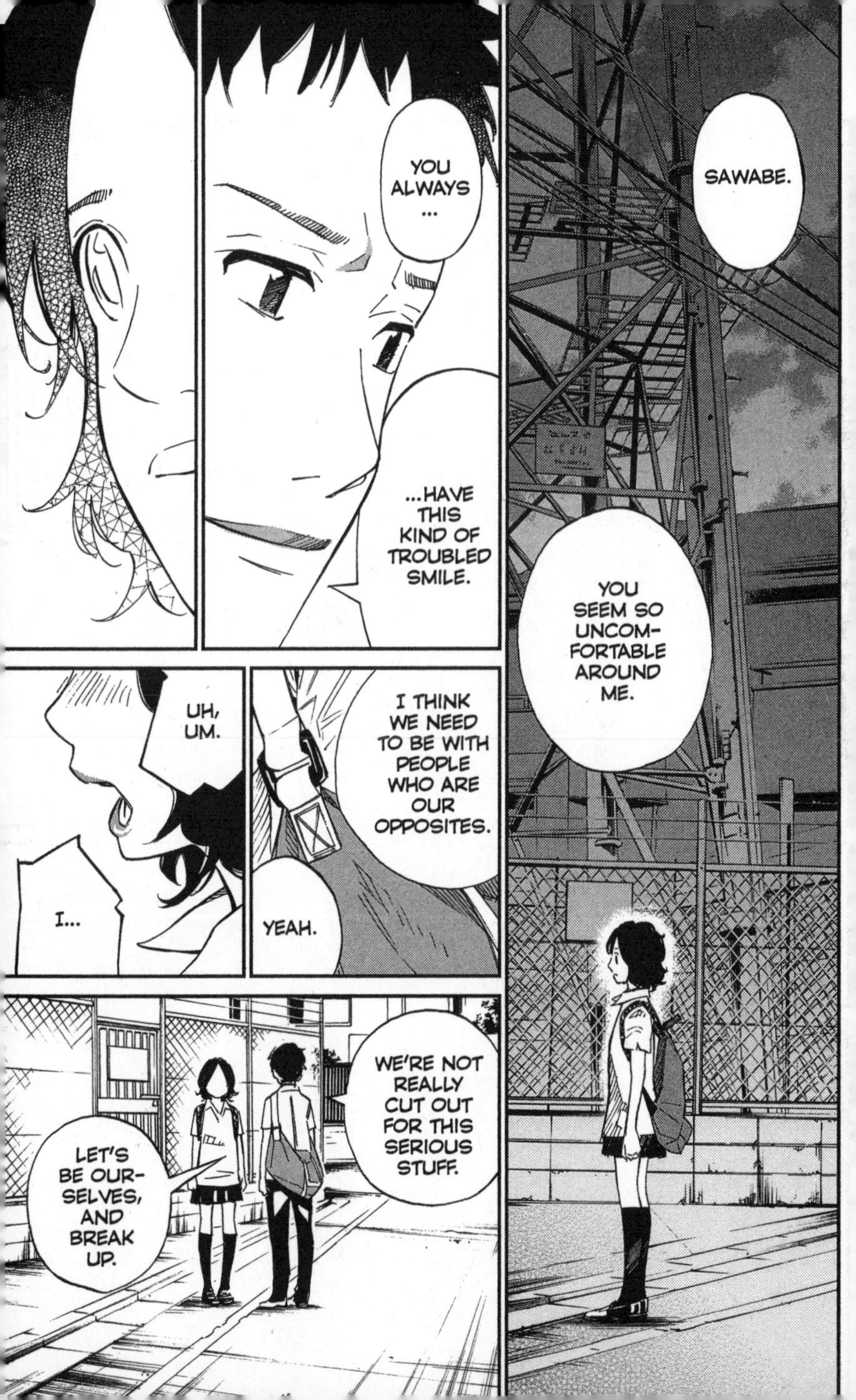
SAWABE.
YOU SEEM SO UNCOM-FORTABLE AROUND ME.
YOU ALWAYS ...
...HAVE THIS KIND OF TROUBLED SMILE.
I THINK WE NEED TO BE WITH PEOPLE WHO ARE OUR OPPOSITES.
YEAH.
UH, UM.
I...
WE'RE NOT REALLY CUT OUT FOR THIS SERIOUS STUFF.
LET'S BE OUR-SELVES, AND BREAK UP.

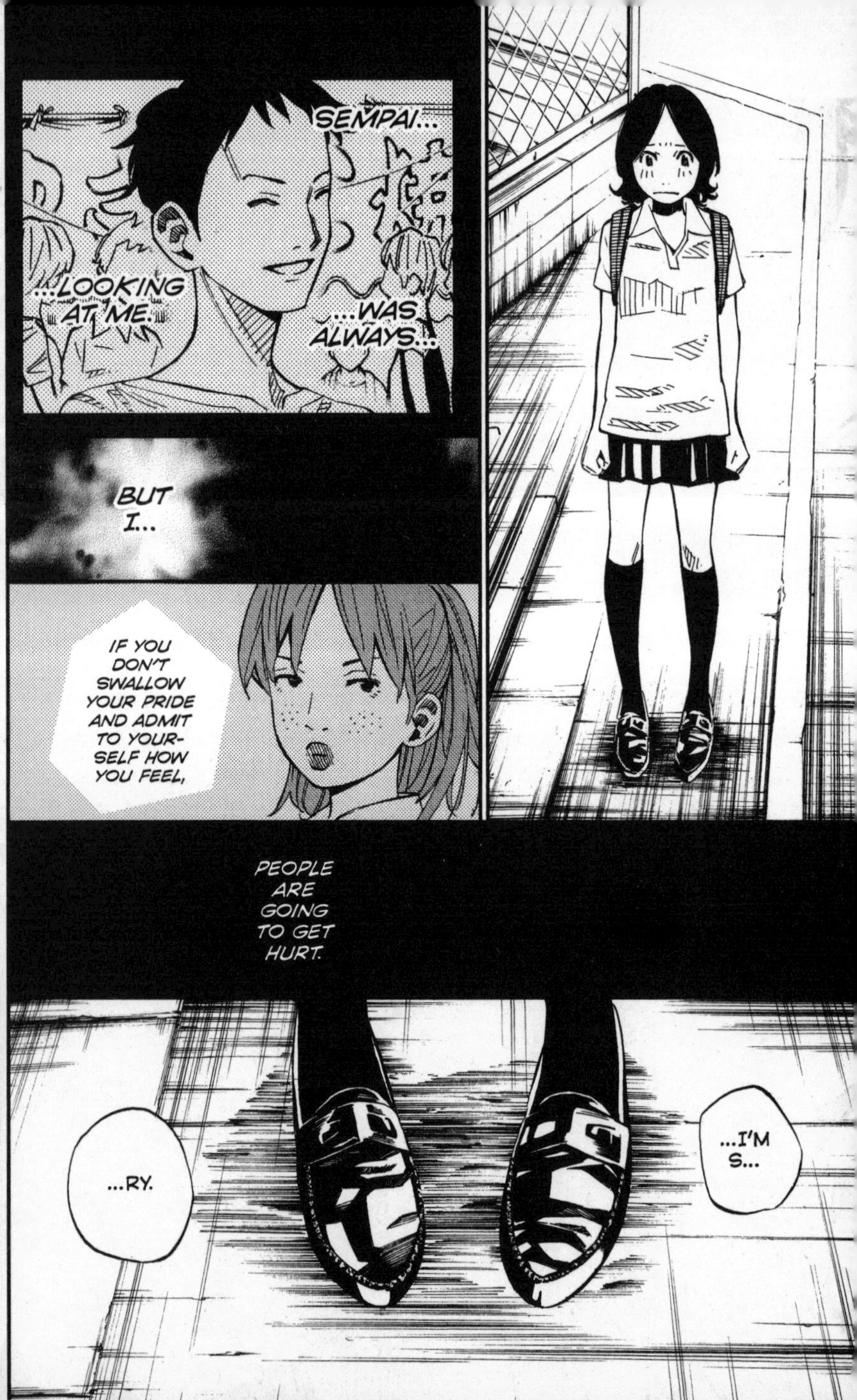
SEMPAI...
...WAS ALWAYS...
...LOOKING AT ME.
BUT I...
IF YOU DON'T SWALLOW YOUR PRIDE AND ADMIT TO YOURSELF HOW YOU FEEL,
PEOPLE ARE GOING TO GET HURT.
...I'M S...
...RY.

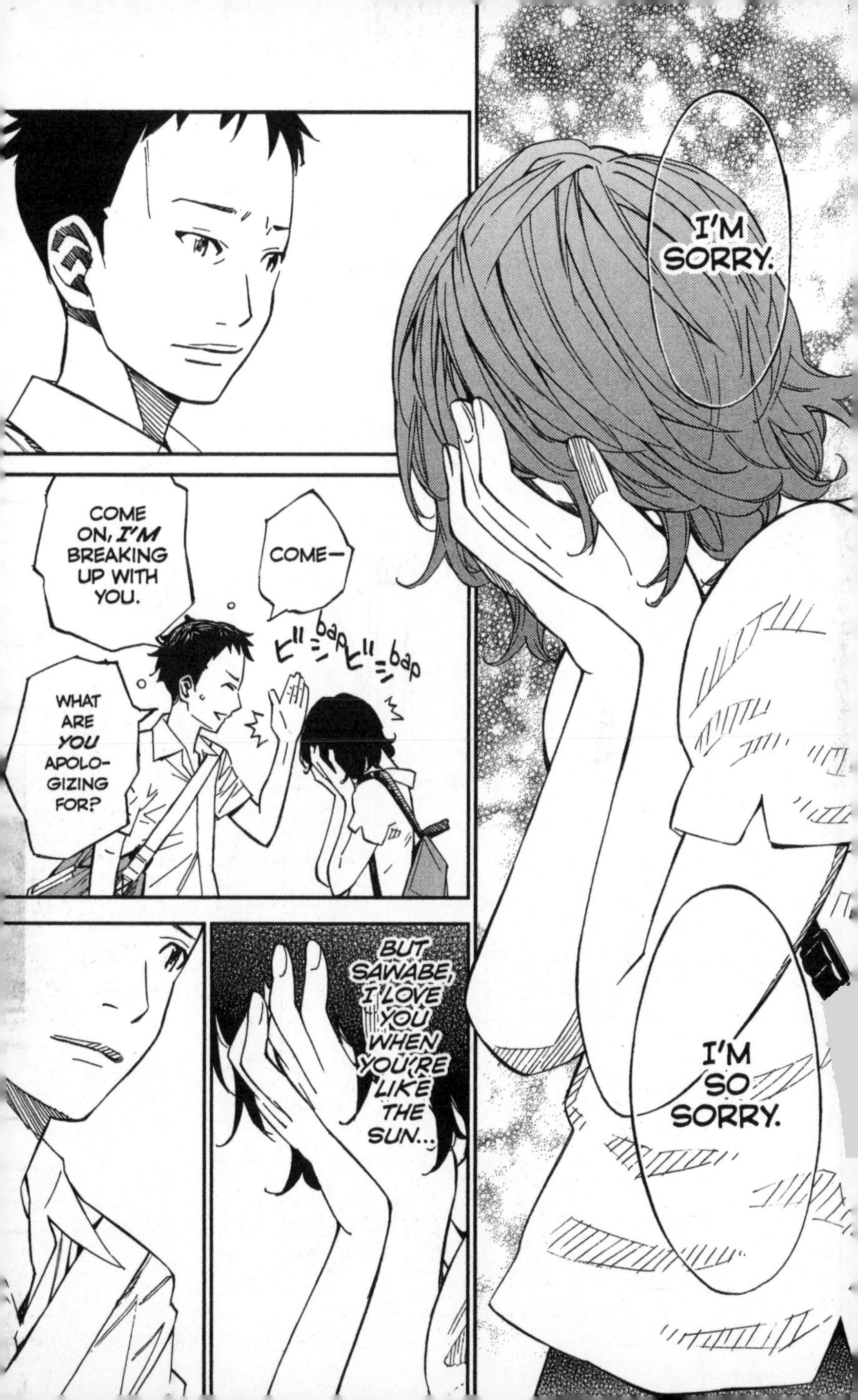
I'M SORRY.
I'M SO SORRY.
COME—
COME ON, *I'M* BREAKING UP WITH YOU.
bap
bap
WHAT ARE *YOU* APOLOGIZING FOR?
BUT SAWABE, I LOVE YOU WHEN YOU'RE LIKE THE SUN...

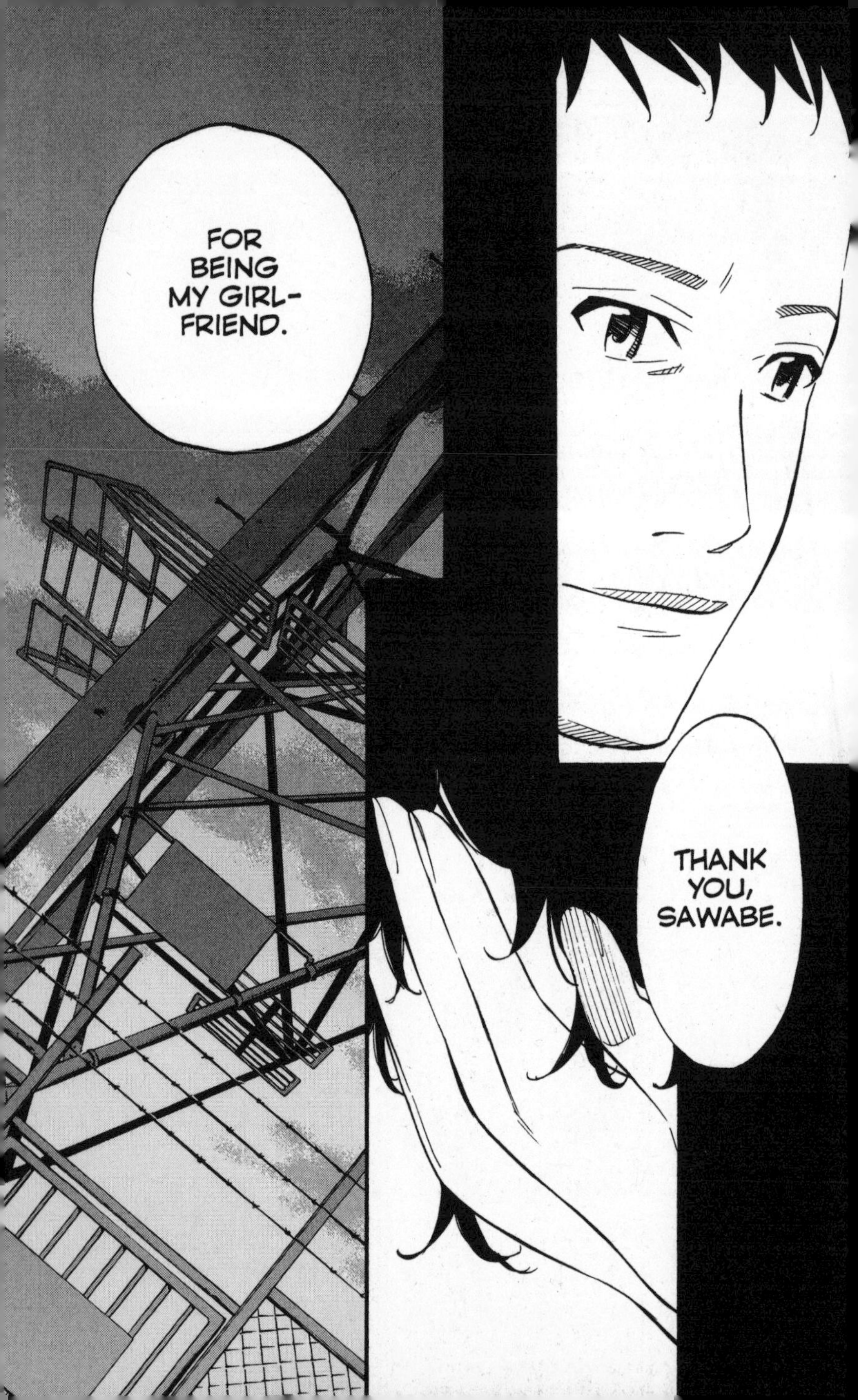
THANK YOU, SAWABE.
FOR BEING MY GIRL-FRIEND.

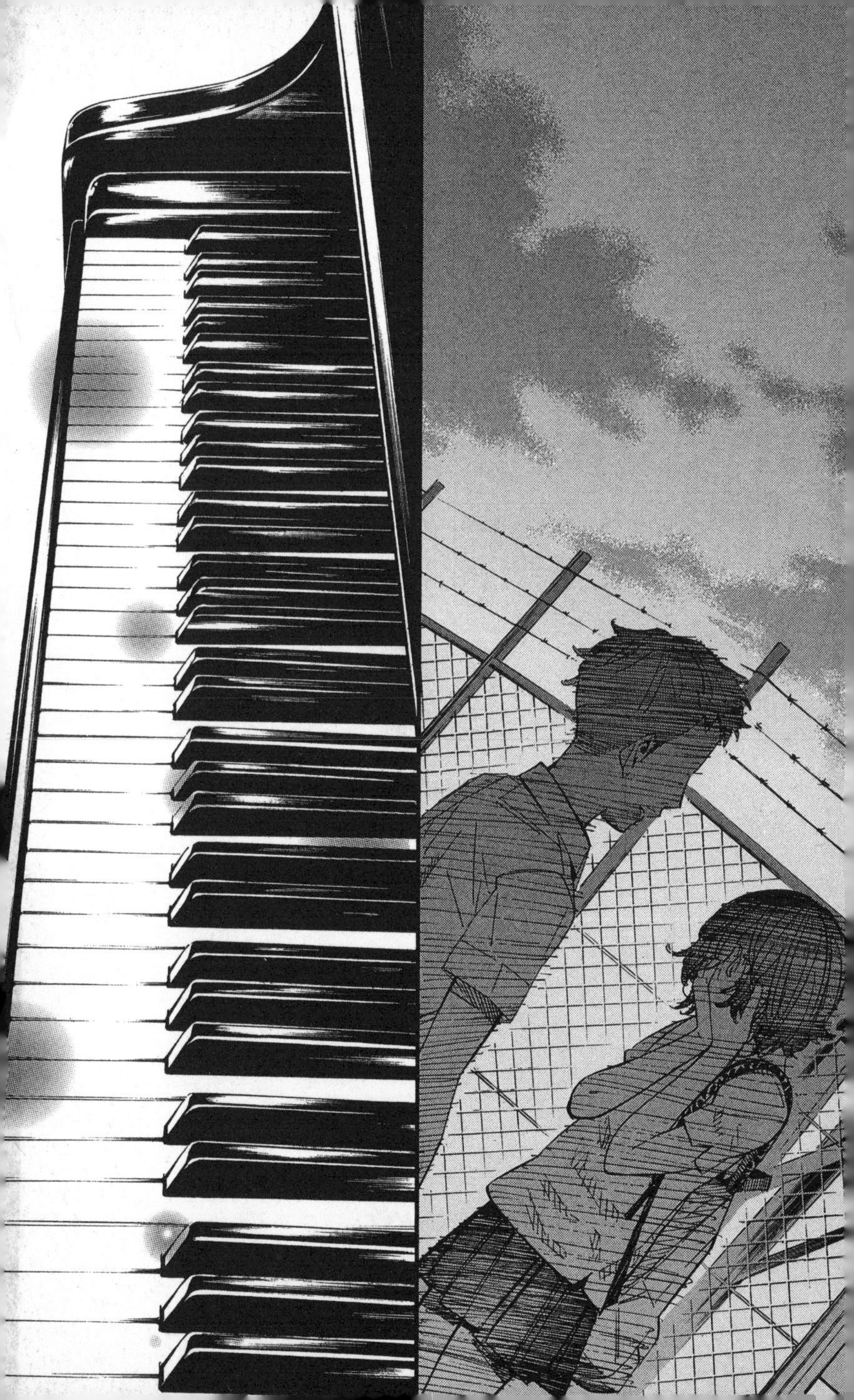

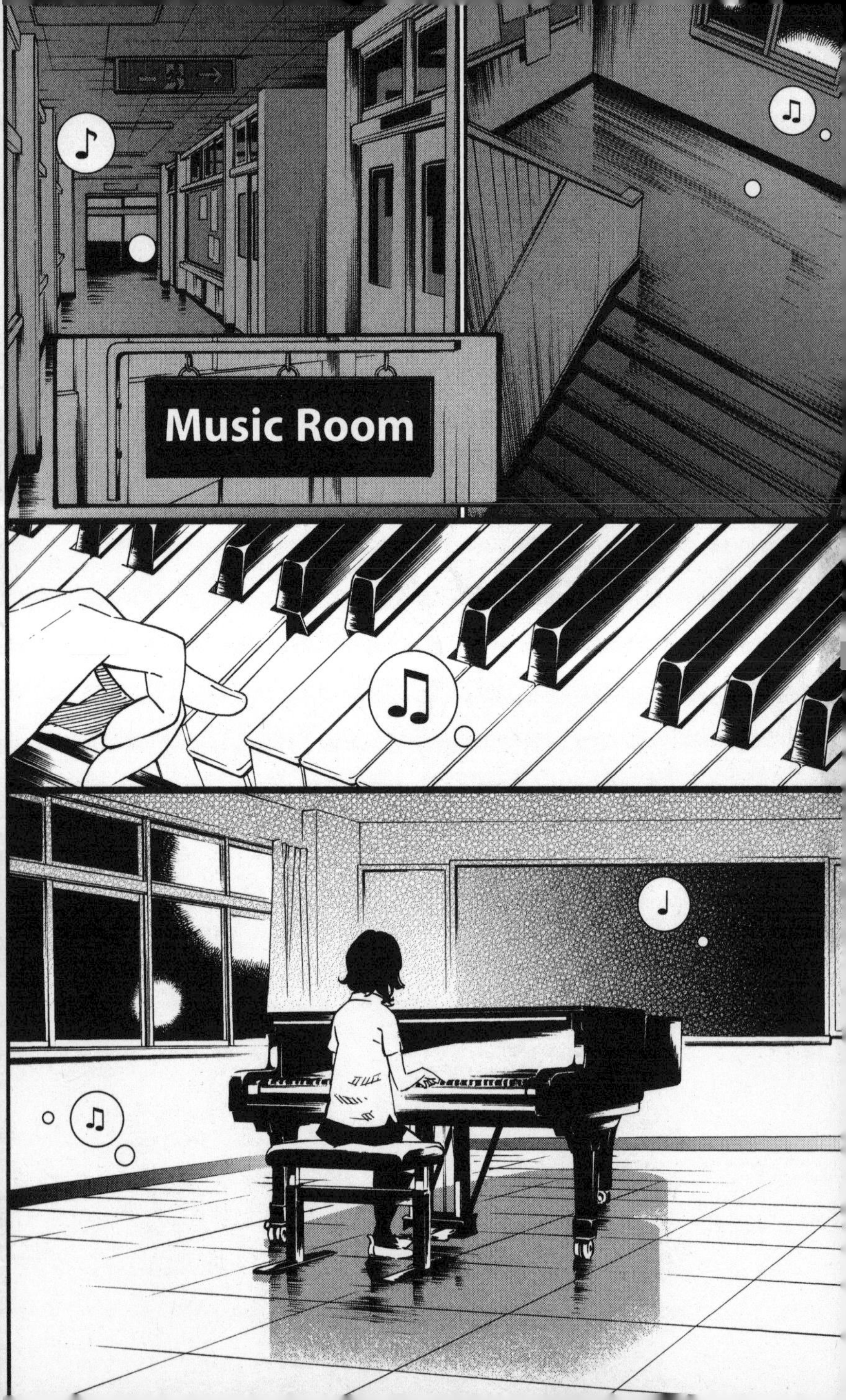
Music Room

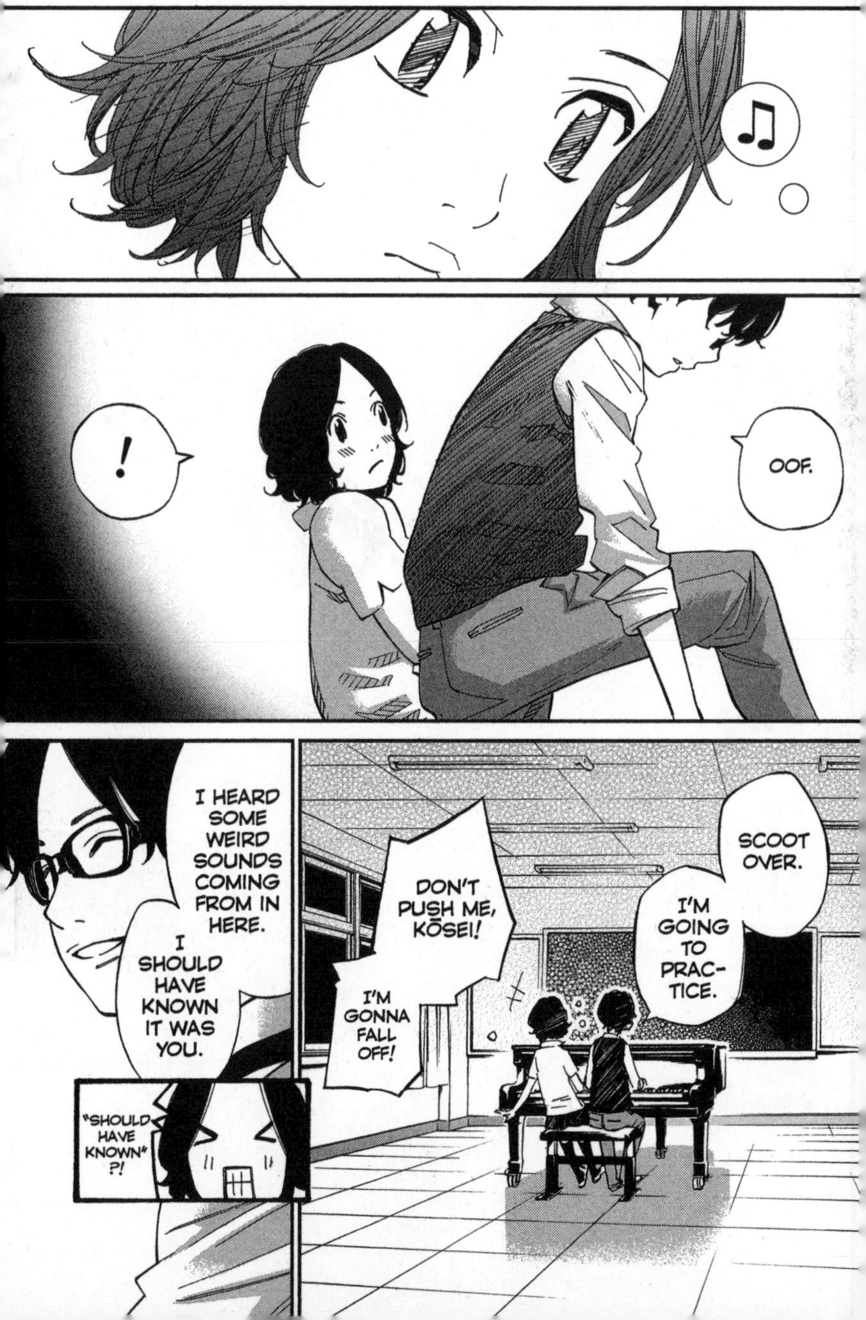
OOF.
!
SCOOT OVER.
I'M GOING TO PRACTICE.
DON'T PUSH ME, KŌSEI!
I'M GONNA FALL OFF!
I HEARD SOME WEIRD SOUNDS COMING FROM IN HERE.
I SHOULD HAVE KNOWN IT WAS YOU.
"SHOULD HAVE KNOWN"?!

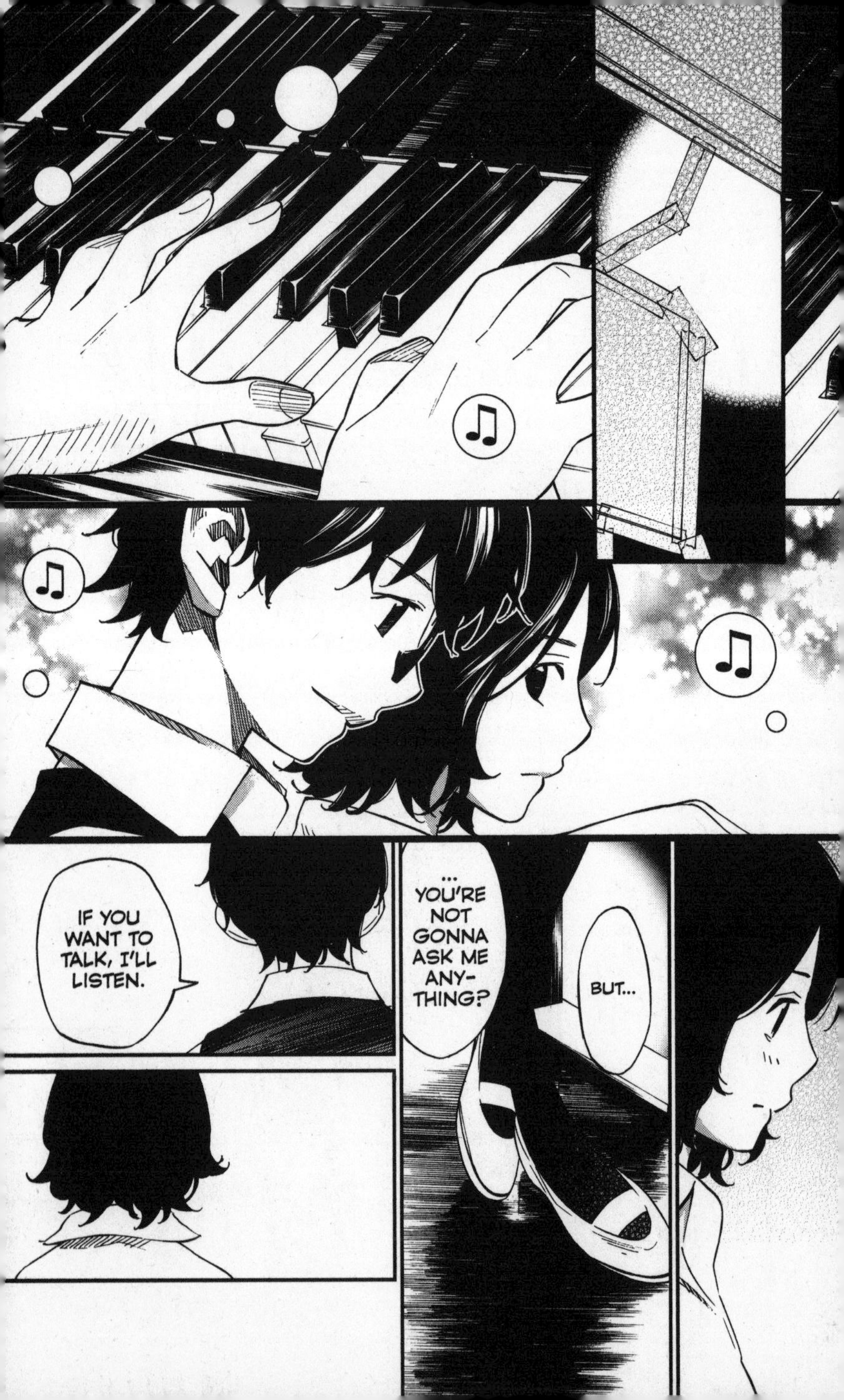
BUT...
...YOU'RE NOT GONNA ASK ME ANY-THING?
IF YOU WANT TO TALK, I'LL LISTEN.

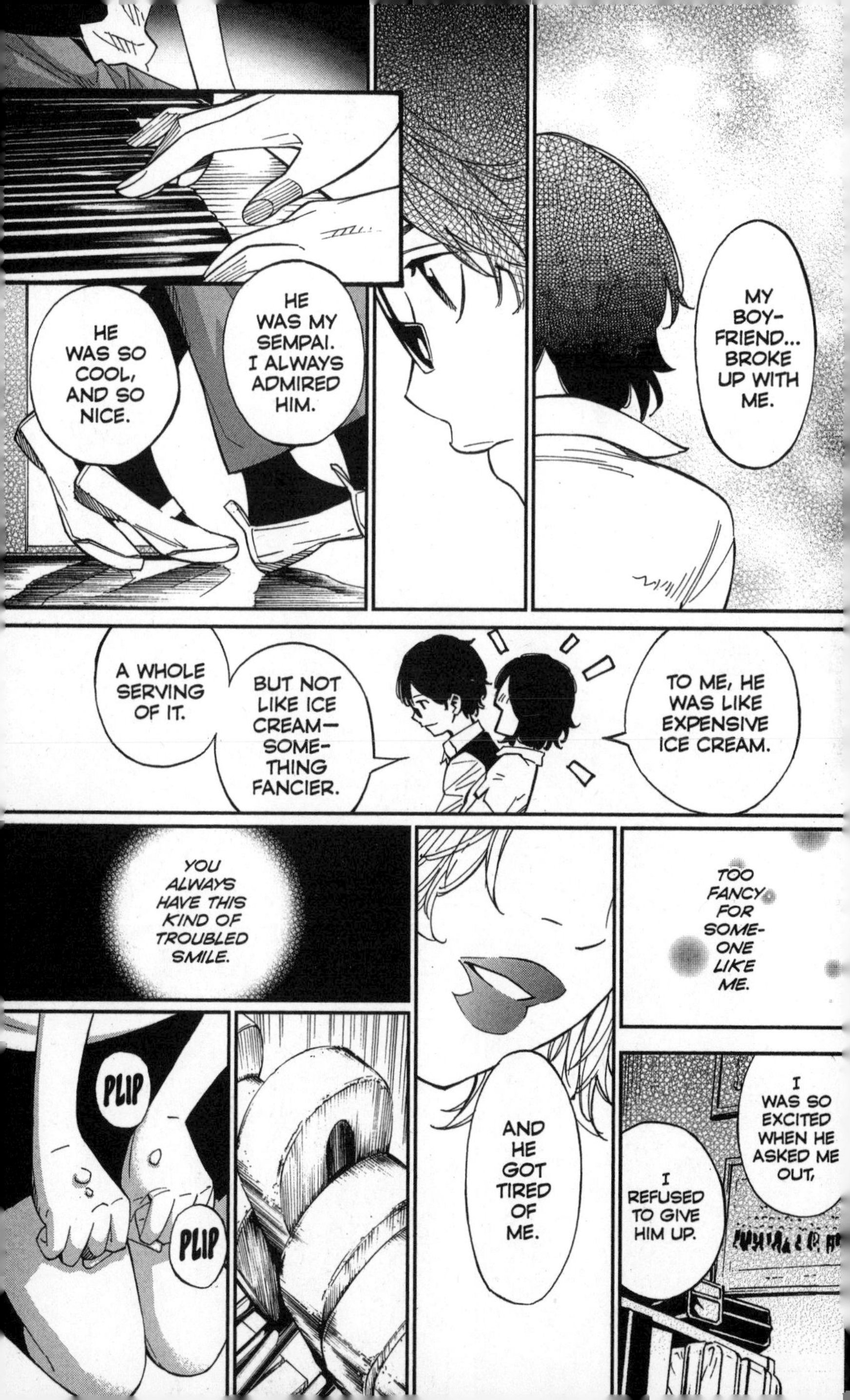
MY BOY-FRIEND... BROKE UP WITH ME.
HE WAS MY SEMPAI. I ALWAYS ADMIRED HIM.
HE WAS SO COOL, AND SO NICE.
TO ME, HE WAS LIKE EXPENSIVE ICE CREAM.
BUT NOT LIKE ICE CREAM—SOME-THING FANCIER.
A WHOLE SERVING OF IT.
TOO FANCY FOR SOME-ONE LIKE ME.
I WAS SO EXCITED WHEN HE ASKED ME OUT,
I REFUSED TO GIVE HIM UP.
AND HE GOT TIRED OF ME.
YOU ALWAYS HAVE THIS KIND OF TROUBLED SMILE.
PLIP
PLIP

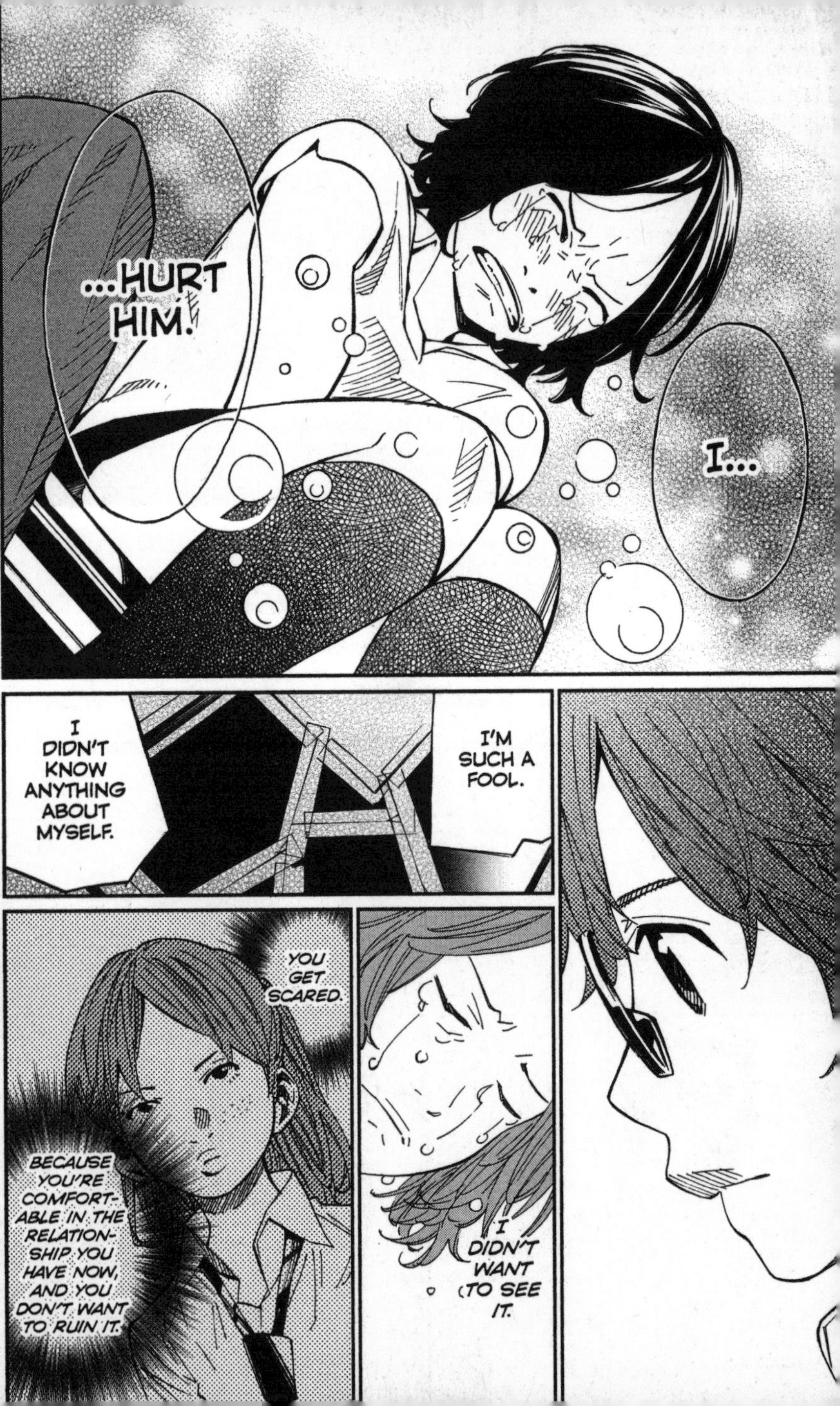
I...
...HURT HIM.
I'M SUCH A FOOL.
I DIDN'T KNOW ANYTHING ABOUT MYSELF.
I DIDN'T WANT TO SEE IT.
YOU GET SCARED.
BECAUSE YOU'RE COMFORTABLE IN THE RELATIONSHIP YOU HAVE NOW, AND YOU DON'T WANT TO RUIN IT.

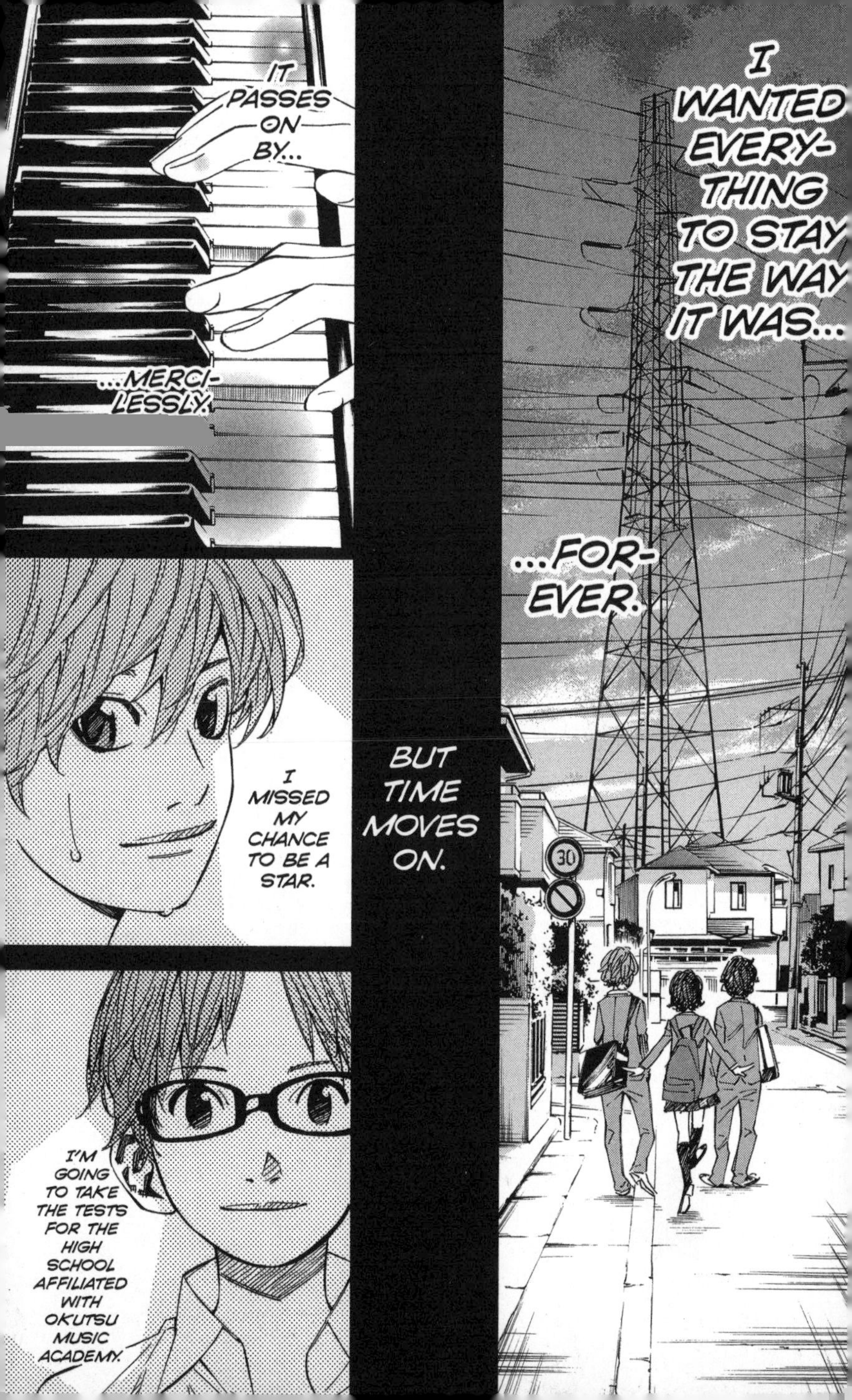
I WANTED EVERYTHING TO STAY THE WAY IT WAS...
...FOREVER.
BUT TIME MOVES ON.
IT PASSES ON BY...
...MERCILESSLY.
I MISSED MY CHANCE TO BE A STAR.
I'M GOING TO TAKE THE TESTS FOR THE HIGH SCHOOL AFFILIATED WITH OKUTSU MUSIC ACADEMY.

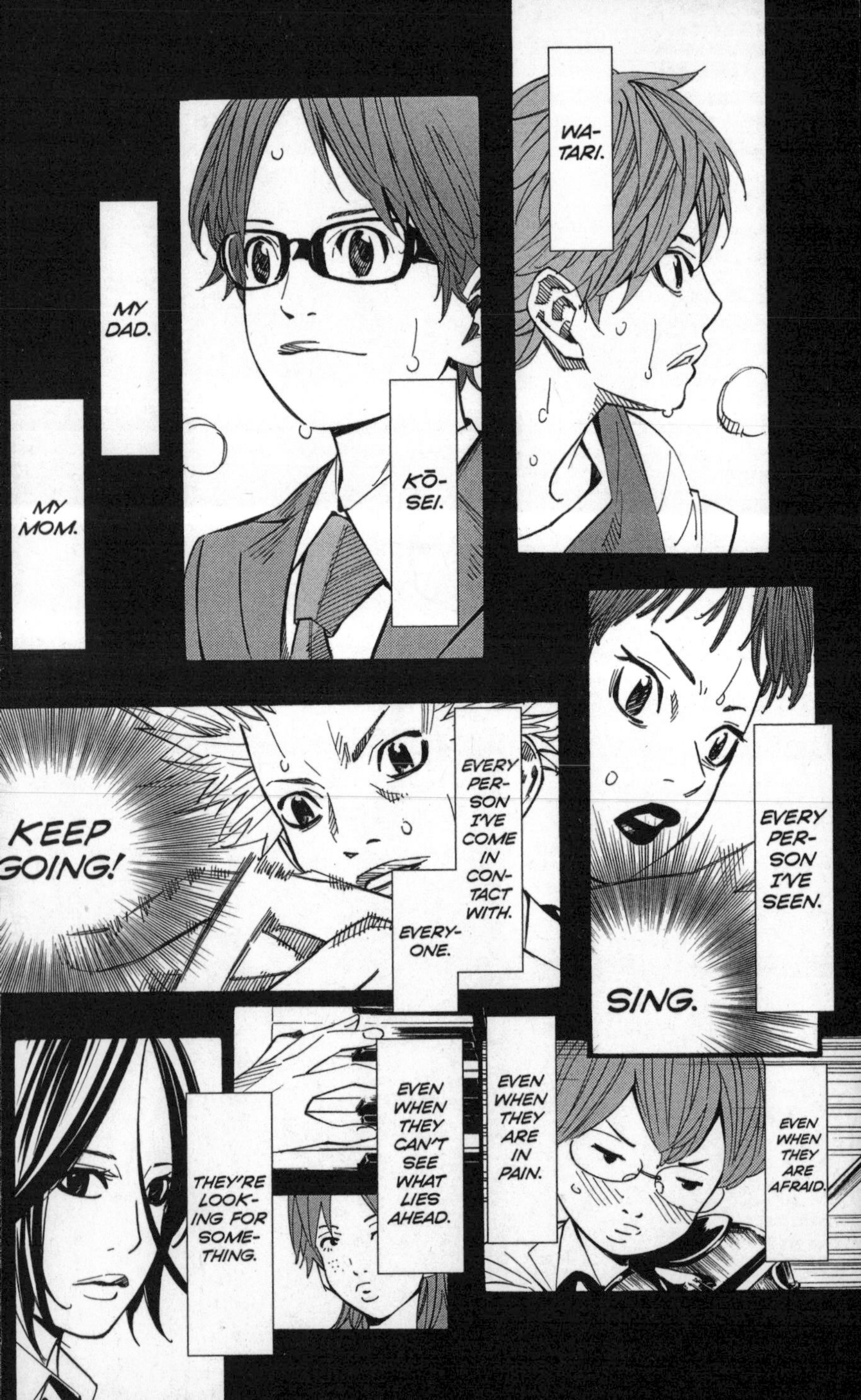
WATARI.
KŌSEI.
MY DAD.
MY MOM.
EVERY PERSON I'VE SEEN.
SING.
EVERY PERSON I'VE COME IN CONTACT WITH.
EVERYONE.
KEEP GOING!
EVEN WHEN THEY ARE AFRAID.
EVEN WHEN THEY ARE IN PAIN.
EVEN WHEN THEY CAN'T SEE WHAT LIES AHEAD.
THEY'RE LOOKING FOR SOMETHING.

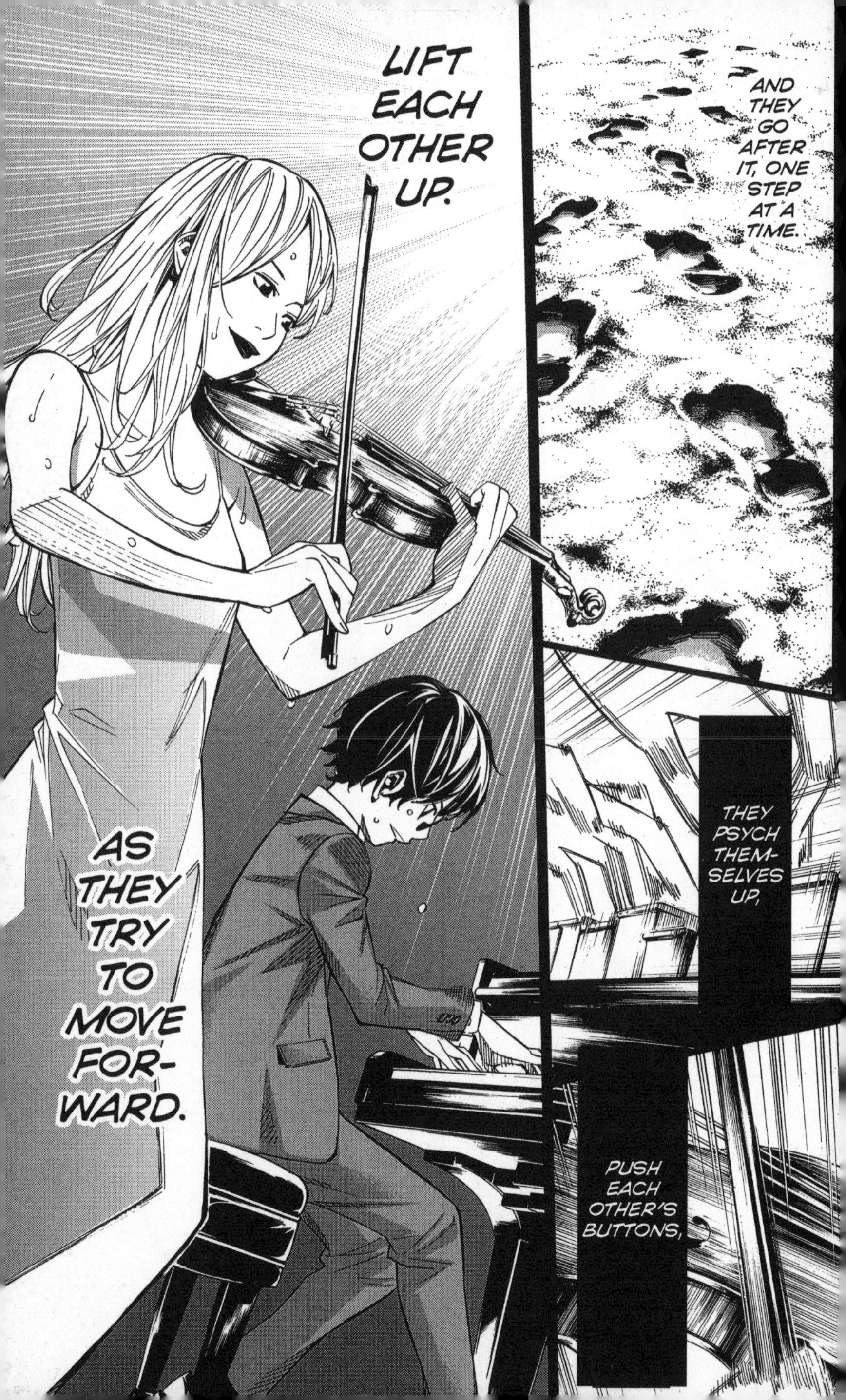
AND THEY GO AFTER IT, ONE STEP AT A TIME.
THEY PSYCH THEM-SELVES UP,
PUSH EACH OTHER'S BUTTONS,
LIFT EACH OTHER UP.
AS THEY TRY TO MOVE FOR-WARD.

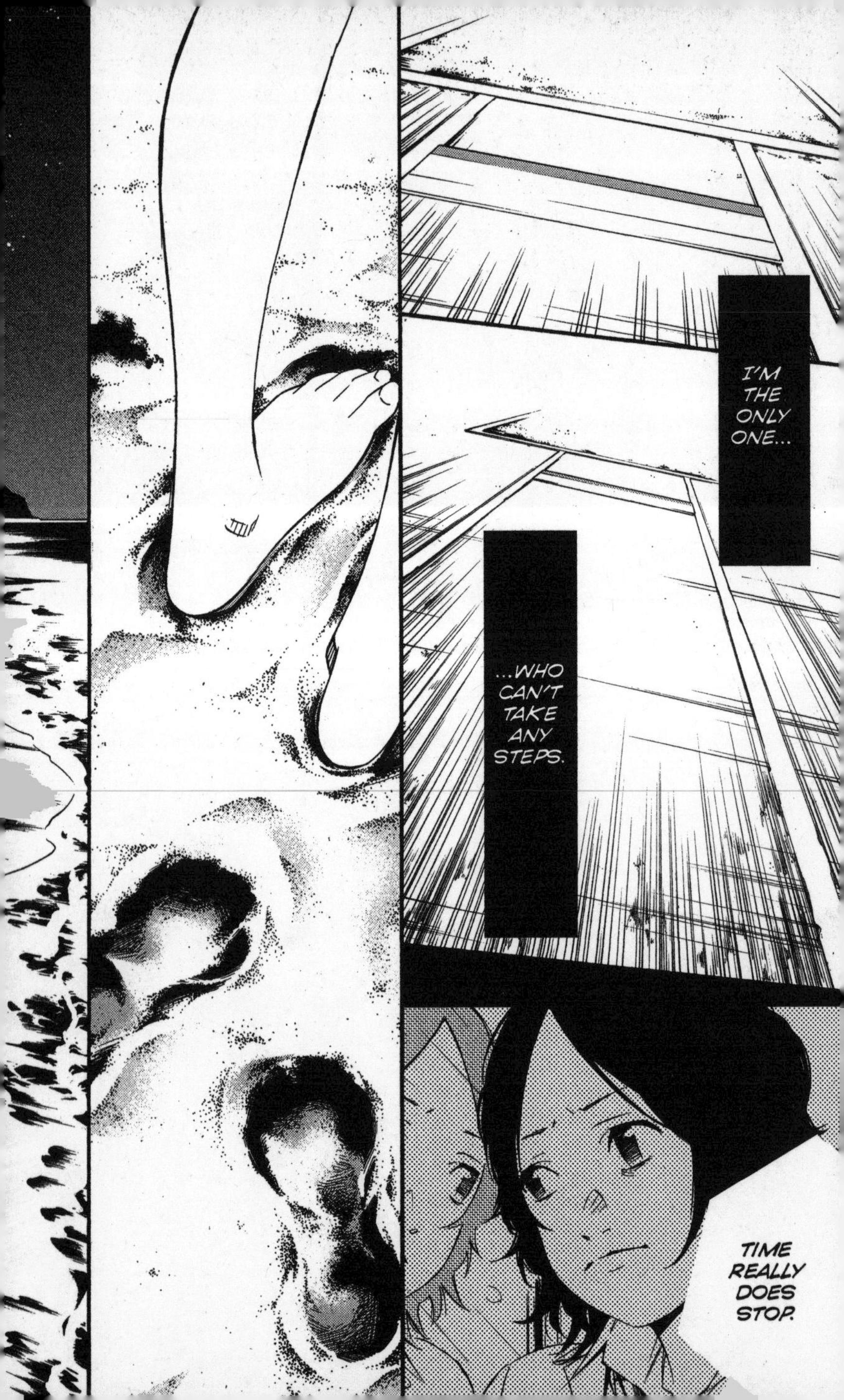
I'M THE ONLY ONE...
...WHO CAN'T TAKE ANY STEPS.
TIME REALLY DOES STOP.

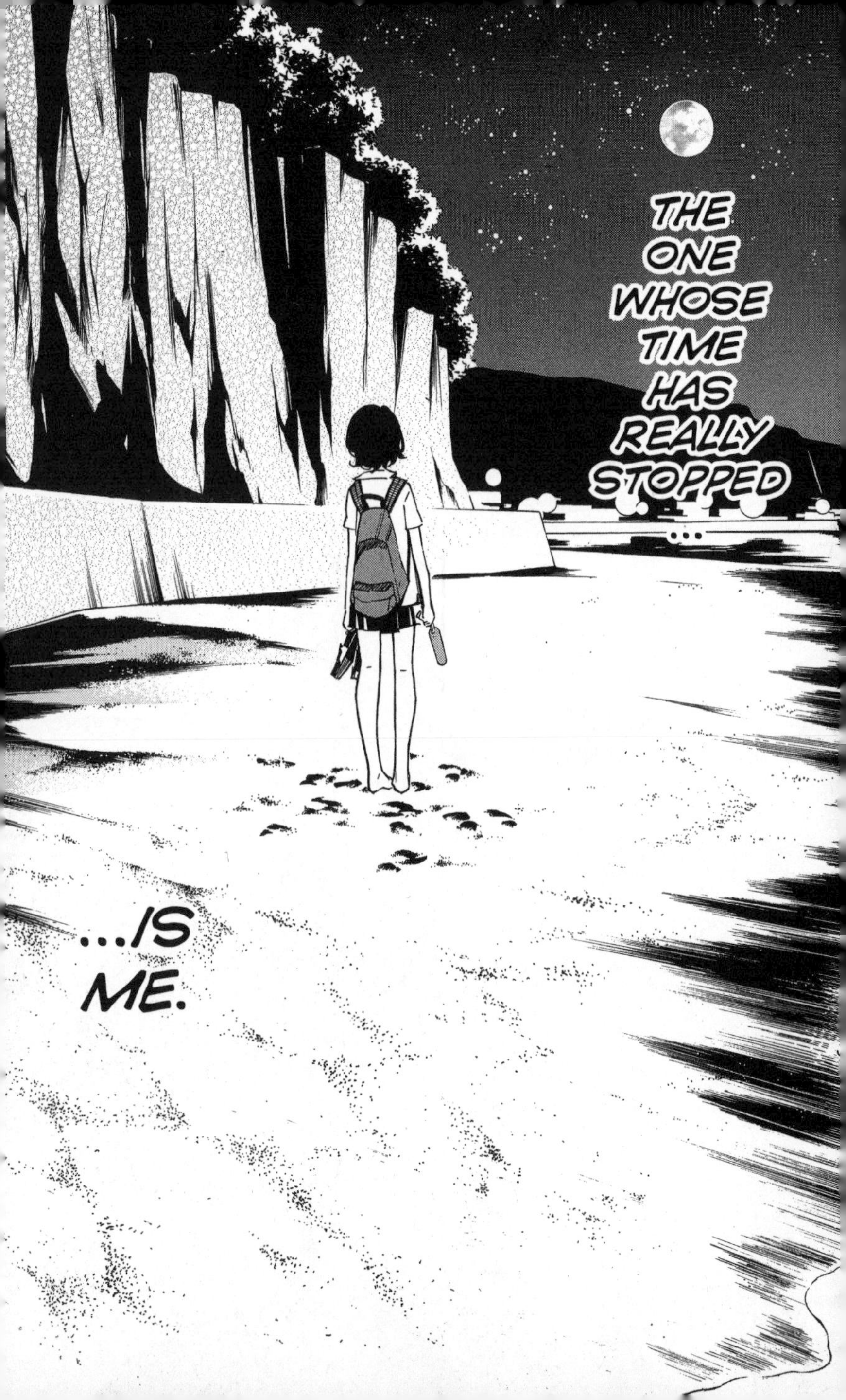
THE ONE WHOSE TIME HAS REALLY STOPPED ...
...IS ME.

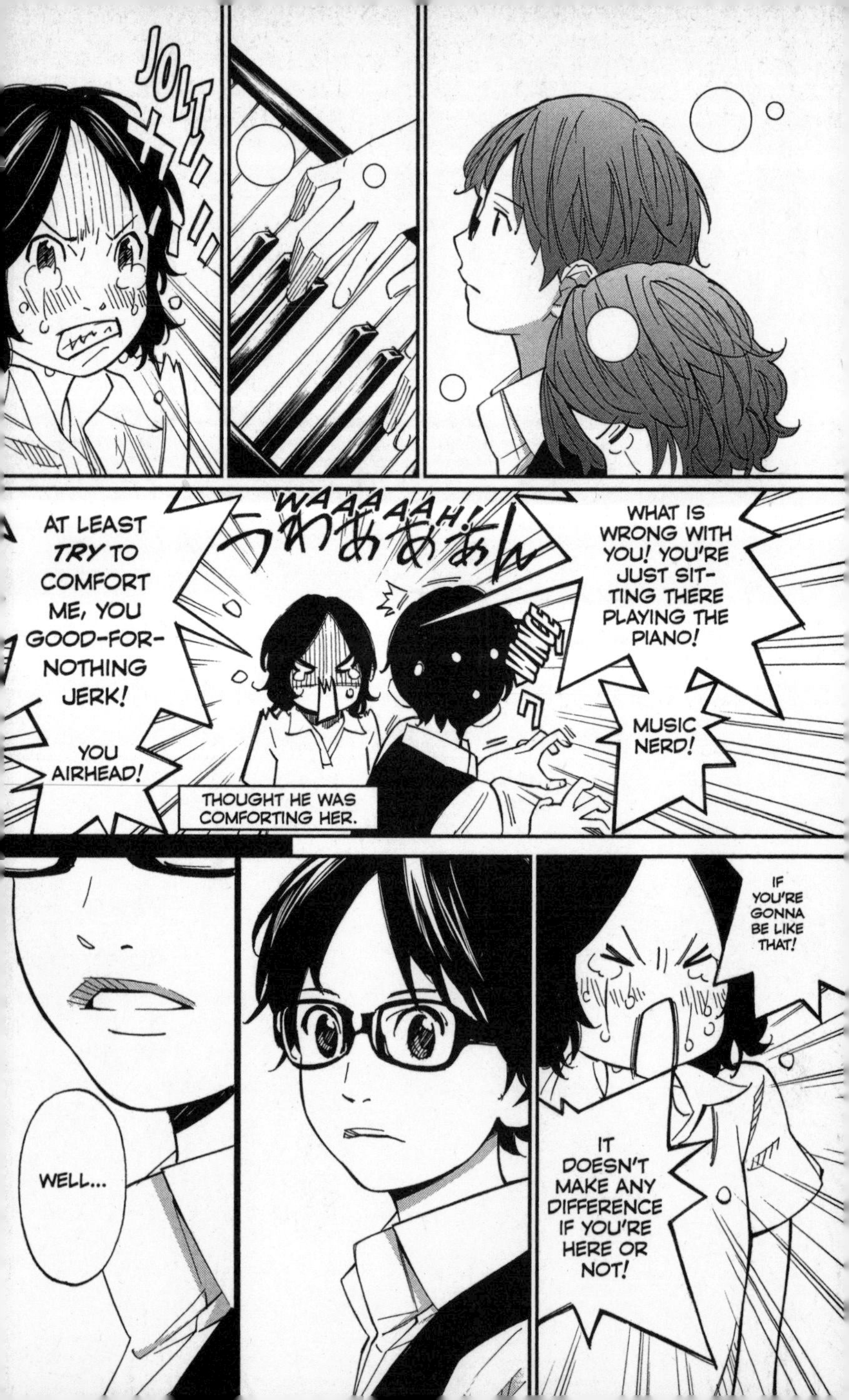
JOLT
WAAAAAAH!
うわあああん
WHAT IS WRONG WITH YOU! YOU'RE JUST SITTING THERE PLAYING THE PIANO!
MUSIC NERD!
AT LEAST *TRY* TO COMFORT ME, YOU GOOD-FOR-NOTHING JERK!
YOU AIRHEAD!
THOUGHT HE WAS COMFORTING HER.
IF YOU'RE GONNA BE LIKE THAT!
IT DOESN'T MAKE ANY DIFFERENCE IF YOU'RE HERE OR NOT!
WELL...

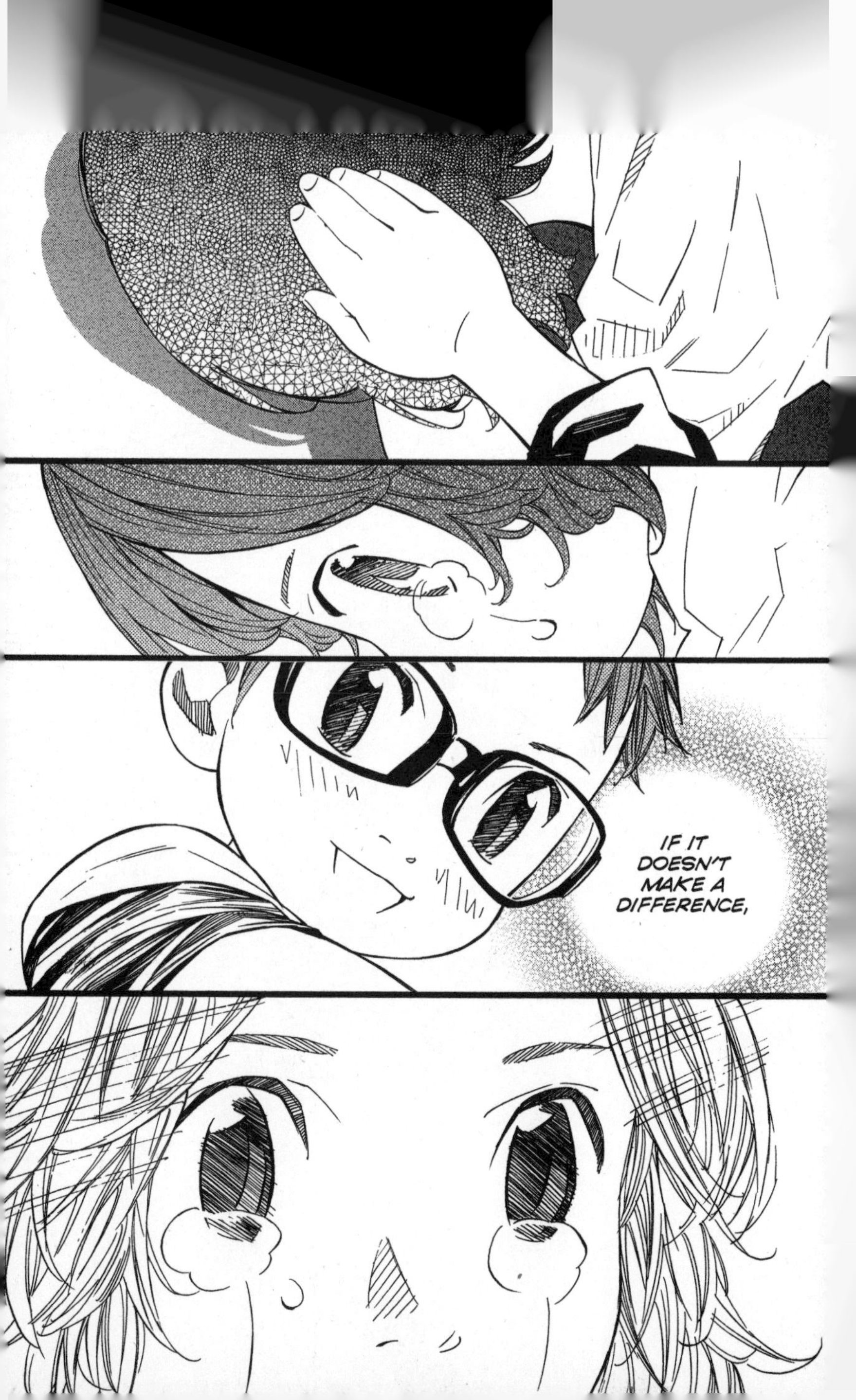
IF IT DOESN'T MAKE A DIFFERENCE,

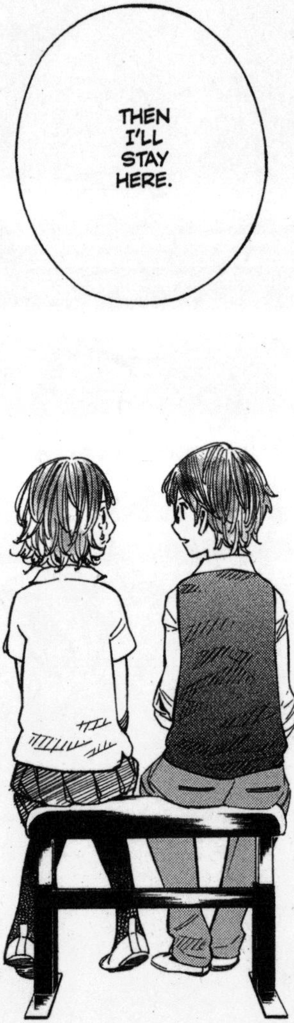
THEN I'LL STAY HERE.

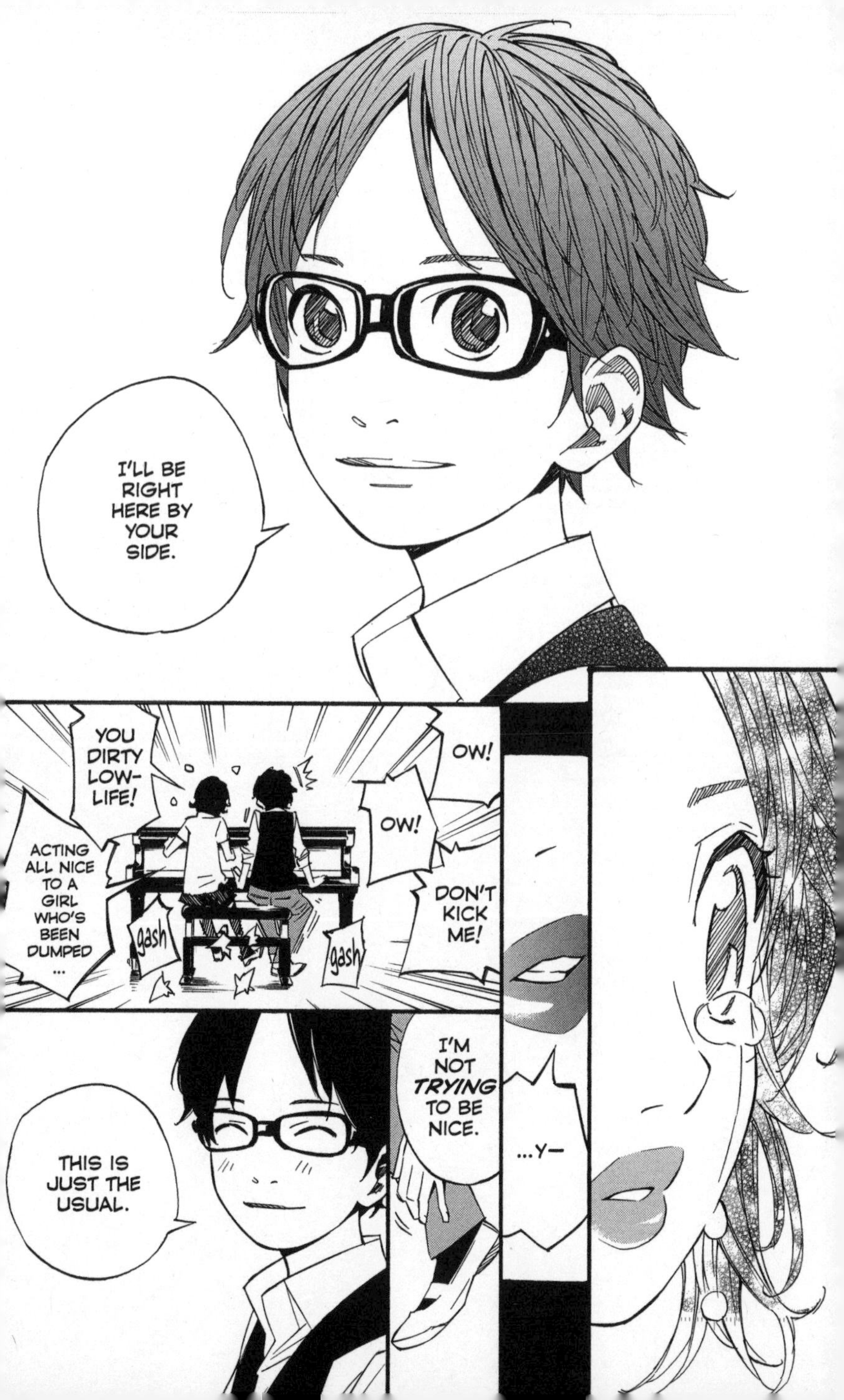
I'LL BE RIGHT HERE BY YOUR SIDE.
...Y—
OW!
OW!
DON'T KICK ME!
YOU DIRTY LOW-LIFE!
ACTING ALL NICE TO A GIRL WHO'S BEEN DUMPED ...
gash
gash
I'M NOT *TRYING* TO BE NICE.
THIS IS JUST THE USUAL.

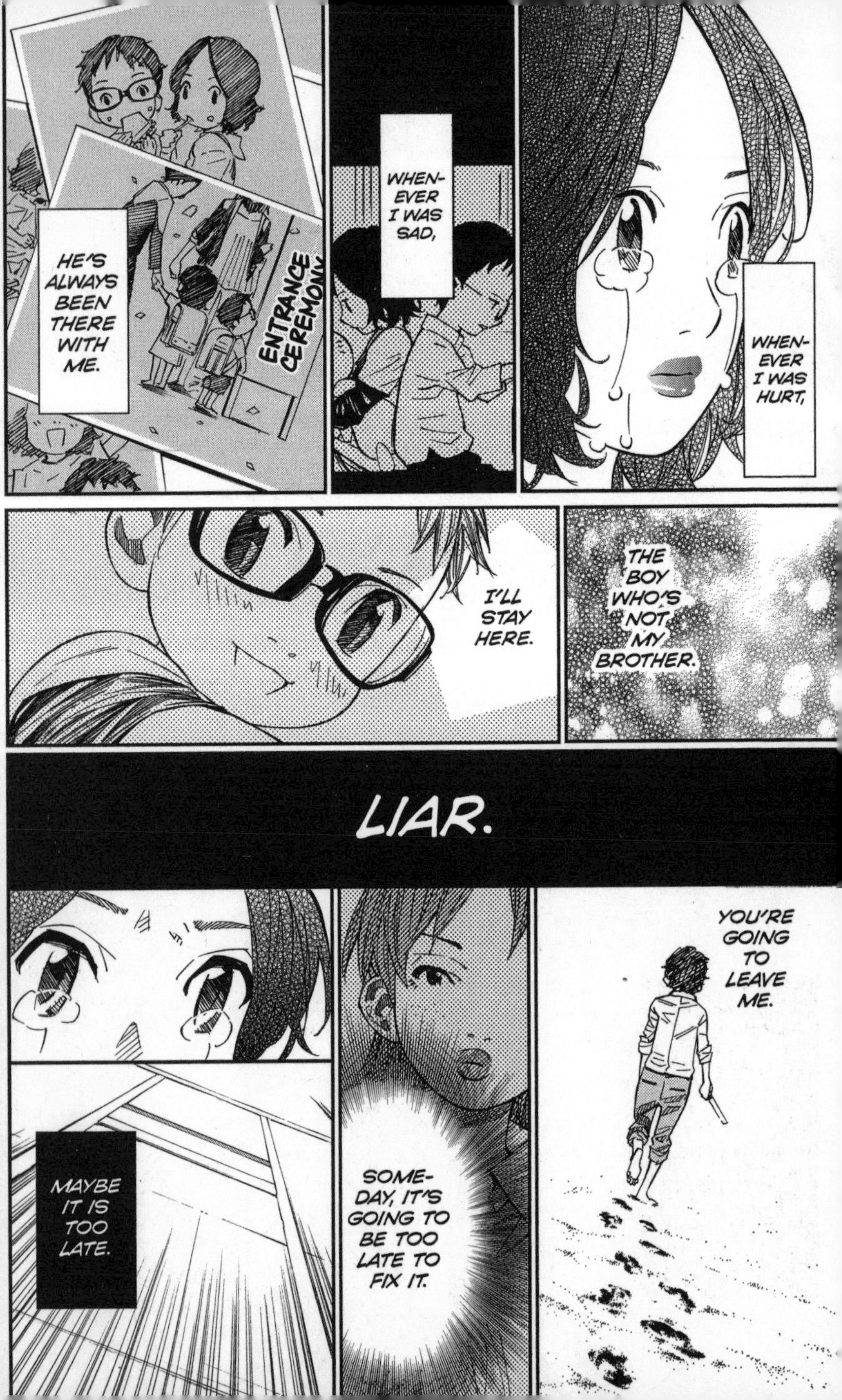
WHEN-EVER I WAS HURT,
WHEN-EVER I WAS SAD,
HE'S ALWAYS BEEN THERE WITH ME.
ENTRANCE CEREMONY
THE BOY WHO'S NOT MY BROTHER.
I'LL STAY HERE.
LIAR.
YOU'RE GOING TO LEAVE ME.
SOME-DAY, IT'S GOING TO BE TOO LATE TO FIX IT.
MAYBE IT IS TOO LATE.

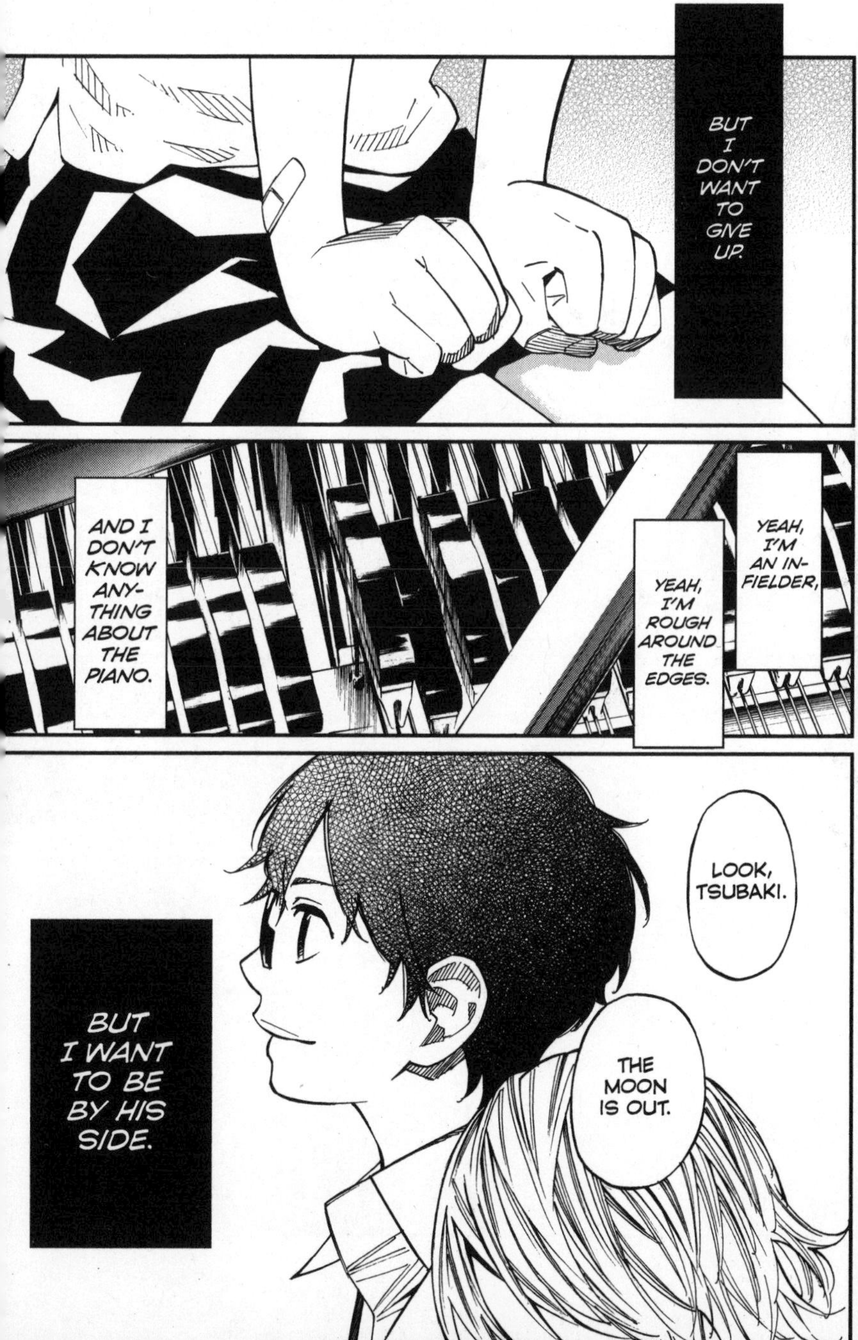
BUT I DON'T WANT TO GIVE UP.
YEAH, I'M AN IN-FIELDER,
YEAH, I'M ROUGH AROUND THE EDGES.
AND I DON'T KNOW ANY-THING ABOUT THE PIANO.
LOOK, TSUBAKI.
THE MOON IS OUT.
BUT I WANT TO BE BY HIS SIDE.

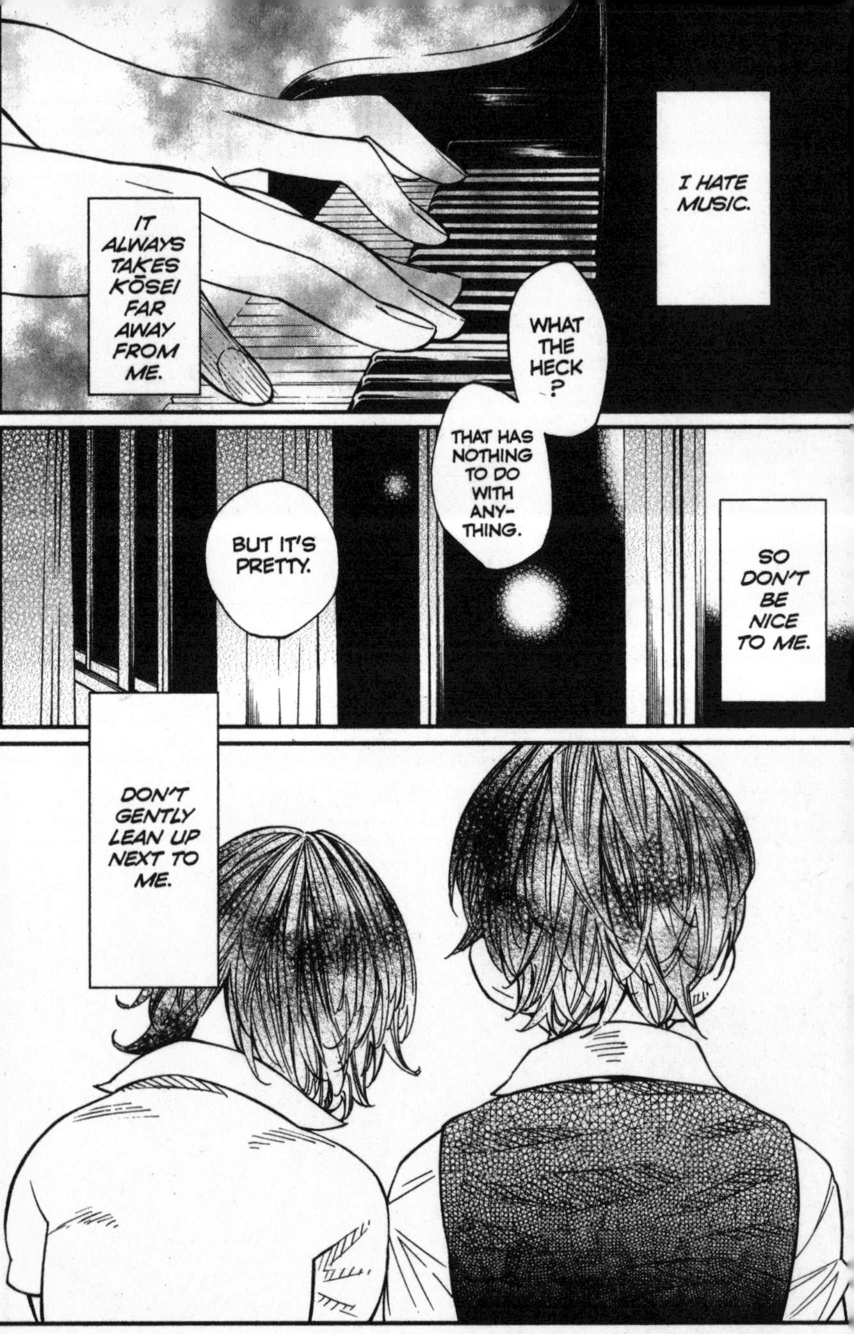
I HATE MUSIC.
WHAT THE HECK?
IT ALWAYS TAKES KŌSEI FAR AWAY FROM ME.
SO DON'T BE NICE TO ME.
THAT HAS NOTHING TO DO WITH ANYTHING.
BUT IT'S PRETTY.
DON'T GENTLY LEAN UP NEXT TO ME.

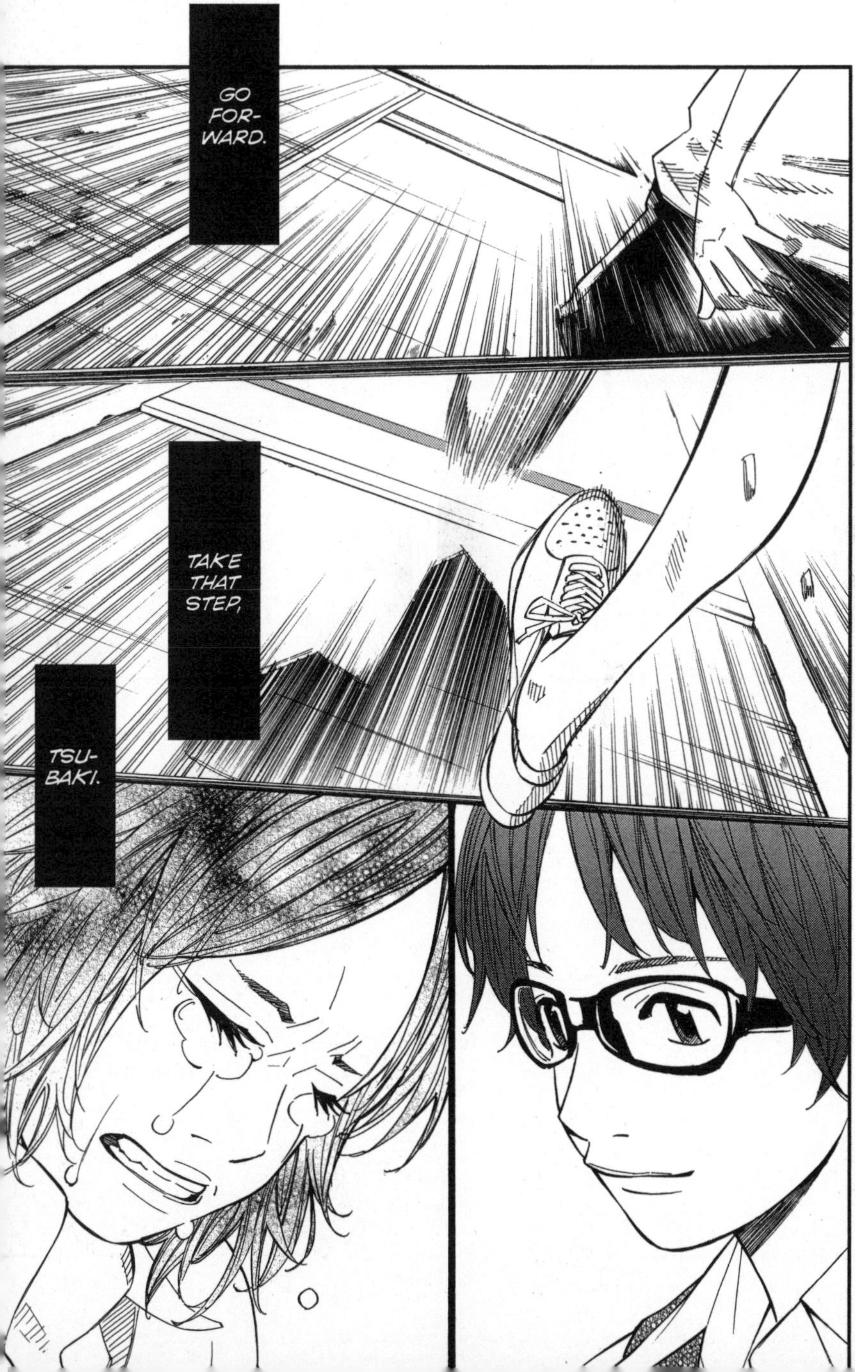
GO FOR-WARD.
TAKE THAT STEP,
TSU-BAKI.

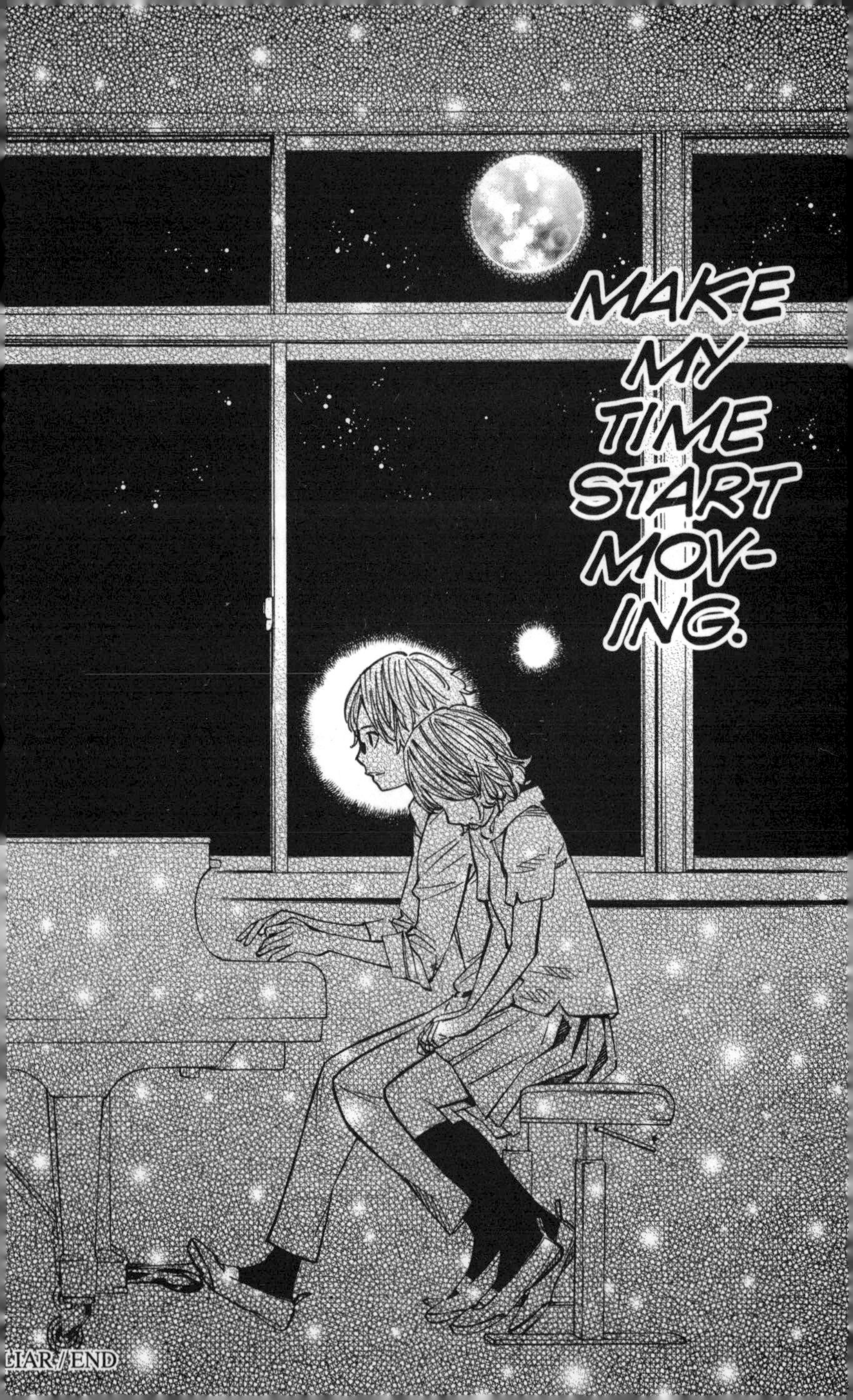
MAKE MY TIME START MOV- ING.
LIAR / END

Your Lie in April

I met the girl under full-bloomed cherry blossoms, and my fate has begun to change.

Your Lie in April

I met the girl under full-bloomed cherry blossoms, and my fate has begun to change.

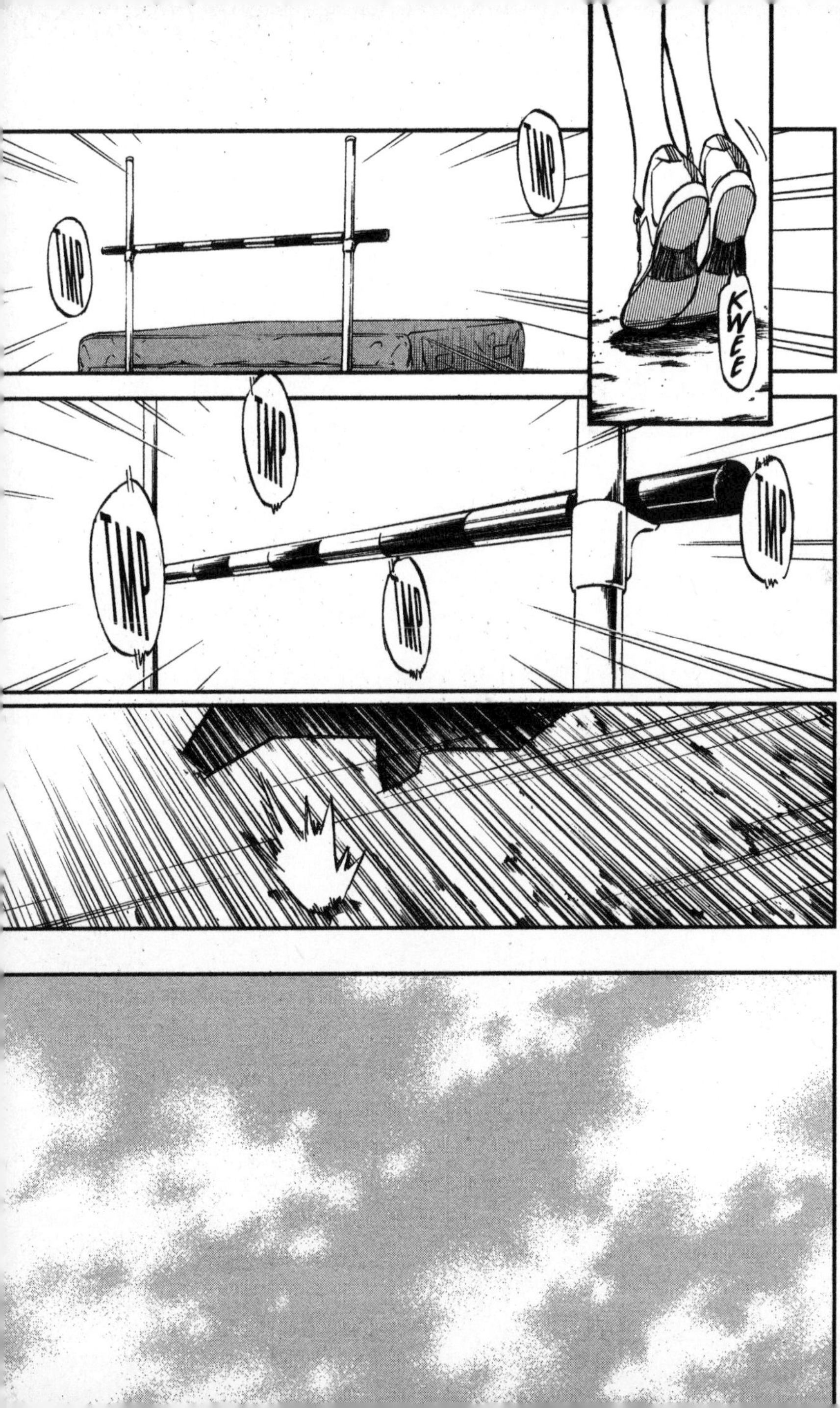
KWEE
TMP
TMP
TMP
TMP
TMP
TMP

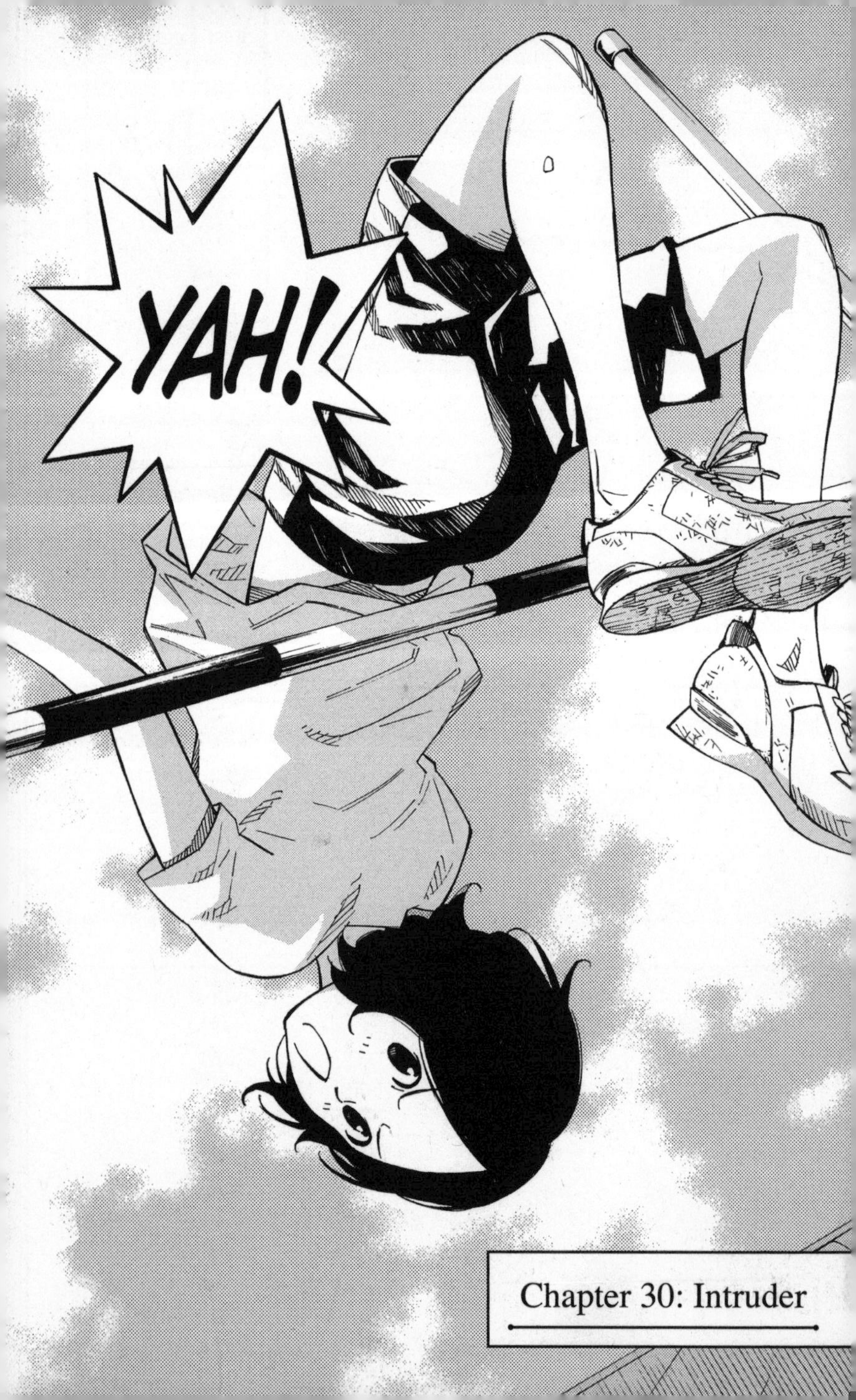
YAH!
Chapter 30: Intruder

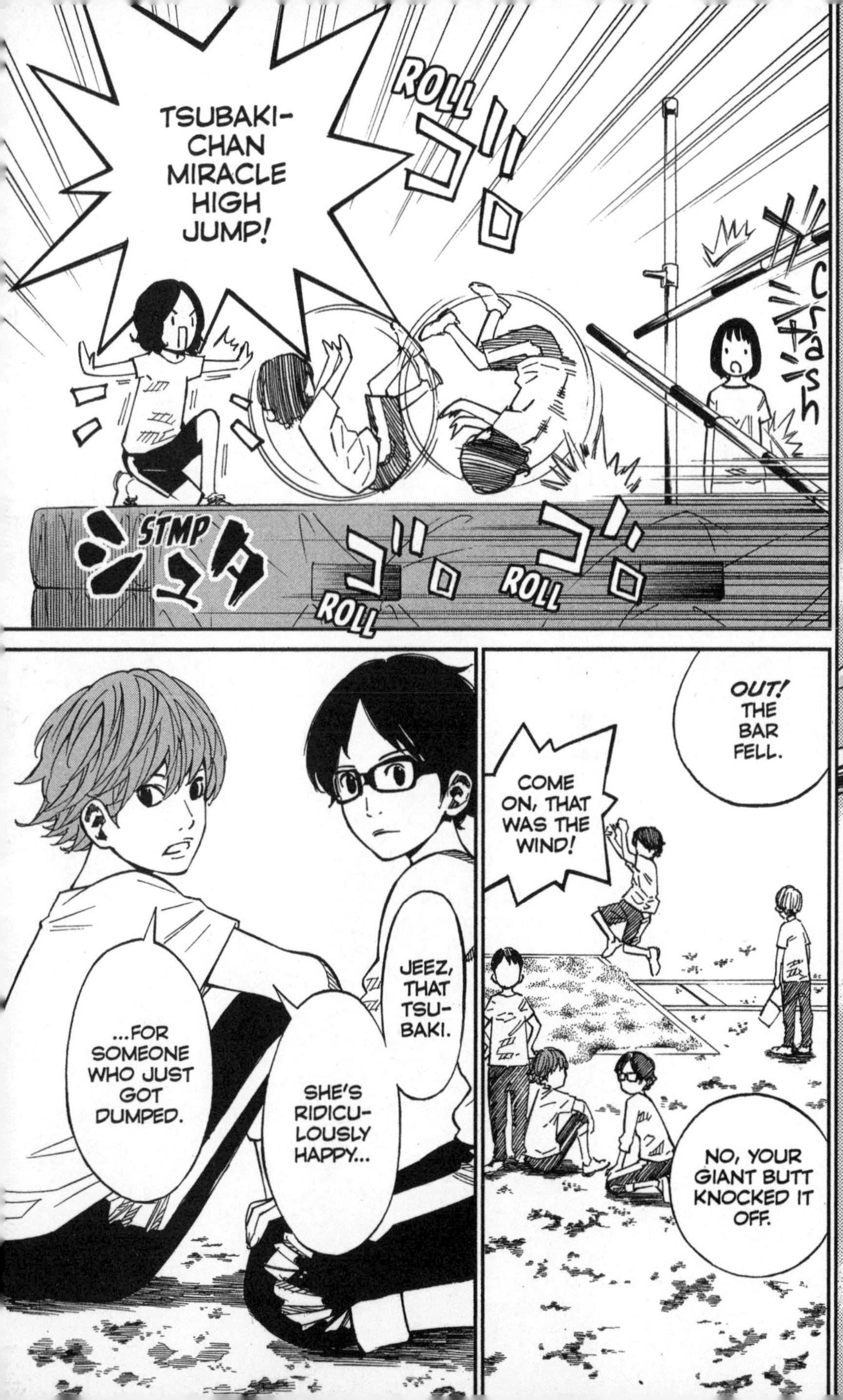
ROLL
crash
TSUBAKI-CHAN MIRACLE HIGH JUMP!
ROLL
ROLL
STMP
OUT! THE BAR FELL.
COME ON, THAT WAS THE WIND!
NO, YOUR GIANT BUTT KNOCKED IT OFF.
JEEZ, THAT TSUBAKI.
SHE'S RIDICULOUSLY HAPPY...
...FOR SOMEONE WHO JUST GOT DUMPED.

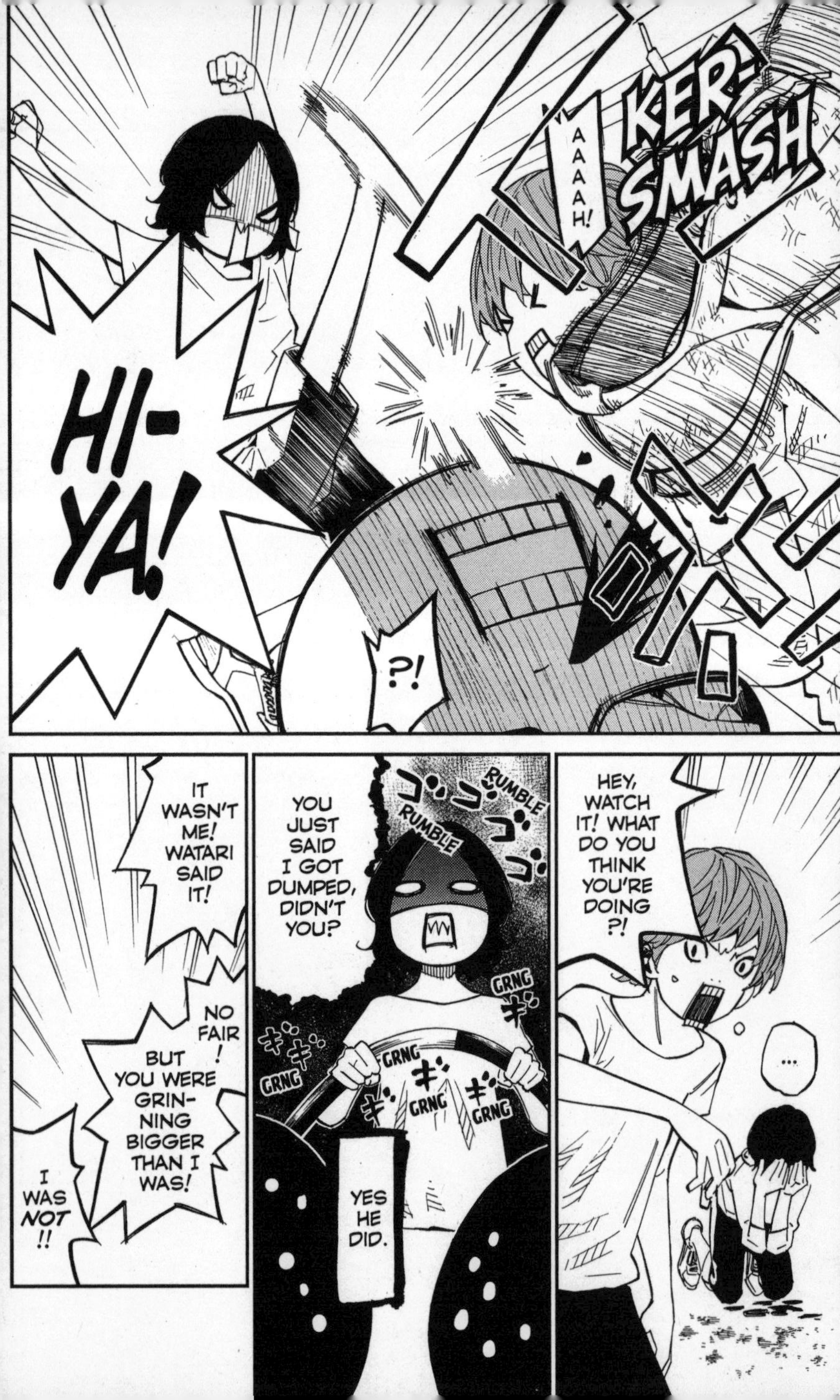
KER-SMASH
AAAAH!
HI-YA!
?!
HEY, WATCH IT! WHAT DO YOU THINK YOU'RE DOING?!
...
RUMBLE
RUMBLE
YOU JUST SAID I GOT DUMPED, DIDN'T YOU?
GRNG GRNG GRNG GRNG GRNG
YES HE DID.
IT WASN'T ME! WATARI SAID IT!
NO FAIR!
BUT YOU WERE GRIN-NING BIGGER THAN I WAS!
I WAS NOT!!

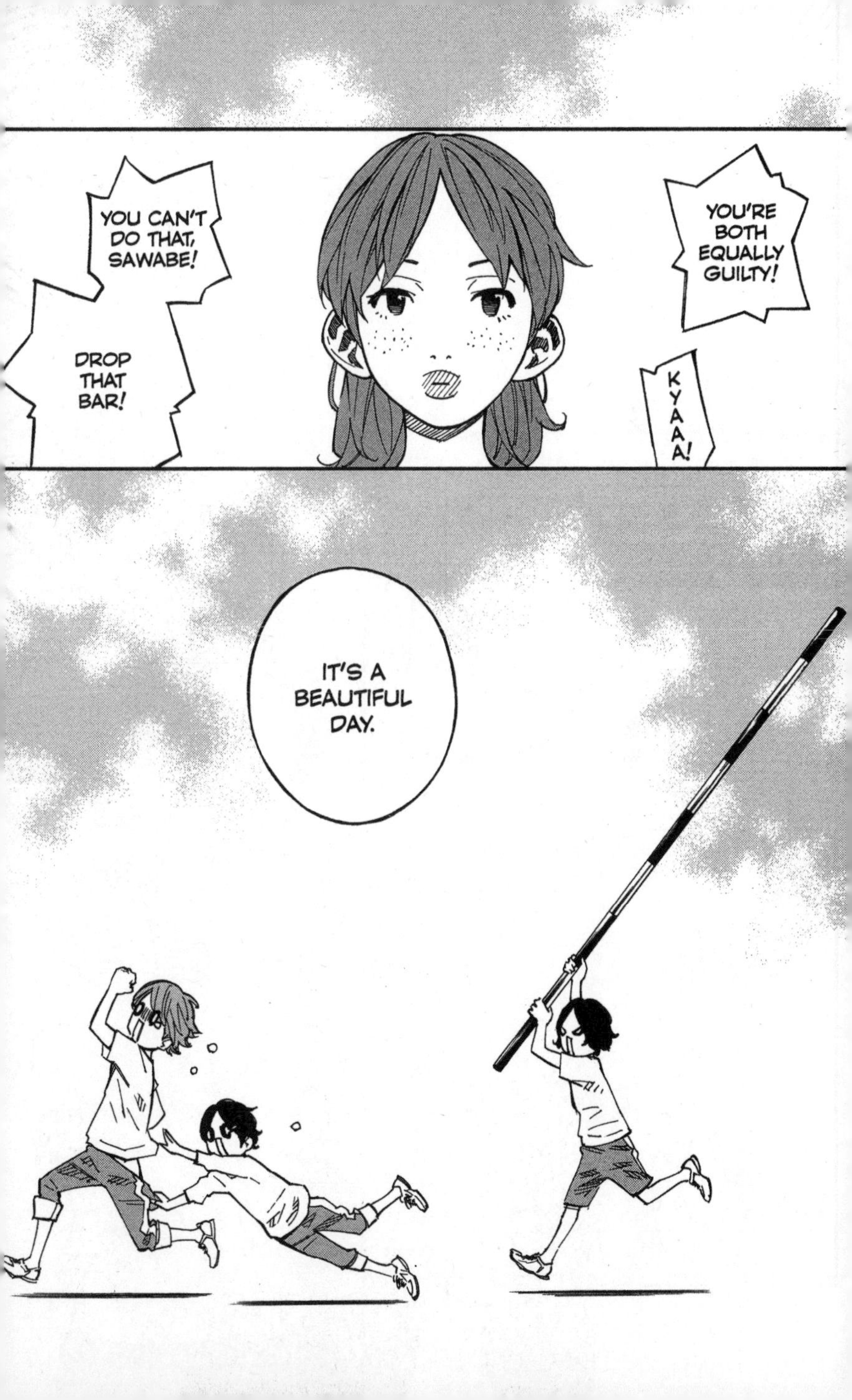
YOU'RE BOTH EQUALLY GUILTY!
KYAAA!
YOU CAN'T DO THAT, SAWABE!
DROP THAT BAR!
IT'S A BEAUTIFUL DAY.

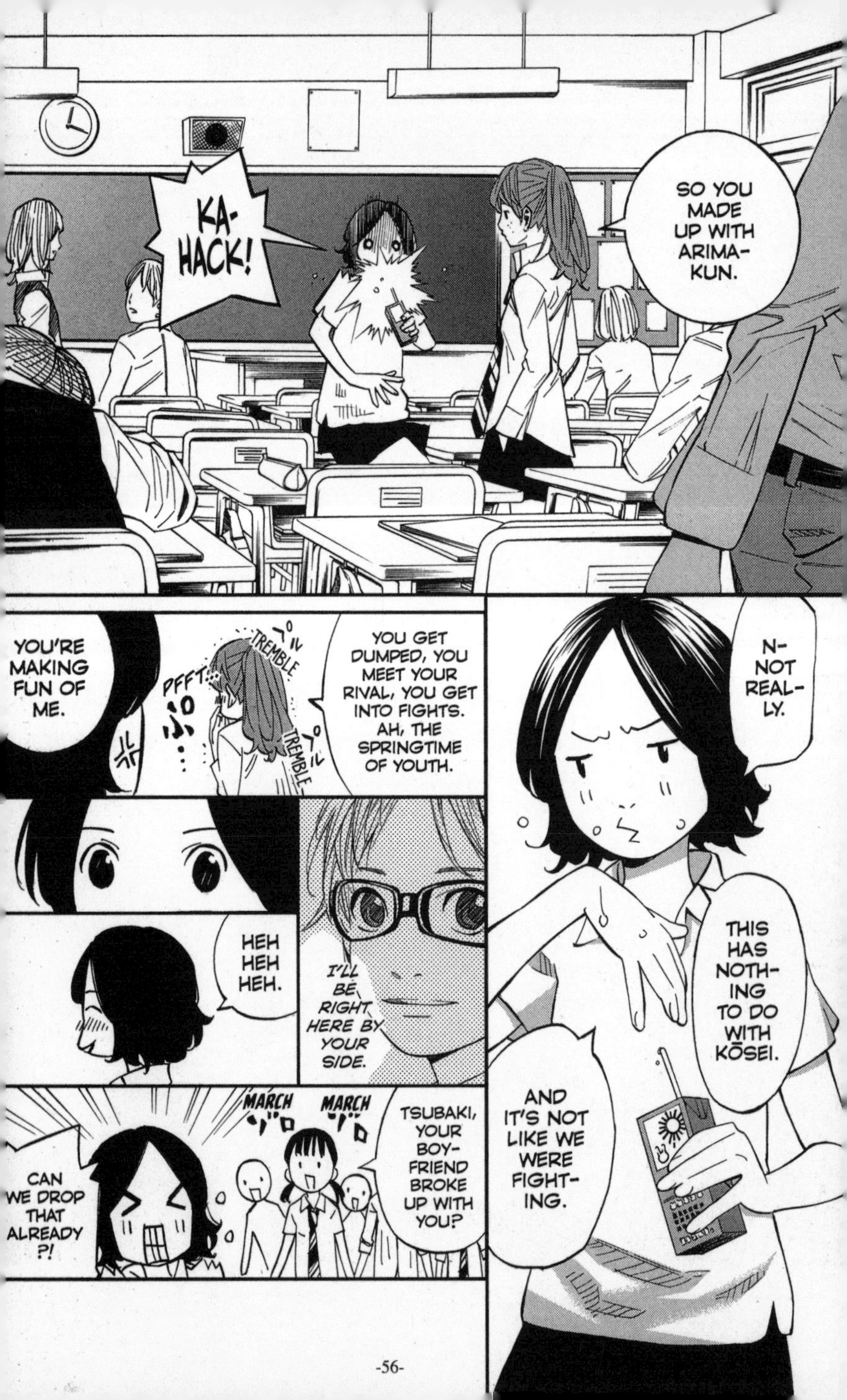
SO YOU MADE UP WITH ARIMA-KUN.
KA-HACK!
N-NOT REALLY.
THIS HAS NOTHING TO DO WITH KŌSEI.
AND IT'S NOT LIKE WE WERE FIGHTING.
YOU GET DUMPED, YOU MEET YOUR RIVAL, YOU GET INTO FIGHTS. AH, THE SPRINGTIME OF YOUTH.
TREMBLE
TREMBLE
PFFT
YOU'RE MAKING FUN OF ME.
I'LL BE RIGHT HERE BY YOUR SIDE.
HEH HEH HEH.
TSUBAKI, YOUR BOY-FRIEND BROKE UP WITH YOU?
MARCH
MARCH
CAN WE DROP THAT ALREADY ?!

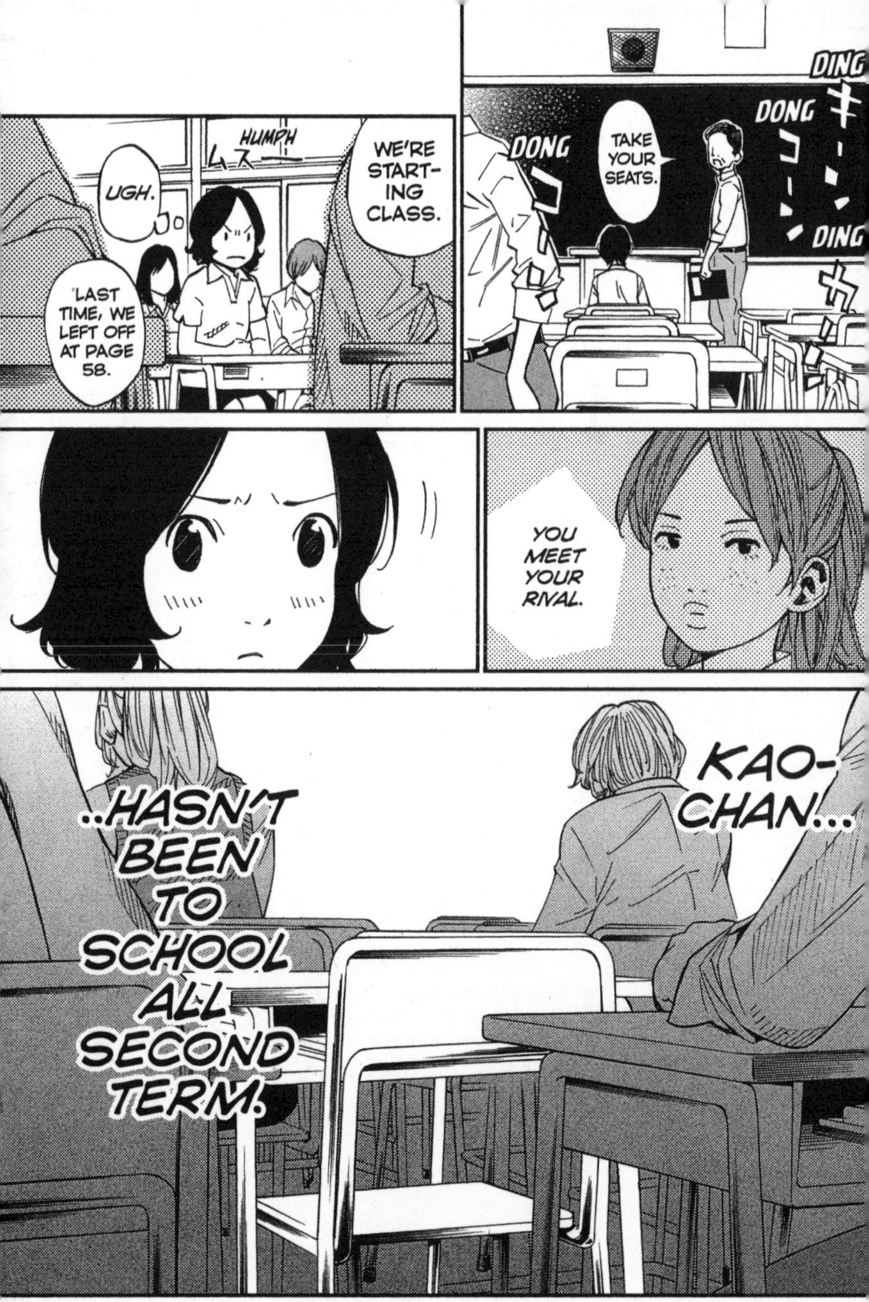

DING
DONG
DONG
TAKE YOUR SEATS.
DING
WE'RE START-ING CLASS.
HUMPH
ムスー
UGH.
LAST TIME, WE LEFT OFF AT PAGE 58.
YOU MEET YOUR RIVAL.
KAO-CHAN...
...HASN'T BEEN TO SCHOOL ALL SECOND TERM.

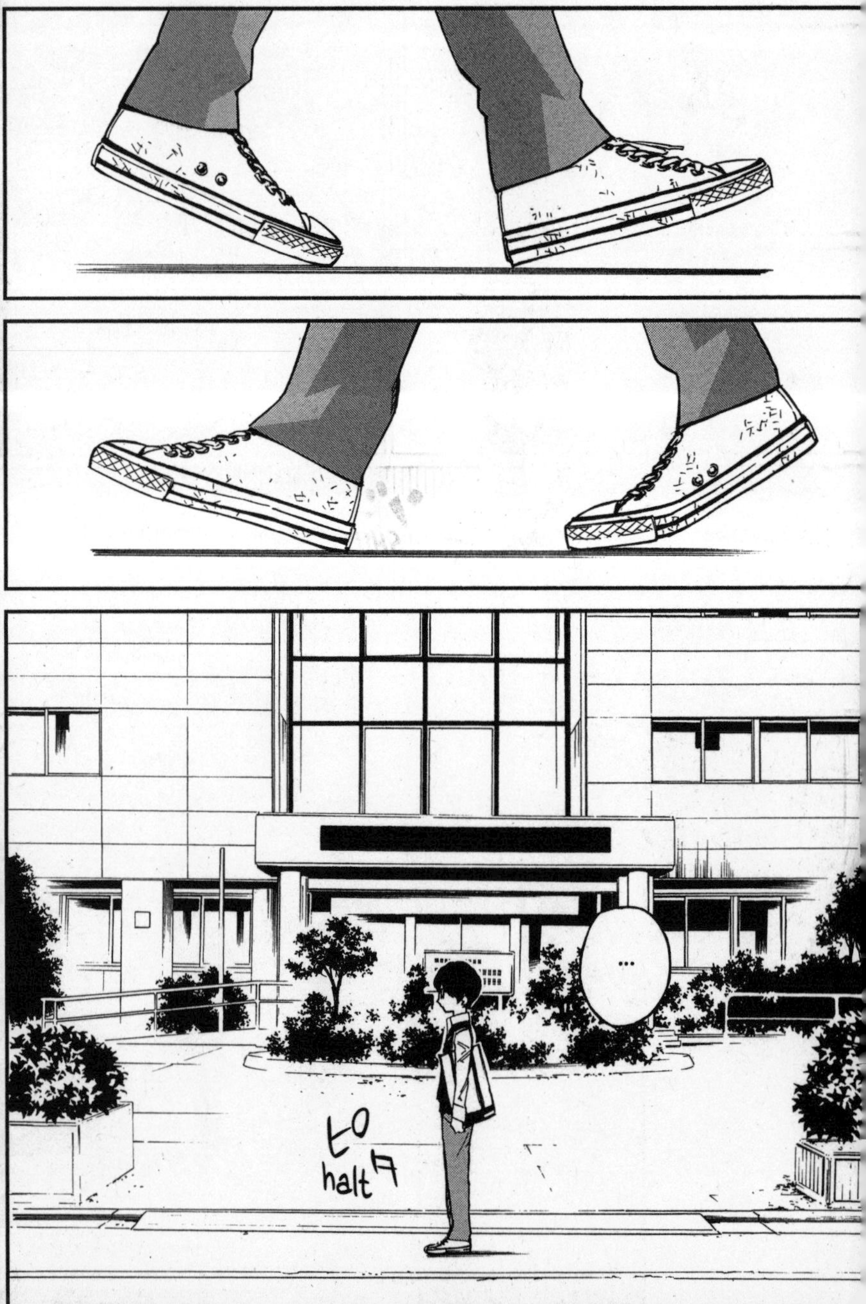
…
ピタ
halt

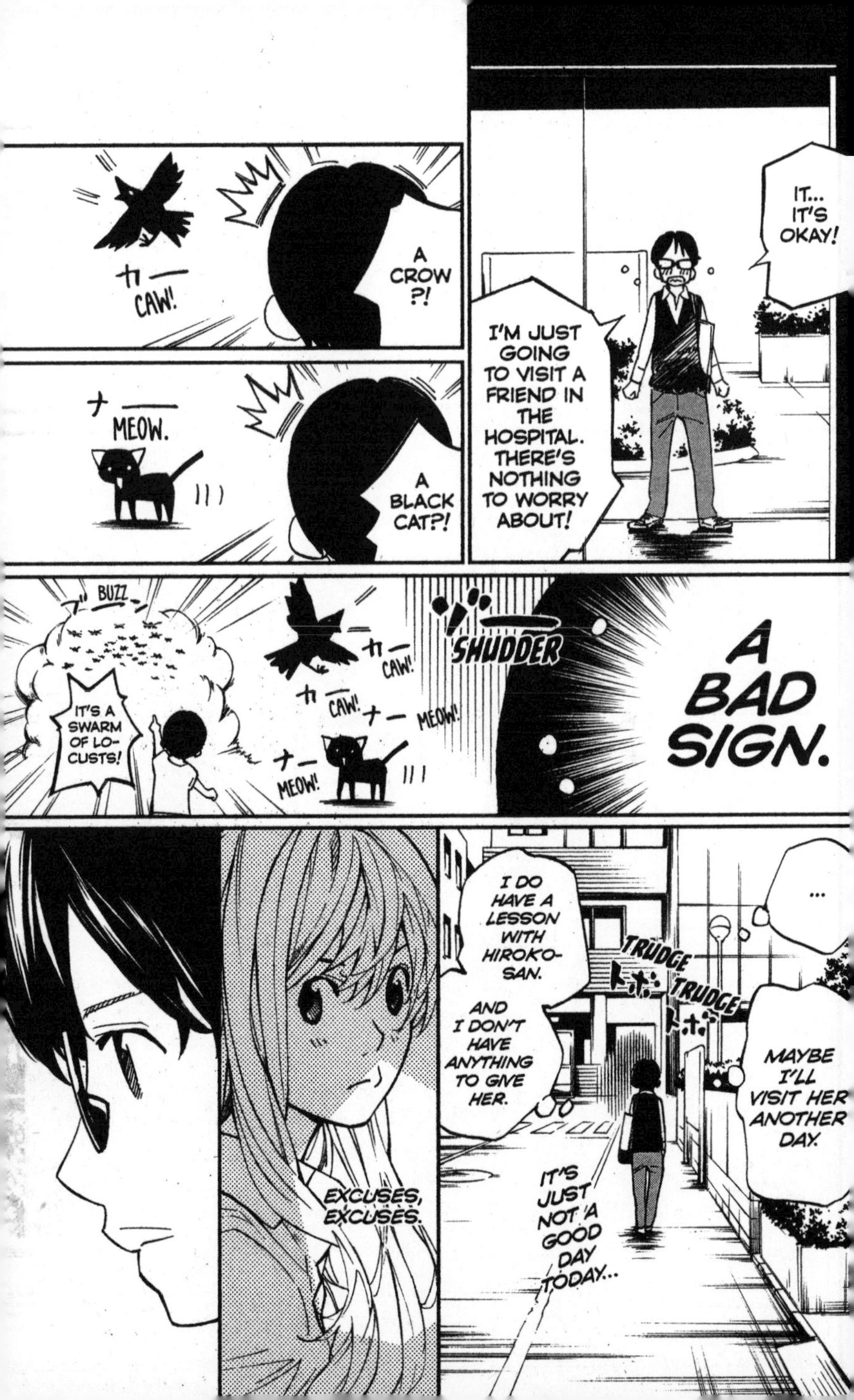
IT... IT'S OKAY!
I'M JUST GOING TO VISIT A FRIEND IN THE HOSPITAL. THERE'S NOTHING TO WORRY ABOUT!
A CROW?!
カー CAW!
A BLACK CAT?!
ナー MEOW.
A BAD SIGN.
SHUDDER
カー CAW!
カー CAW!
ナー MEOW!
ナー MEOW!
BUZZ
IT'S A SWARM OF LO-CUSTS!
...
MAYBE I'LL VISIT HER ANOTHER DAY.
TRUDGE
TRUDGE
I DO HAVE A LESSON WITH HIROKO-SAN.
AND I DON'T HAVE ANYTHING TO GIVE HER.
IT'S JUST NOT A GOOD DAY TODAY...
EXCUSES, EXCUSES.

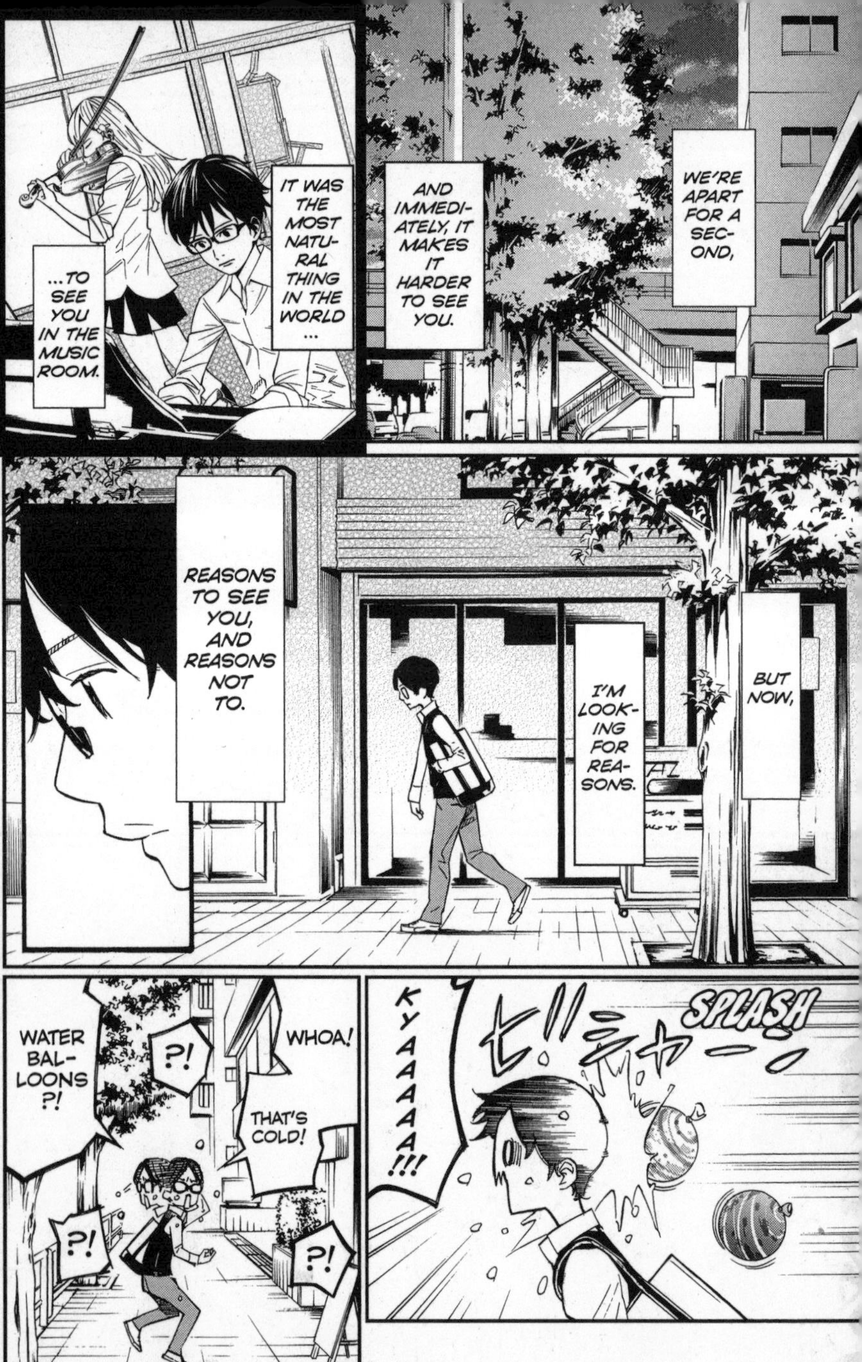
WE'RE APART FOR A SECOND,
AND IMMEDIATELY, IT MAKES IT HARDER TO SEE YOU.
IT WAS THE MOST NATURAL THING IN THE WORLD ...
...TO SEE YOU IN THE MUSIC ROOM.
BUT NOW,
I'M LOOKING FOR REASONS.
REASONS TO SEE YOU, AND REASONS NOT TO.
SPLASH
KYAAAAAA!!!
WHOA!
?!
WATER BALLOONS ?!
THAT'S COLD!
?!
?!

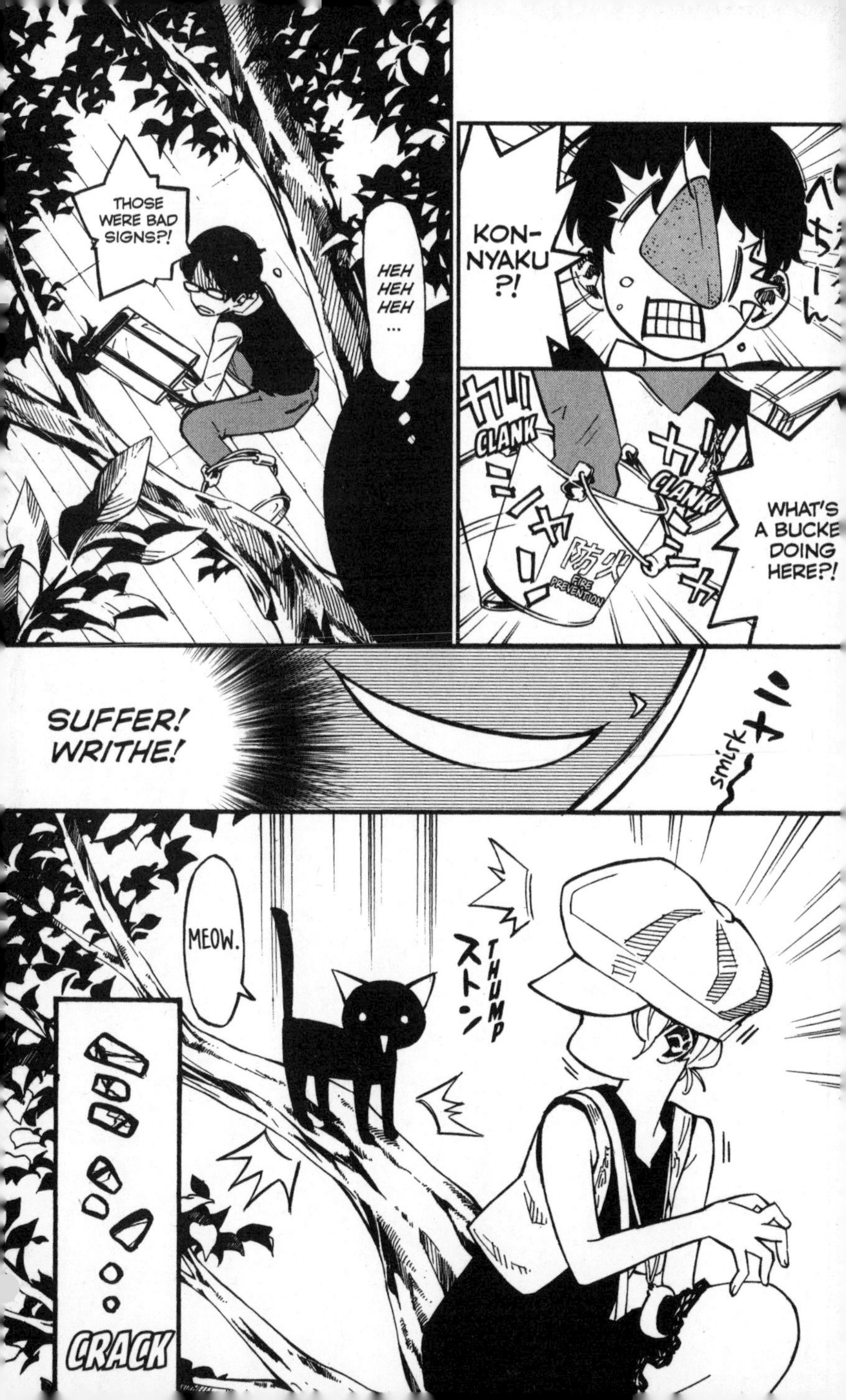
へちーん
KON-NYAKU?!
CLANK
CLANK
防火
FIRE PREVENTION
WHAT'S A BUCKE DOING HERE?!
HEH HEH HEH ...
THOSE WERE BAD SIGNS?!
smirk
SUFFER! WRITHE!
THUMP
MEOW.
CRACK

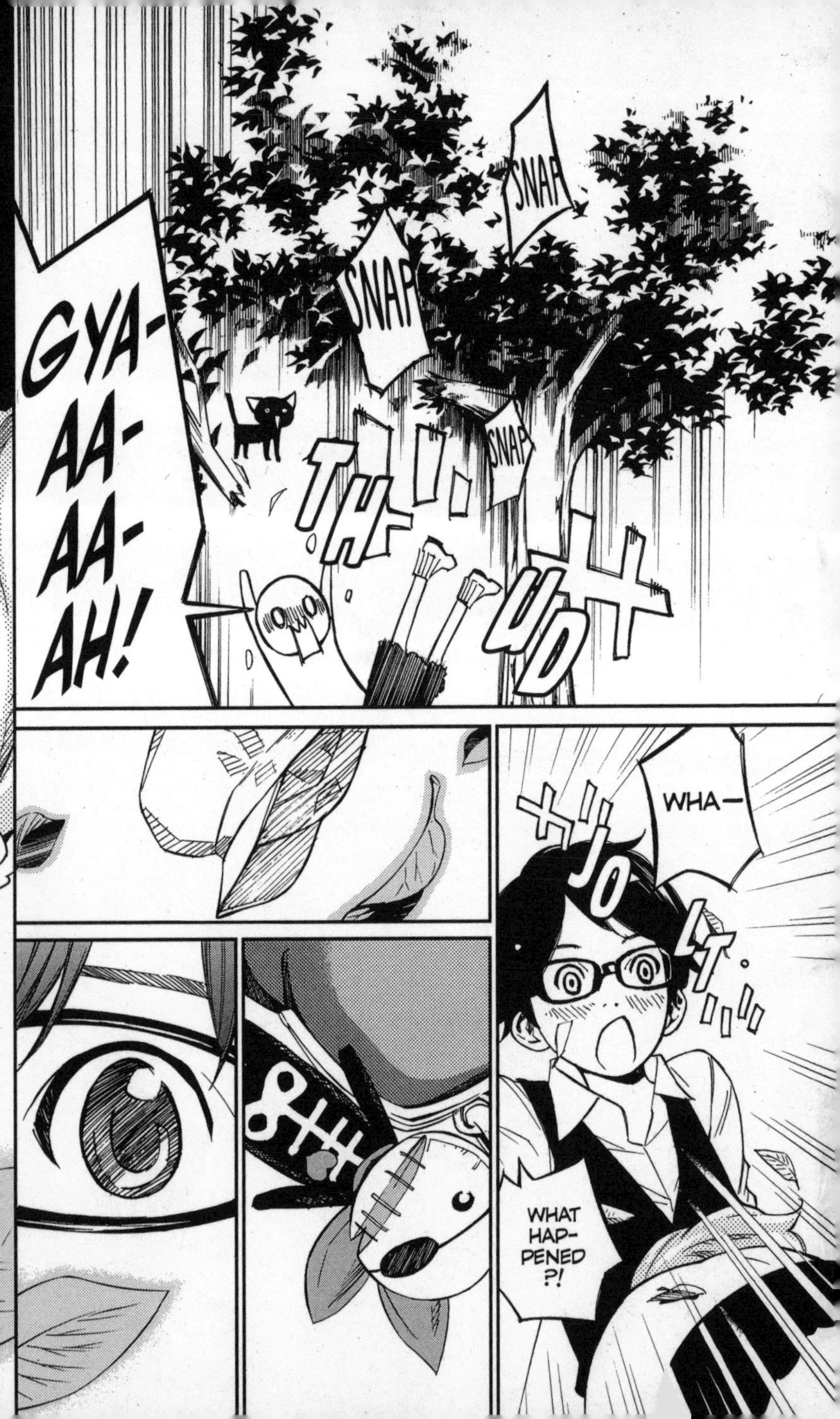
SNAP
SNAP
SNAP
GYA-AA-AA-AH!
THUD
WHA—
JOLT
WHAT HAP-PENED?!

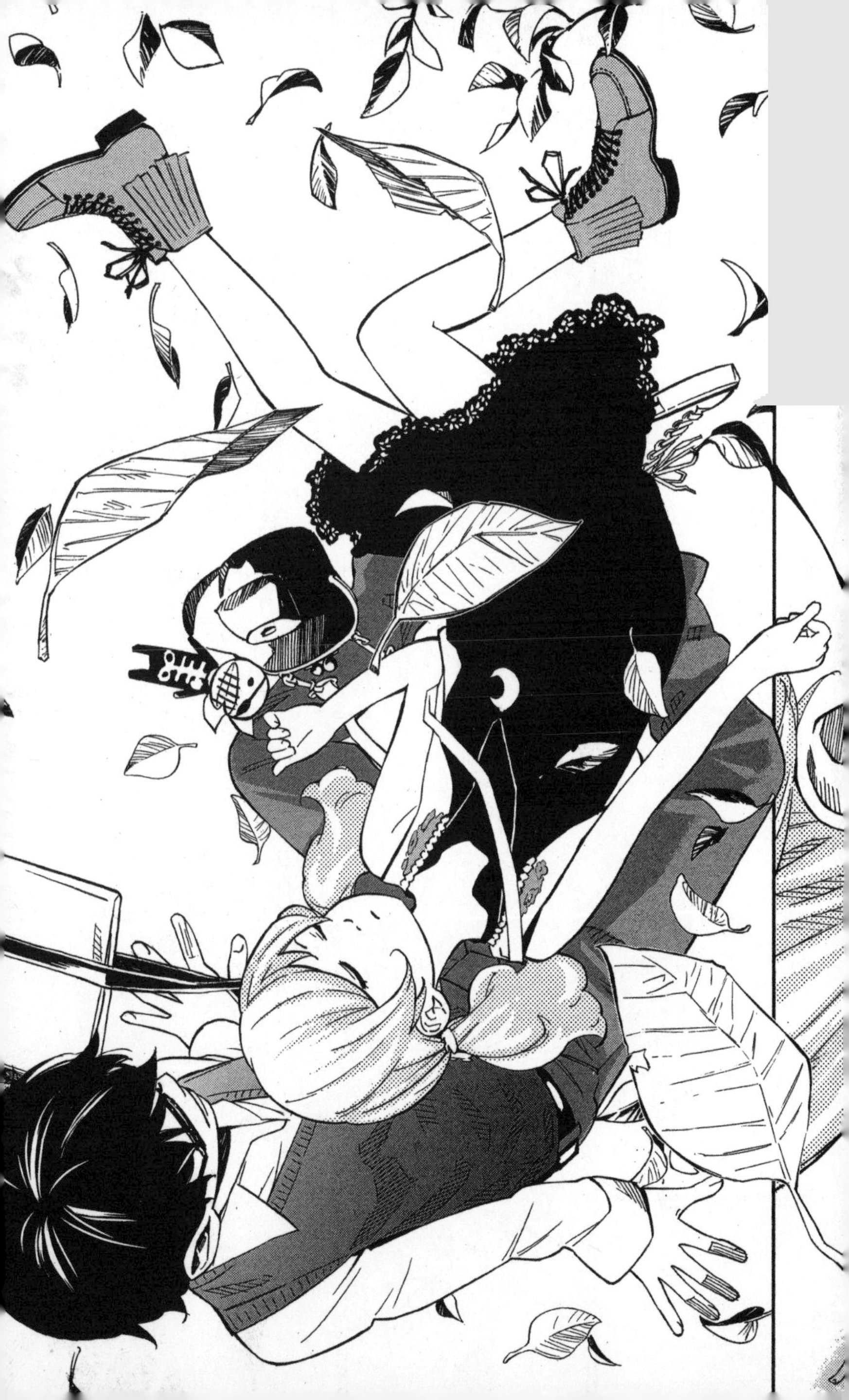

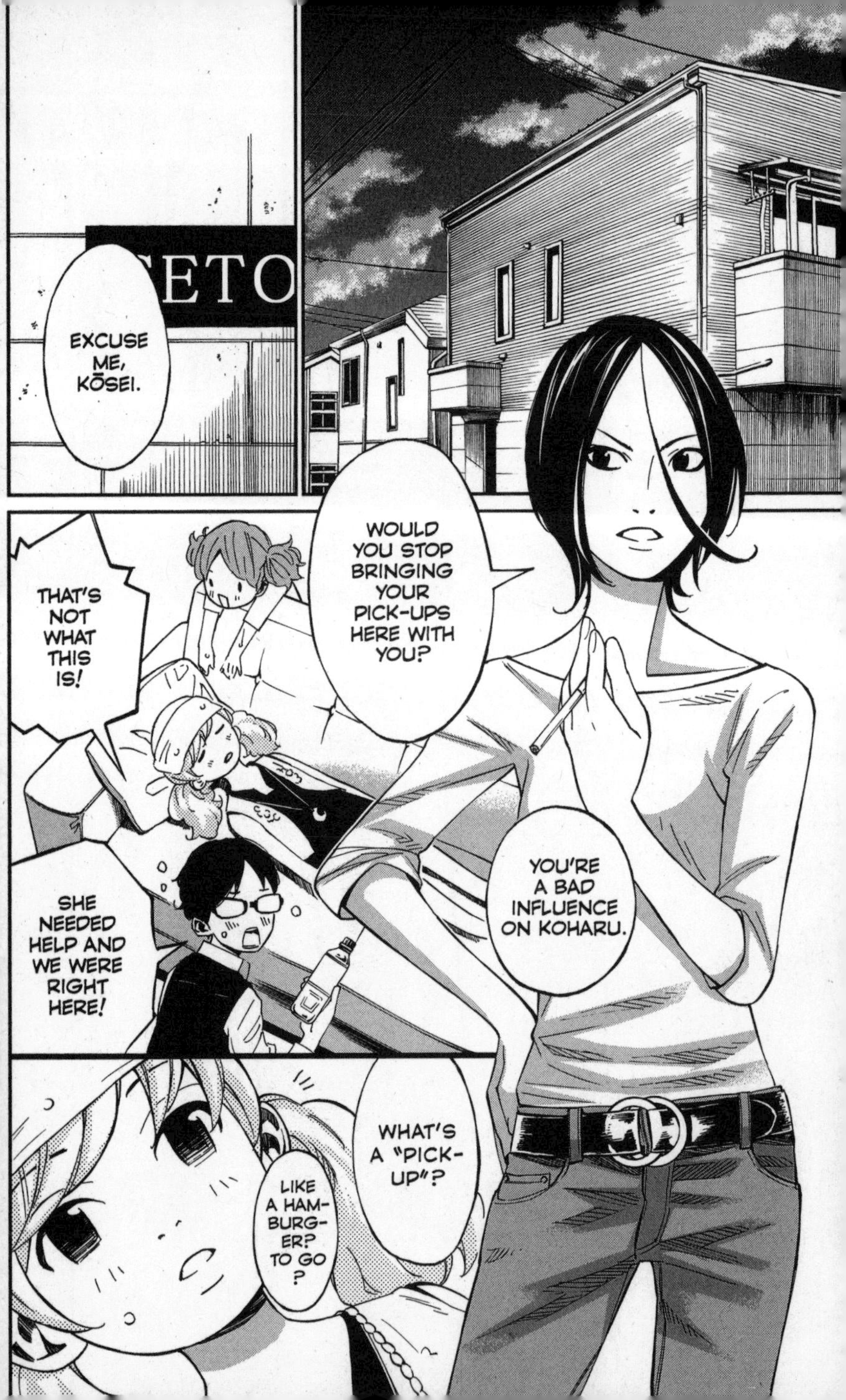
SETO
EXCUSE ME, KŌSEI.
WOULD YOU STOP BRINGING YOUR PICK-UPS HERE WITH YOU?
YOU'RE A BAD INFLUENCE ON KOHARU.
THAT'S NOT WHAT THIS IS!
SHE NEEDED HELP AND WE WERE RIGHT HERE!
WHAT'S A "PICK-UP"?
LIKE A HAMBURGER? TO GO?

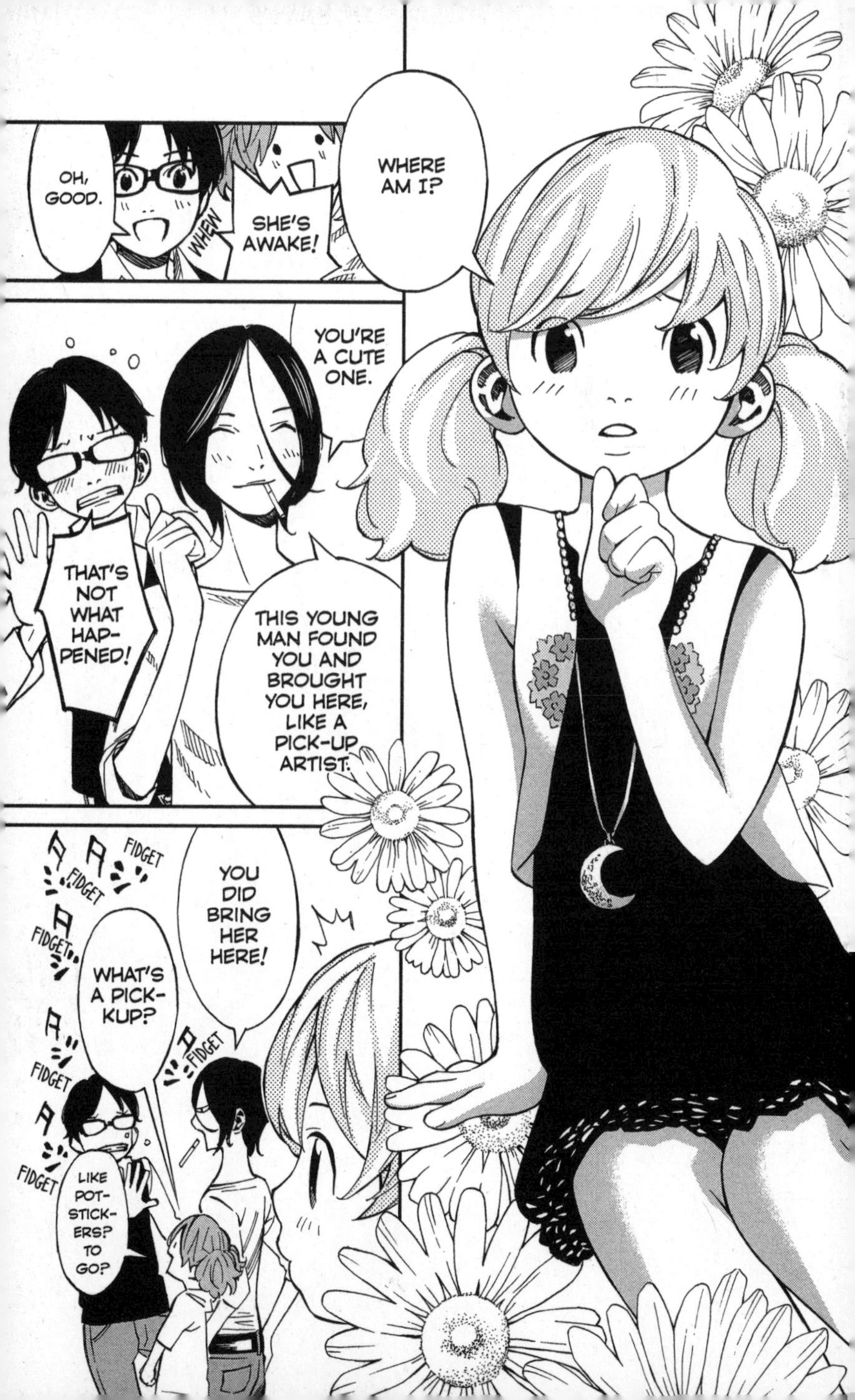
WHERE AM I?
SHE'S AWAKE!
WHEW
OH, GOOD.
YOU'RE A CUTE ONE.
THIS YOUNG MAN FOUND YOU AND BROUGHT YOU HERE, LIKE A PICK-UP ARTIST.
THAT'S NOT WHAT HAP-PENED!
YOU DID BRING HER HERE!
FIDGET
FIDGET
FIDGET
WHAT'S A PICK-KUP?
FIDGET
FIDGET
FIDGET
LIKE POT-STICK-ERS? TO GO?

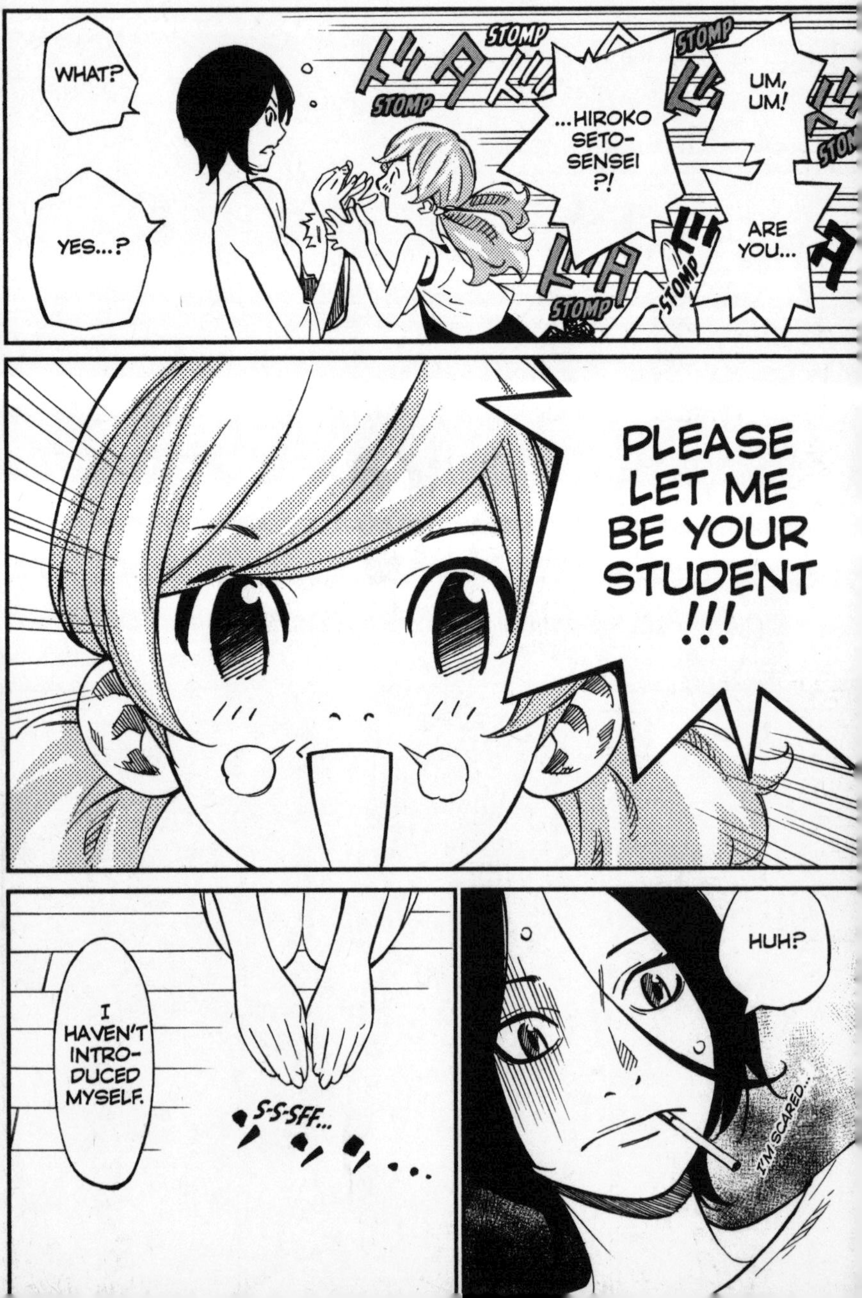
UM, UM!
ARE YOU...
STOMP
STOMP
...HIROKO SETO-SENSEI?!
STOMP
STOMP
STOMP
WHAT?
YES...?
PLEASE LET ME BE YOUR STUDENT!!!
HUH?
I'M SCARED...
I HAVEN'T INTRO-DUCED MYSELF.
S-S-SFF...

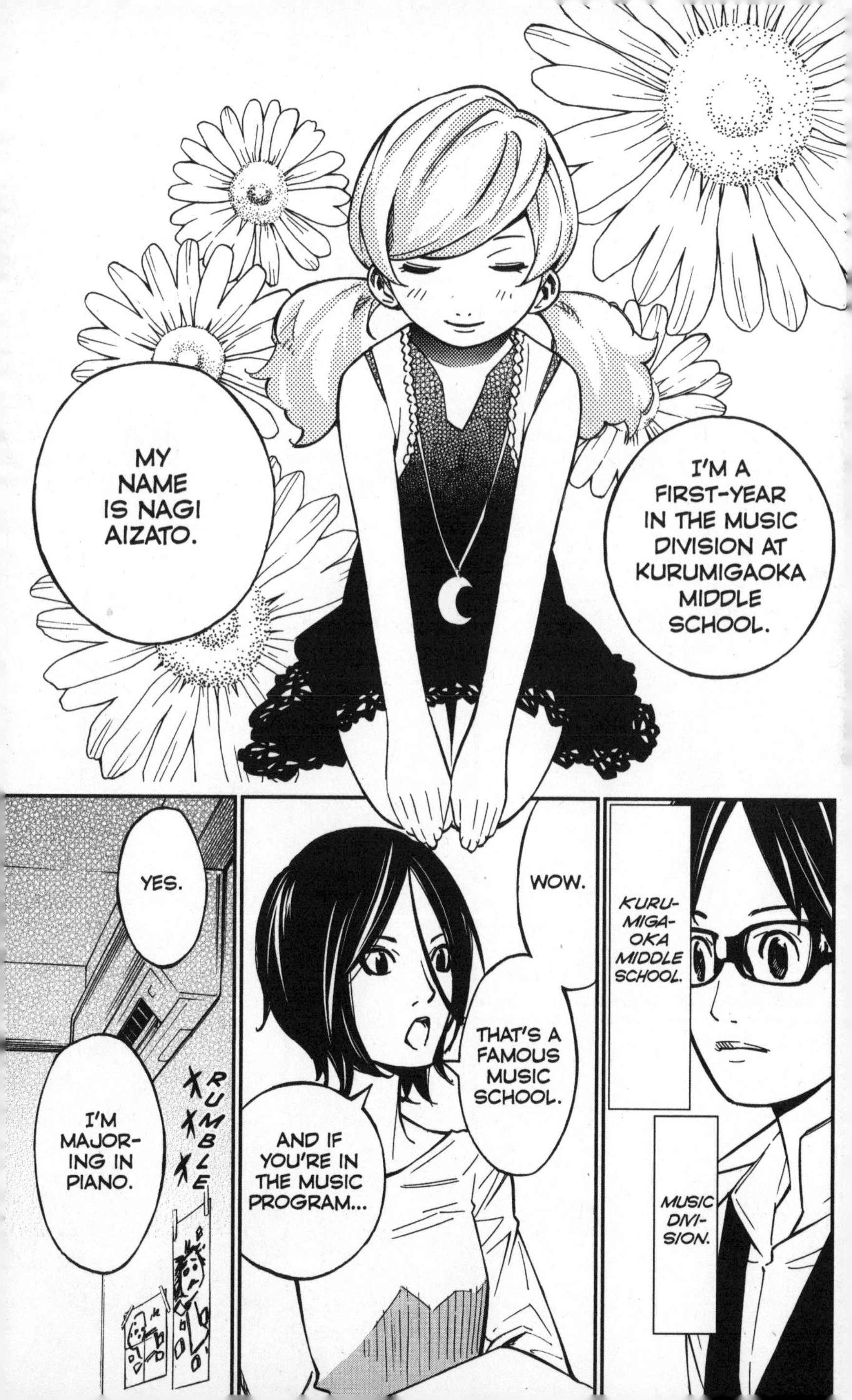
MY NAME IS NAGI AIZATO.
I'M A FIRST-YEAR IN THE MUSIC DIVISION AT KURUMIGAOKA MIDDLE SCHOOL.
KURU-MIGA-OKA MIDDLE SCHOOL.
MUSIC DIVI-SION.
WOW.
THAT'S A FAMOUS MUSIC SCHOOL.
AND IF YOU'RE IN THE MUSIC PROGRAM...
YES.
I'M MAJOR-ING IN PIANO.
RUMBLE

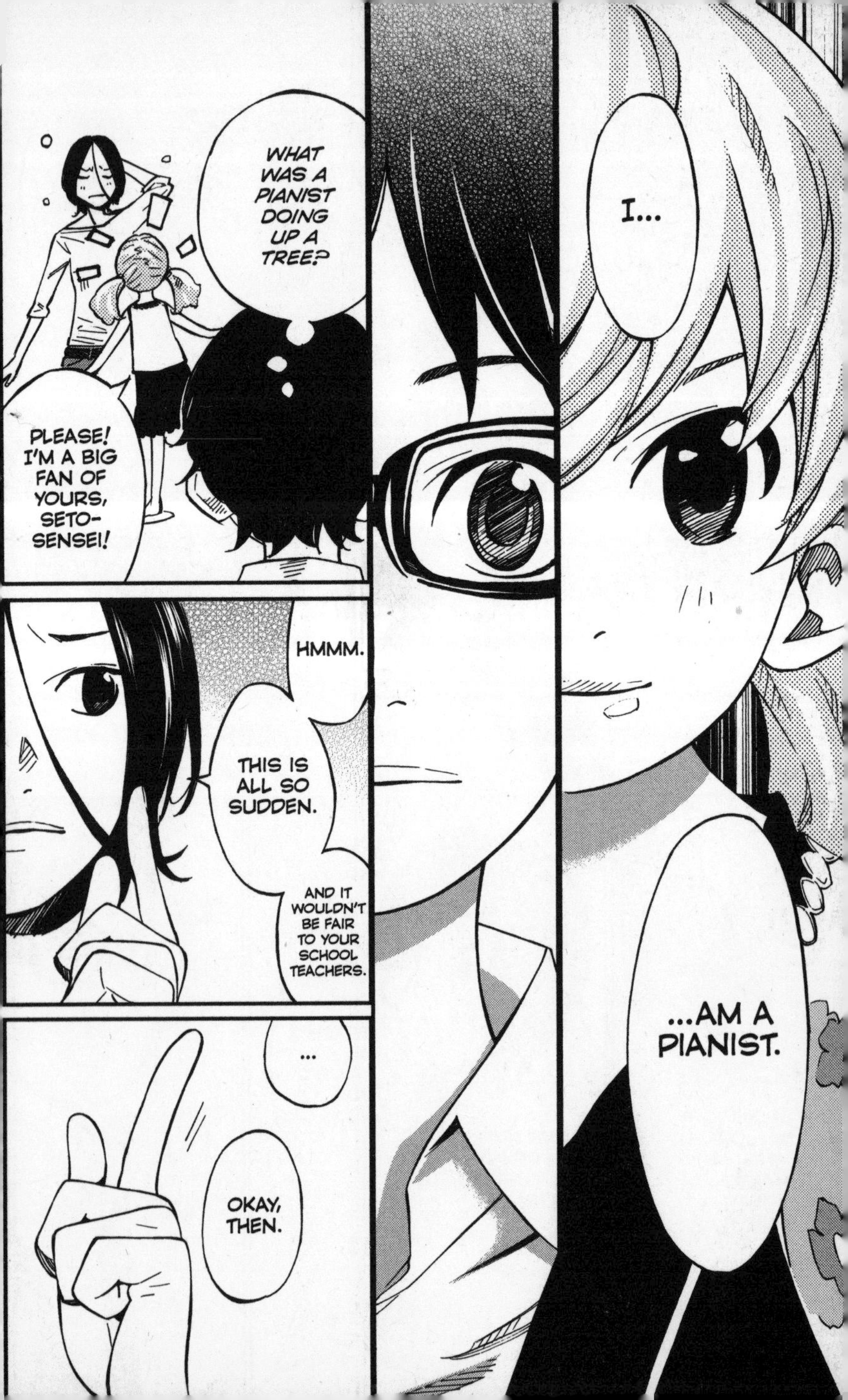
I...
...AM A PIANIST.
WHAT WAS A PIANIST DOING UP A TREE?
PLEASE! I'M A BIG FAN OF YOURS, SETO-SENSEI!
HMMM.
THIS IS ALL SO SUDDEN.
AND IT WOULDN'T BE FAIR TO YOUR SCHOOL TEACHERS.
...
OKAY, THEN.

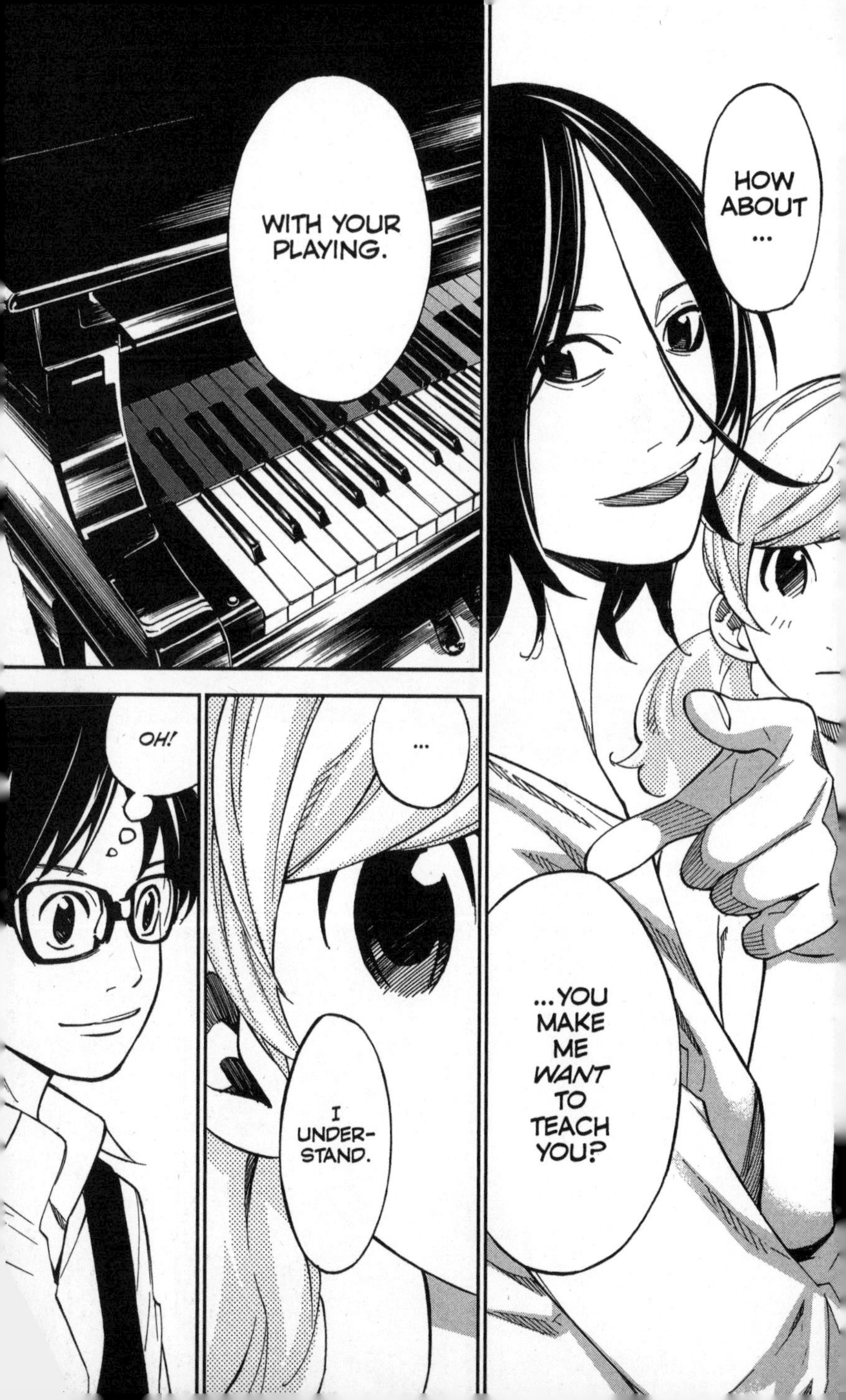
HOW ABOUT ...
...YOU MAKE ME *WANT* TO TEACH YOU?
WITH YOUR PLAYING.
...
I UNDER-STAND.
OH!

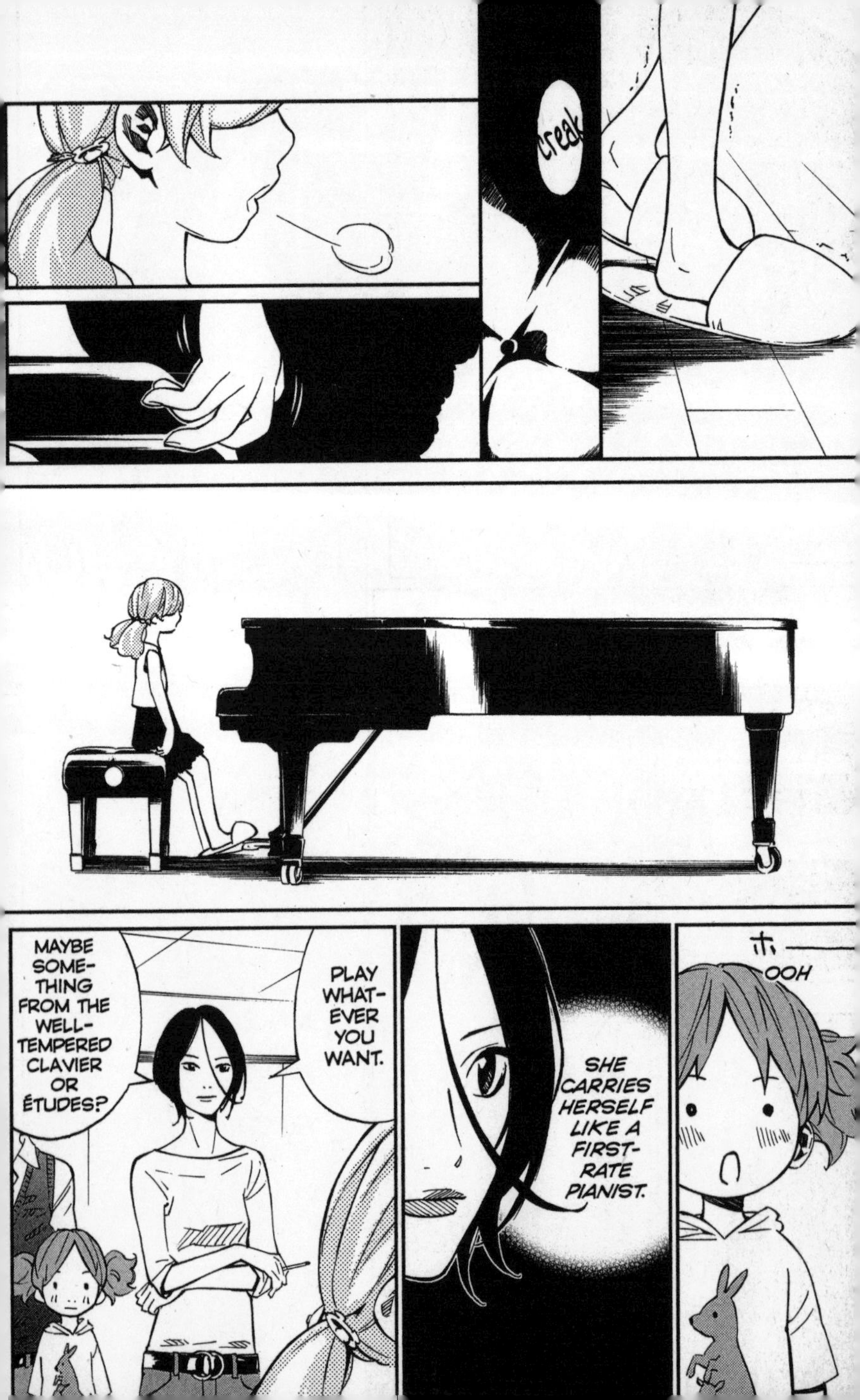
creak
OOH
SHE CARRIES HERSELF LIKE A FIRST-RATE PIANIST.
PLAY WHATEVER YOU WANT.
MAYBE SOMETHING FROM THE WELL-TEMPERED CLAVIER OR ÉTUDES?

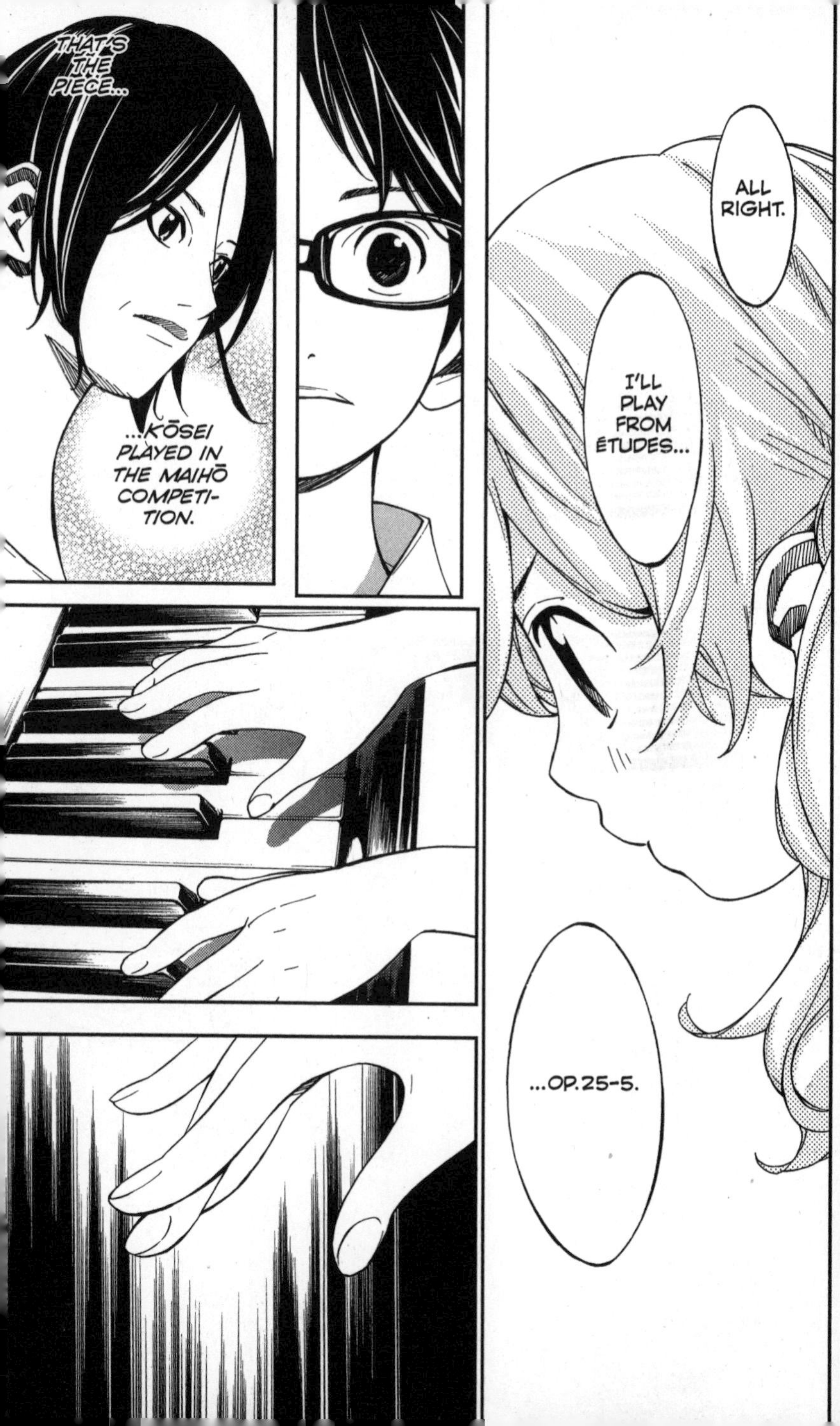
ALL RIGHT.
I'LL PLAY FROM ÉTUDES...
...OP.25-5.
THAT'S THE PIECE...
...KŌSEI PLAYED IN THE MAIHŌ COMPETI-TION.

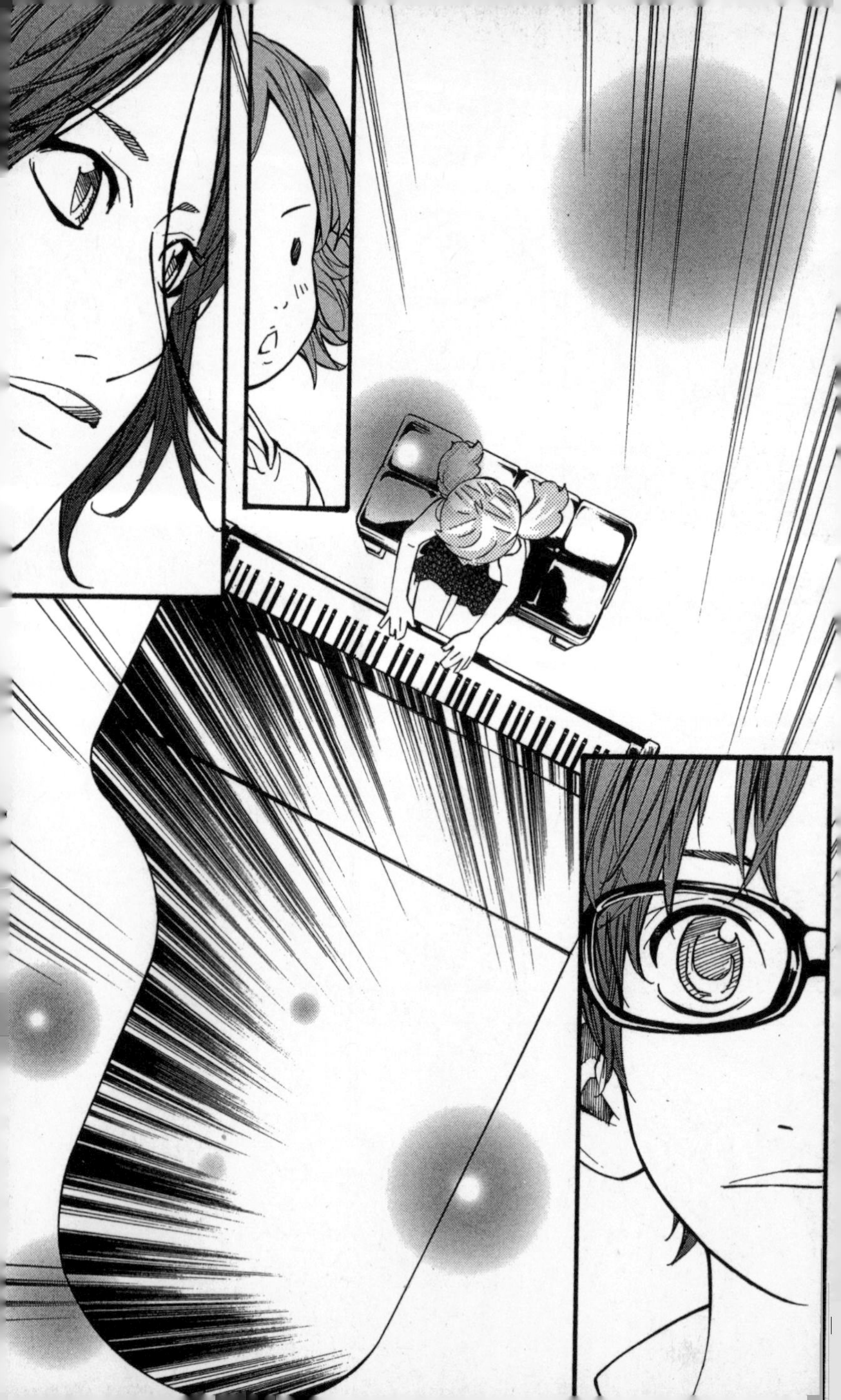

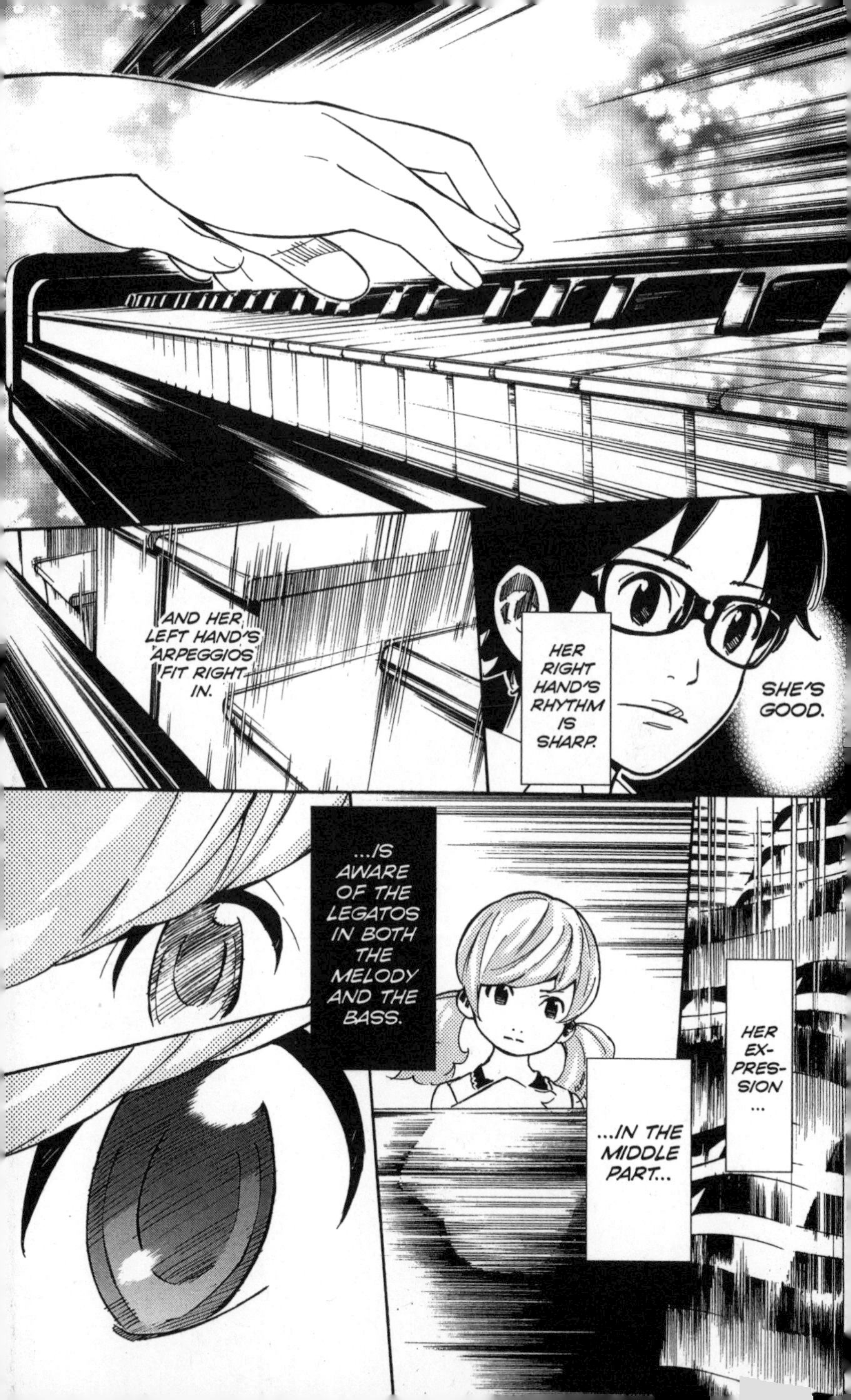
SHE'S GOOD.
HER RIGHT HAND'S RHYTHM IS SHARP.
AND HER LEFT HAND'S ARPEGGIOS FIT RIGHT IN.
HER EXPRESSION...
...IN THE MIDDLE PART...
...IS AWARE OF THE LEGATOS IN BOTH THE MELODY AND THE BASS.

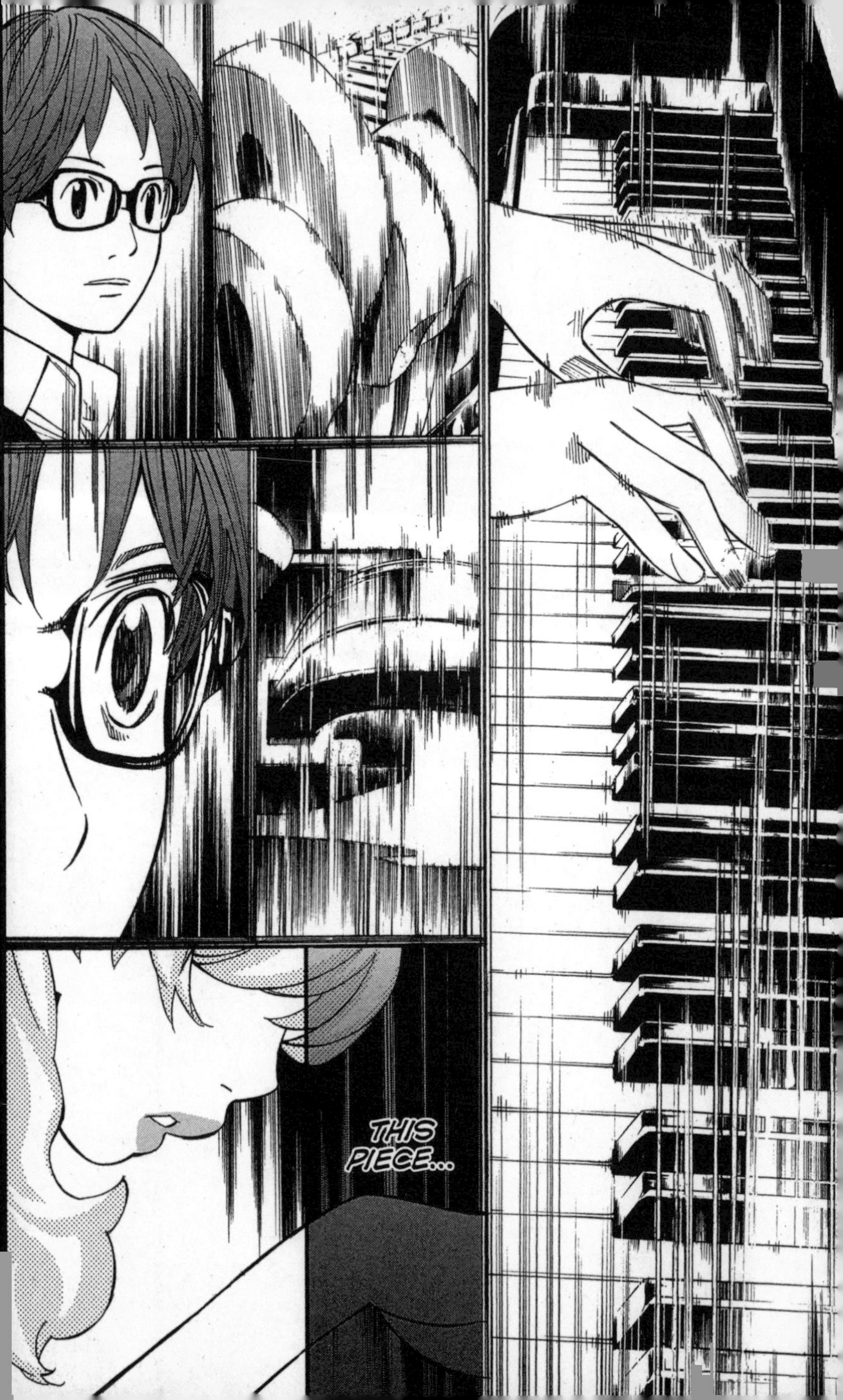
THIS PIECE...

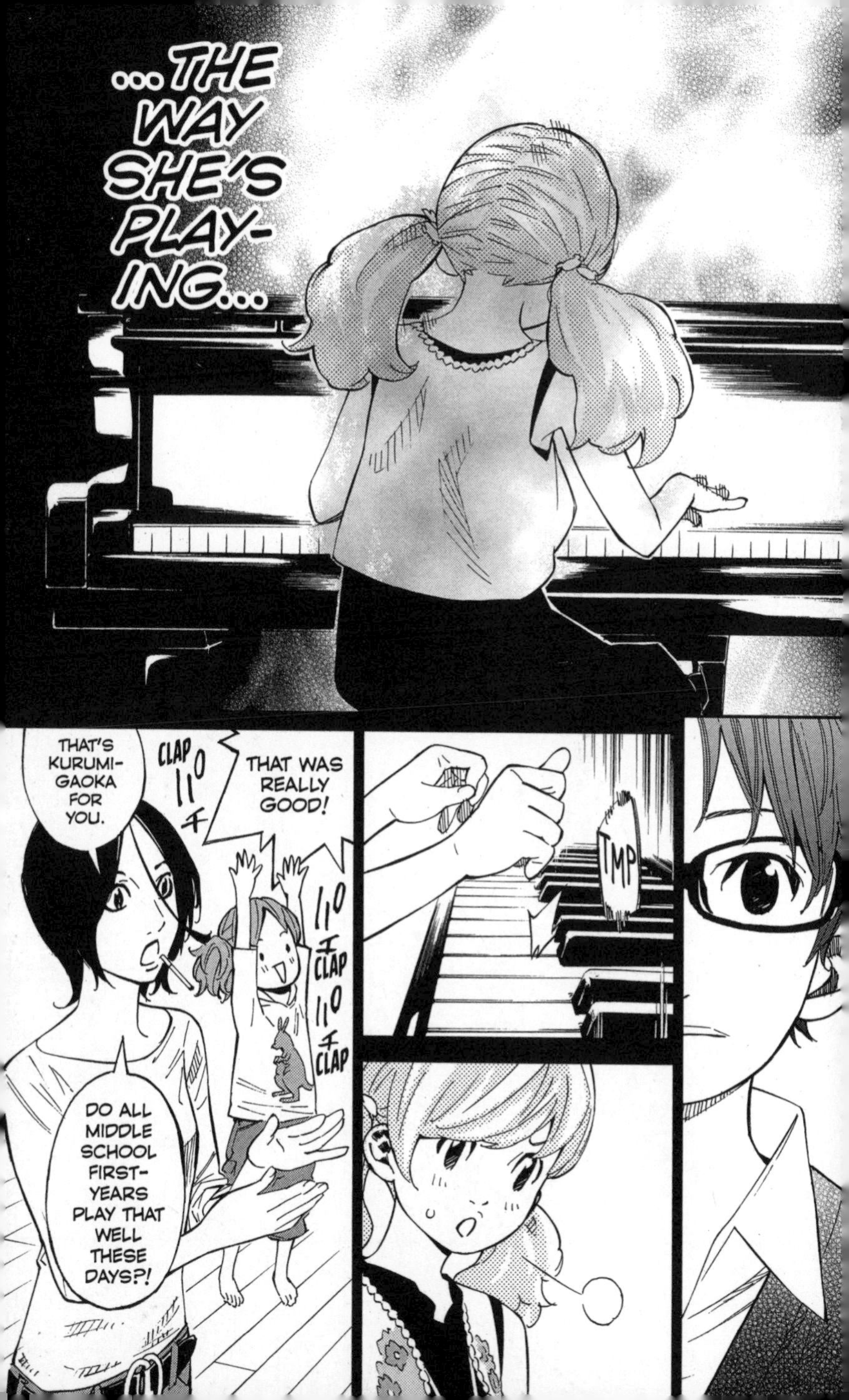
...THE WAY SHE'S PLAY-ING...
TMP
THAT WAS REALLY GOOD!
CLAP
THAT'S KURUMI-GAOKA FOR YOU.
CLAP
CLAP
DO ALL MIDDLE SCHOOL FIRST-YEARS PLAY THAT WELL THESE DAYS?!

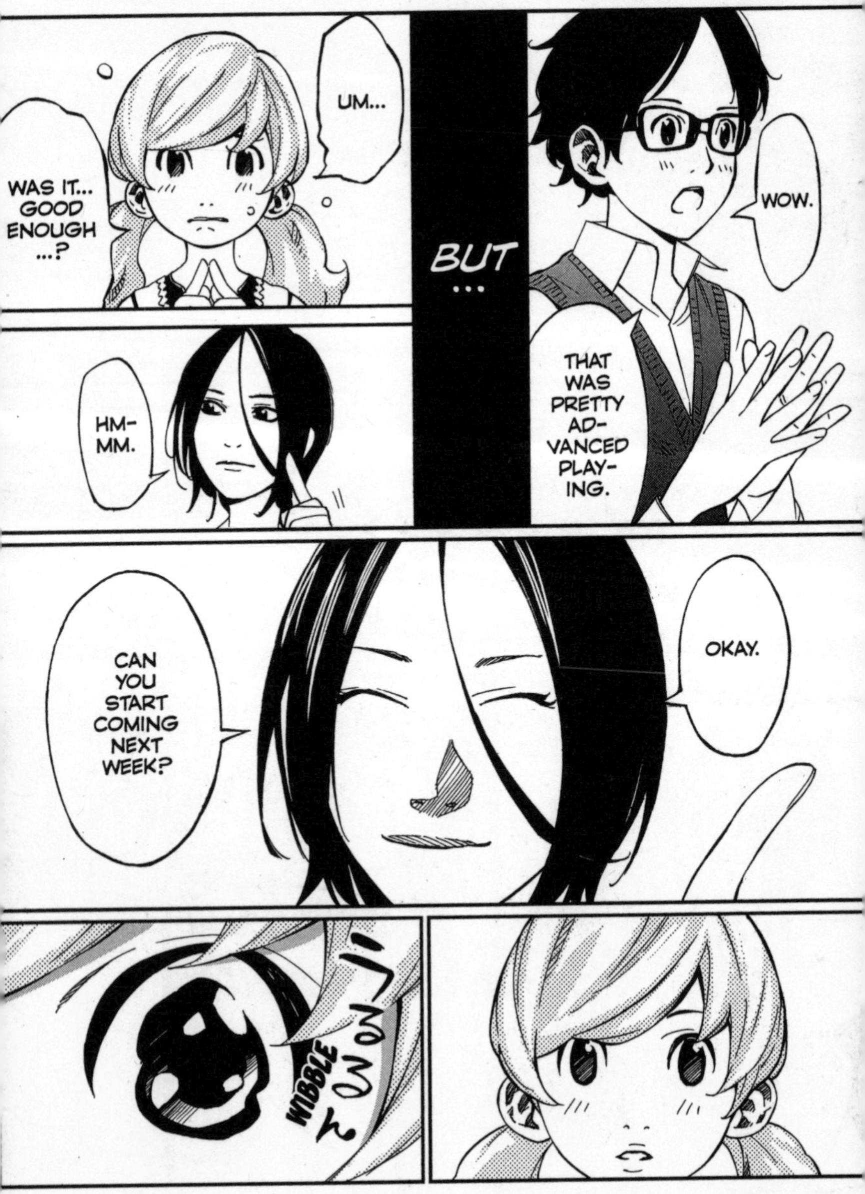
WOW.
THAT WAS PRETTY AD-VANCED PLAY-ING.
BUT ...
UM...
WAS IT... GOOD ENOUGH ...?
HM-MM.
OKAY.
CAN YOU START COMING NEXT WEEK?
WIBBLE

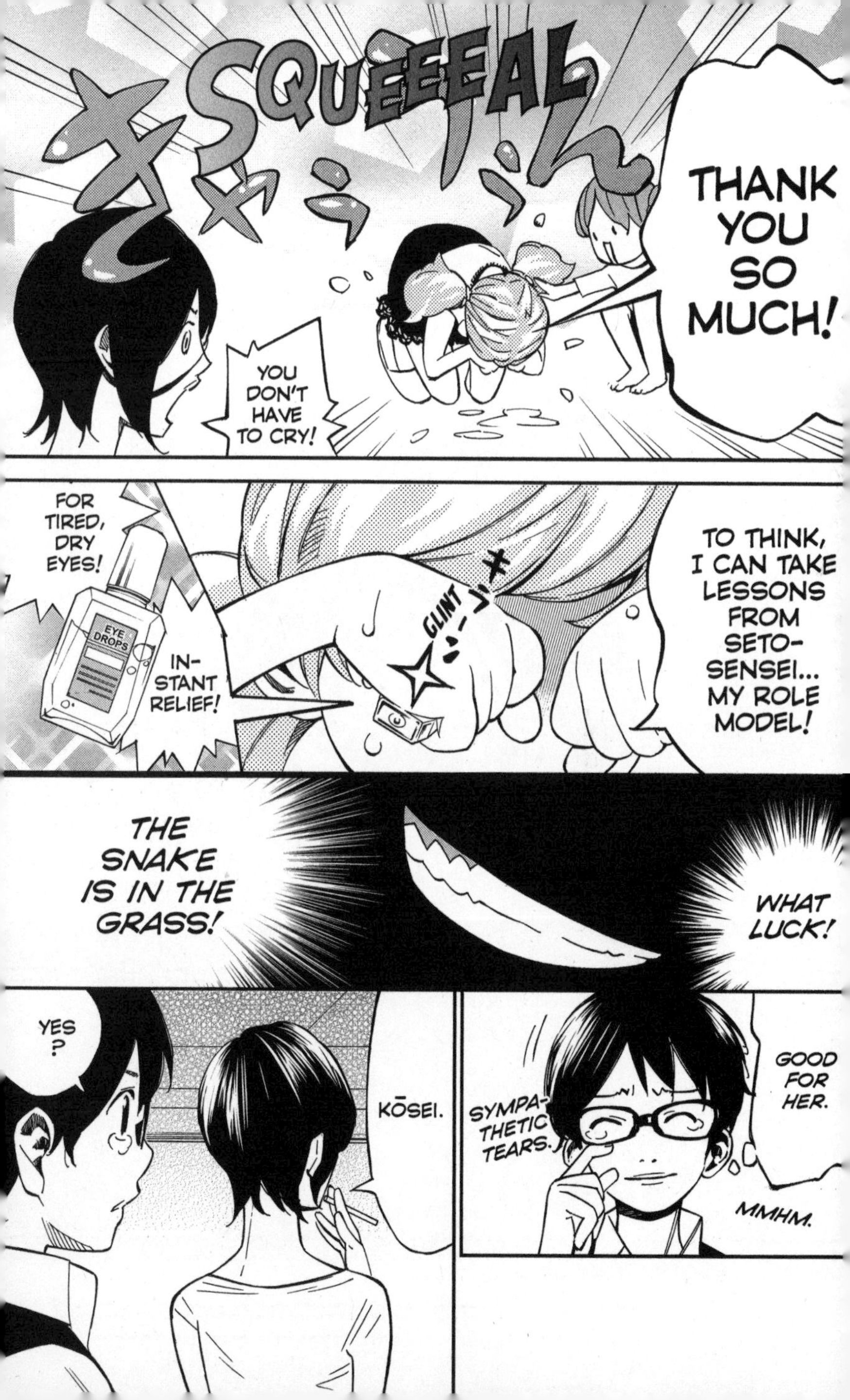
THANK YOU SO MUCH!
SQUEEEAL
YOU DON'T HAVE TO CRY!
TO THINK, I CAN TAKE LESSONS FROM SETO-SENSEI... MY ROLE MODEL!
GLINT
IN-STANT RELIEF!
FOR TIRED, DRY EYES!
EYE DROPS
WHAT LUCK!
THE SNAKE IS IN THE GRASS!
GOOD FOR HER.
MMHM.
SYMPA-THETIC TEARS.
KŌSEI.
YES?

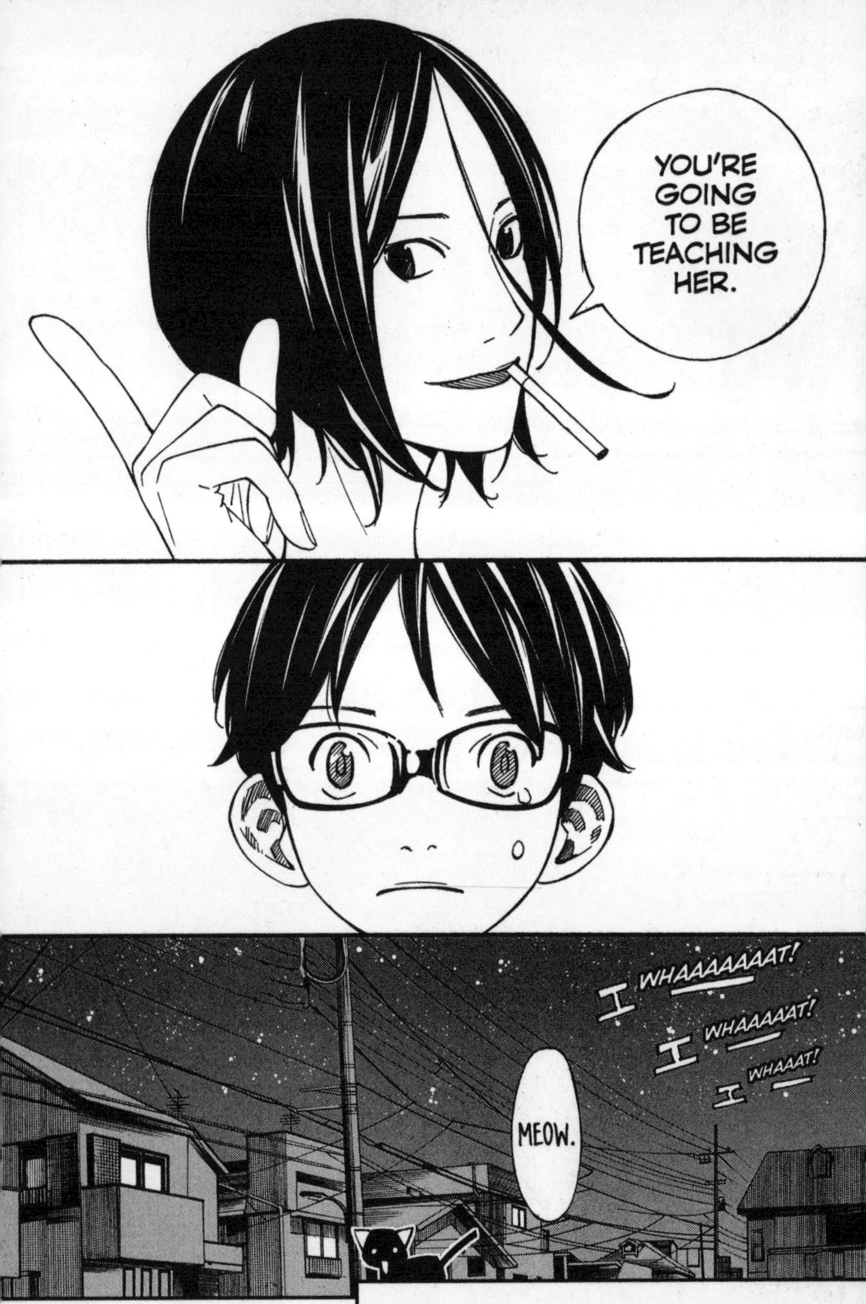
YOU'RE GOING TO BE TEACHING HER.
WHAAAAAAAT!
WHAAAAAT!
WHAAAT!
MEOW.

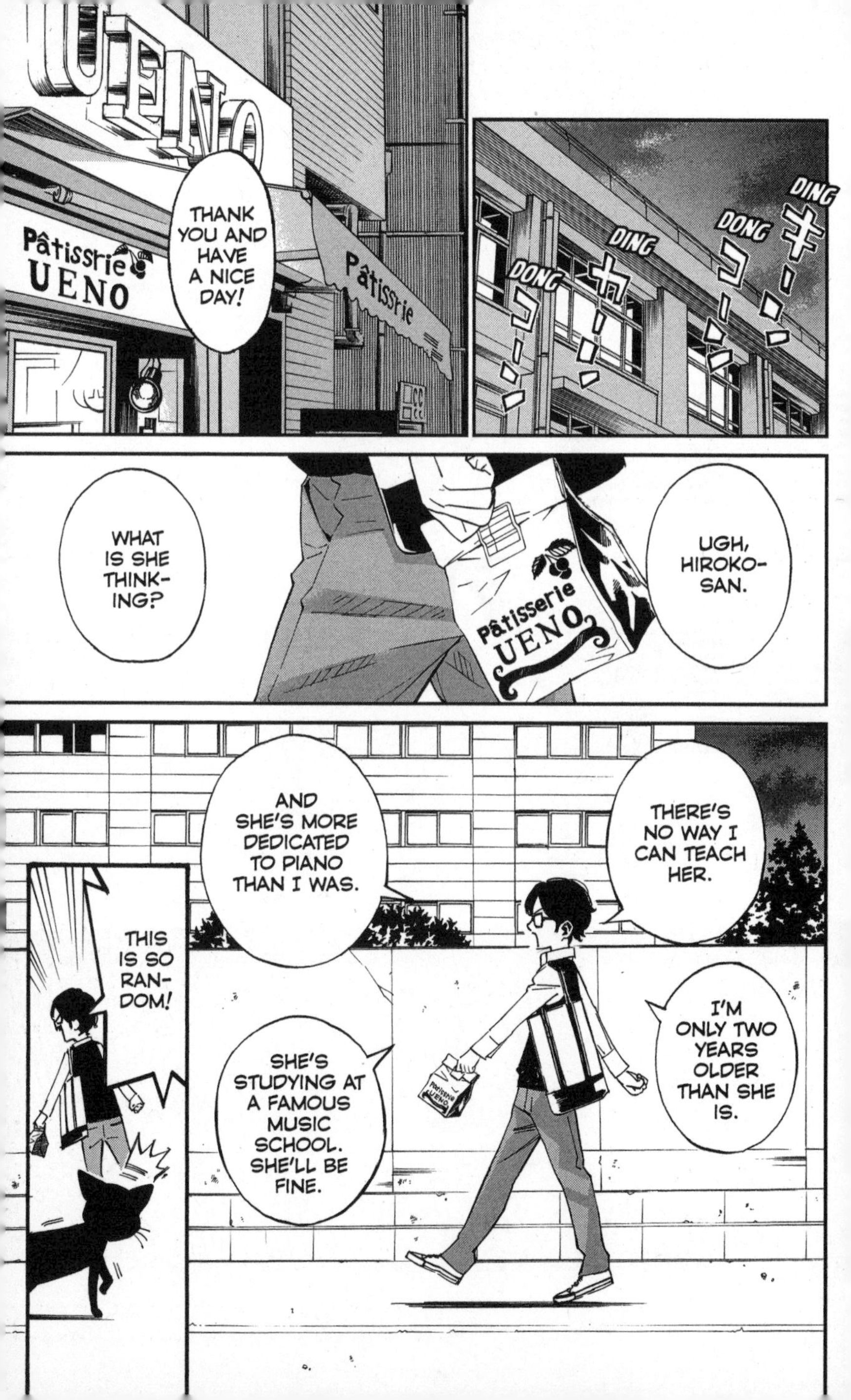
DING
DONG
DING
DONG
UENO
Pâtissrie UENO
Pâtissrie
THANK YOU AND HAVE A NICE DAY!
UGH, HIROKO-SAN.
Pâtisserie UENO
WHAT IS SHE THINKING?
THERE'S NO WAY I CAN TEACH HER.
AND SHE'S MORE DEDICATED TO PIANO THAN I WAS.
I'M ONLY TWO YEARS OLDER THAN SHE IS.
SHE'S STUDYING AT A FAMOUS MUSIC SCHOOL. SHE'LL BE FINE.
THIS IS SO RAN-DOM!

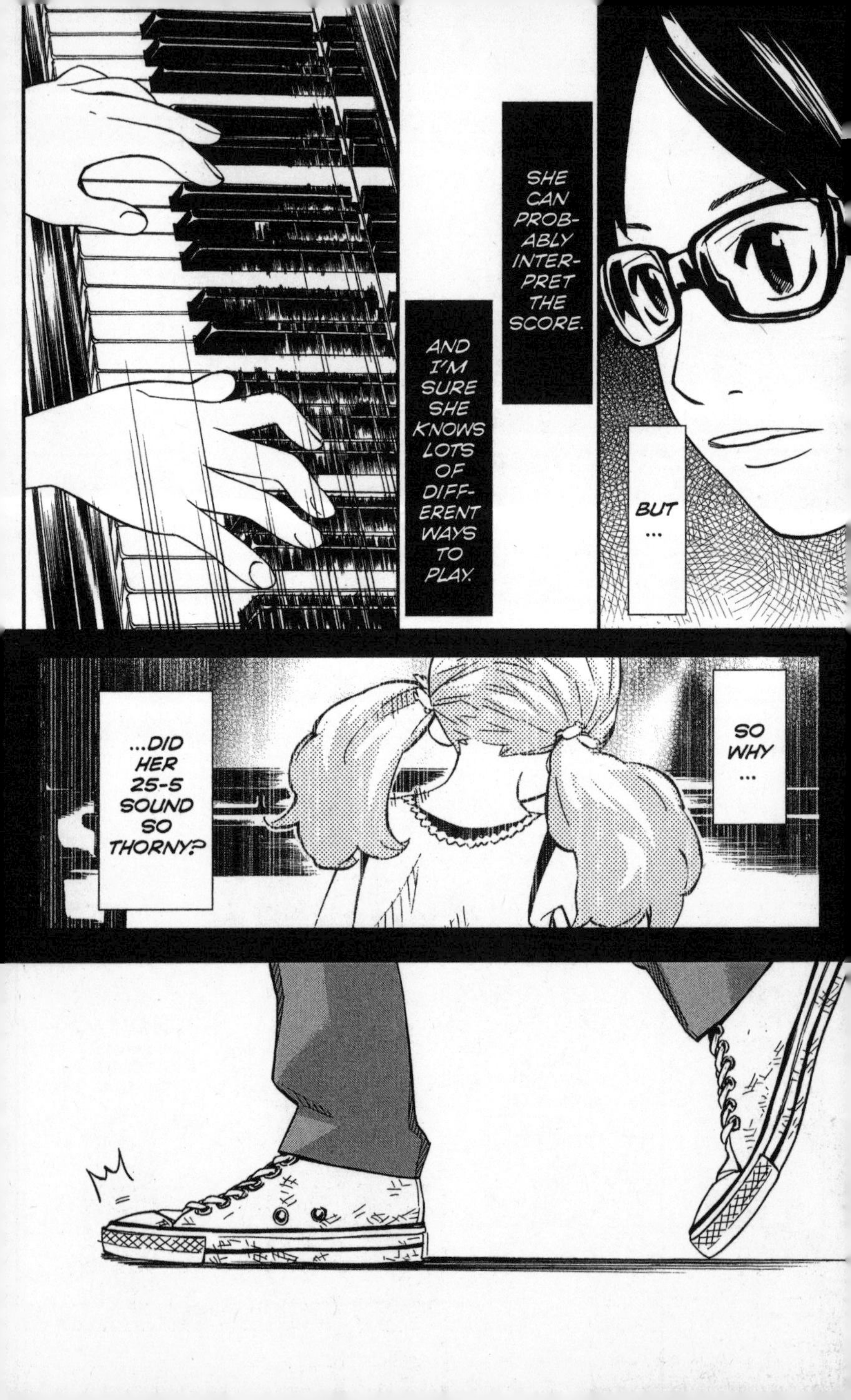
SHE CAN PROB-ABLY INTER-PRET THE SCORE.
AND I'M SURE SHE KNOWS LOTS OF DIFF-ERENT WAYS TO PLAY.
BUT ...
SO WHY ...
...DID HER 25-5 SOUND SO THORNY?

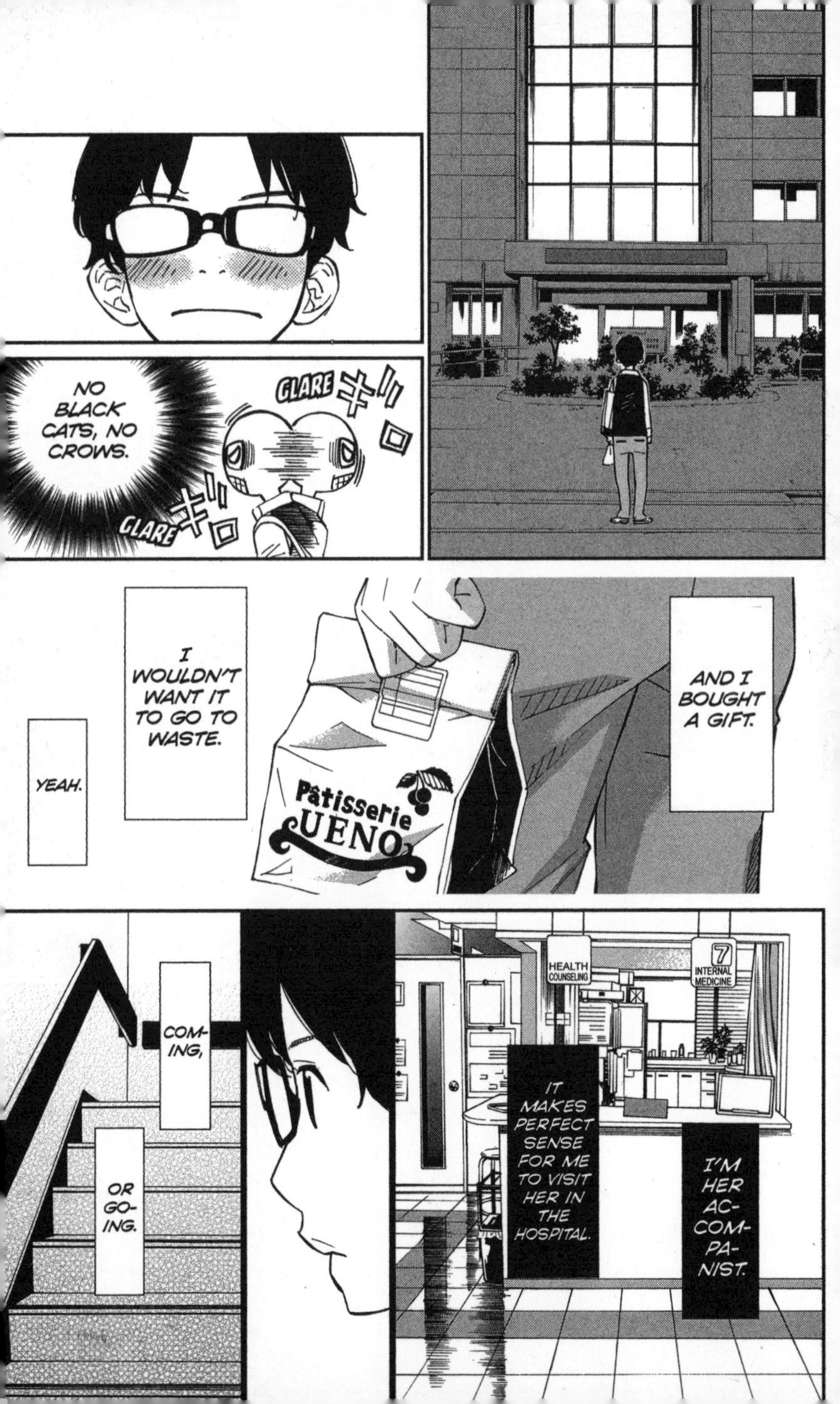
GLARE
NO BLACK CATS, NO CROWS.
GLARE
AND I BOUGHT A GIFT.
Pâtisserie UENO
I WOULDN'T WANT IT TO GO TO WASTE.
YEAH.
HEALTH COUNSELING
7 INTERNAL MEDICINE
I'M HER AC-COM-PA-NIST.
IT MAKES PERFECT SENSE FOR ME TO VISIT HER IN THE HOSPITAL.
COM-ING,
OR GO-ING.

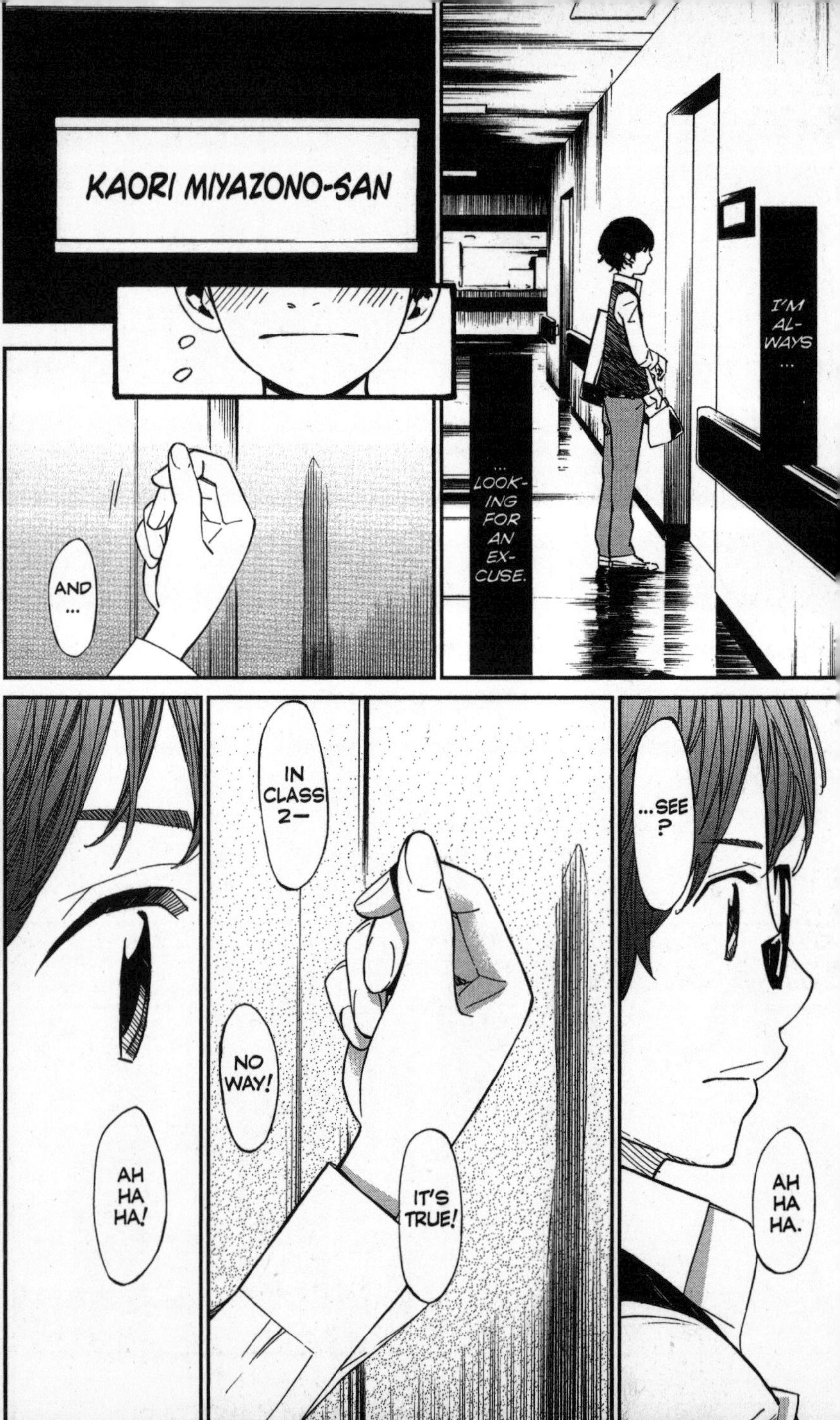
I'M ALWAYS...
...LOOKING FOR AN EXCUSE.
KAORI MIYAZONO-SAN
AND...
...SEE?
AH HA HA.
IN CLASS 2—
NO WAY!
IT'S TRUE!
AH HA HA!

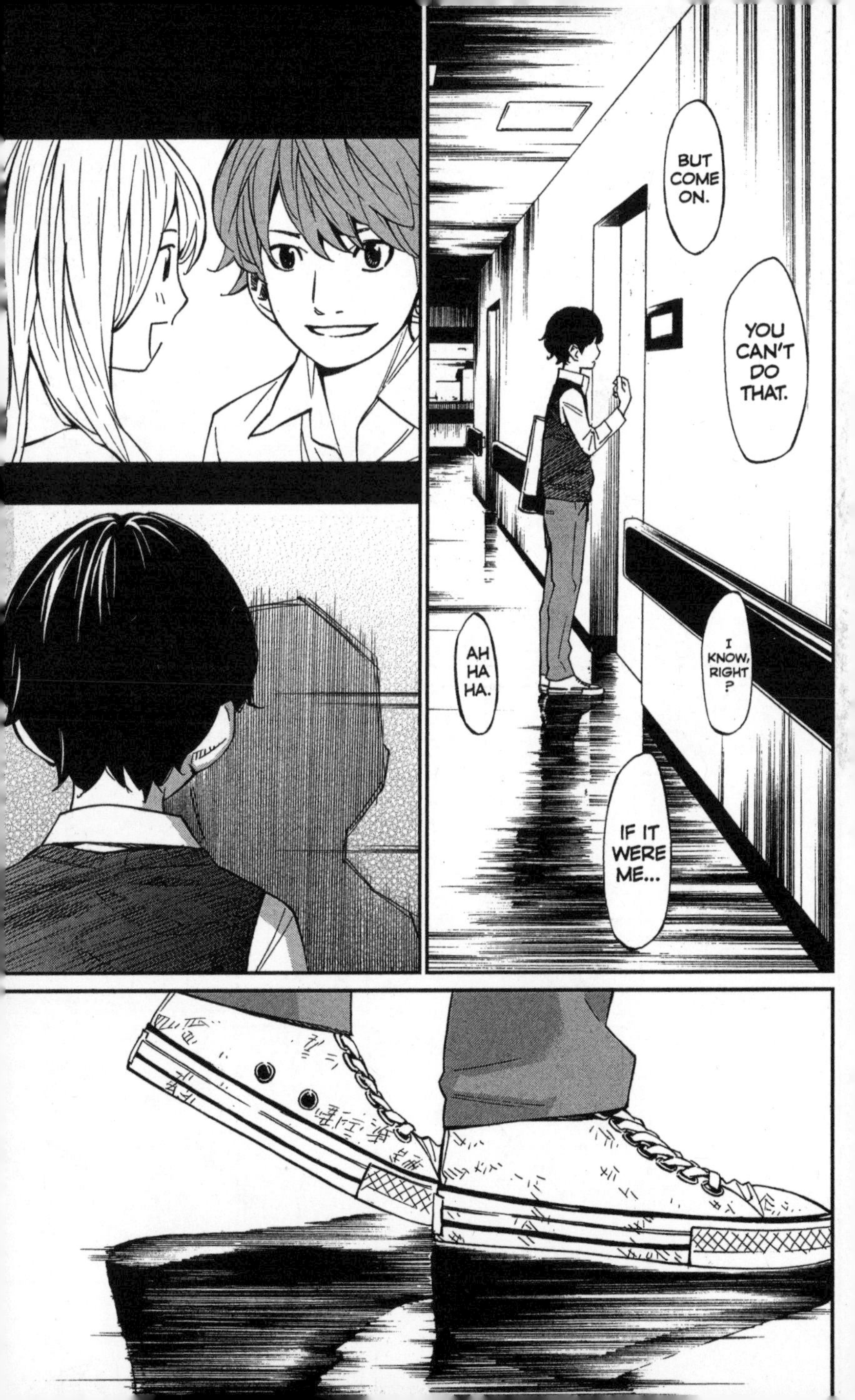
BUT COME ON.
YOU CAN'T DO THAT.
I KNOW, RIGHT?
AH HA HA.
IF IT WERE ME...

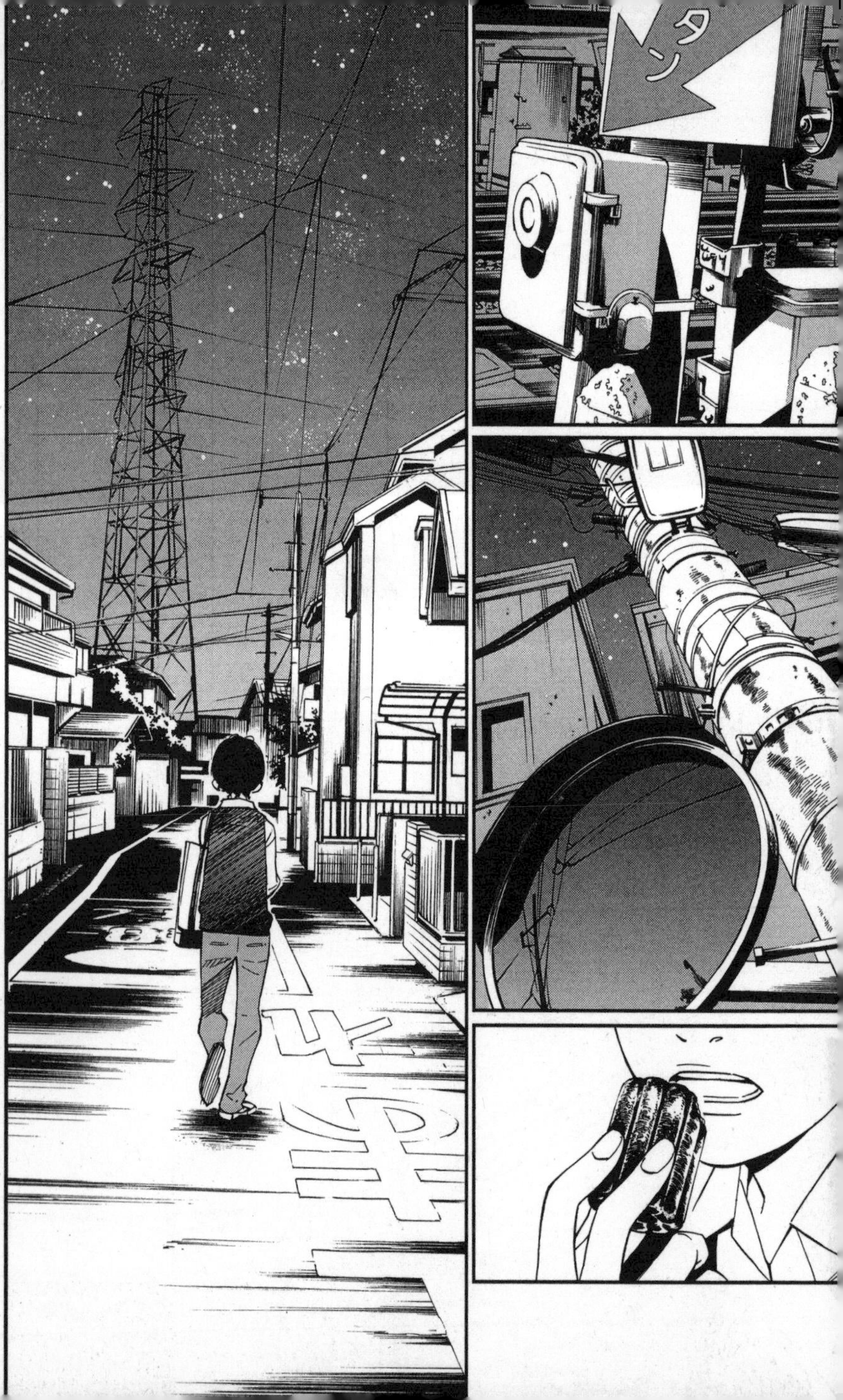
タン

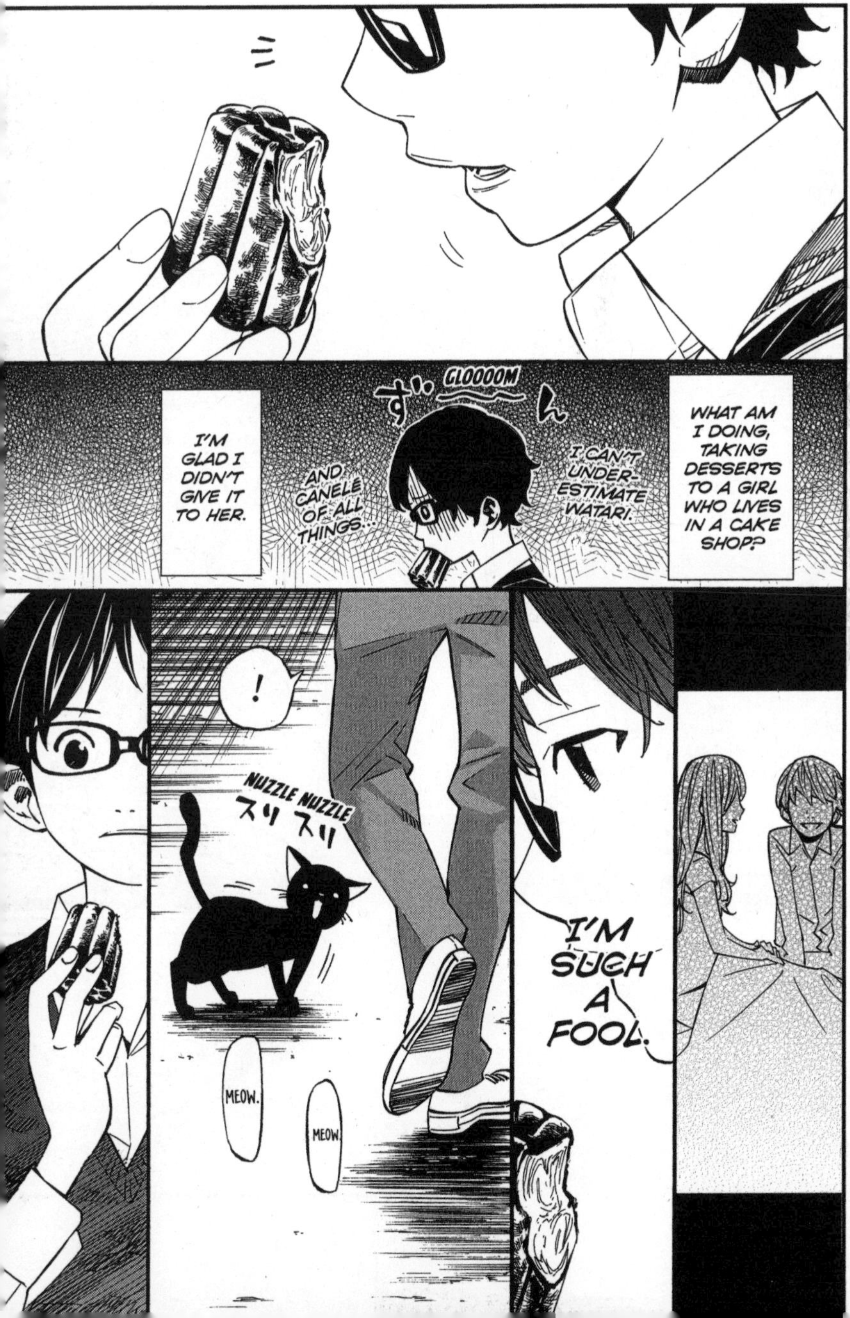
WHAT AM I DOING, TAKING DESSERTS TO A GIRL WHO LIVES IN A CAKE SHOP?
ずーん GLOOOOM
I CAN'T UNDER-ESTIMATE WATARI.
AND CANELE OF ALL THINGS...
I'M GLAD I DIDN'T GIVE IT TO HER.
I'M SUCH A FOOL.
!
NUZZLE NUZZLE スリスリ
MEOW.
MEOW.

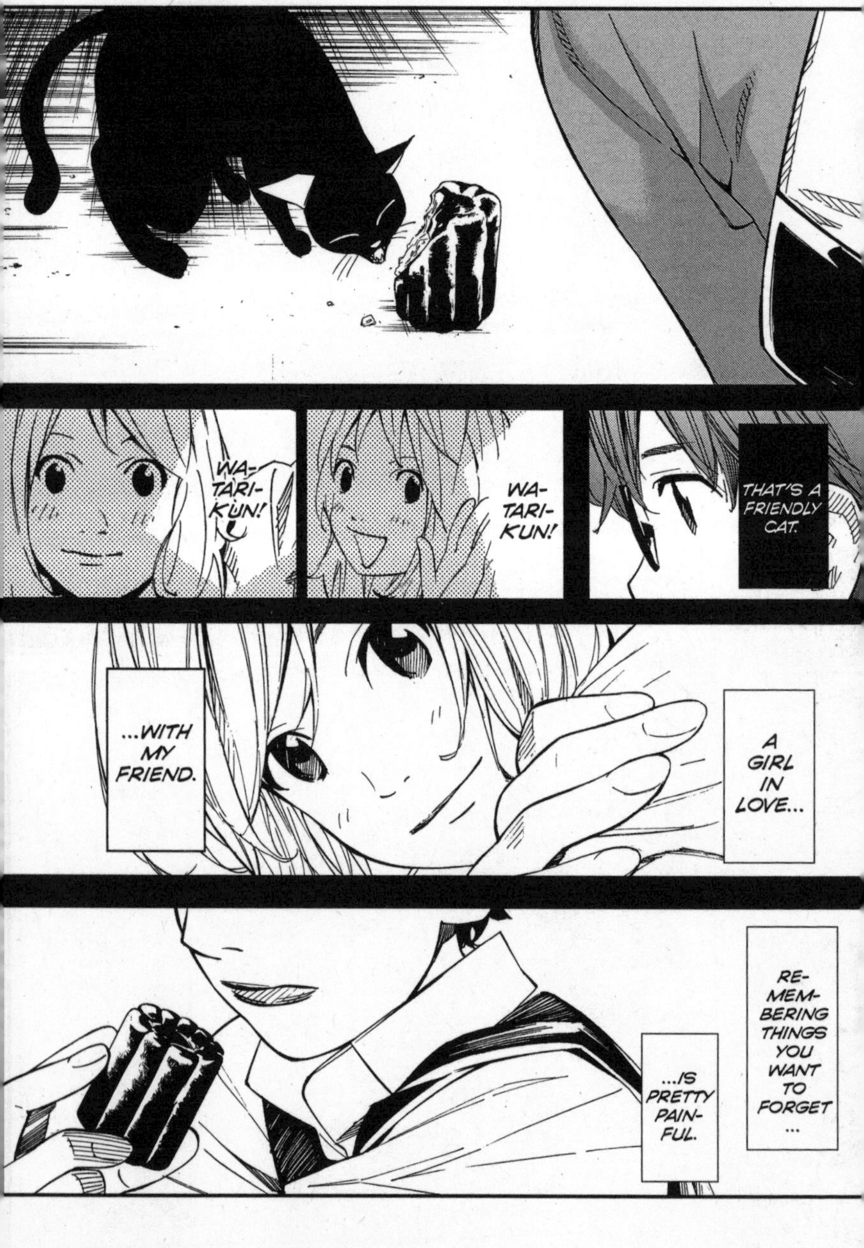
THAT'S A FRIENDLY CAT.
WA-TARI-KUN!
WA-TARI-KUN!
A GIRL IN LOVE...
...WITH MY FRIEND.
RE-MEM-BERING THINGS YOU WANT TO FORGET ...
...IS PRETTY PAIN-FUL.

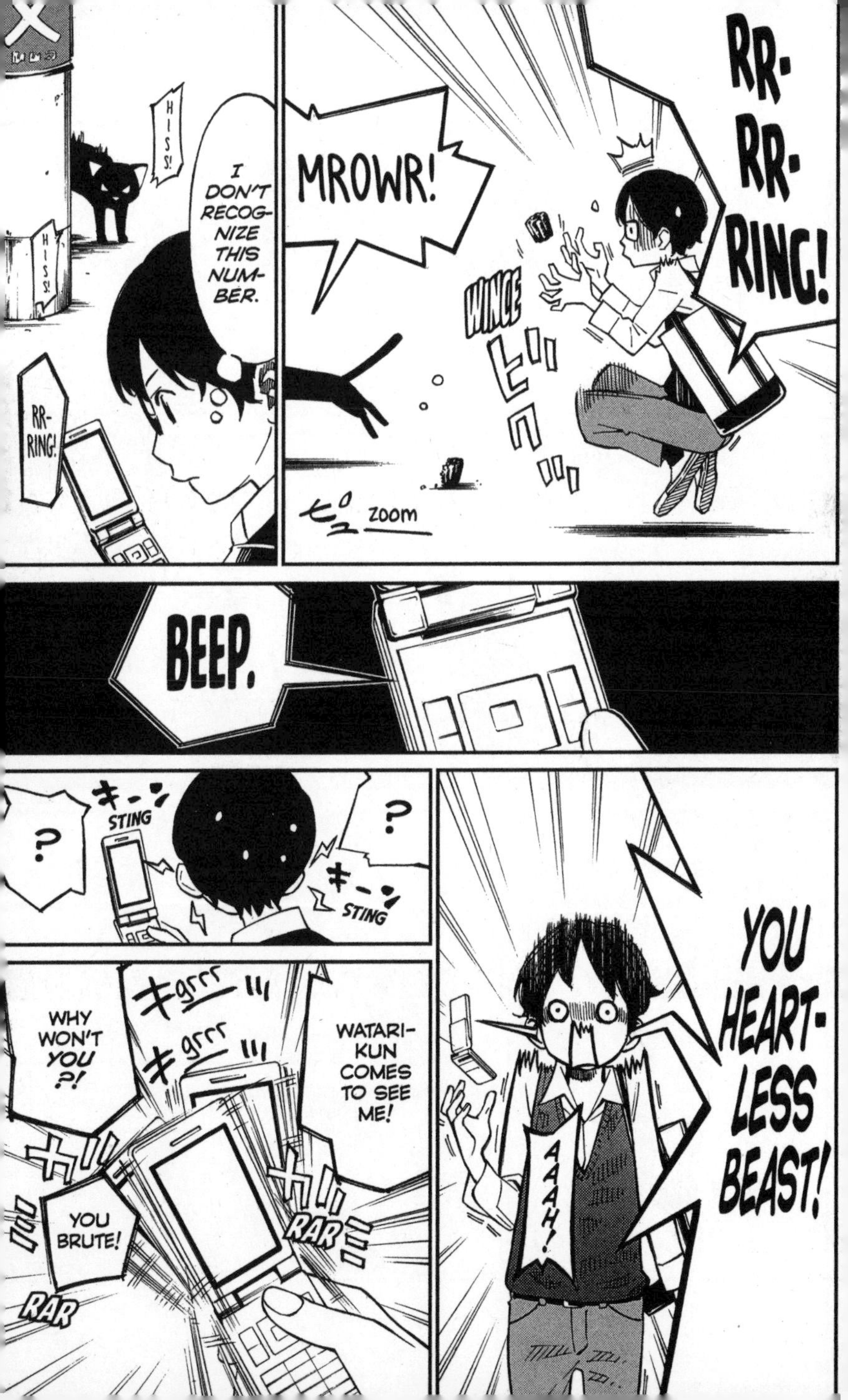
RR-RR-RING!
MROWR!
WINCE
ZOOM
I DON'T RECOGNIZE THIS NUMBER.
HISS!
HISS!
RR-RING!
BEEP.
YOU HEARTLESS BEAST!
AAAH!
?
?
STING
STING
WATARI-KUN COMES TO SEE ME!
WHY WON'T YOU?!
grrr
grrr
RAR
YOU BRUTE!
RAR

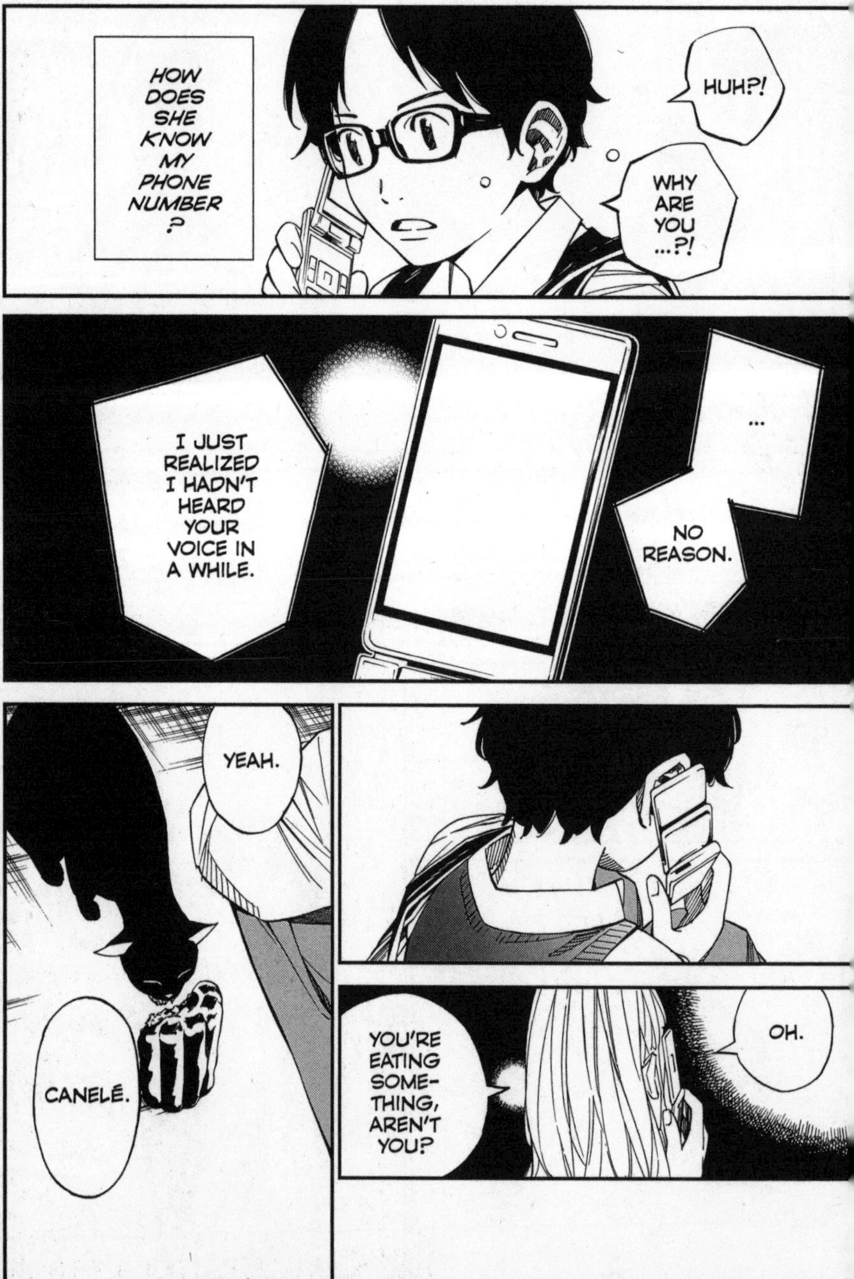
HUH?!
WHY ARE YOU ...?!
HOW DOES SHE KNOW MY PHONE NUMBER?
...
NO REASON.
I JUST REALIZED I HADN'T HEARD YOUR VOICE IN A WHILE.
OH.
YOU'RE EATING SOME-THING, AREN'T YOU?
YEAH.
CANELÉ.

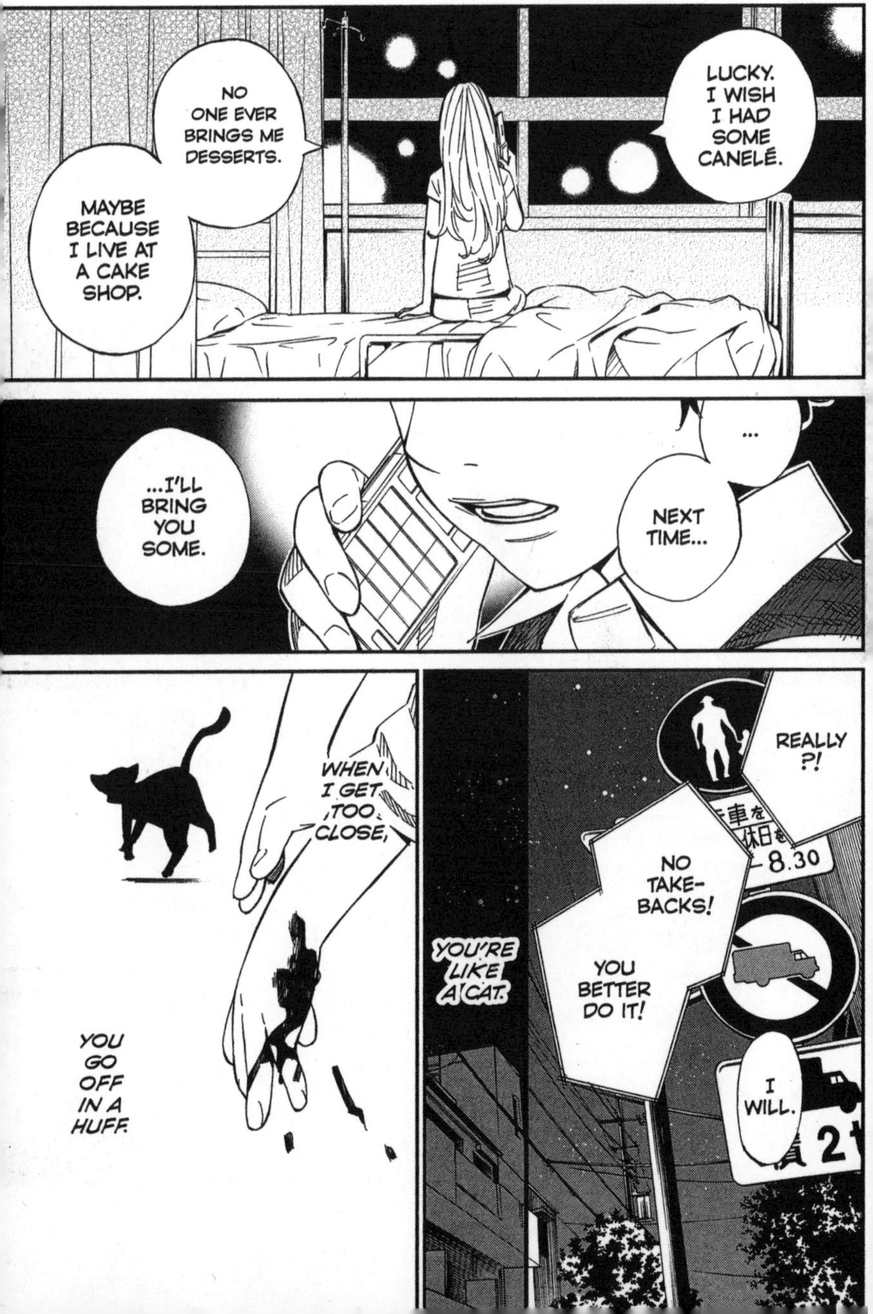
LUCKY. I WISH I HAD SOME CANELÉ.
NO ONE EVER BRINGS ME DESSERTS.
MAYBE BECAUSE I LIVE AT A CAKE SHOP.
...
NEXT TIME...
...I'LL BRING YOU SOME.
REALLY?!
NO TAKE-BACKS!
YOU BETTER DO IT!
I WILL.
YOU'RE LIKE A CAT.
WHEN I GET TOO CLOSE,
YOU GO OFF IN A HUFF.

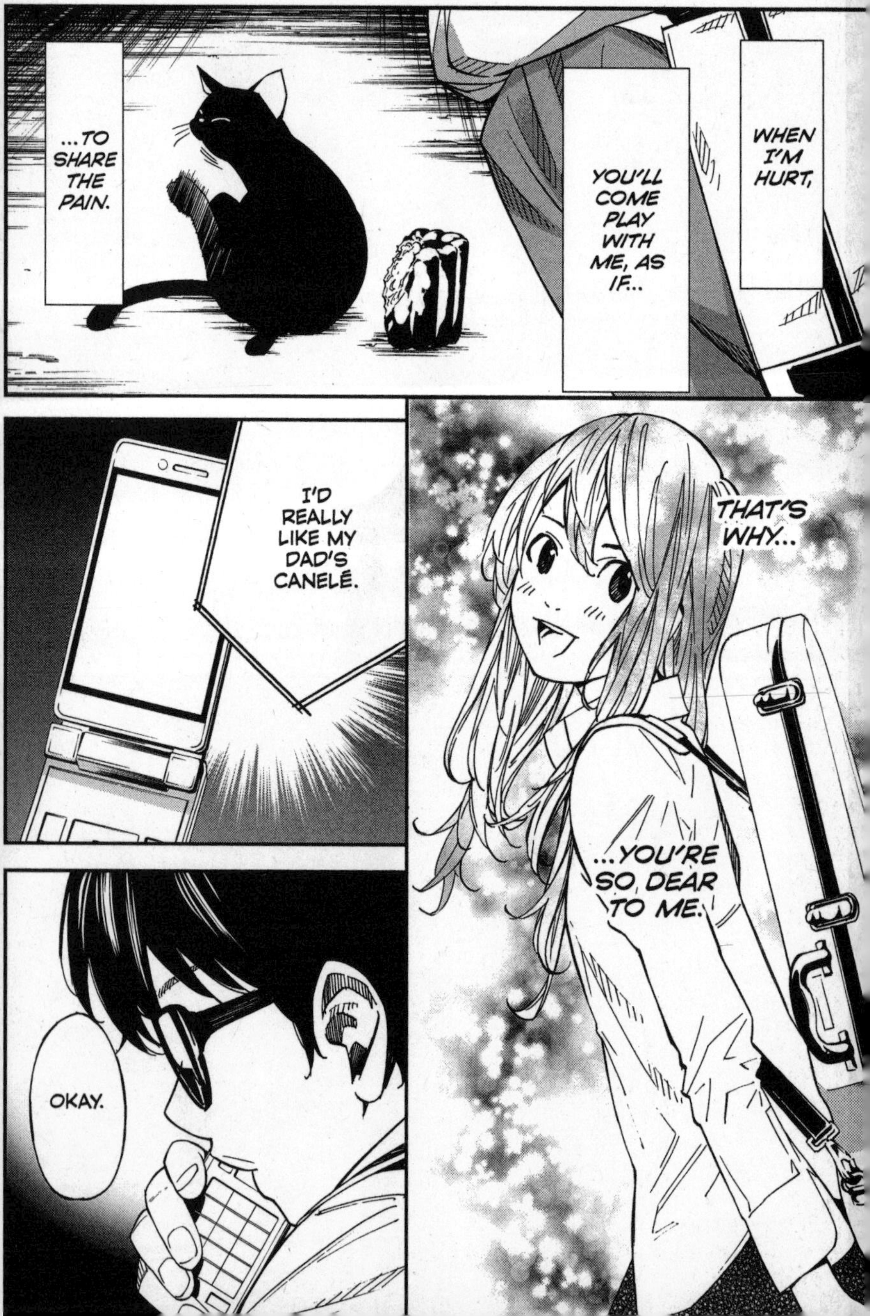
WHEN I'M HURT,
YOU'LL COME PLAY WITH ME, AS IF...
...TO SHARE THE PAIN.
THAT'S WHY...
...YOU'RE SO DEAR TO ME.
I'D REALLY LIKE MY DAD'S CANELÉ.
OKAY.

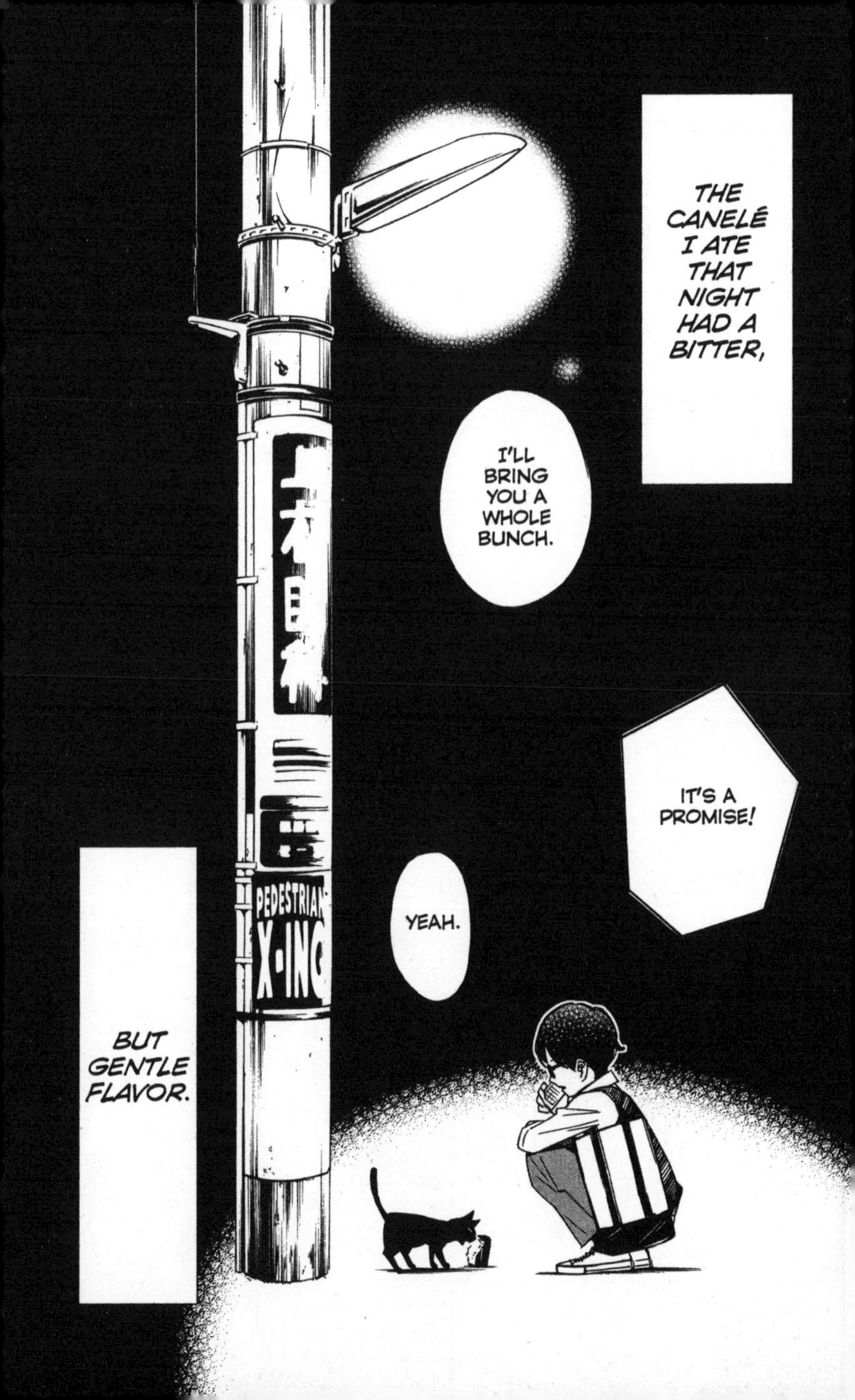
THE CANELÉ I ATE THAT NIGHT HAD A BITTER,
I'LL BRING YOU A WHOLE BUNCH.
IT'S A PROMISE!
YEAH.
PEDESTRIAN X-ING
BUT GENTLE FLAVOR.

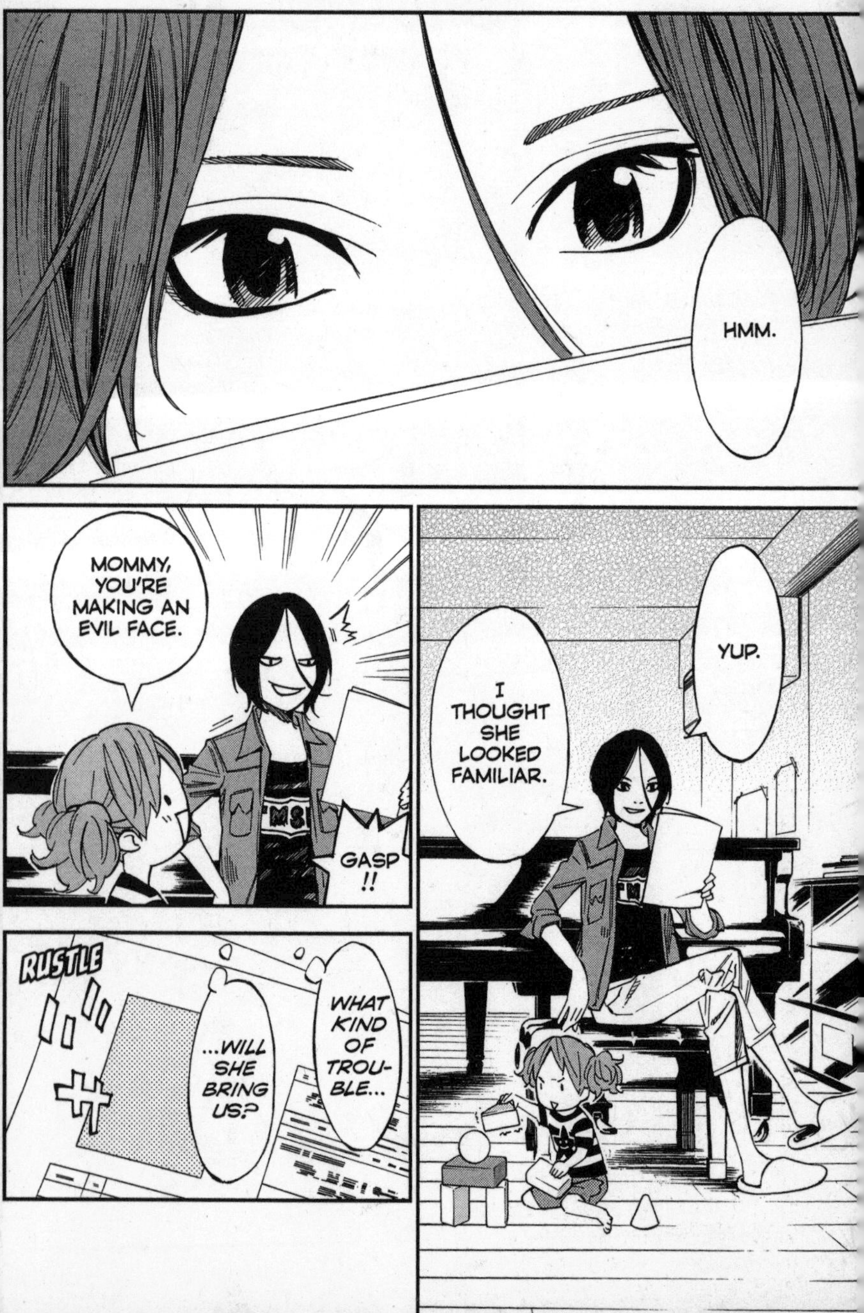
HMM.
YUP.
I THOUGHT SHE LOOKED FAMILIAR.
MOMMY, YOU'RE MAKING AN EVIL FACE.
GASP !!
RUSTLE
WHAT KIND OF TROUBLE...
...WILL SHE BRING US?

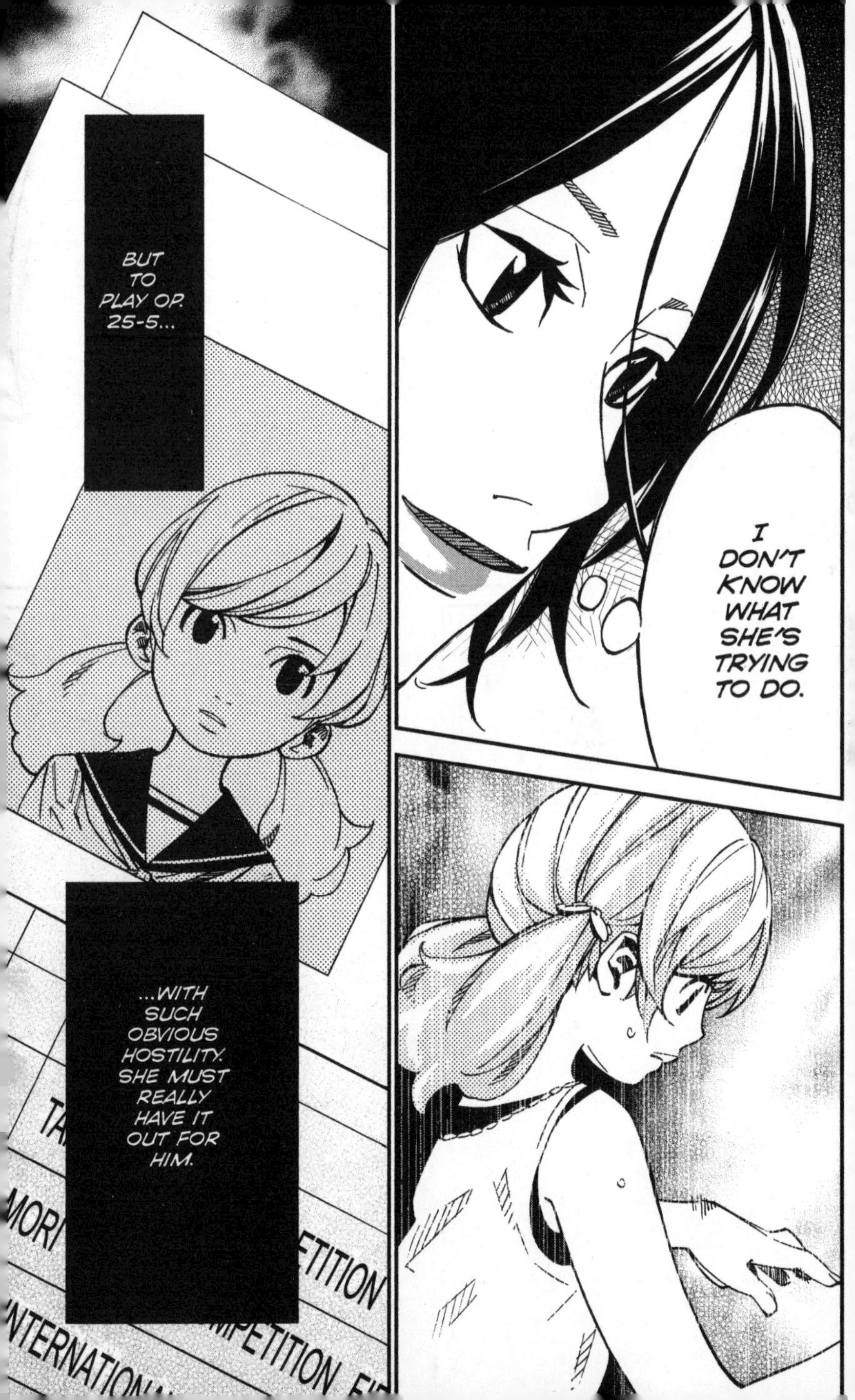
I DON'T KNOW WHAT SHE'S TRYING TO DO.
BUT TO PLAY OP. 25-5...
...WITH SUCH OBVIOUS HOSTILITY. SHE MUST REALLY HAVE IT OUT FOR HIM.

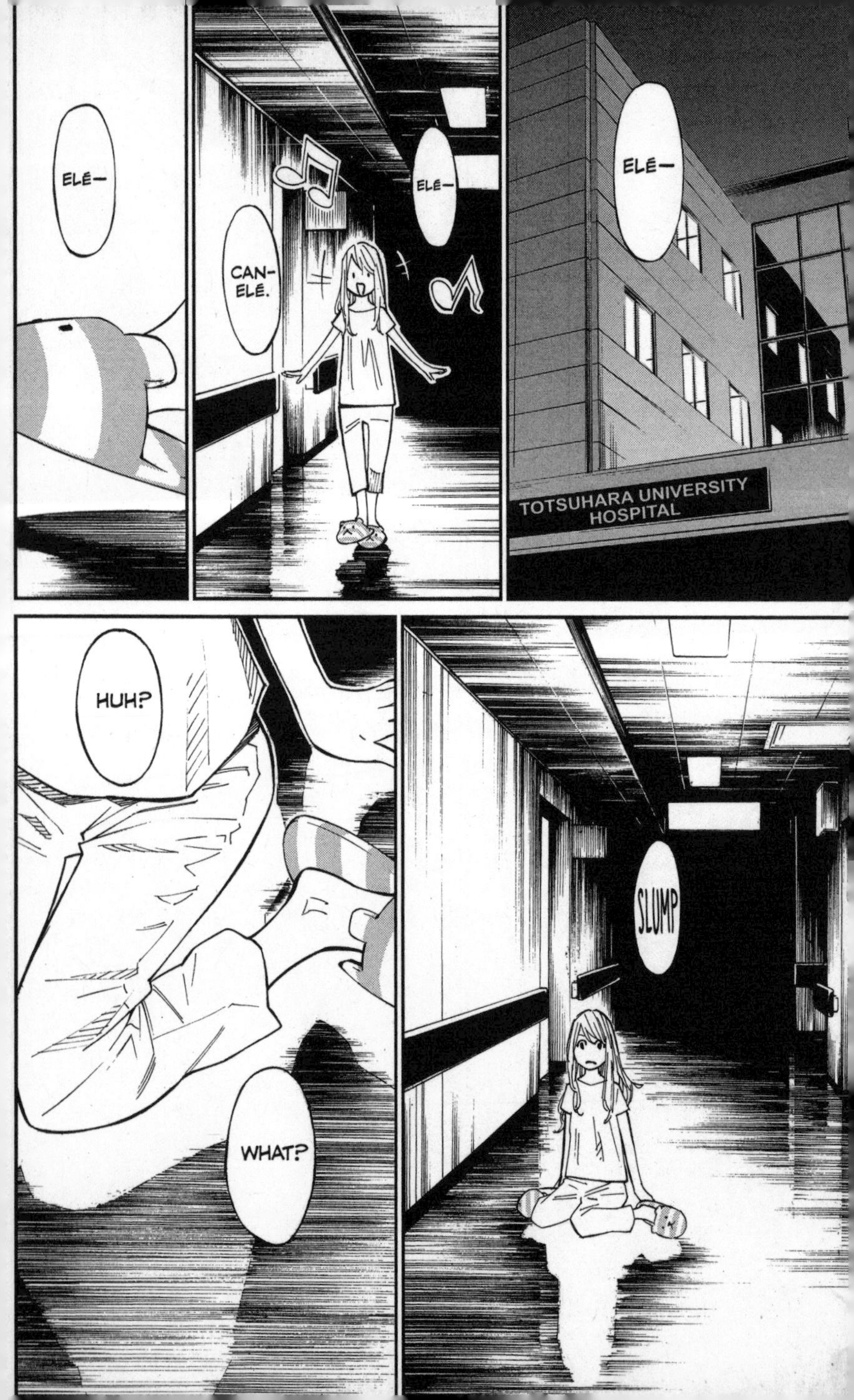
ELÉ—
TOTSUHARA UNIVERSITY HOSPITAL
ELÉ—
CAN-ELÉ.
ELÉ—
SLUMP
HUH?
WHAT?

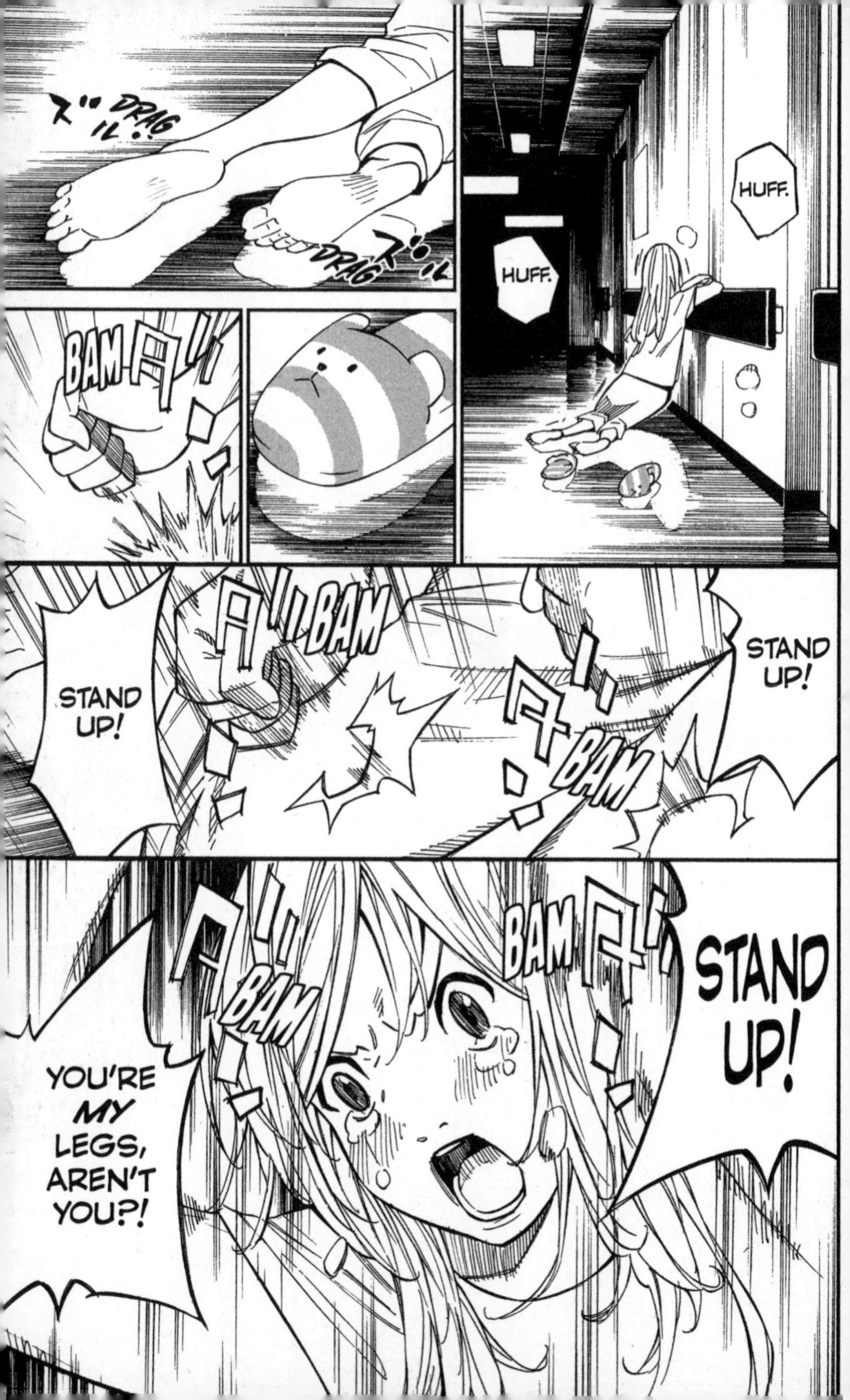
HUFF.
HUFF.
DRAG
DRAG
BAM
STAND UP!
BAM
BAM
STAND UP!
STAND UP!
BAM
BAM
YOU'RE *MY* LEGS, AREN'T YOU?!

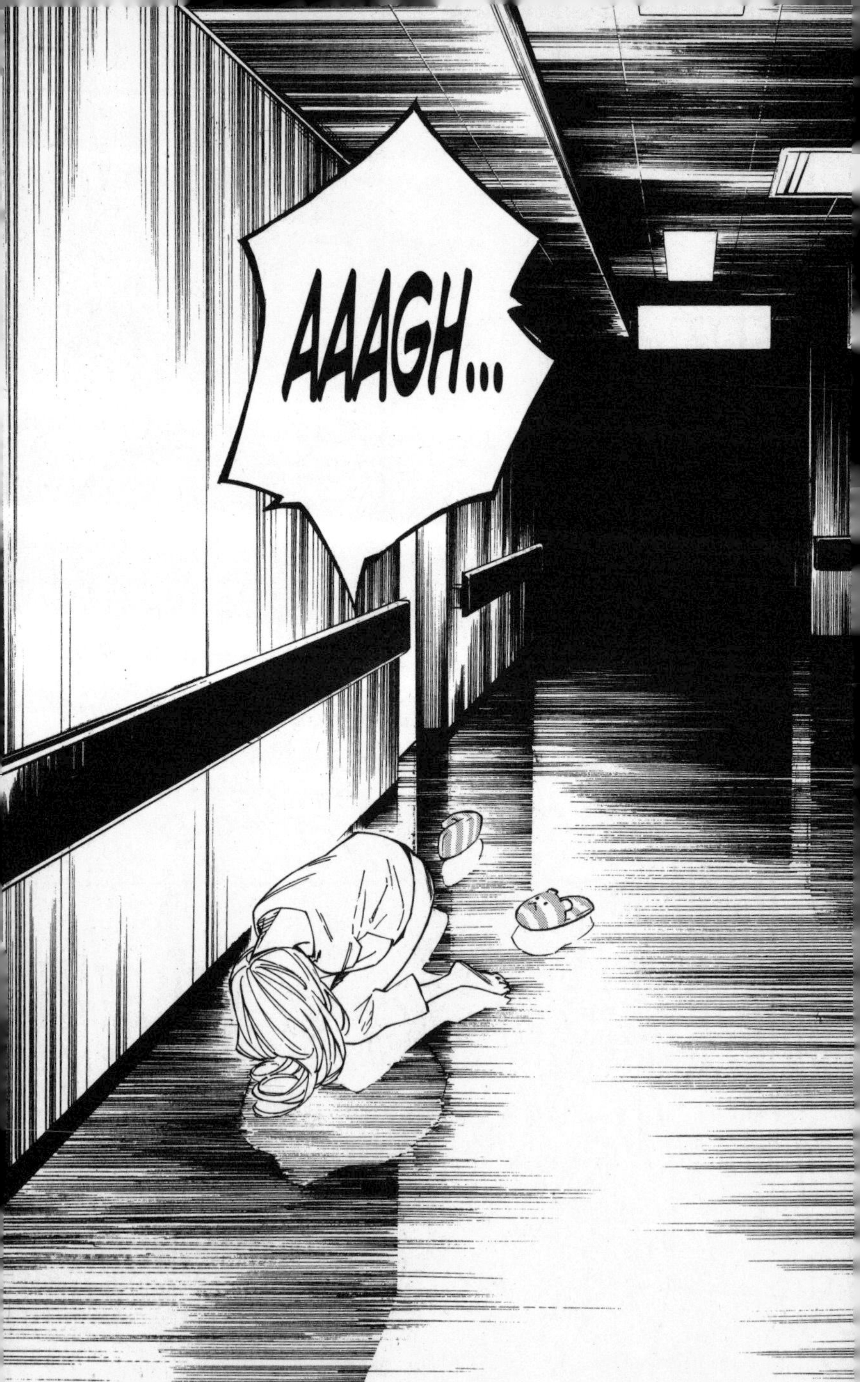
AAAGH...

INTRUDER / END

Your Lie in April
I met the girl under full-bloomed cherry blossoms, and my fate has begun to change.

Chapter 31: You'll Do

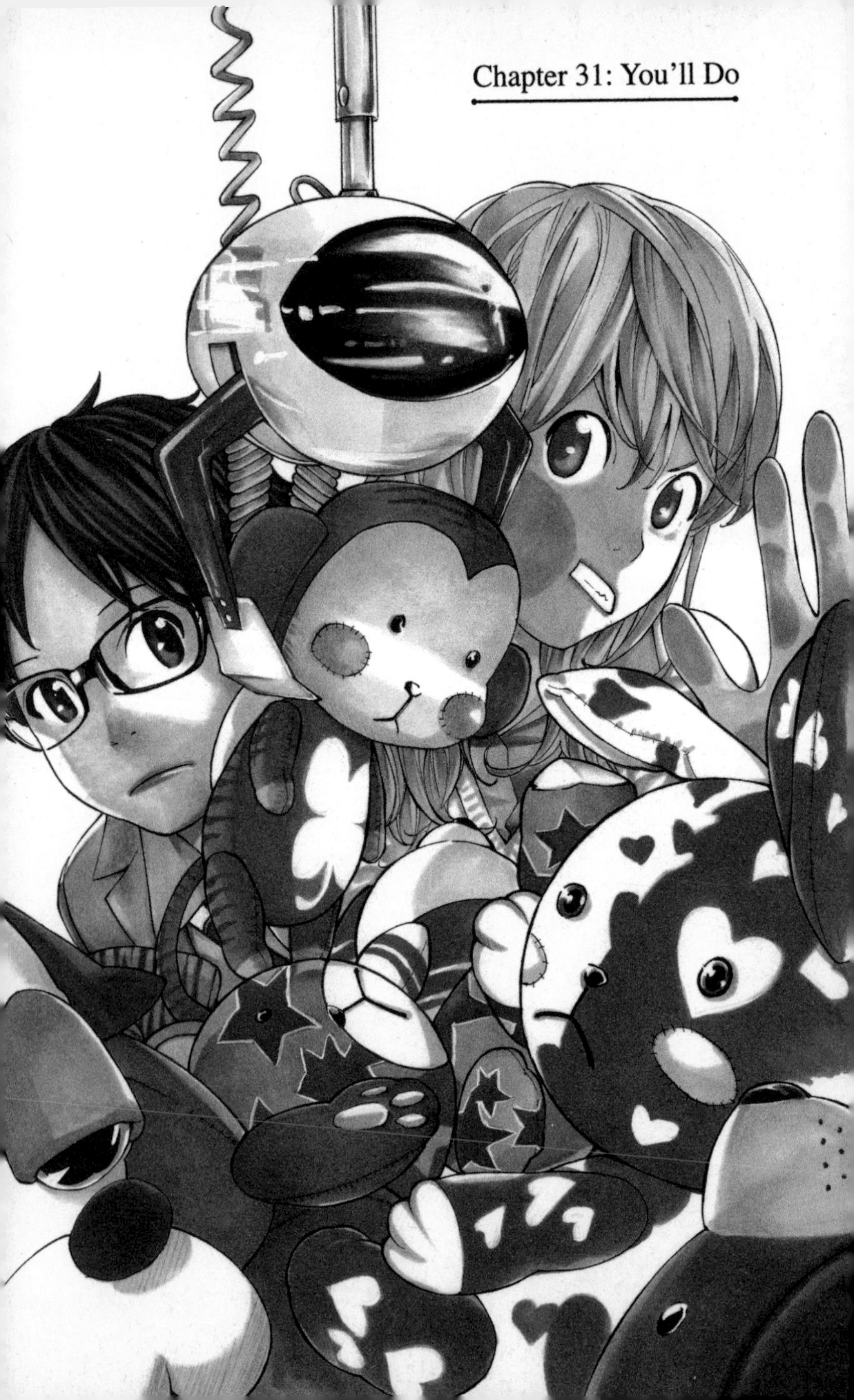

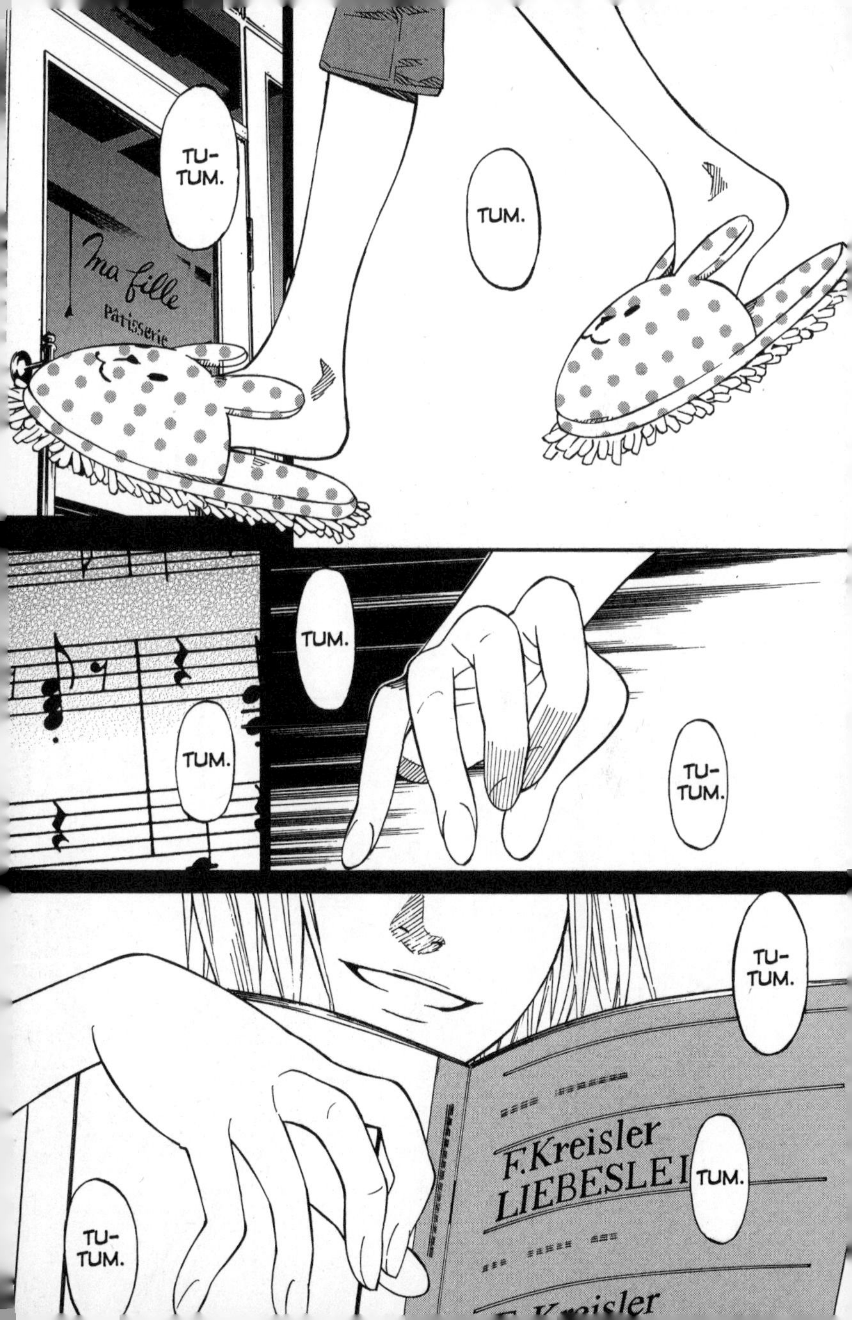
TUM.
TU-
TUM.
ma fille
pâtisserie
TUM.
TU-
TUM.
TUM.
TU-
TUM.
TUM.
F.Kreisler
LIEBESLEI
TU-
TUM.
F.Kreisler

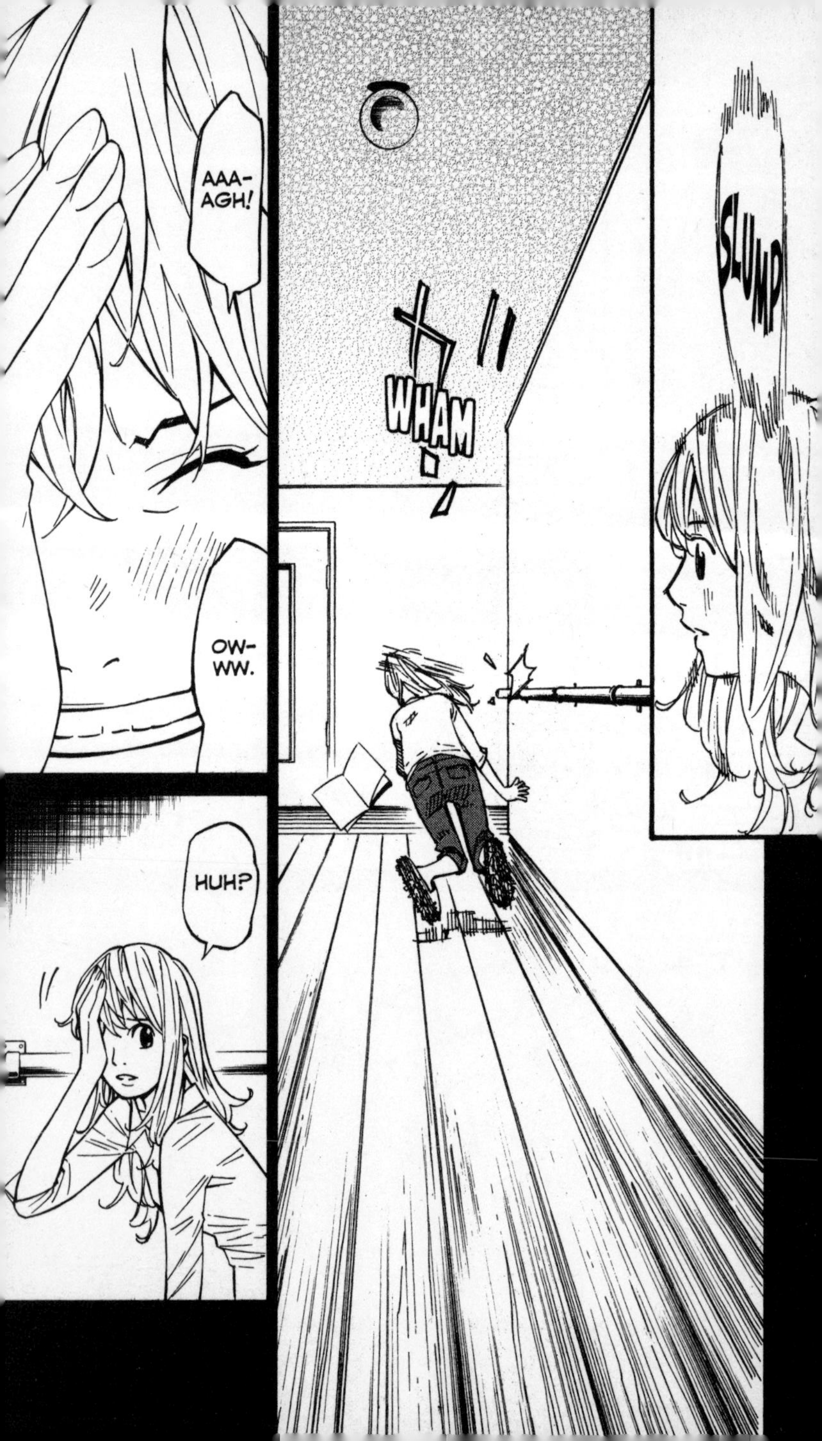
SLUMP
WHAM
AAA-AGH!
OW-WW.
HUH?

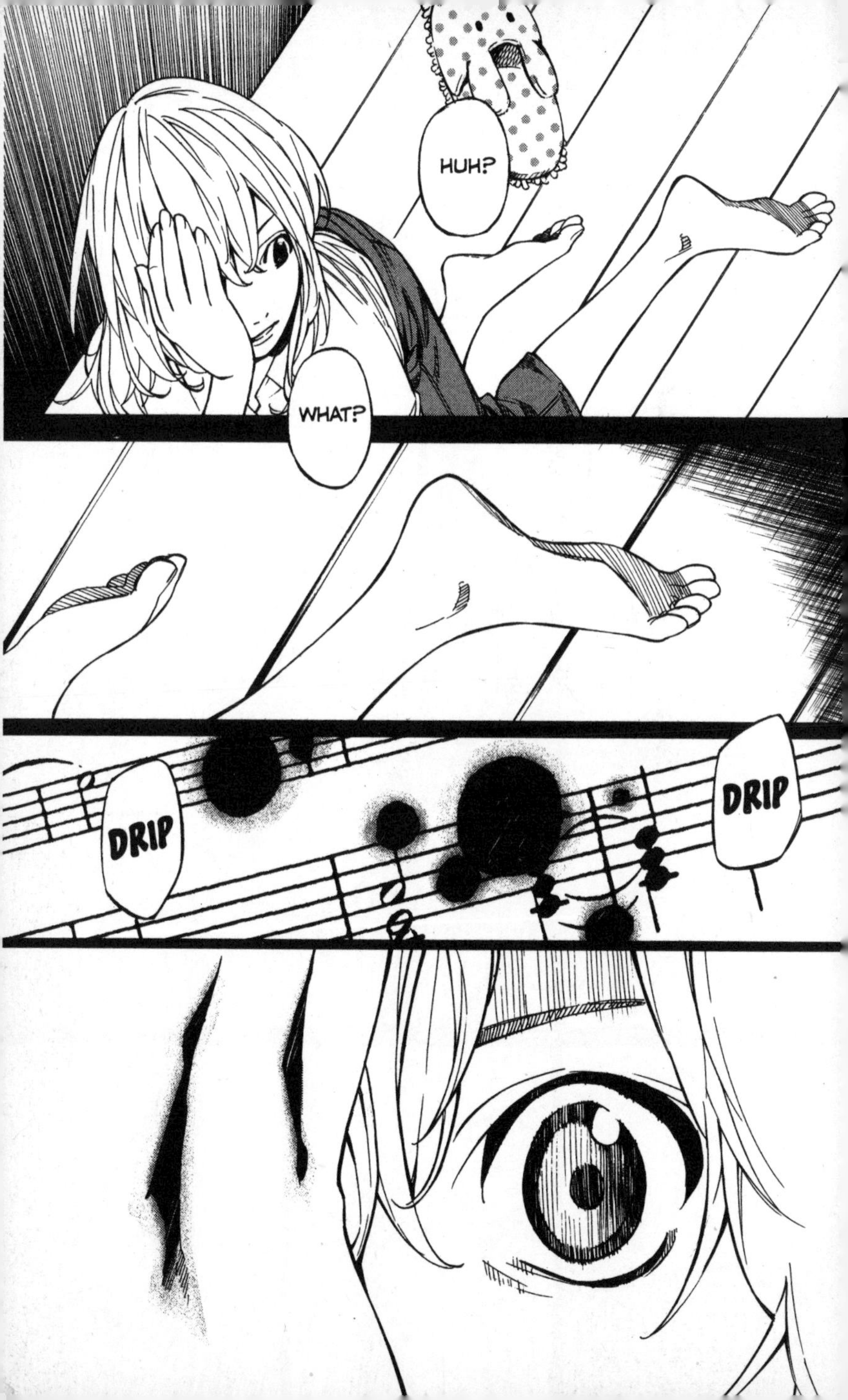
HUH?
WHAT?
DRIP
DRIP

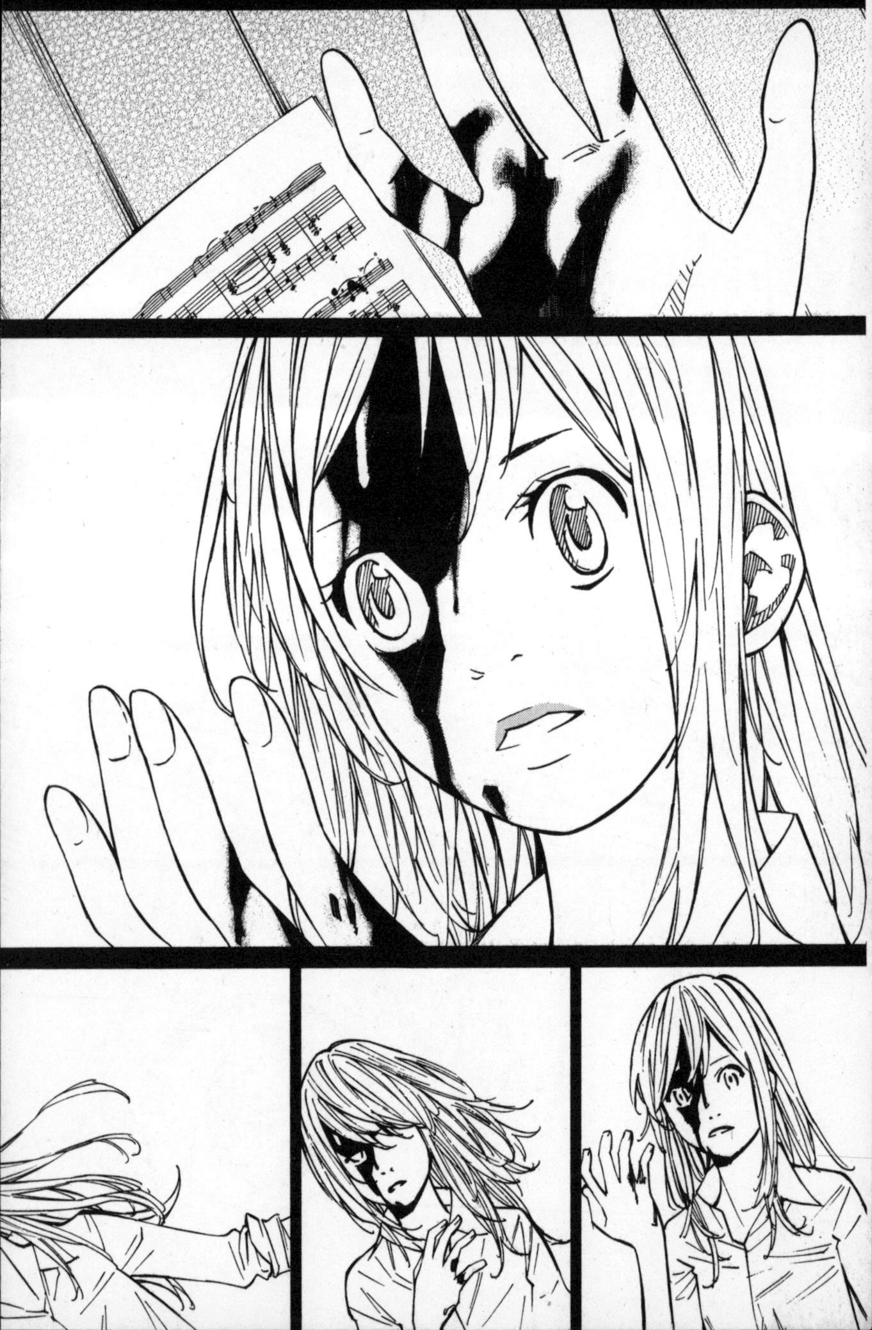

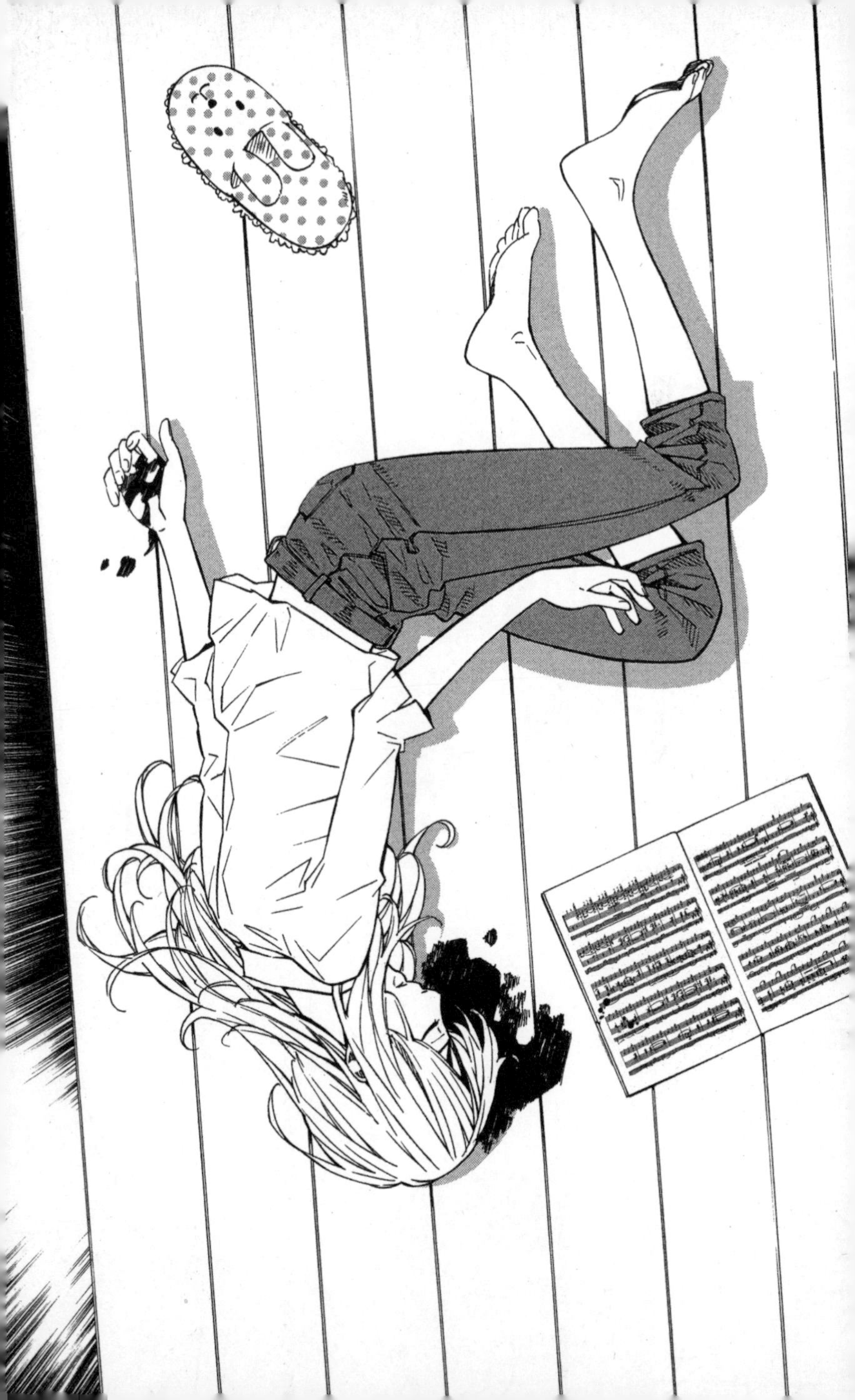

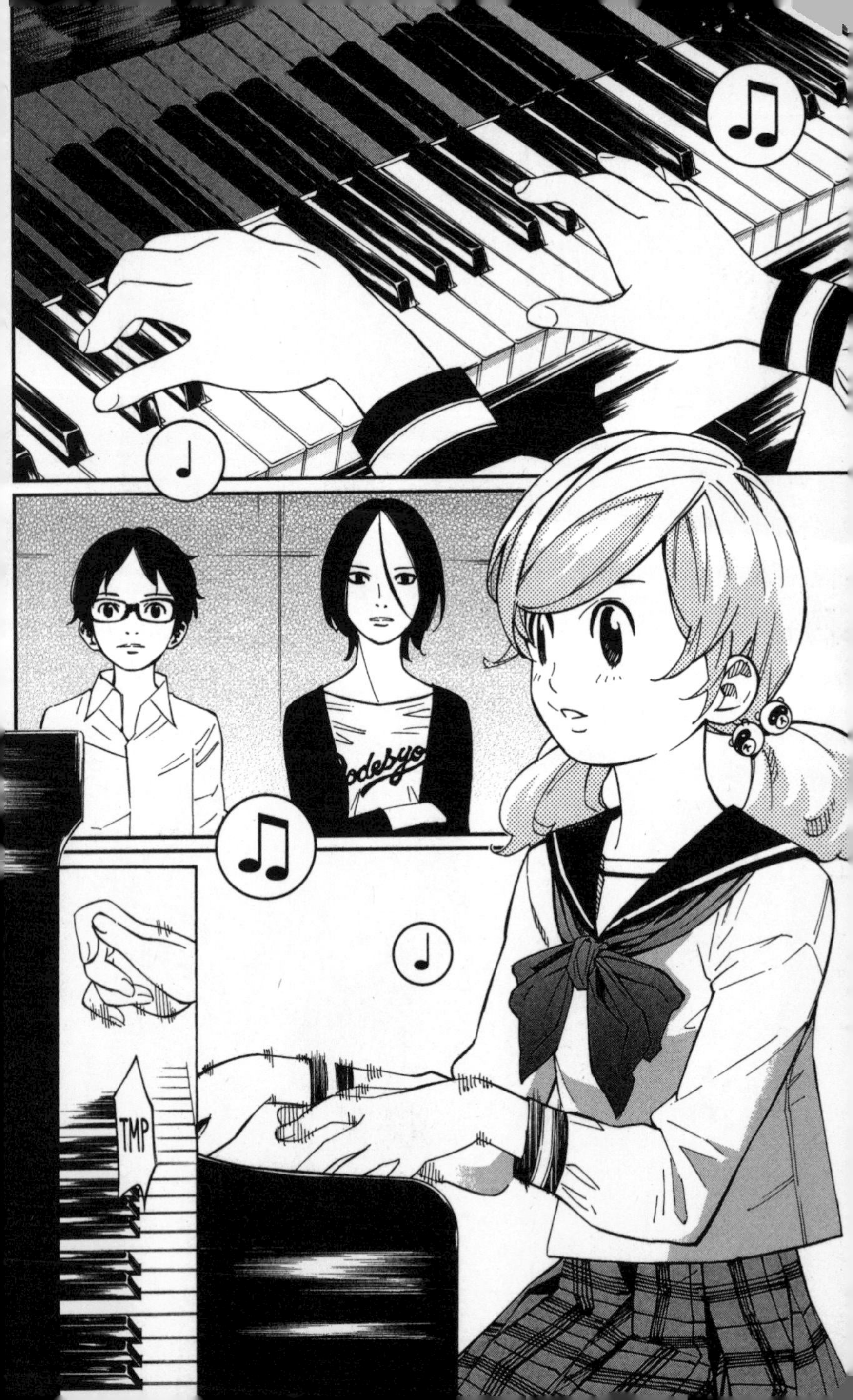
TMP

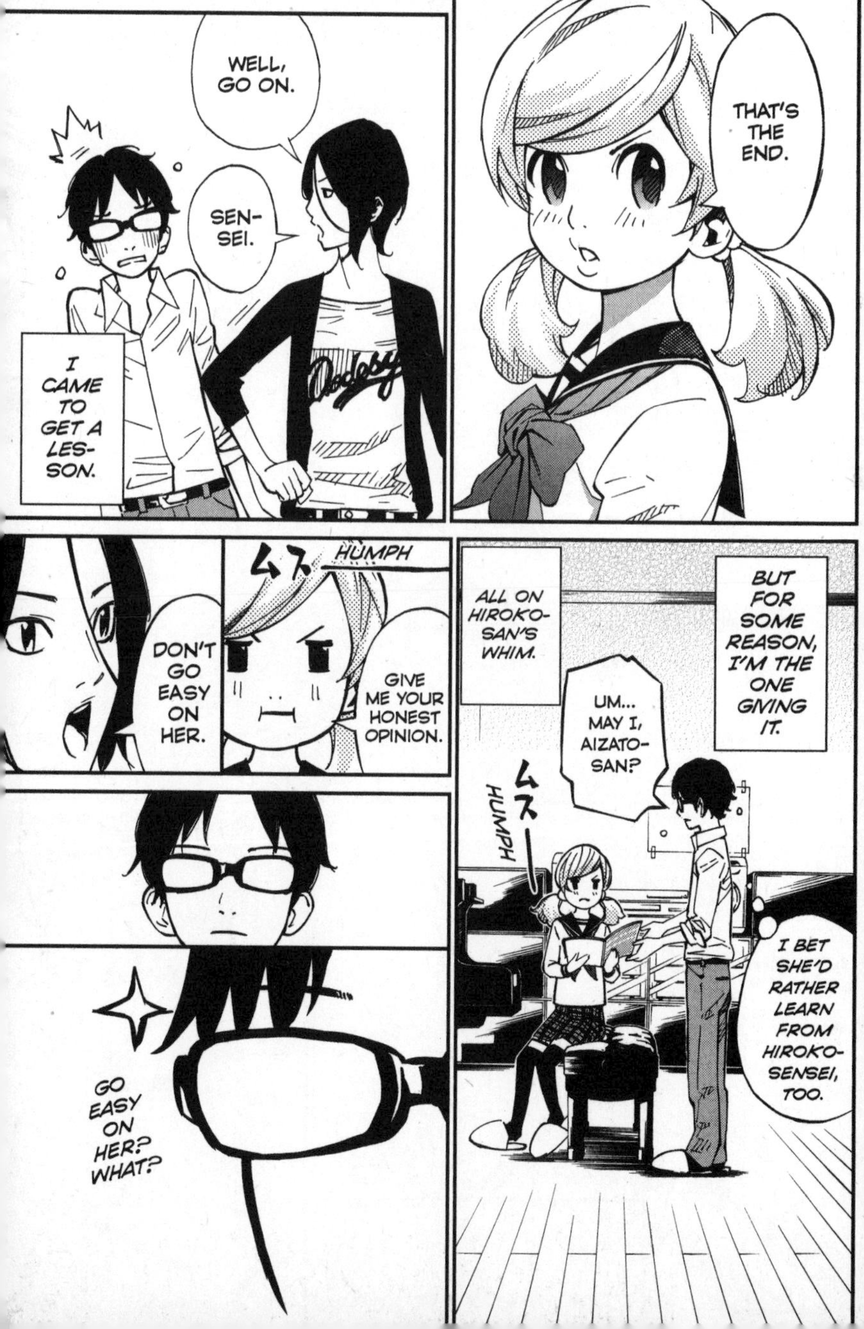
THAT'S THE END.
WELL, GO ON.
SEN-SEI.
I CAME TO GET A LES-SON.
BUT FOR SOME REASON, I'M THE ONE GIVING IT.
ALL ON HIROKO-SAN'S WHIM.
UM... MAY I, AIZATO-SAN?
ムスー HUMPH
I BET SHE'D RATHER LEARN FROM HIROKO-SENSEI, TOO.
ムス HUMPH
GIVE ME YOUR HONEST OPINION.
DON'T GO EASY ON HER.
GO EASY ON HER? WHAT?

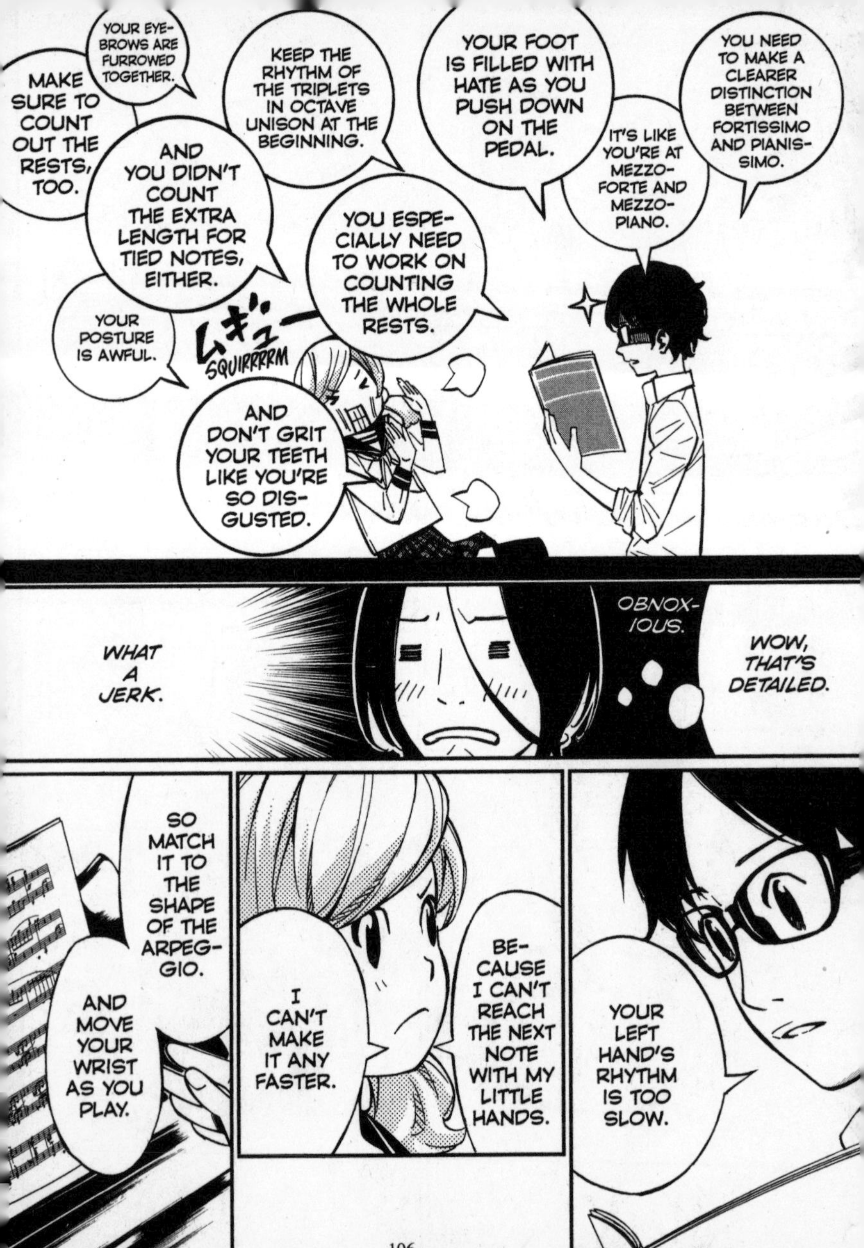
YOU NEED TO MAKE A CLEARER DISTINCTION BETWEEN FORTISSIMO AND PIANISSIMO.
IT'S LIKE YOU'RE AT MEZZOFORTE AND MEZZOPIANO.
YOUR FOOT IS FILLED WITH HATE AS YOU PUSH DOWN ON THE PEDAL.
KEEP THE RHYTHM OF THE TRIPLETS IN OCTAVE UNISON AT THE BEGINNING.
YOUR EYEBROWS ARE FURROWED TOGETHER.
MAKE SURE TO COUNT OUT THE RESTS, TOO.
AND YOU DIDN'T COUNT THE EXTRA LENGTH FOR TIED NOTES, EITHER.
YOU ESPECIALLY NEED TO WORK ON COUNTING THE WHOLE RESTS.
YOUR POSTURE IS AWFUL.
ムギュー
SQUIRRRRM
AND DON'T GRIT YOUR TEETH LIKE YOU'RE SO DISGUSTED.
WOW, THAT'S DETAILED.
OBNOXIOUS.
WHAT A JERK.
YOUR LEFT HAND'S RHYTHM IS TOO SLOW.
BECAUSE I CAN'T REACH THE NEXT NOTE WITH MY LITTLE HANDS.
I CAN'T MAKE IT ANY FASTER.
SO MATCH IT TO THE SHAPE OF THE ARPEGGIO.
AND MOVE YOUR WRIST AS YOU PLAY.

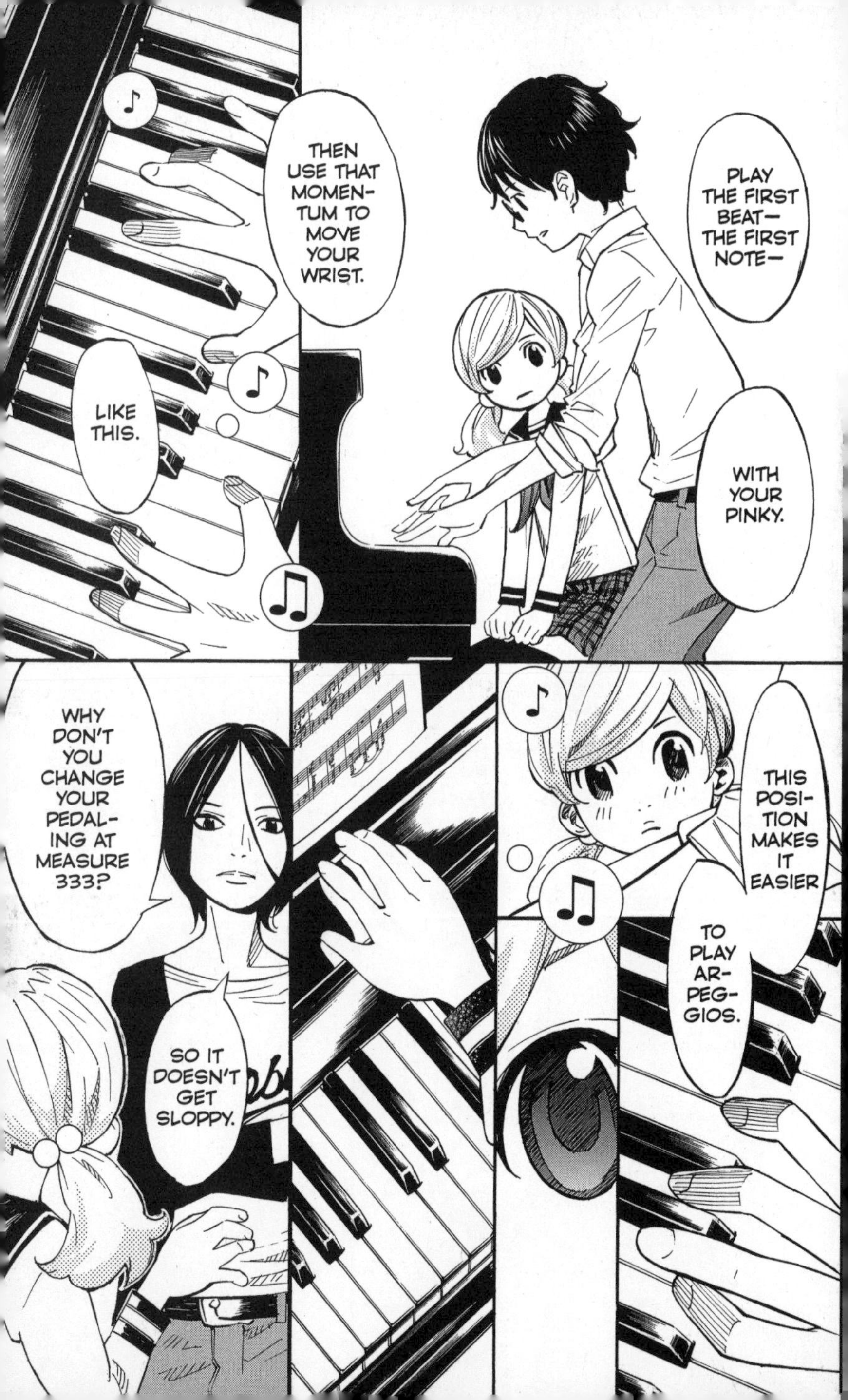
PLAY THE FIRST BEAT—THE FIRST NOTE—
WITH YOUR PINKY.
THEN USE THAT MOMENTUM TO MOVE YOUR WRIST.
LIKE THIS.
THIS POSITION MAKES IT EASIER
TO PLAY ARPEGGIOS.
WHY DON'T YOU CHANGE YOUR PEDALING AT MEASURE 333?
SO IT DOESN'T GET SLOPPY.

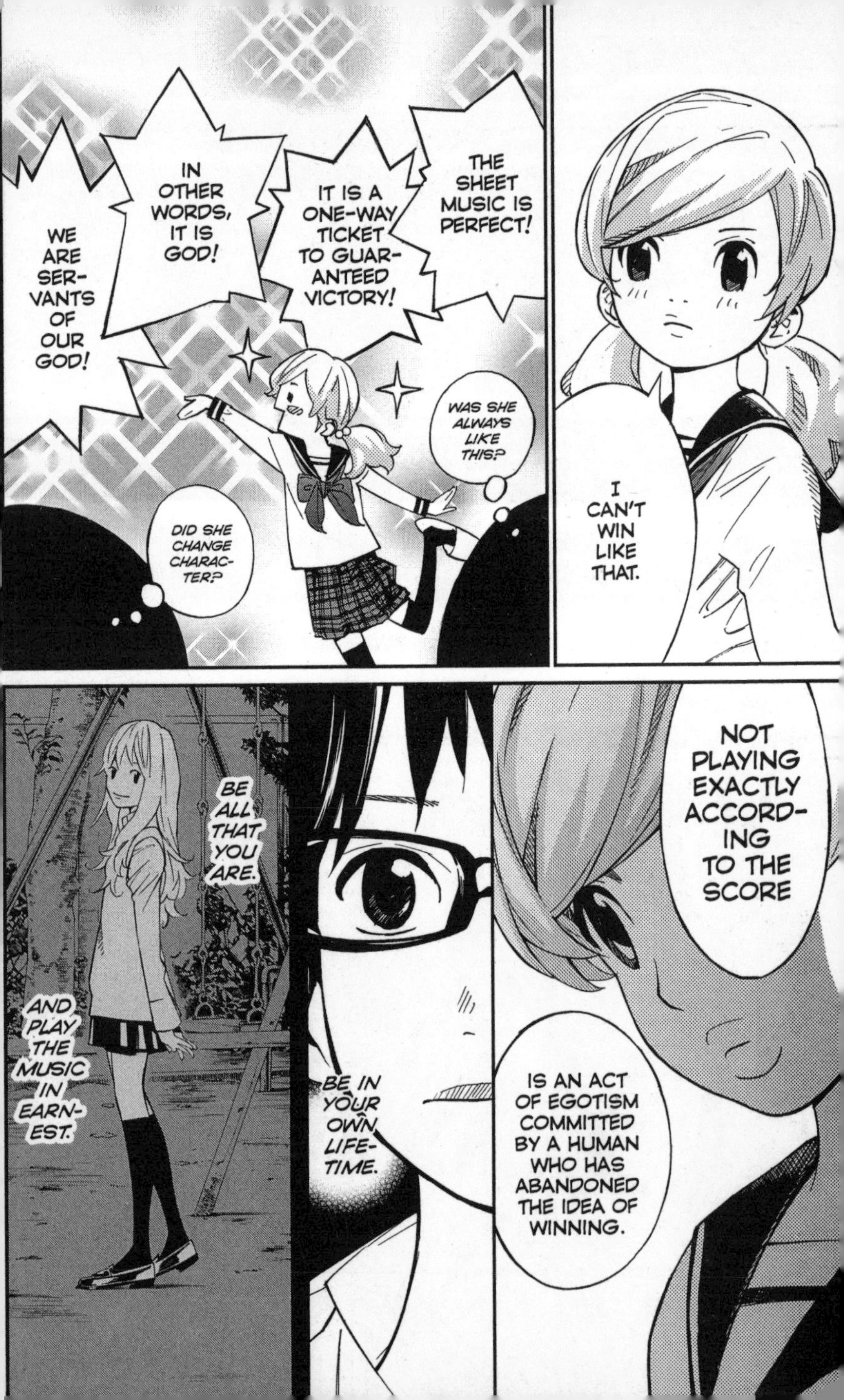
I CAN'T WIN LIKE THAT.
THE SHEET MUSIC IS PERFECT!
IT IS A ONE-WAY TICKET TO GUARANTEED VICTORY!
IN OTHER WORDS, IT IS GOD!
WE ARE SERVANTS OF OUR GOD!
WAS SHE ALWAYS LIKE THIS?
DID SHE CHANGE CHARACTER?
NOT PLAYING EXACTLY ACCORDING TO THE SCORE
IS AN ACT OF EGOTISM COMMITTED BY A HUMAN WHO HAS ABANDONED THE IDEA OF WINNING.
BE IN YOUR OWN LIFETIME.
BE ALL THAT YOU ARE.
AND PLAY THE MUSIC IN EARNEST.

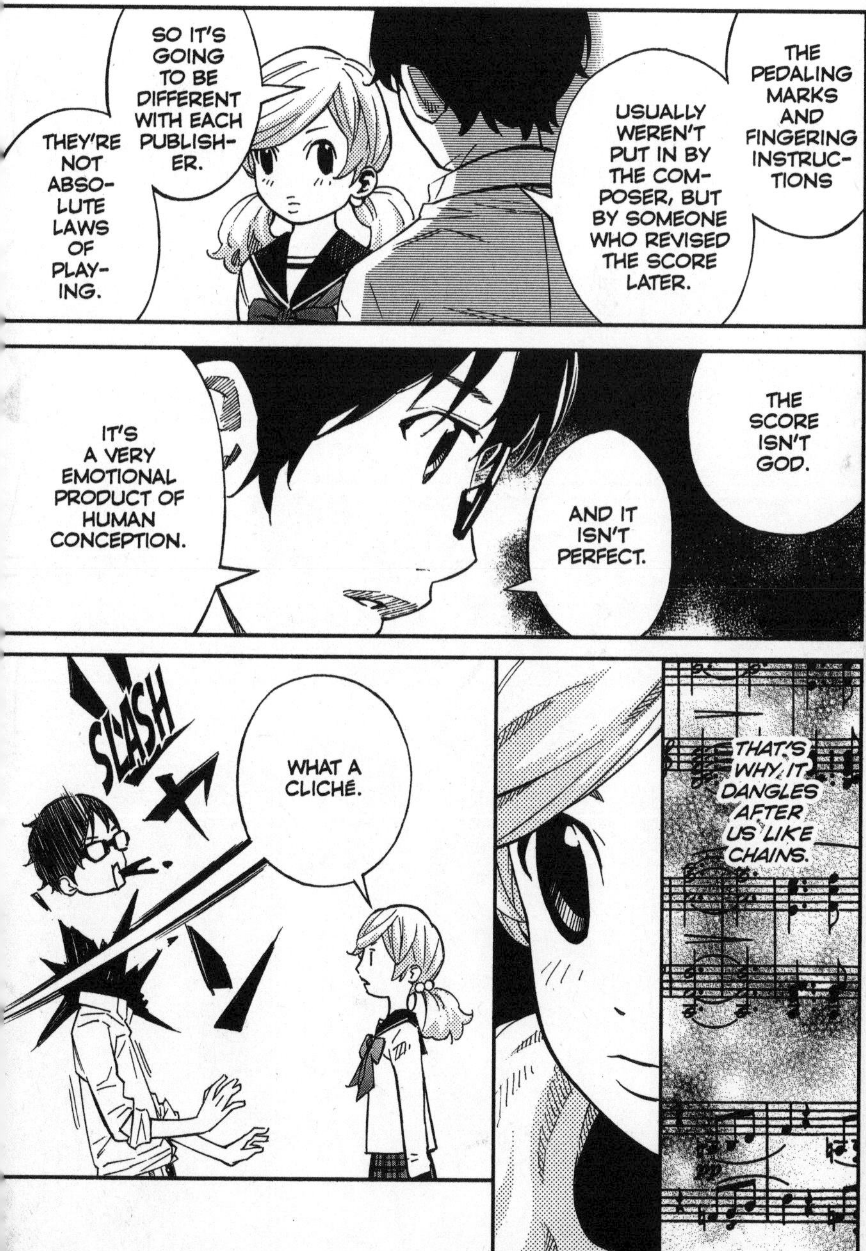
THE PEDALING MARKS AND FINGERING INSTRUCTIONS
USUALLY WEREN'T PUT IN BY THE COMPOSER, BUT BY SOMEONE WHO REVISED THE SCORE LATER.
SO IT'S GOING TO BE DIFFERENT WITH EACH PUBLISHER.
THEY'RE NOT ABSOLUTE LAWS OF PLAYING.
THE SCORE ISN'T GOD.
AND IT ISN'T PERFECT.
IT'S A VERY EMOTIONAL PRODUCT OF HUMAN CONCEPTION.
THAT'S WHY IT DANGLES AFTER US LIKE CHAINS.
WHAT A CLICHÉ.
SLASH

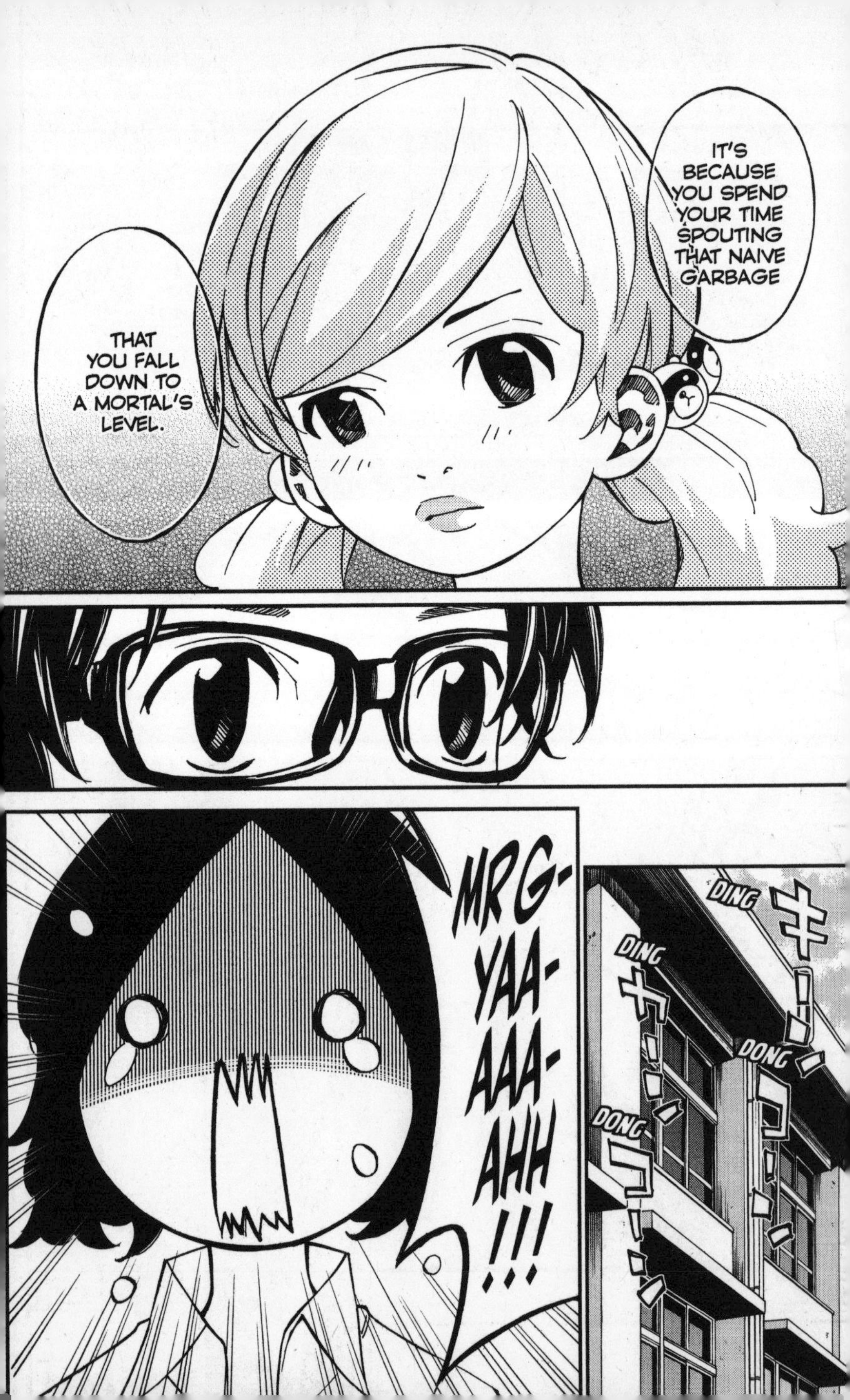
IT'S BECAUSE YOU SPEND YOUR TIME SPOUTING THAT NAIVE GARBAGE
THAT YOU FALL DOWN TO A MORTAL'S LEVEL.
DING
DING
DONG
DONG
MRG-YAA-AAA-AHH!!!

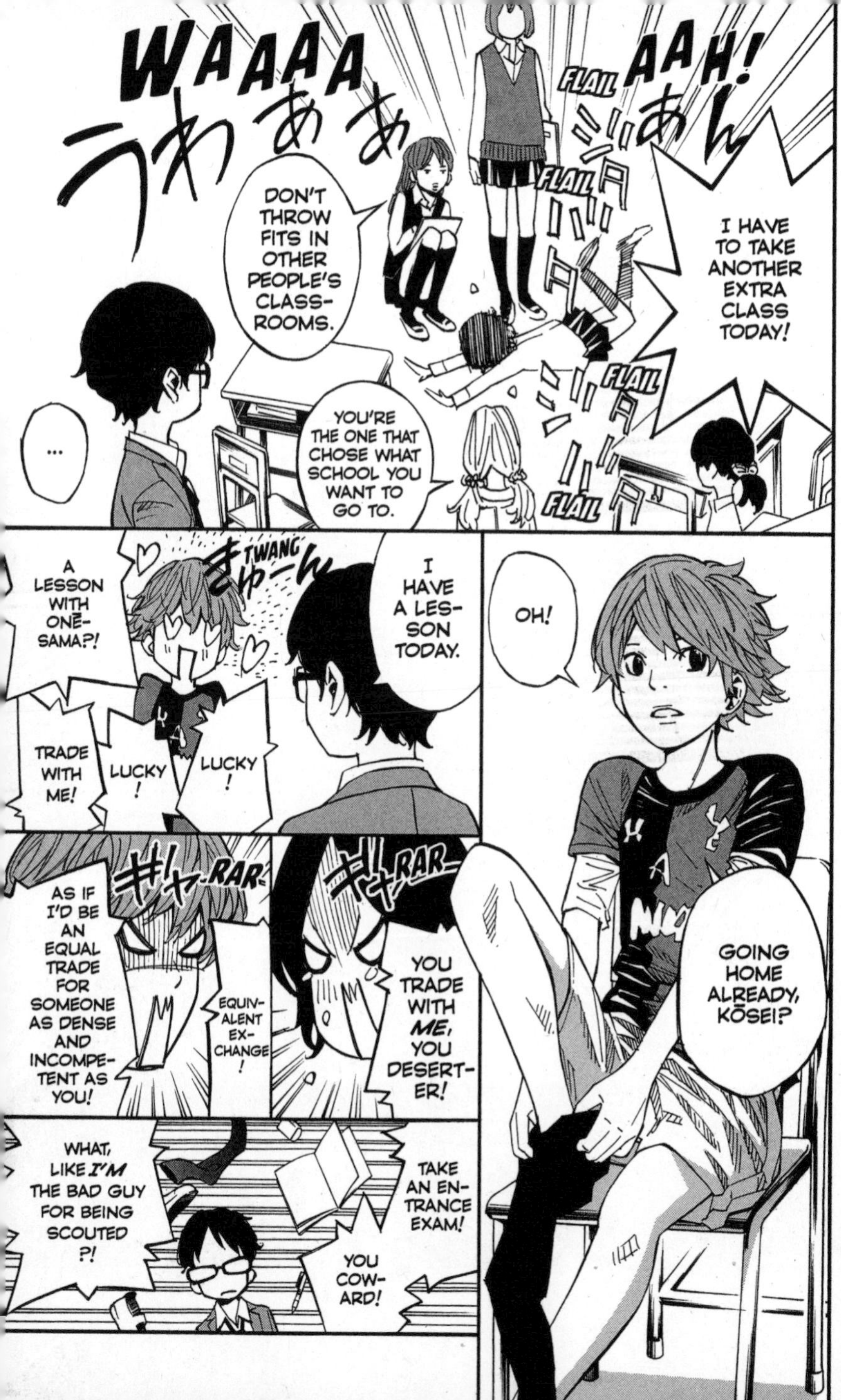

WAAAAAAH!
FLAIL
FLAIL
I HAVE TO TAKE ANOTHER EXTRA CLASS TODAY!
DON'T THROW FITS IN OTHER PEOPLE'S CLASSROOMS.
FLAIL
FLAIL
YOU'RE THE ONE THAT CHOSE WHAT SCHOOL YOU WANT TO GO TO.
...
OH!
GOING HOME ALREADY, KŌSEI?
I HAVE A LESSON TODAY.
TWANG
A LESSON WITH ONĒ-SAMA?!
LUCKY!
LUCKY!
TRADE WITH ME!
RAR
YOU TRADE WITH *ME*, YOU DESERTER!
EQUIVALENT EXCHANGE!
RAR
AS IF I'D BE AN EQUAL TRADE FOR SOMEONE AS DENSE AND INCOMPETENT AS YOU!
TAKE AN ENTRANCE EXAM!
YOU COWARD!
WHAT, LIKE *I'M* THE BAD GUY FOR BEING SCOUTED?!

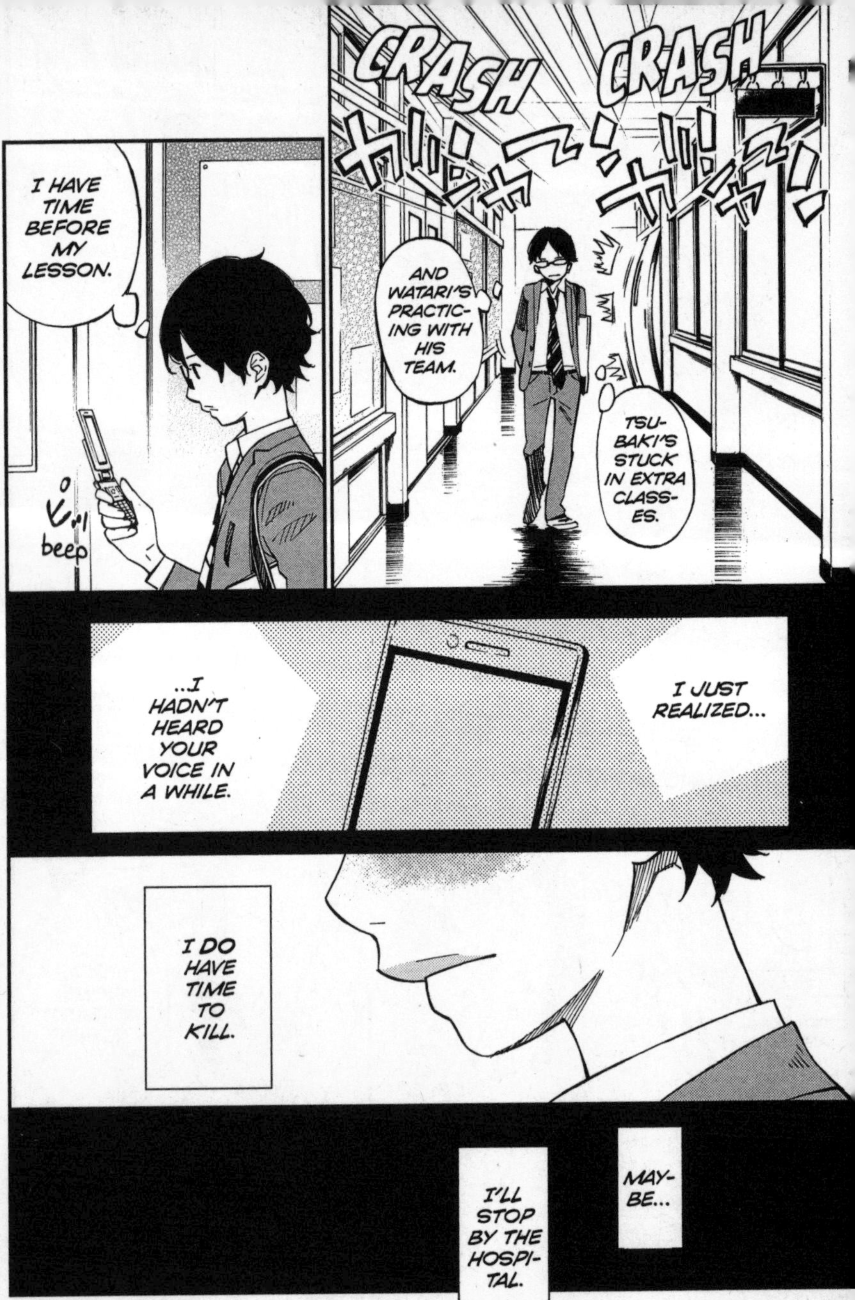
CRASH
CRASH
TSU-BAKI'S STUCK IN EXTRA CLASS-ES.
AND WATARI'S PRACTIC-ING WITH HIS TEAM.
I HAVE TIME BEFORE MY LESSON.
beep
I JUST REALIZED...
...I HADN'T HEARD YOUR VOICE IN A WHILE.
I DO HAVE TIME TO KILL.
MAY-BE...
I'LL STOP BY THE HOSPI-TAL.

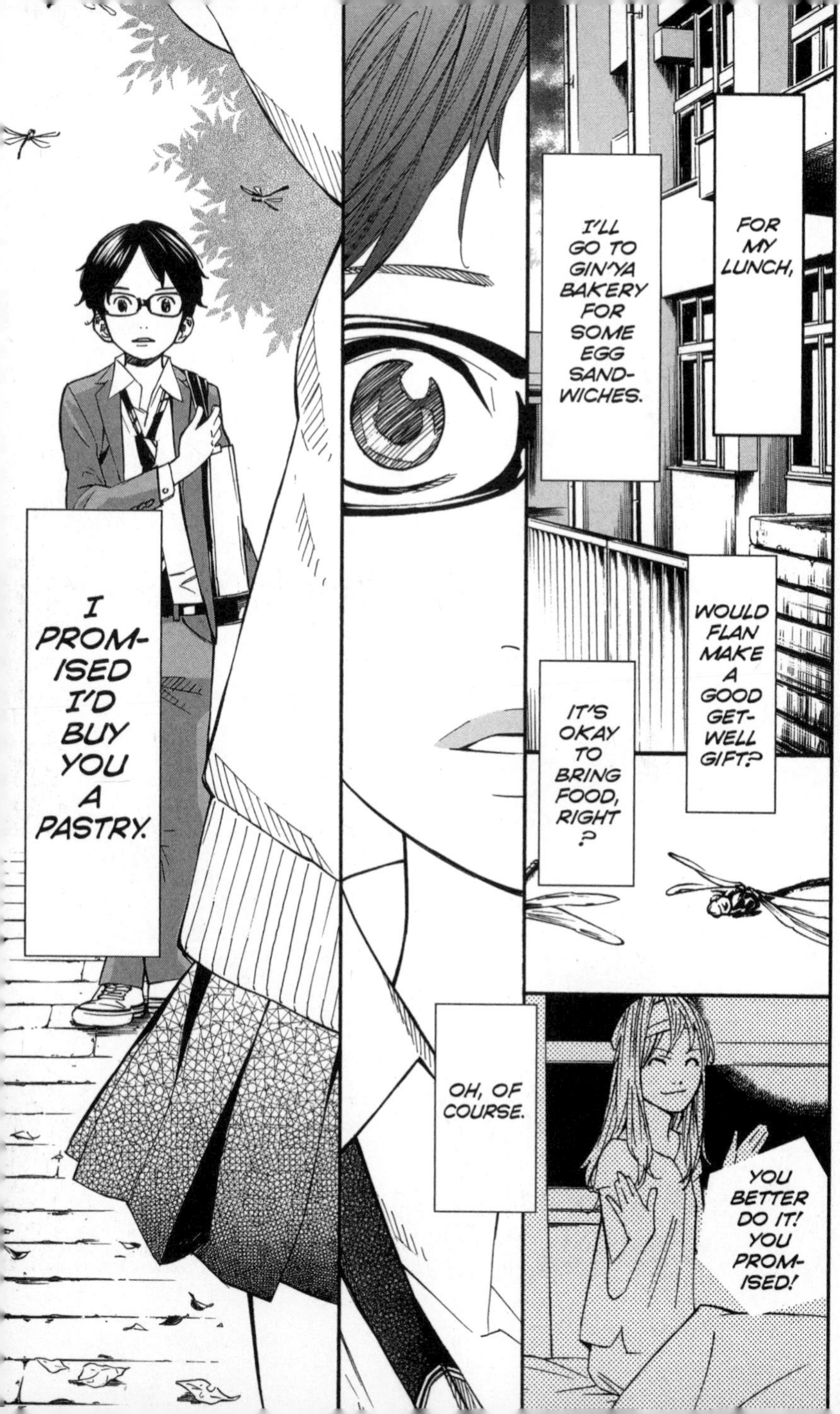
FOR MY LUNCH,
I'LL GO TO GIN'YA BAKERY FOR SOME EGG SANDWICHES.
WOULD FLAN MAKE A GOOD GET-WELL GIFT?
IT'S OKAY TO BRING FOOD, RIGHT?
YOU BETTER DO IT! YOU PROMISED!
OH, OF COURSE.
I PROMISED I'D BUY YOU A PASTRY.

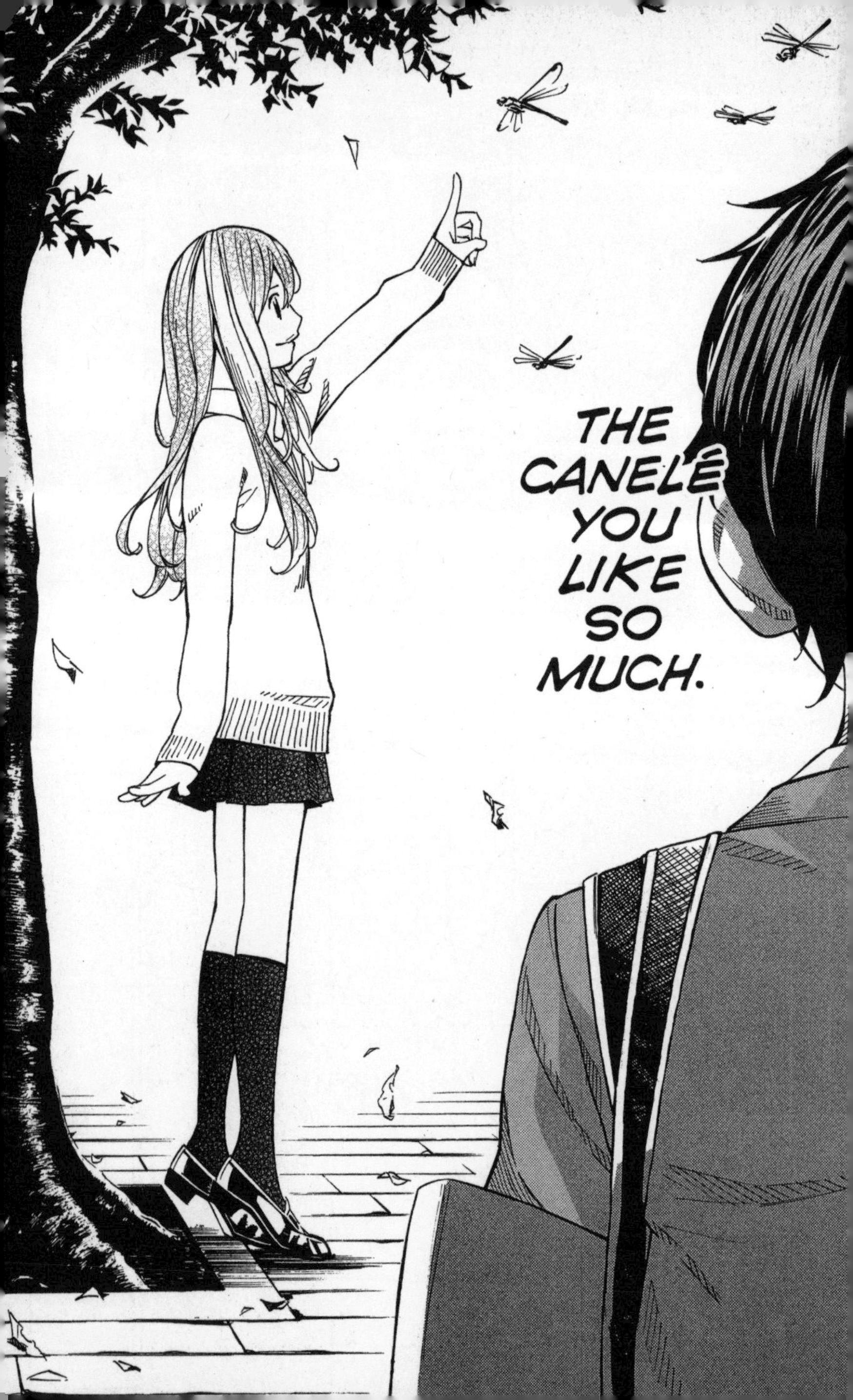
THE CANELÉ YOU LIKE SO MUCH.

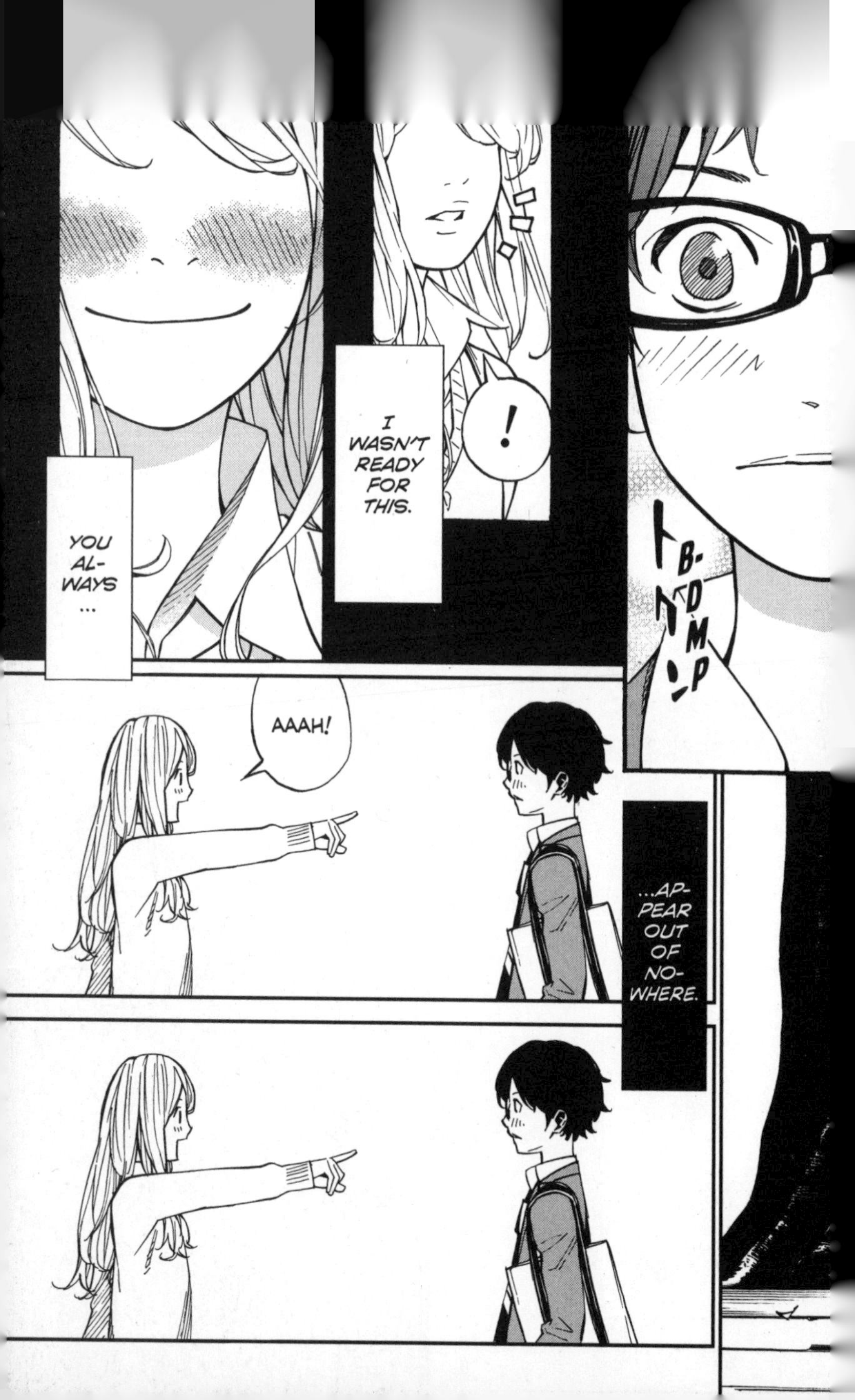

B-DMP
!
I WASN'T READY FOR THIS.
YOU AL-WAYS ...
...AP-PEAR OUT OF NO-WHERE.
AAAH!

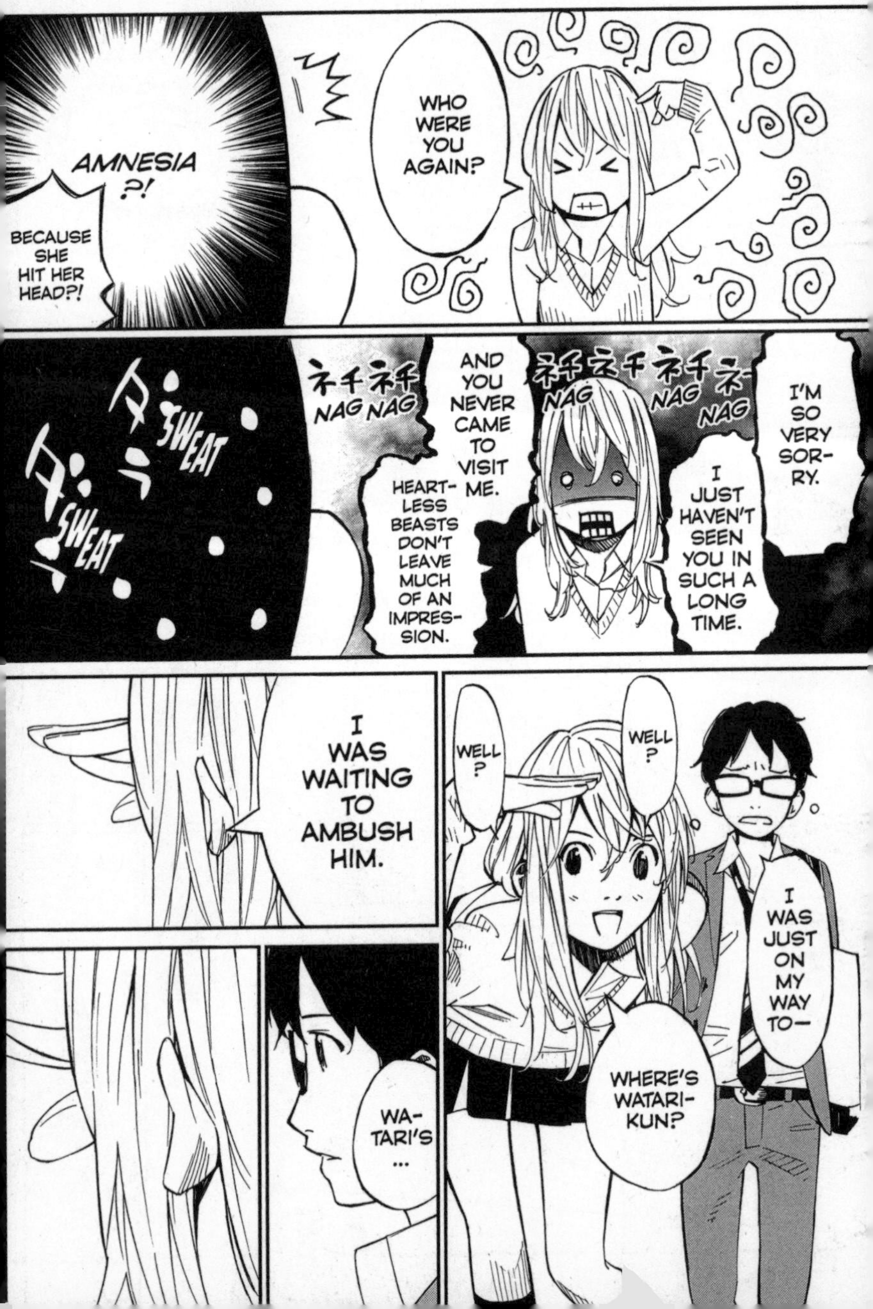
WHO WERE YOU AGAIN?
AMNESIA ?!
BECAUSE SHE HIT HER HEAD?!
I'M SO VERY SORRY.
I JUST HAVEN'T SEEN YOU IN SUCH A LONG TIME.
NAG NAG NAG
AND YOU NEVER CAME TO VISIT ME.
NAG NAG
HEART-LESS BEASTS DON'T LEAVE MUCH OF AN IMPRES-SION.
SWEAT
SWEAT
WELL?
WELL?
I WAS JUST ON MY WAY TO—
WHERE'S WATARI-KUN?
I WAS WAITING TO AMBUSH HIM.
WA-TARI'S ...

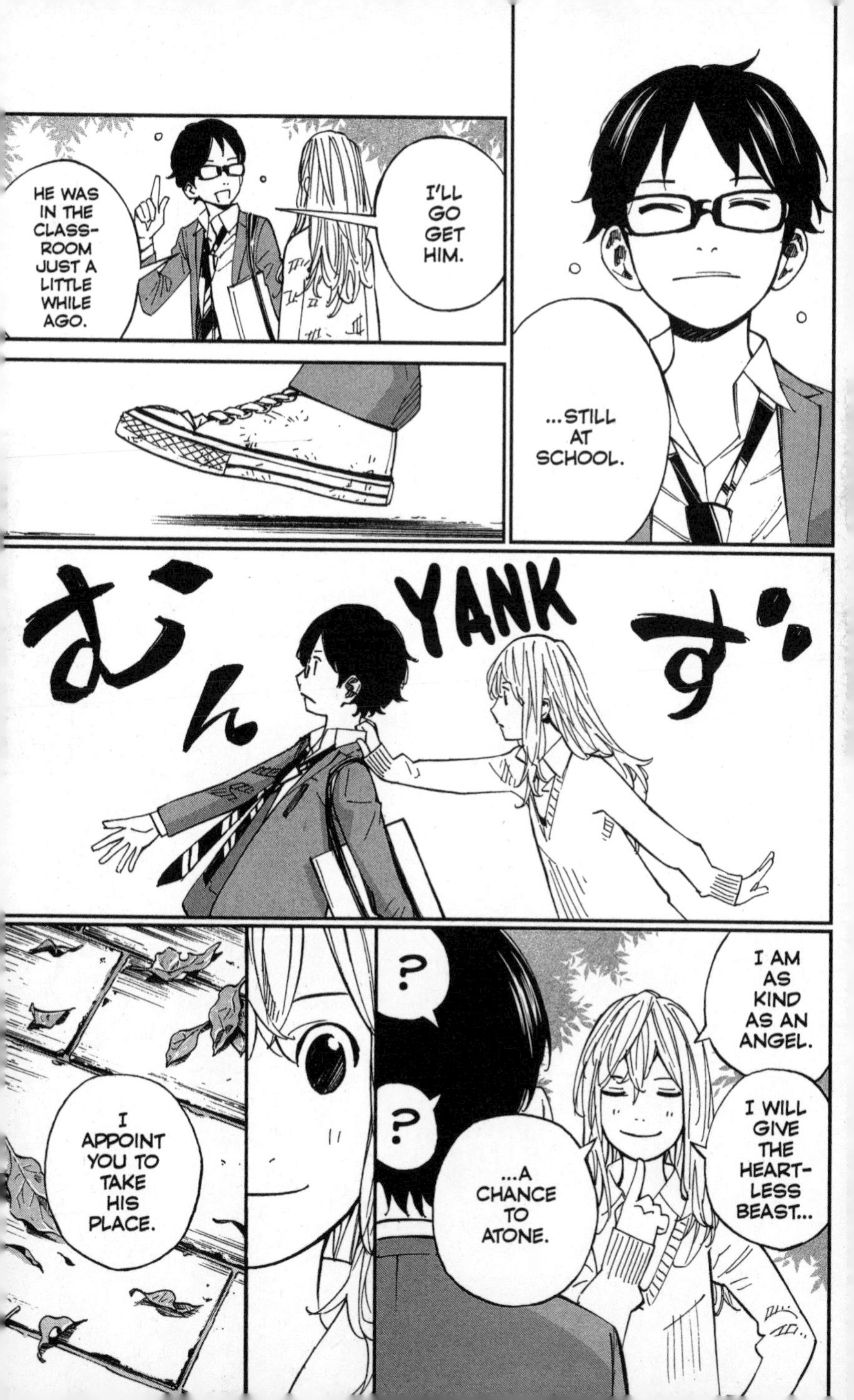
...STILL AT SCHOOL.
HE WAS IN THE CLASSROOM JUST A LITTLE WHILE AGO.
I'LL GO GET HIM.
YANK
むんず
I AM AS KIND AS AN ANGEL.
I WILL GIVE THE HEARTLESS BEAST...
...A CHANCE TO ATONE.
?
?
I APPOINT YOU TO TAKE HIS PLACE.

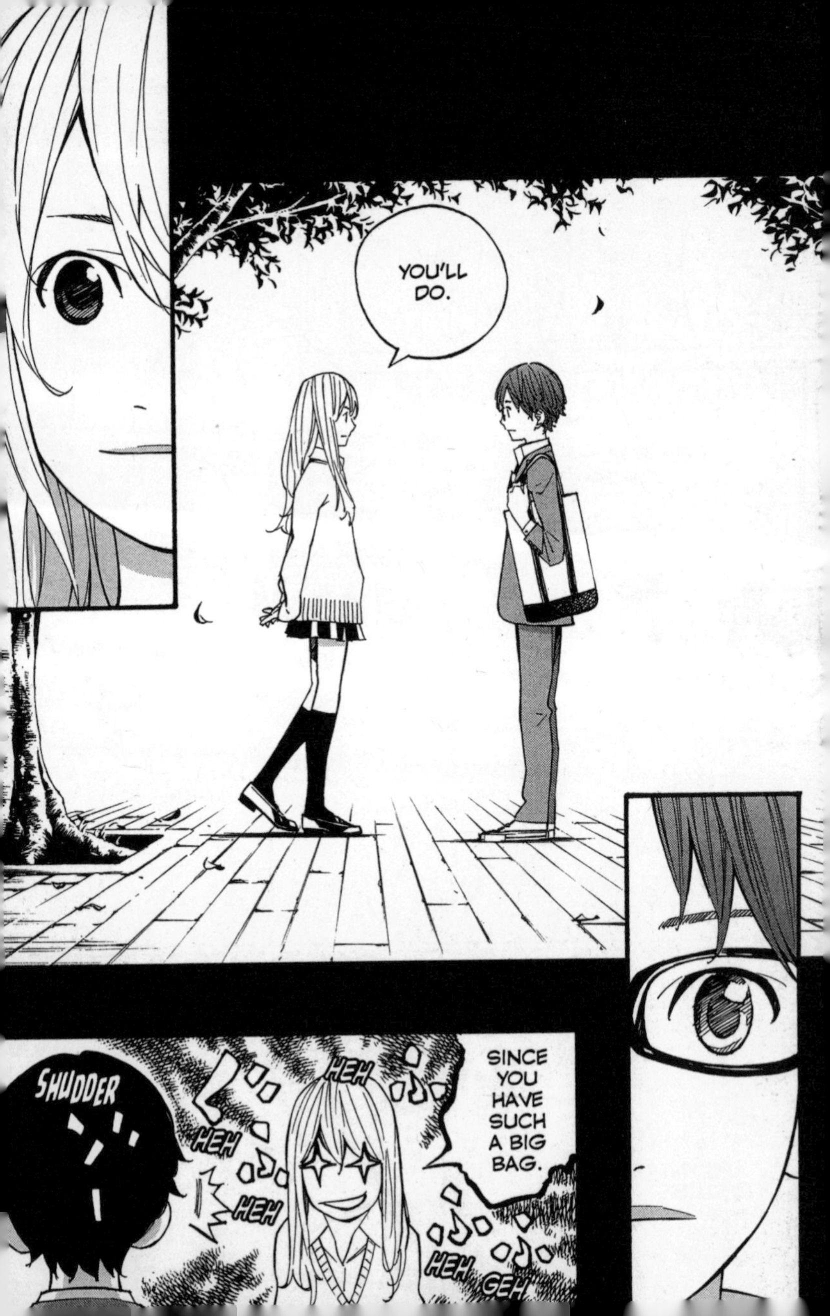
YOU'LL DO.
SINCE YOU HAVE SUCH A BIG BAG.
HEH
HEH
HEH
HEH
GEH
SHUDDER

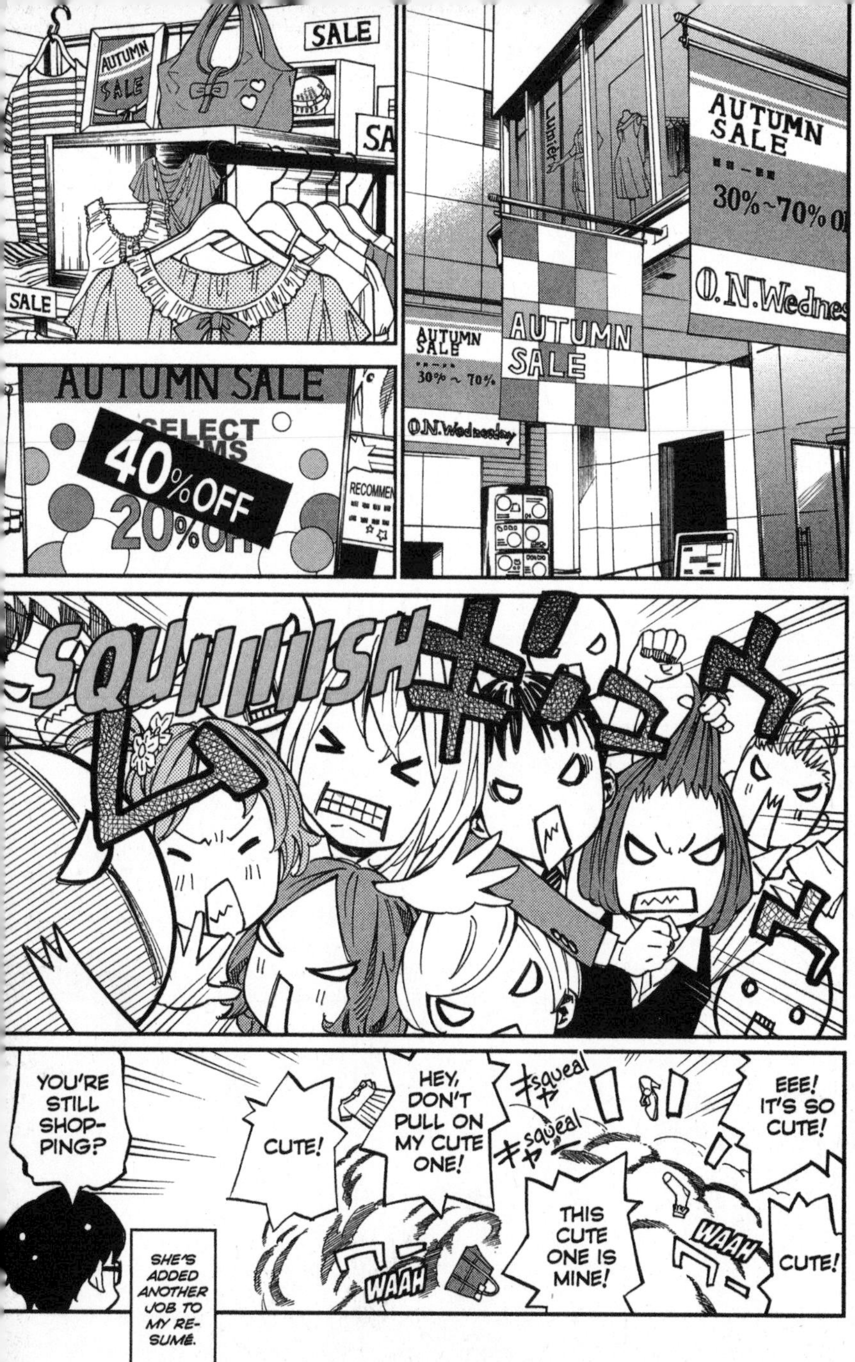
AUTUMN SALE
30%~70% O
O.N.Wednes
AUTUMN SALE
30% ~ 70%
O.N.Wednesday
AUTUMN SALE
SALE
AUTUMN SALE
SALE
SALE
AUTUMN SALE
40%OFF
SQUIIIIIISH
EEE! IT'S SO CUTE!
CUTE!
WAAH
squeal
squeal
THIS CUTE ONE IS MINE!
HEY, DON'T PULL ON MY CUTE ONE!
CUTE!
WAAH
YOU'RE STILL SHOP-PING?
SHE'S ADDED ANOTHER JOB TO MY RE-SUMÉ.

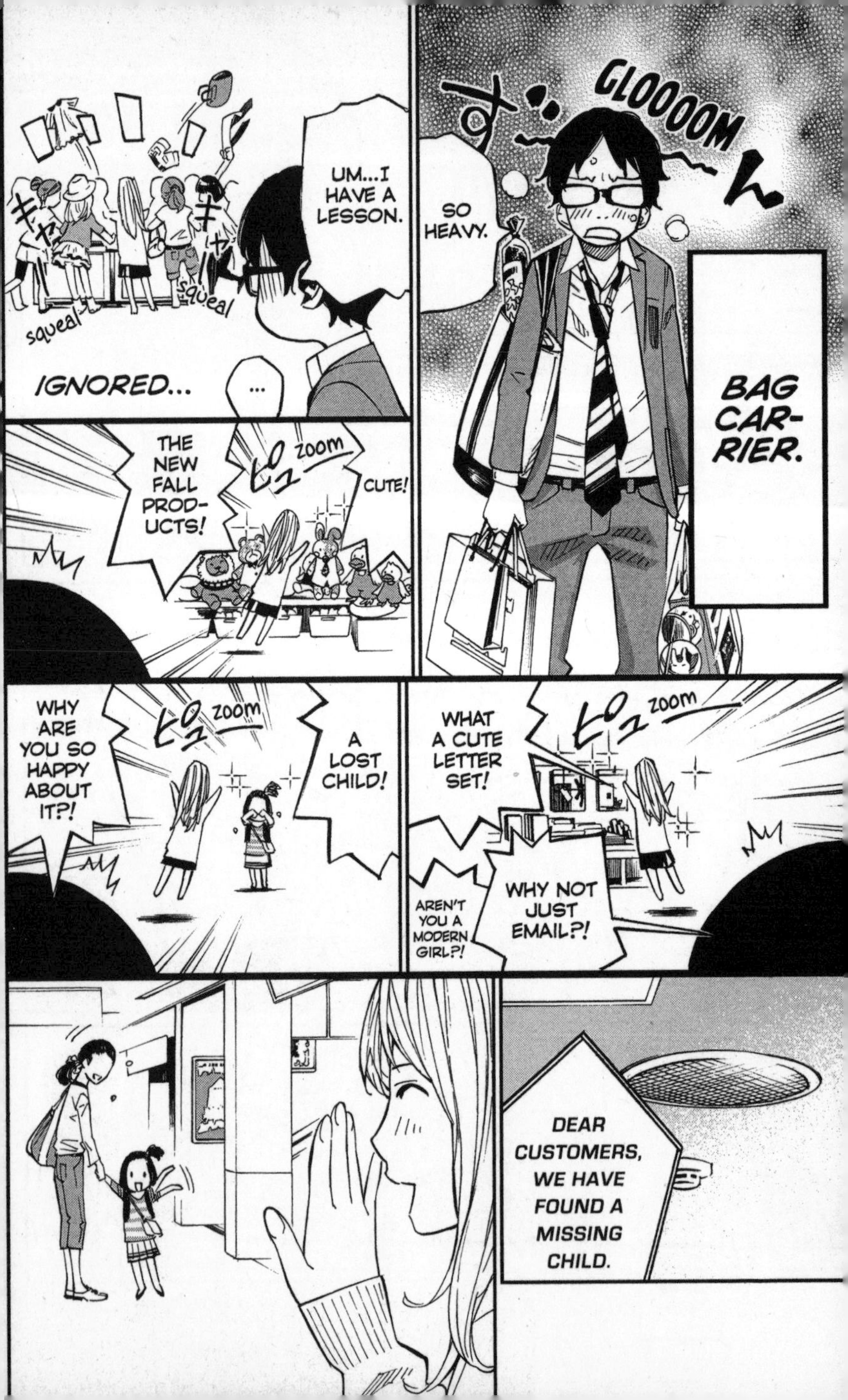
GLOOOOM
SO HEAVY.
BAG CARRIER.
UM...I HAVE A LESSON.
squeal
squeal
...
IGNORED...
THE NEW FALL PRODUCTS!
zoom
CUTE!
WHAT A CUTE LETTER SET!
zoom
WHY NOT JUST EMAIL?!
AREN'T YOU A MODERN GIRL?!
A LOST CHILD!
zoom
WHY ARE YOU SO HAPPY ABOUT IT?!
DEAR CUSTOMERS, WE HAVE FOUND A MISSING CHILD.

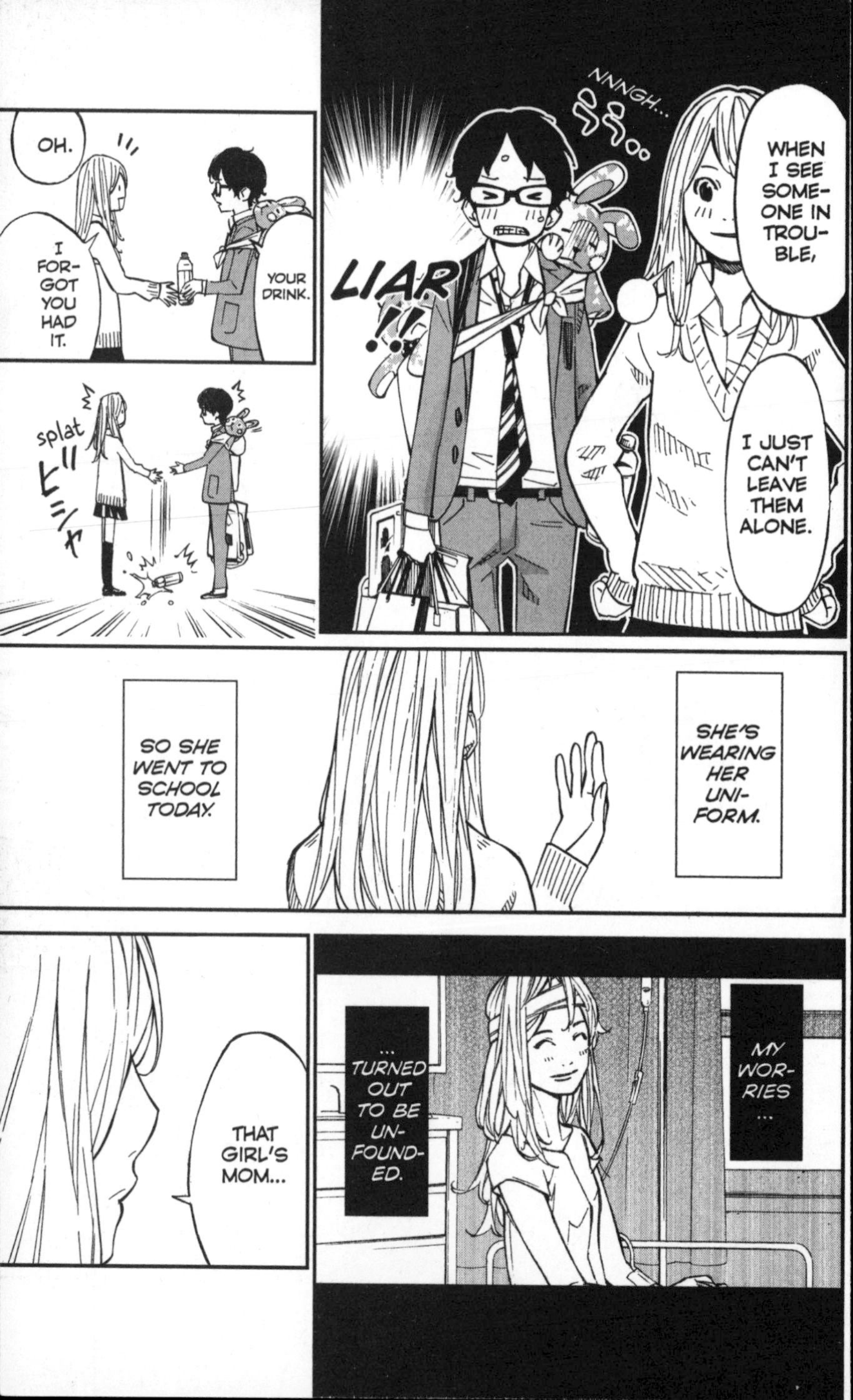
WHEN I SEE SOMEONE IN TROUBLE,
I JUST CAN'T LEAVE THEM ALONE.
NNNGH...
LIAR!!
YOUR DRINK.
OH.
I FORGOT YOU HAD IT.
splat
SHE'S WEARING HER UNIFORM.
SO SHE WENT TO SCHOOL TODAY.
MY WORRIES...
...TURNED OUT TO BE UNFOUNDED.
THAT GIRL'S MOM...

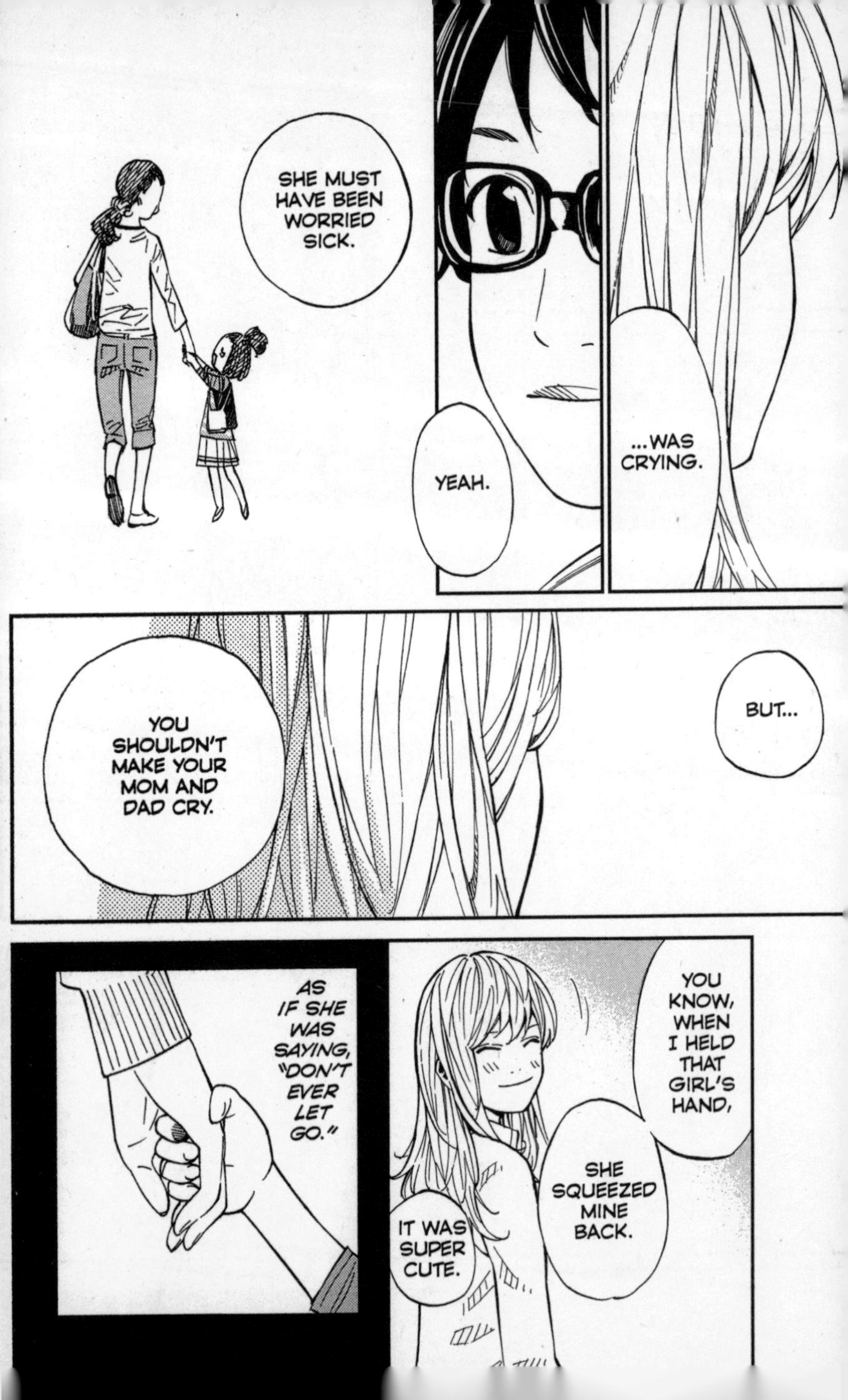
...WAS CRYING.
YEAH.
SHE MUST HAVE BEEN WORRIED SICK.
BUT...
YOU SHOULDN'T MAKE YOUR MOM AND DAD CRY.
YOU KNOW, WHEN I HELD THAT GIRL'S HAND,
SHE SQUEEZED MINE BACK.
IT WAS SUPER CUTE.
AS IF SHE WAS SAYING, "DON'T EVER LET GO."

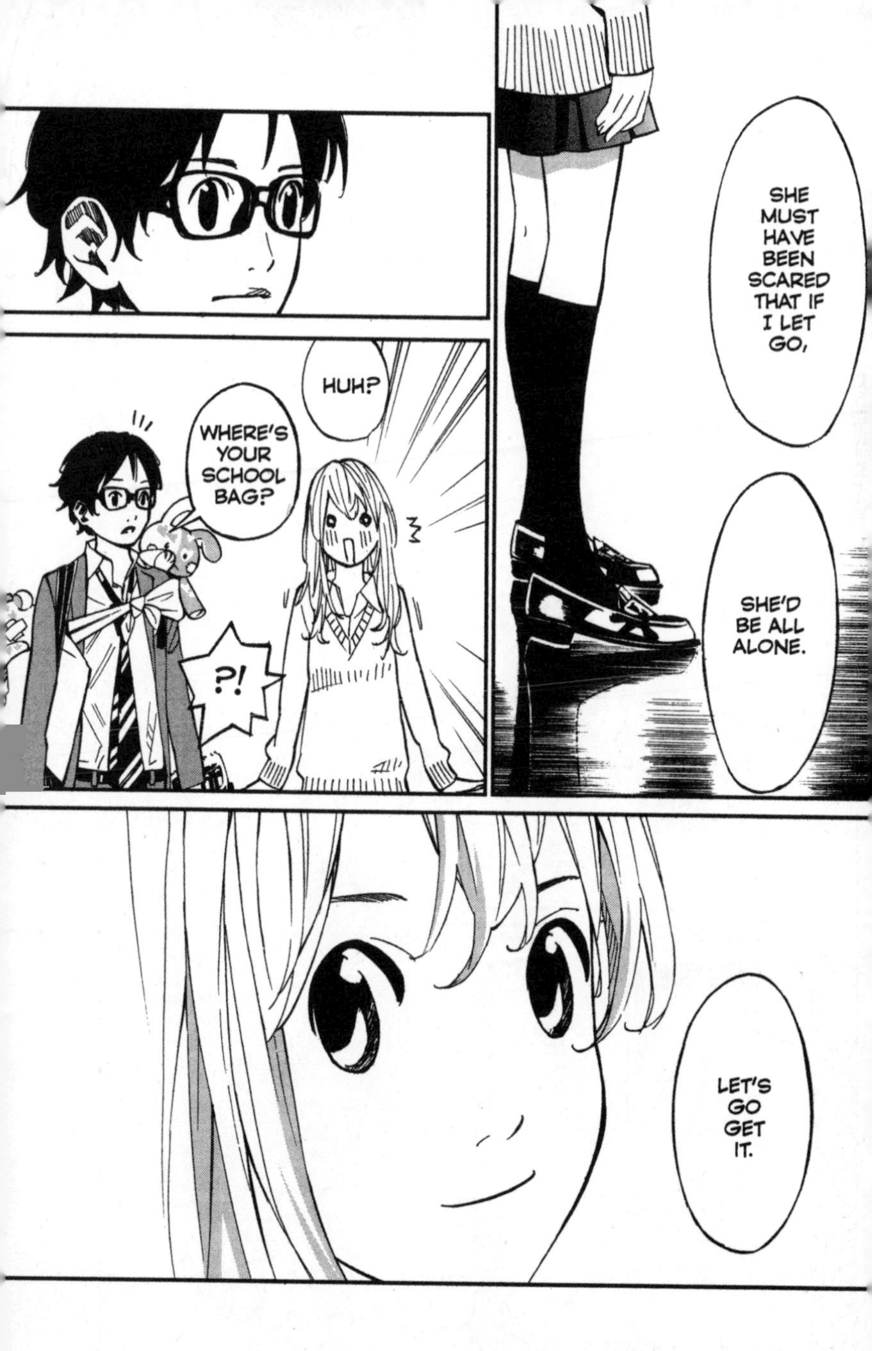
SHE MUST HAVE BEEN SCARED THAT IF I LET GO,
SHE'D BE ALL ALONE.
HUH?
WHERE'S YOUR SCHOOL BAG?
?!
LET'S GO GET IT.

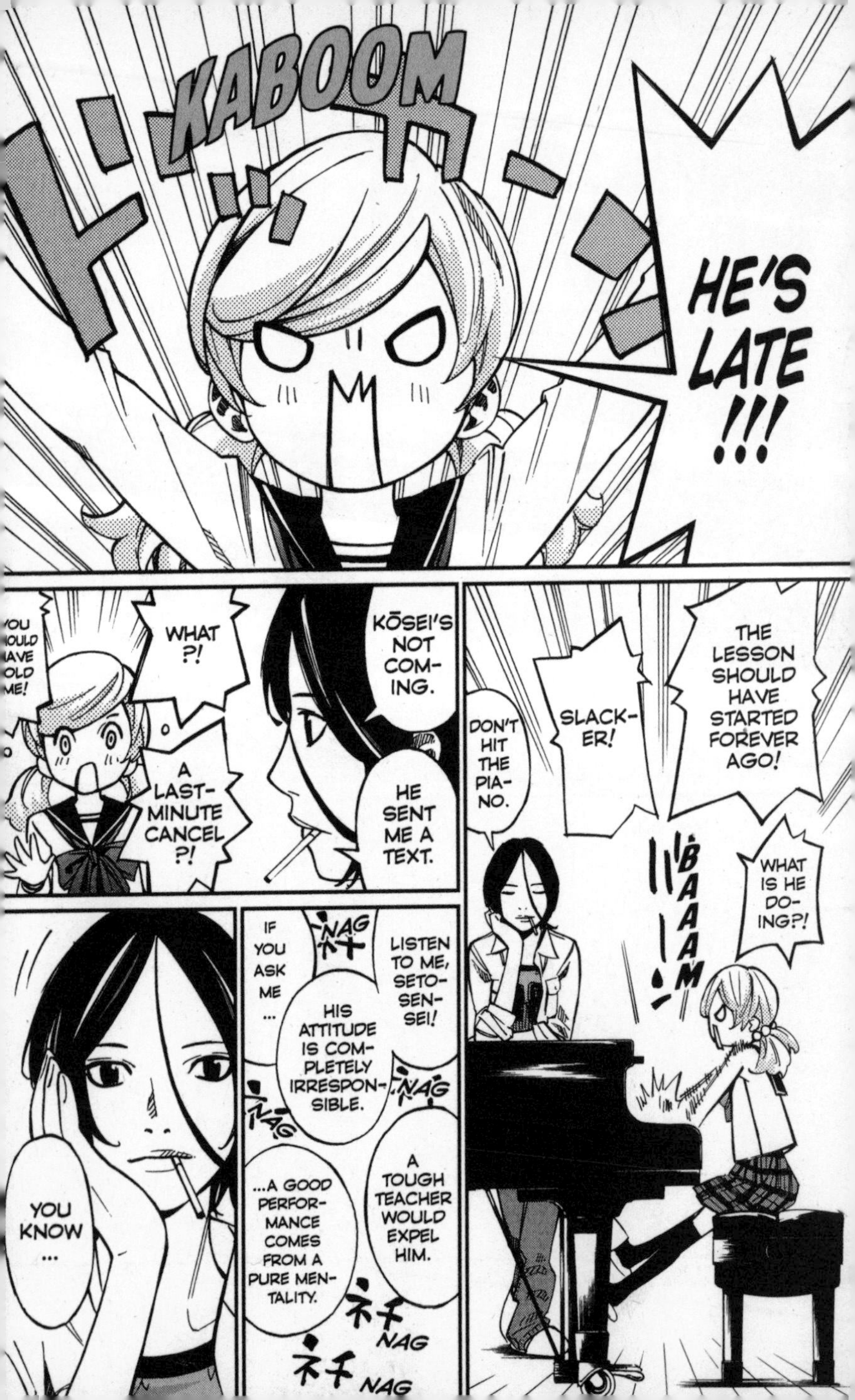
KABOOM
HE'S LATE!!!
THE LESSON SHOULD HAVE STARTED FOREVER AGO!
SLACKER!
DON'T HIT THE PIANO.
BAAAAM
WHAT IS HE DOING?!
KŌSEI'S NOT COMING.
HE SENT ME A TEXT.
WHAT?!
A LAST-MINUTE CANCEL?!
YOU HOULD HAVE OLD ME!
NAG
LISTEN TO ME, SETO-SENSEI!
IF YOU ASK ME...
HIS ATTITUDE IS COMPLETELY IRRESPONSIBLE.
NAG
NAG
A TOUGH TEACHER WOULD EXPEL HIM.
...A GOOD PERFORMANCE COMES FROM A PURE MENTALITY.
NAG
NAG
YOU KNOW...

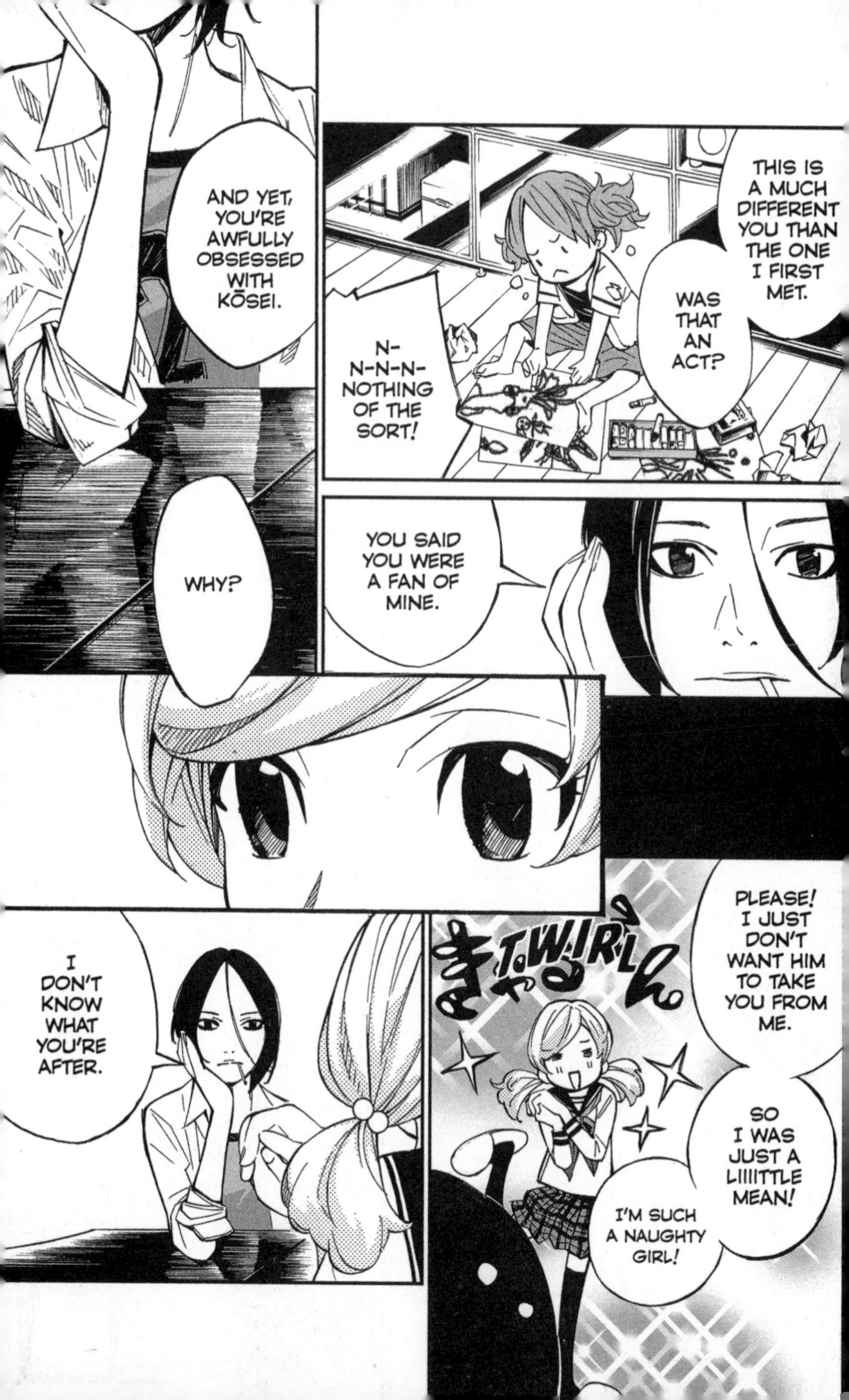
THIS IS A MUCH DIFFERENT YOU THAN THE ONE I FIRST MET.
WAS THAT AN ACT?
N-N-N-N-NOTHING OF THE SORT!
YOU SAID YOU WERE A FAN OF MINE.
AND YET, YOU'RE AWFULLY OBSESSED WITH KŌSEI.
WHY?
TWIRL
PLEASE! I JUST DON'T WANT HIM TO TAKE YOU FROM ME.
SO I WAS JUST A LIIIITTLE MEAN!
I'M SUCH A NAUGHTY GIRL!
I DON'T KNOW WHAT YOU'RE AFTER.

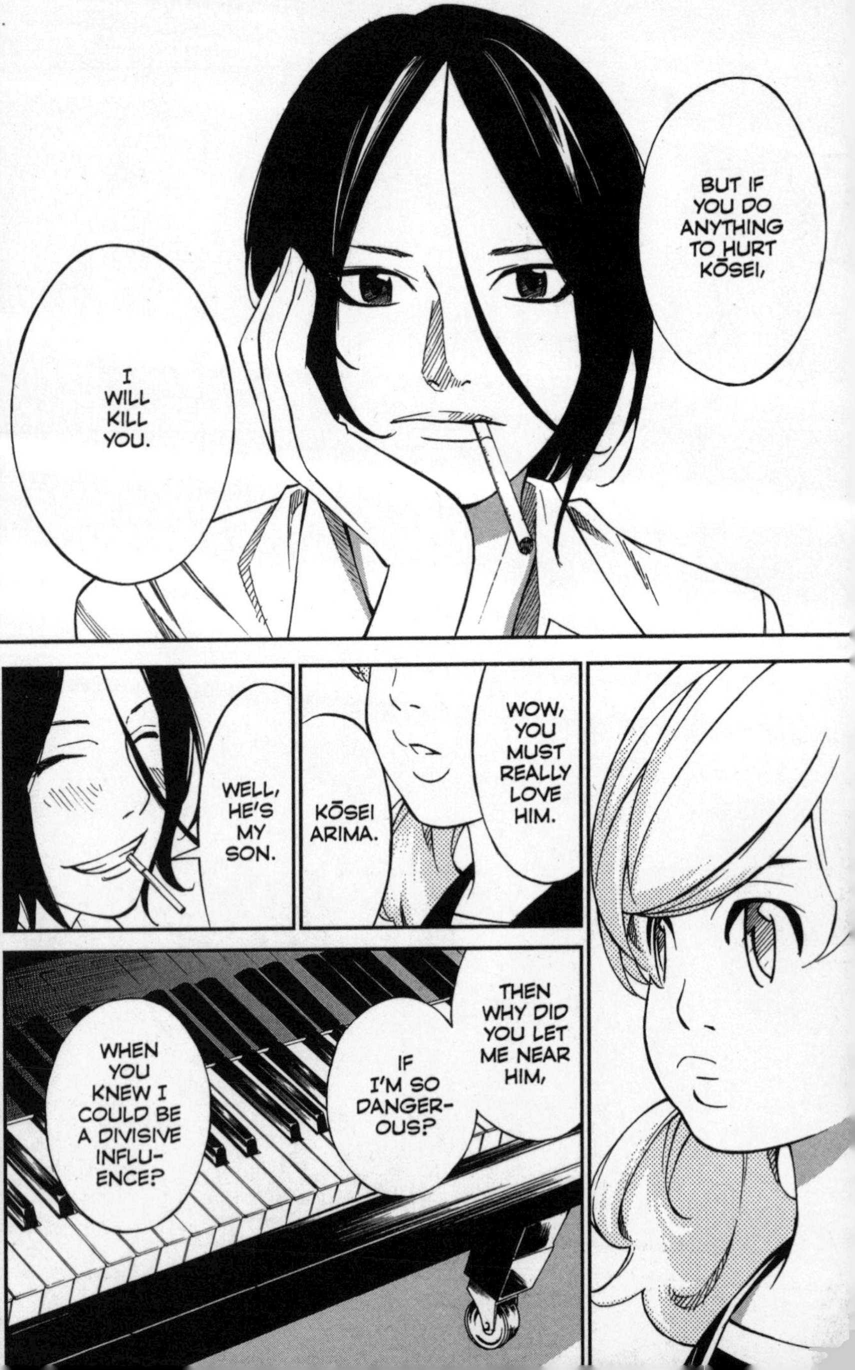
BUT IF YOU DO ANYTHING TO HURT KŌSEI,
I WILL KILL YOU.
WOW, YOU MUST REALLY LOVE HIM.
KŌSEI ARIMA.
WELL, HE'S MY SON.
THEN WHY DID YOU LET ME NEAR HIM,
IF I'M SO DANGER-OUS?
WHEN YOU KNEW I COULD BE A DIVISIVE INFLU-ENCE?

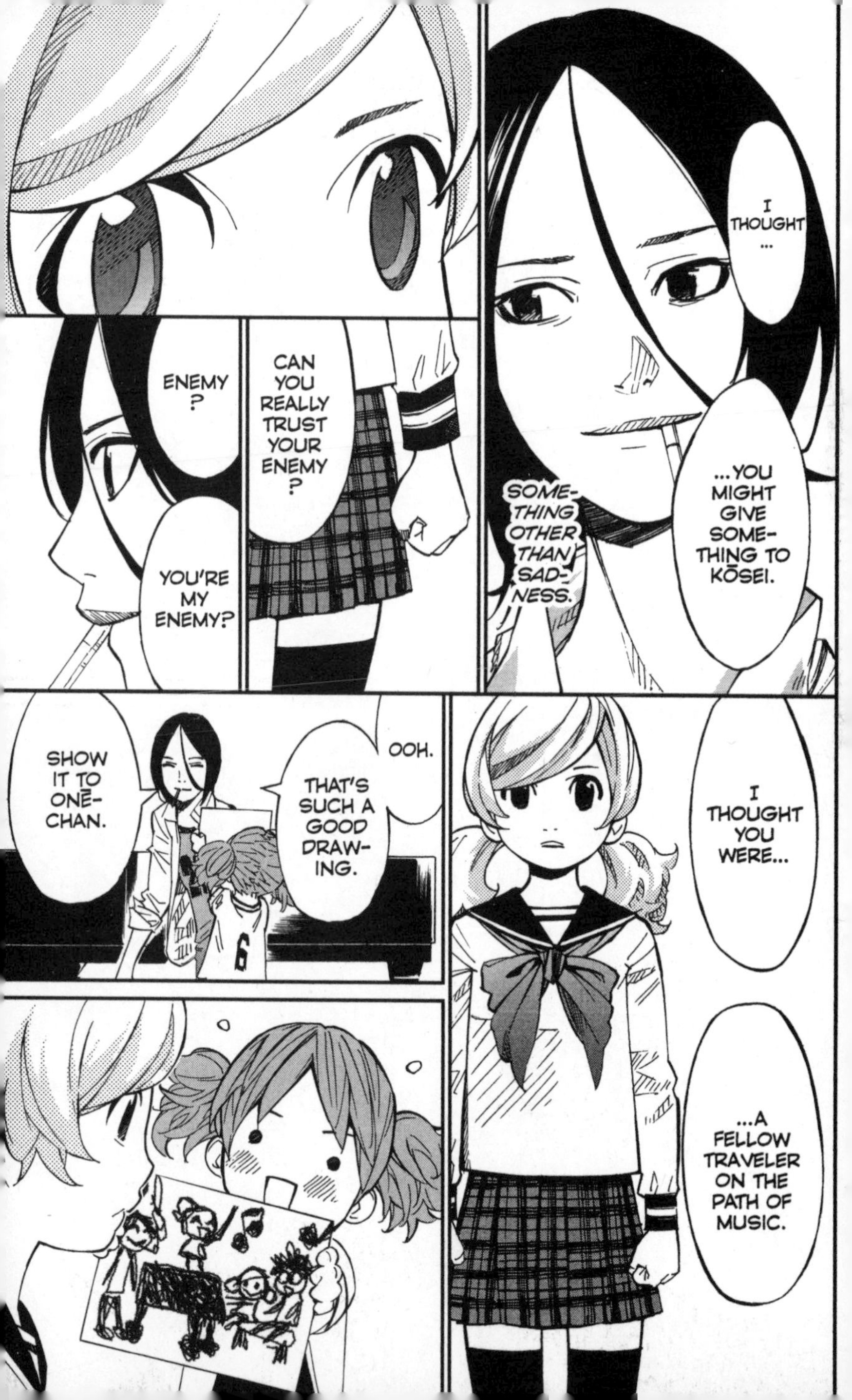
I THOUGHT ...
...YOU MIGHT GIVE SOME-THING TO KŌSEI.
SOME-THING OTHER THAN SAD-NESS.
CAN YOU REALLY TRUST YOUR ENEMY?
ENEMY?
YOU'RE MY ENEMY?
I THOUGHT YOU WERE...
...A FELLOW TRAVELER ON THE PATH OF MUSIC.
OOH.
THAT'S SUCH A GOOD DRAW-ING.
SHOW IT TO ONĒ-CHAN.

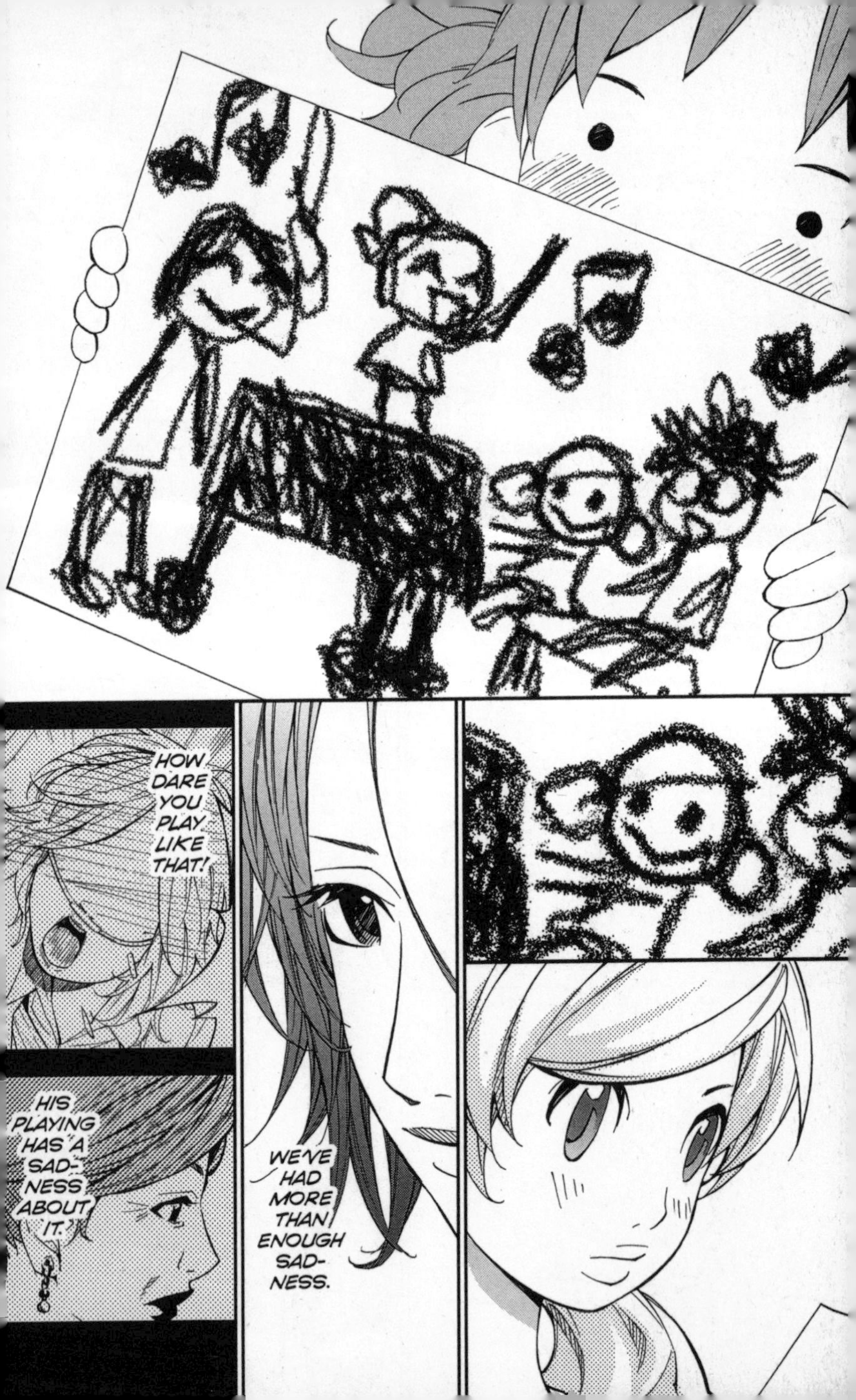
WE'VE HAD MORE THAN ENOUGH SAD-NESS.
HOW DARE YOU PLAY LIKE THAT!
HIS PLAYING HAS A SAD-NESS ABOUT IT.

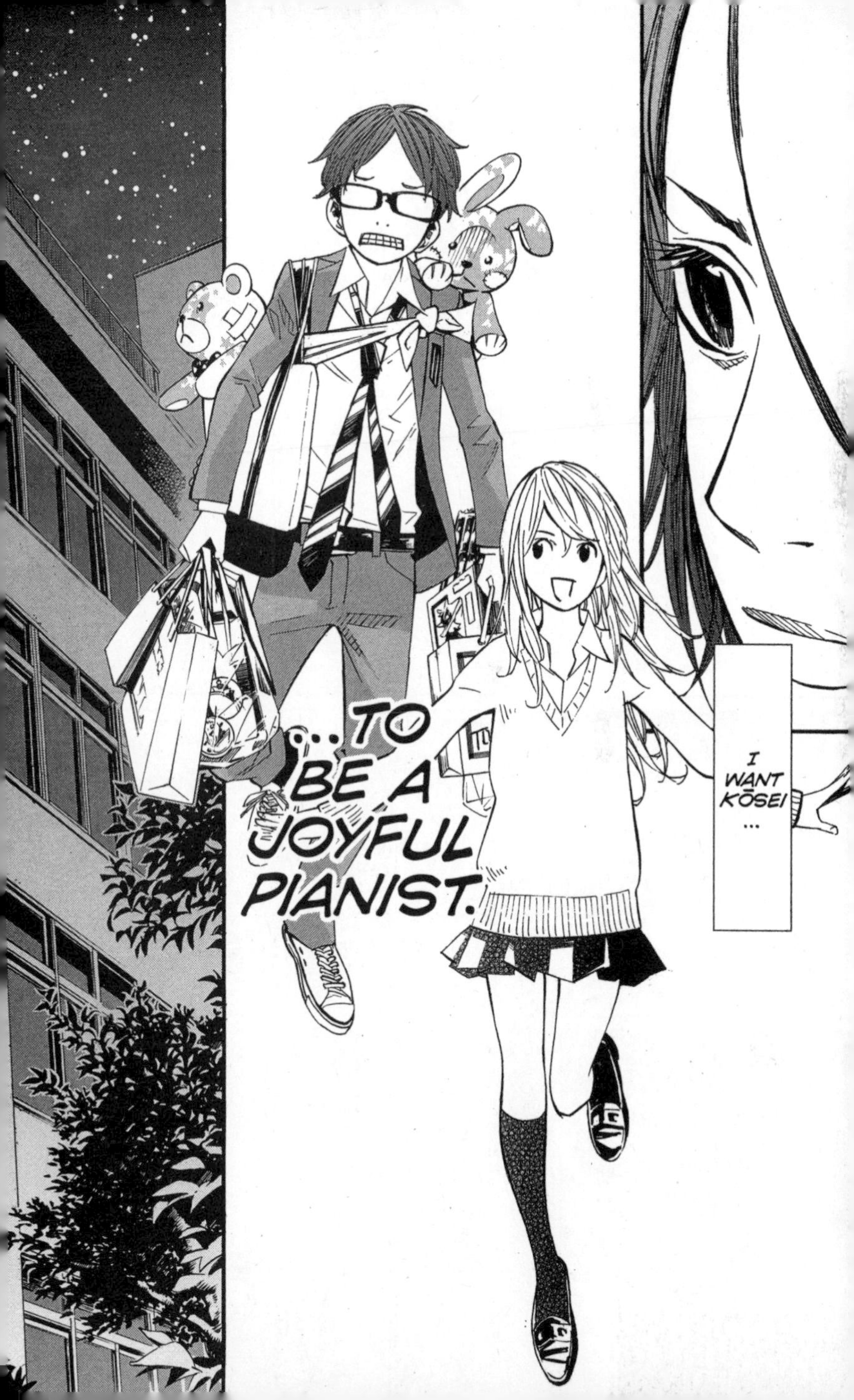
I WANT KŌSEI ...
... TO BE A JOYFUL PIANIST.

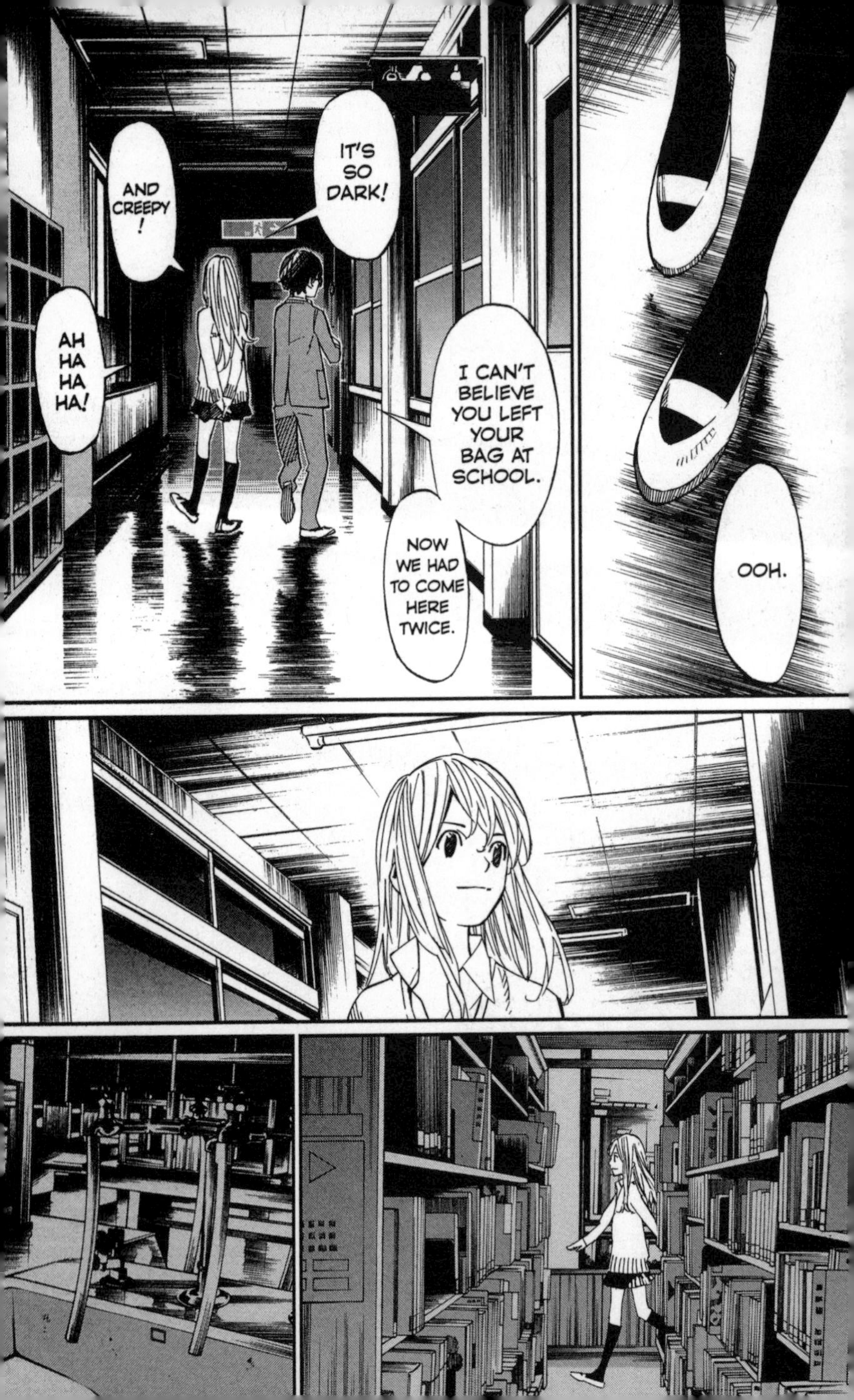
OOH.
IT'S SO DARK!
AND CREEPY!
I CAN'T BELIEVE YOU LEFT YOUR BAG AT SCHOOL.
NOW WE HAD TO COME HERE TWICE.
AH HA HA HA!

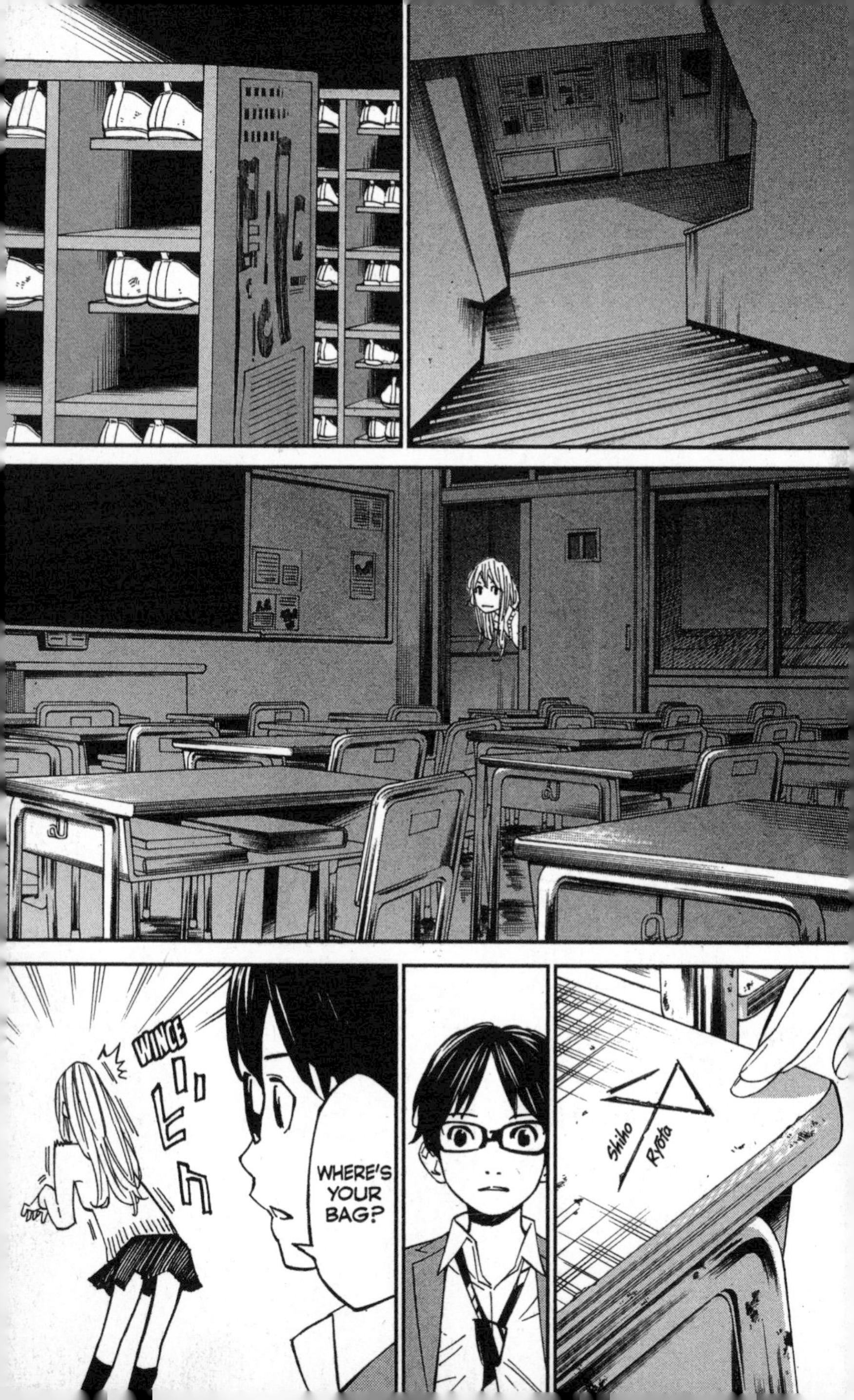
Shiho
Ryota
WHERE'S YOUR BAG?
WINCE
ビクッ

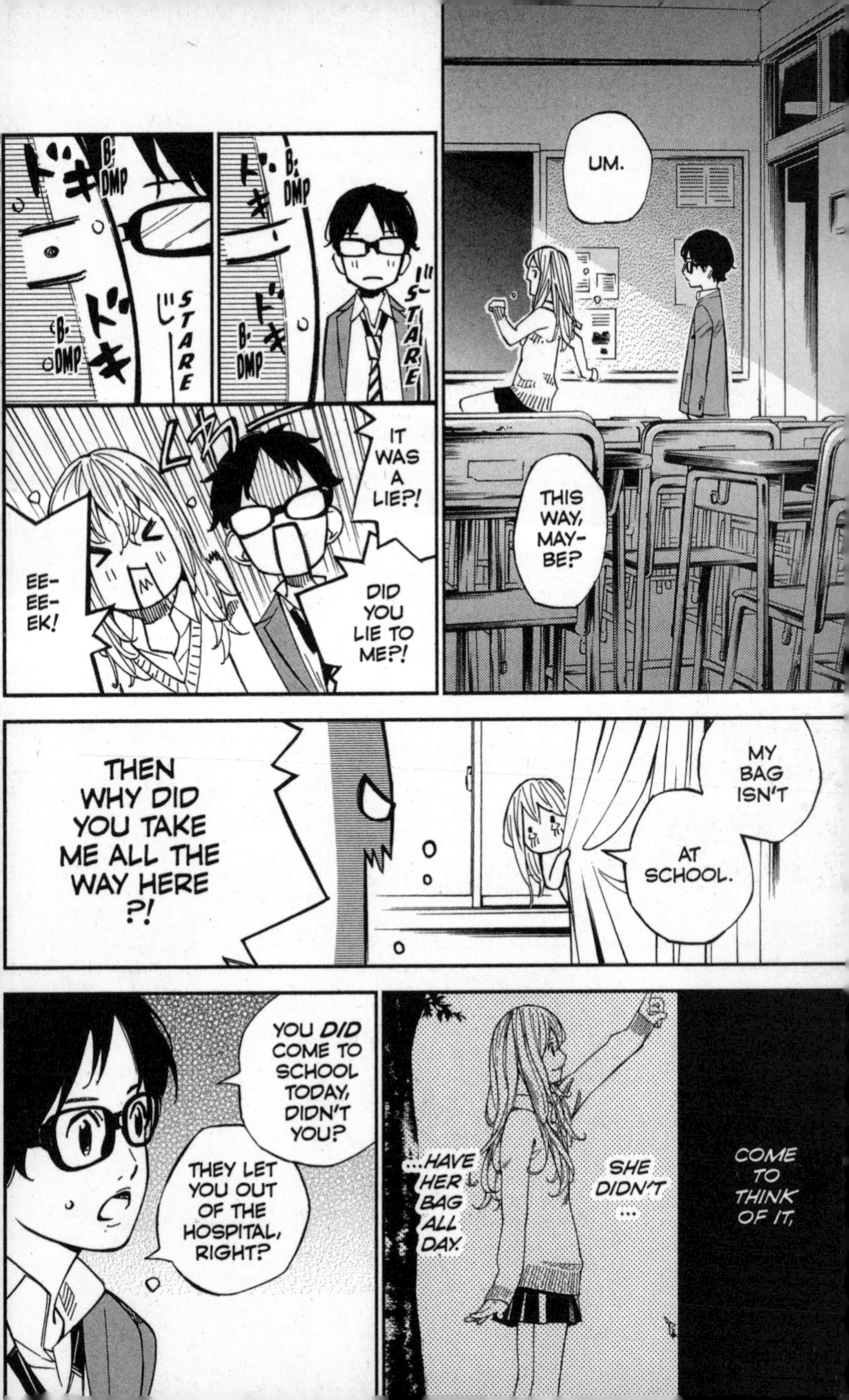
UM.
THIS WAY, MAYBE?
B-DMP
B-DMP
STARE
B-DMP
B-DMP
STARE
IT WAS A LIE?!
DID YOU LIE TO ME?!
EE-EE-EK!
MY BAG ISN'T
AT SCHOOL.
THEN WHY DID YOU TAKE ME ALL THE WAY HERE?!
COME TO THINK OF IT,
SHE DIDN'T ...
...HAVE HER BAG ALL DAY.
YOU DID COME TO SCHOOL TODAY, DIDN'T YOU?
THEY LET YOU OUT OF THE HOSPITAL, RIGHT?

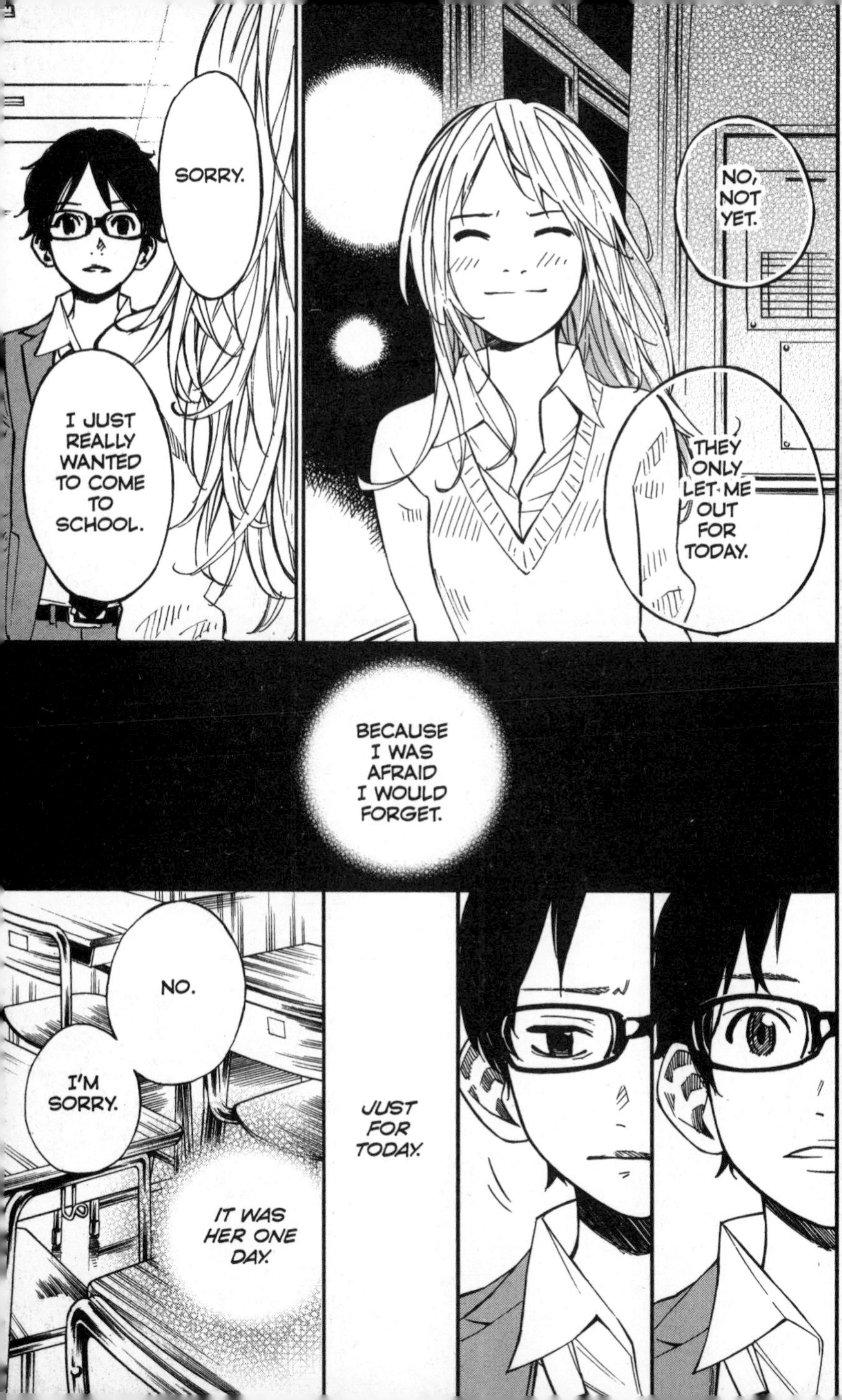
NO, NOT YET.
THEY ONLY LET ME OUT FOR TODAY.
SORRY.
I JUST REALLY WANTED TO COME TO SCHOOL.
BECAUSE I WAS AFRAID I WOULD FORGET.
JUST FOR TODAY.
NO.
I'M SORRY.
IT WAS HER ONE DAY.

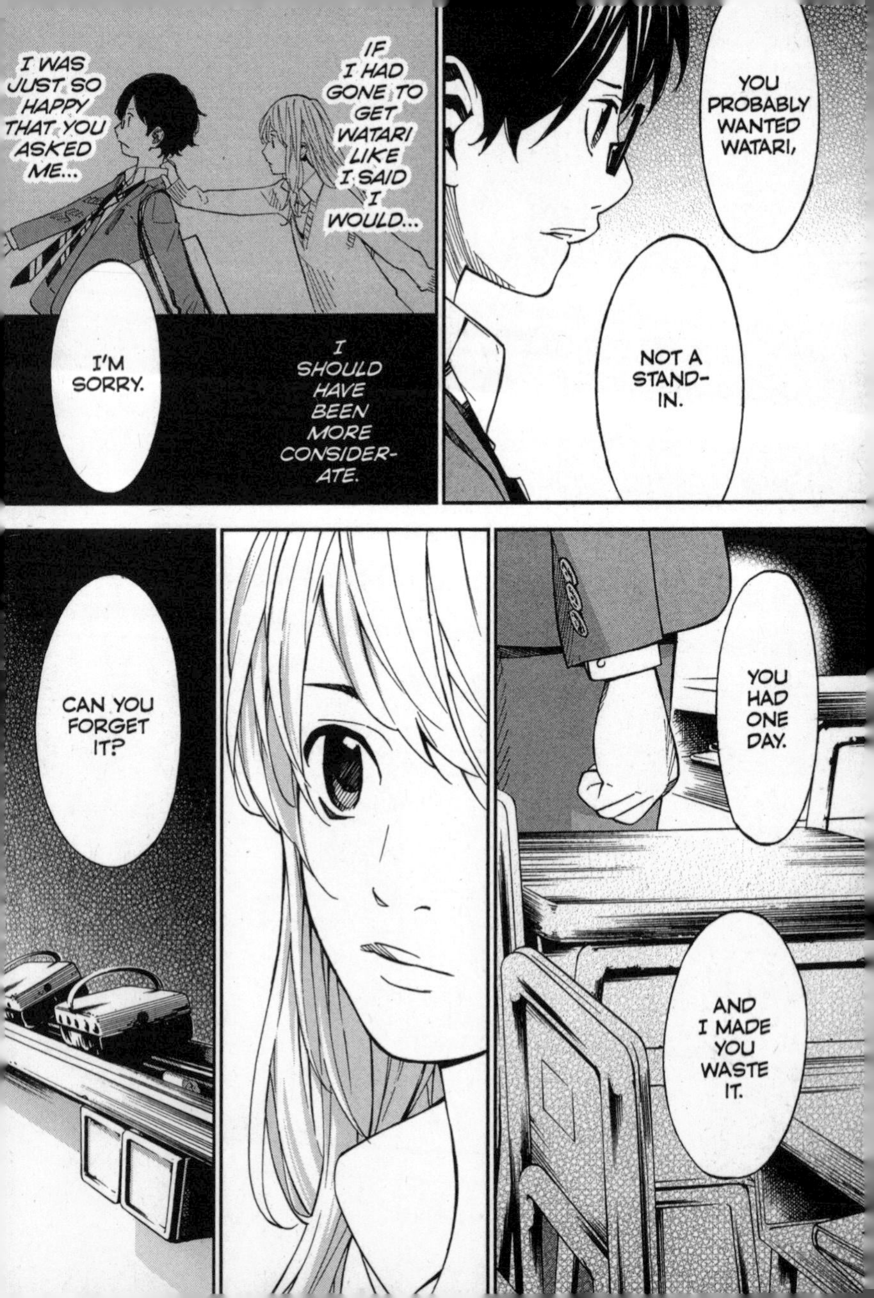
YOU PROBABLY WANTED WATARI,
NOT A STAND-IN.
IF I HAD GONE TO GET WATARI LIKE I SAID I WOULD...
I WAS JUST SO HAPPY THAT YOU ASKED ME...
I SHOULD HAVE BEEN MORE CONSIDER-ATE.
I'M SORRY.
YOU HAD ONE DAY.
AND I MADE YOU WASTE IT.
CAN YOU FORGET IT?

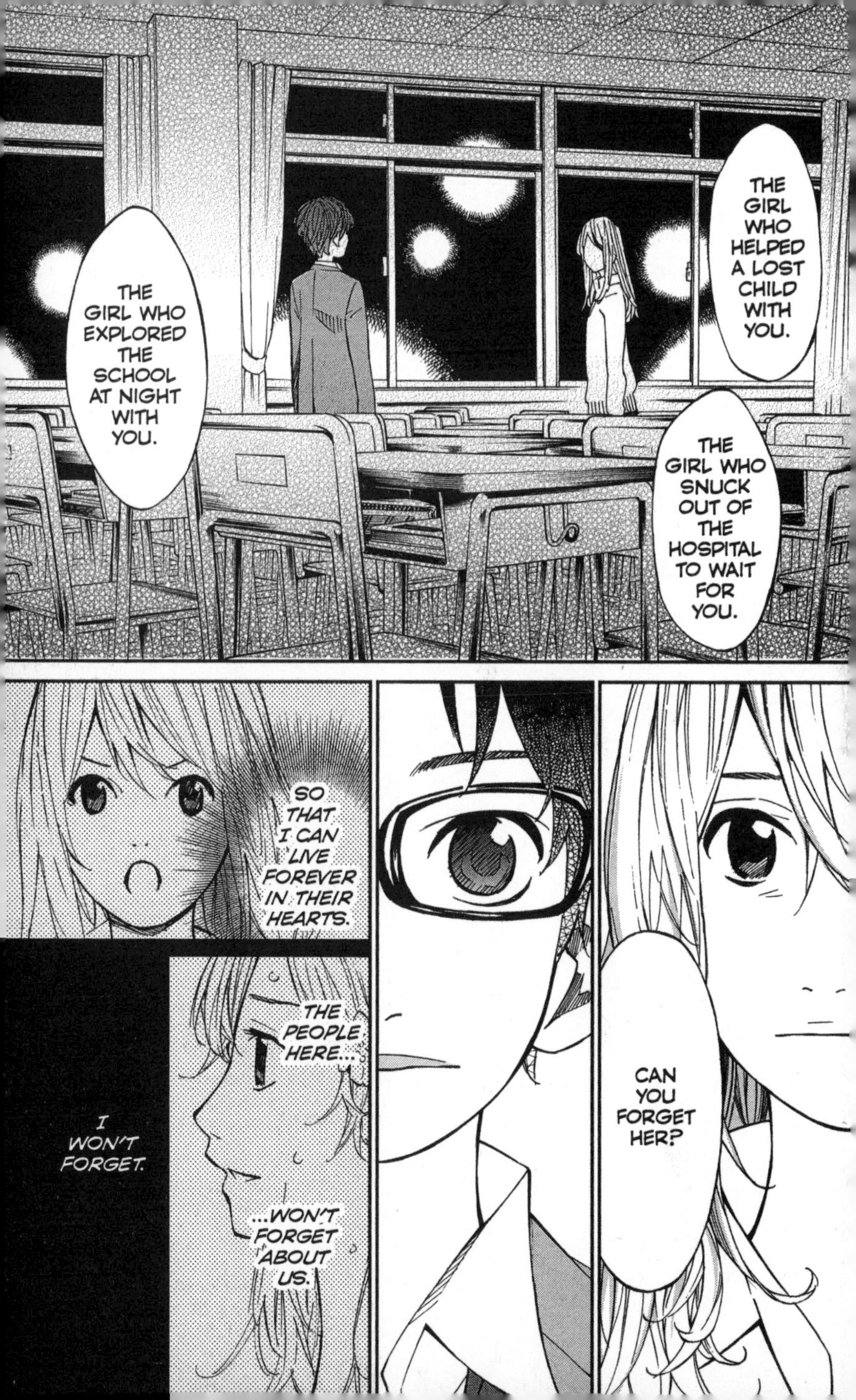
THE GIRL WHO HELPED A LOST CHILD WITH YOU.
THE GIRL WHO EXPLORED THE SCHOOL AT NIGHT WITH YOU.
THE GIRL WHO SNUCK OUT OF THE HOSPITAL TO WAIT FOR YOU.
CAN YOU FORGET HER?
SO THAT I CAN LIVE FOREVER IN THEIR HEARTS.
THE PEOPLE HERE...
...WON'T FORGET ABOUT US.
I WON'T FORGET.

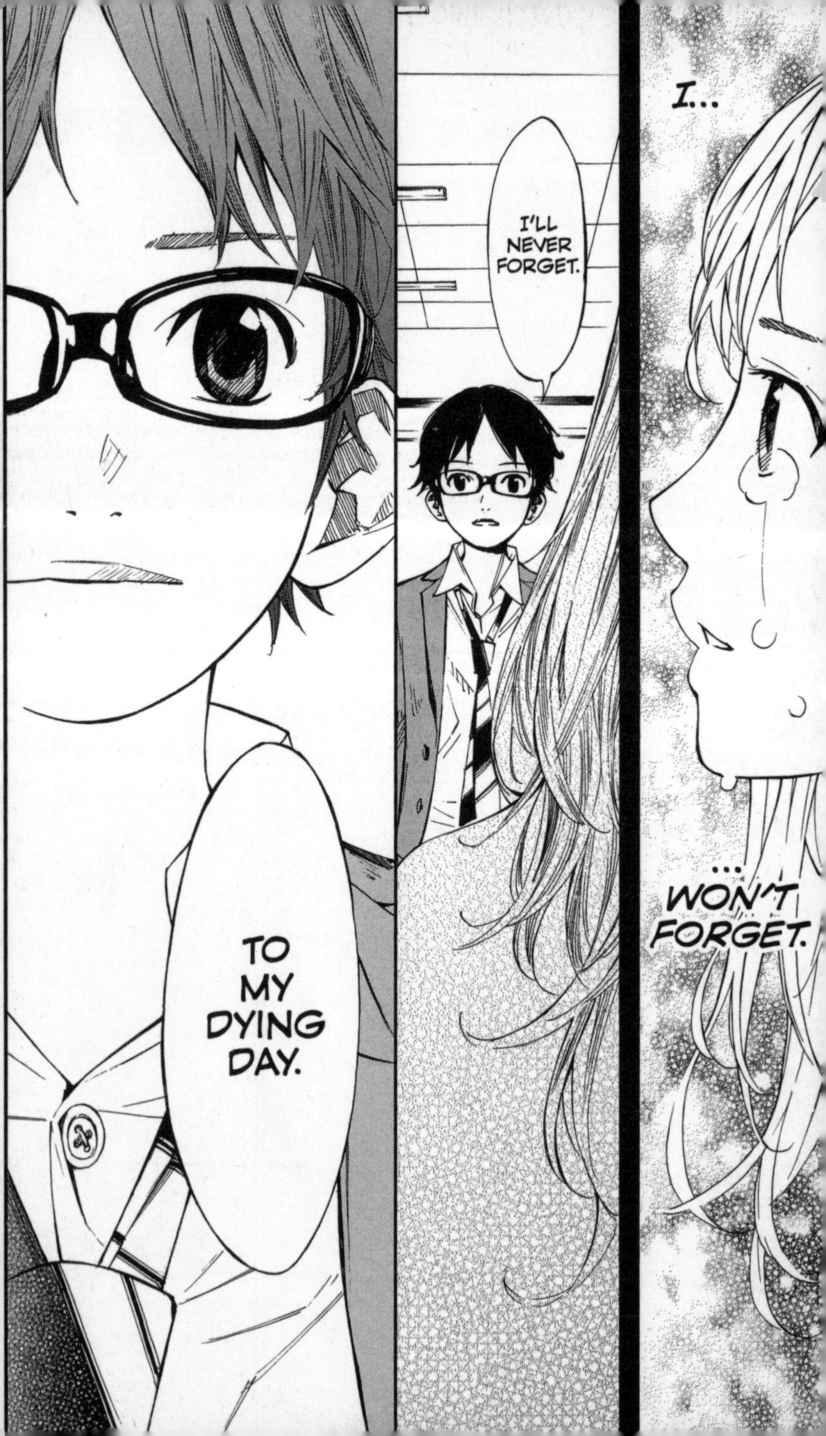
I...
...WON'T FORGET.
I'LL NEVER FORGET.
TO MY DYING DAY.

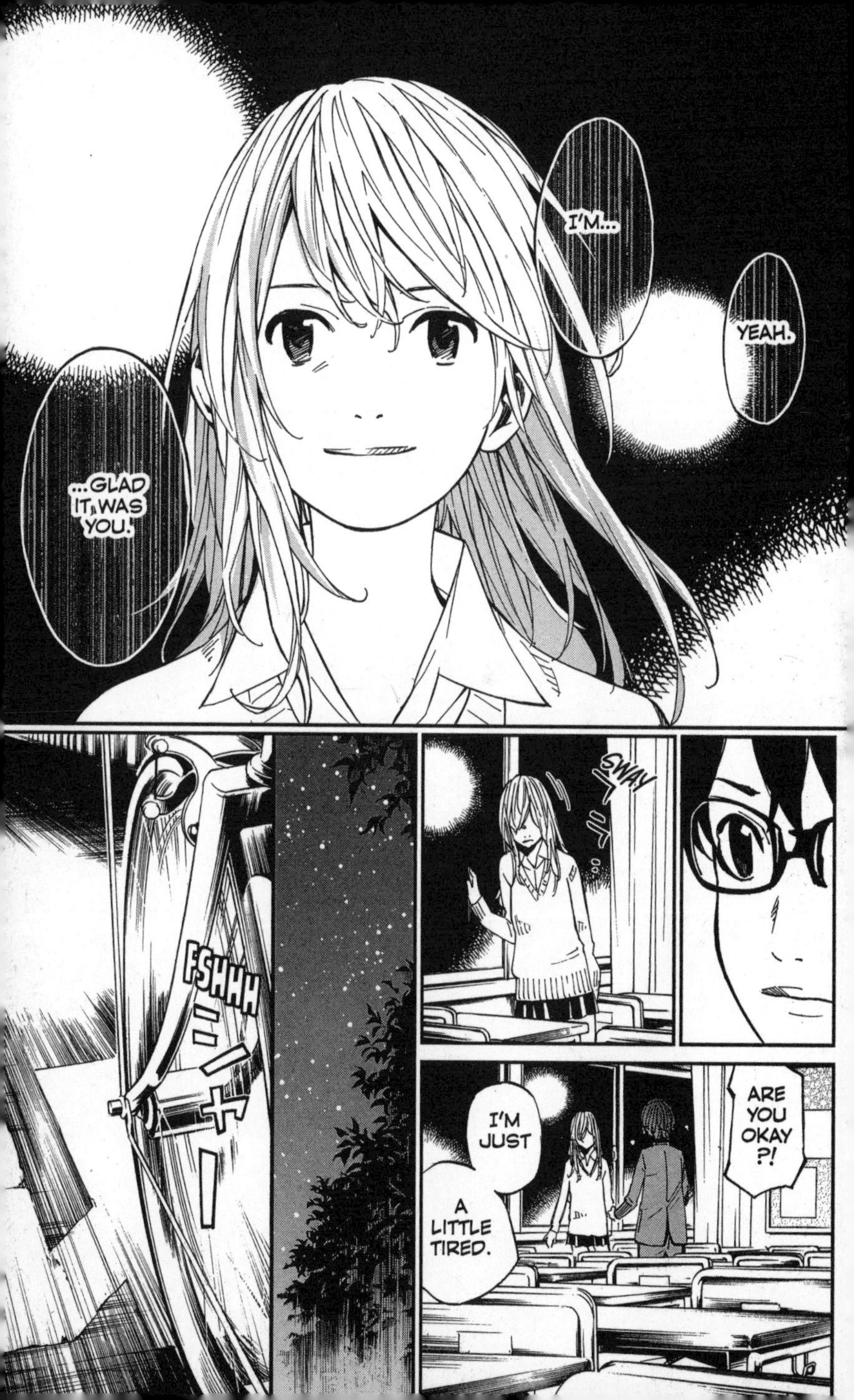
I'M...
YEAH.
...GLAD IT WAS YOU.
SWAY
ARE YOU OKAY?!
I'M JUST A LITTLE TIRED.
FSHHH

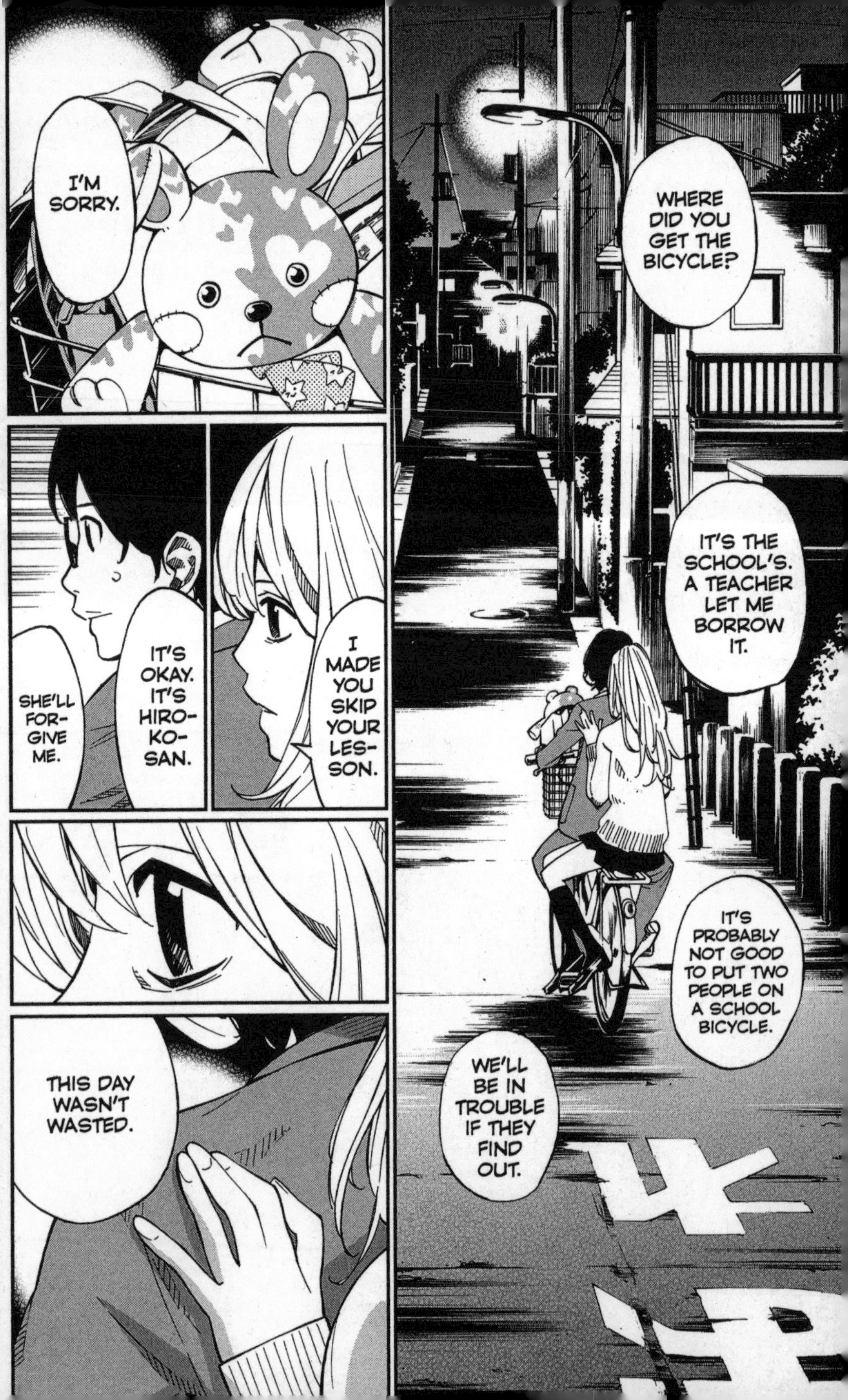
WHERE DID YOU GET THE BICYCLE?
IT'S THE SCHOOL'S. A TEACHER LET ME BORROW IT.
IT'S PROBABLY NOT GOOD TO PUT TWO PEOPLE ON A SCHOOL BICYCLE.
WE'LL BE IN TROUBLE IF THEY FIND OUT.
I'M SORRY.
I MADE YOU SKIP YOUR LES-SON.
IT'S OKAY. IT'S HIRO-KO-SAN.
SHE'LL FOR-GIVE ME.
THIS DAY WASN'T WASTED.

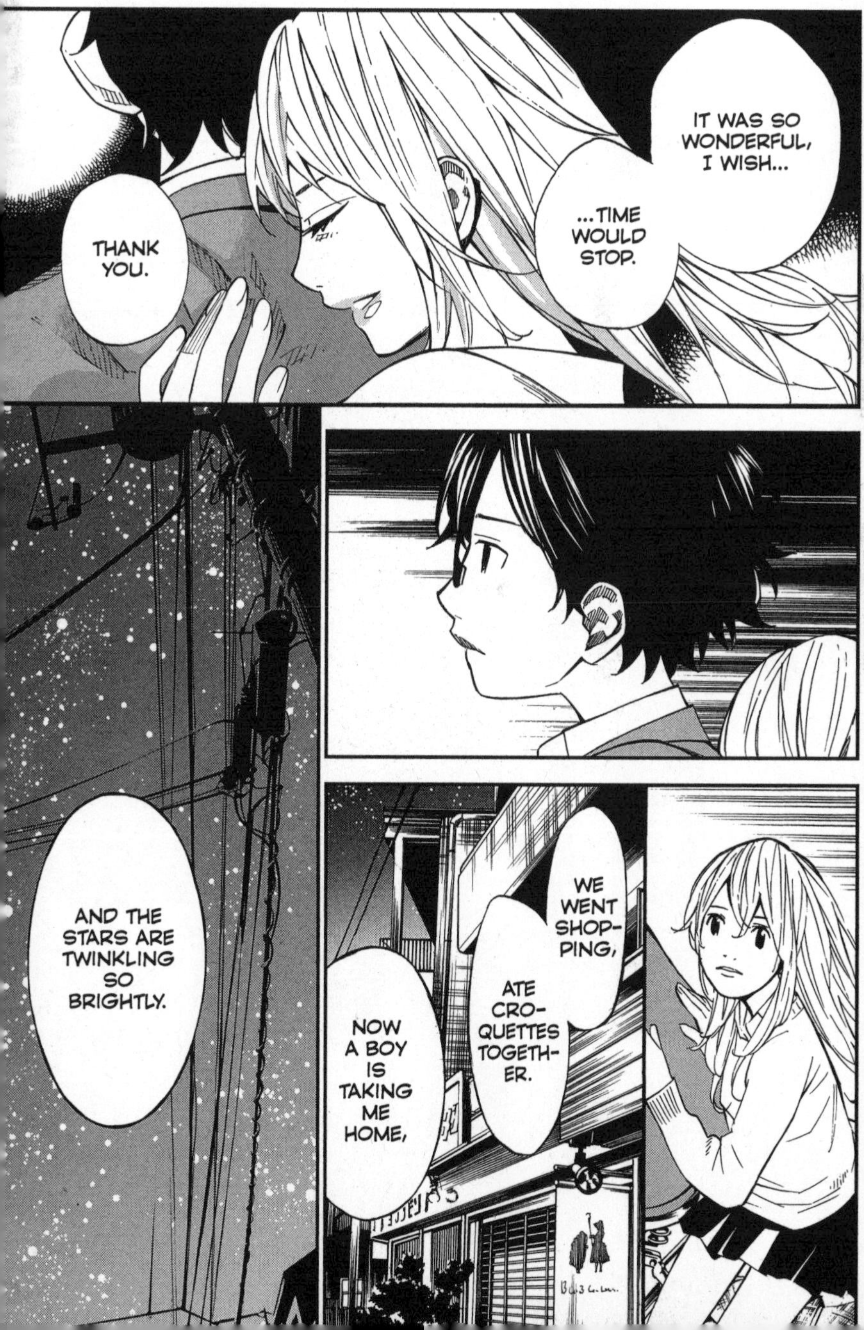
IT WAS SO WONDERFUL, I WISH...
...TIME WOULD STOP.
THANK YOU.
WE WENT SHOP-PING,
ATE CRO-QUETTES TOGETH-ER.
NOW A BOY IS TAKING ME HOME,
AND THE STARS ARE TWINKLING SO BRIGHTLY.

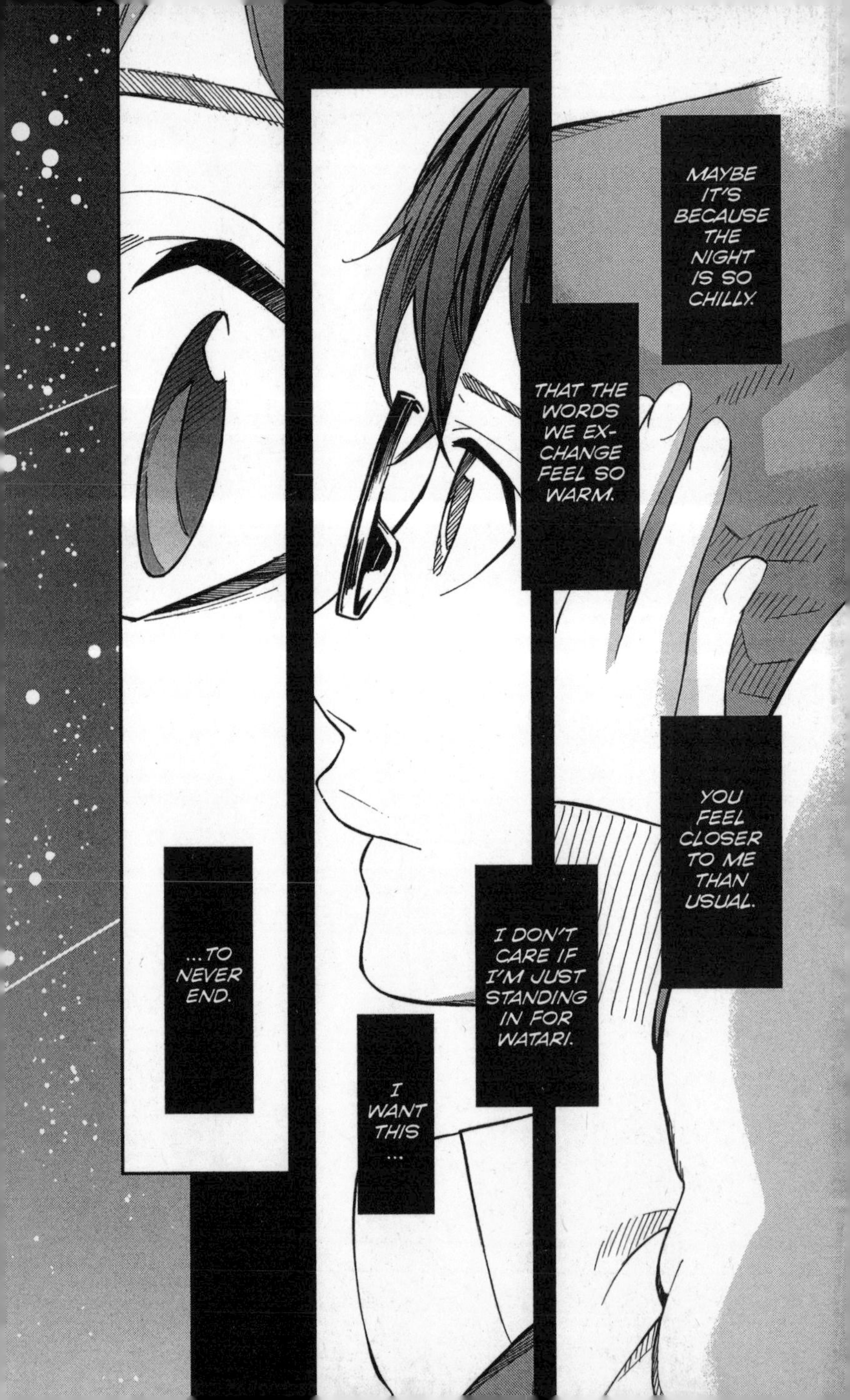
MAYBE IT'S BECAUSE THE NIGHT IS SO CHILLY.
THAT THE WORDS WE EX-CHANGE FEEL SO WARM.
YOU FEEL CLOSER TO ME THAN USUAL.
I DON'T CARE IF I'M JUST STANDING IN FOR WATARI.
I WANT THIS ...
...TO NEVER END.

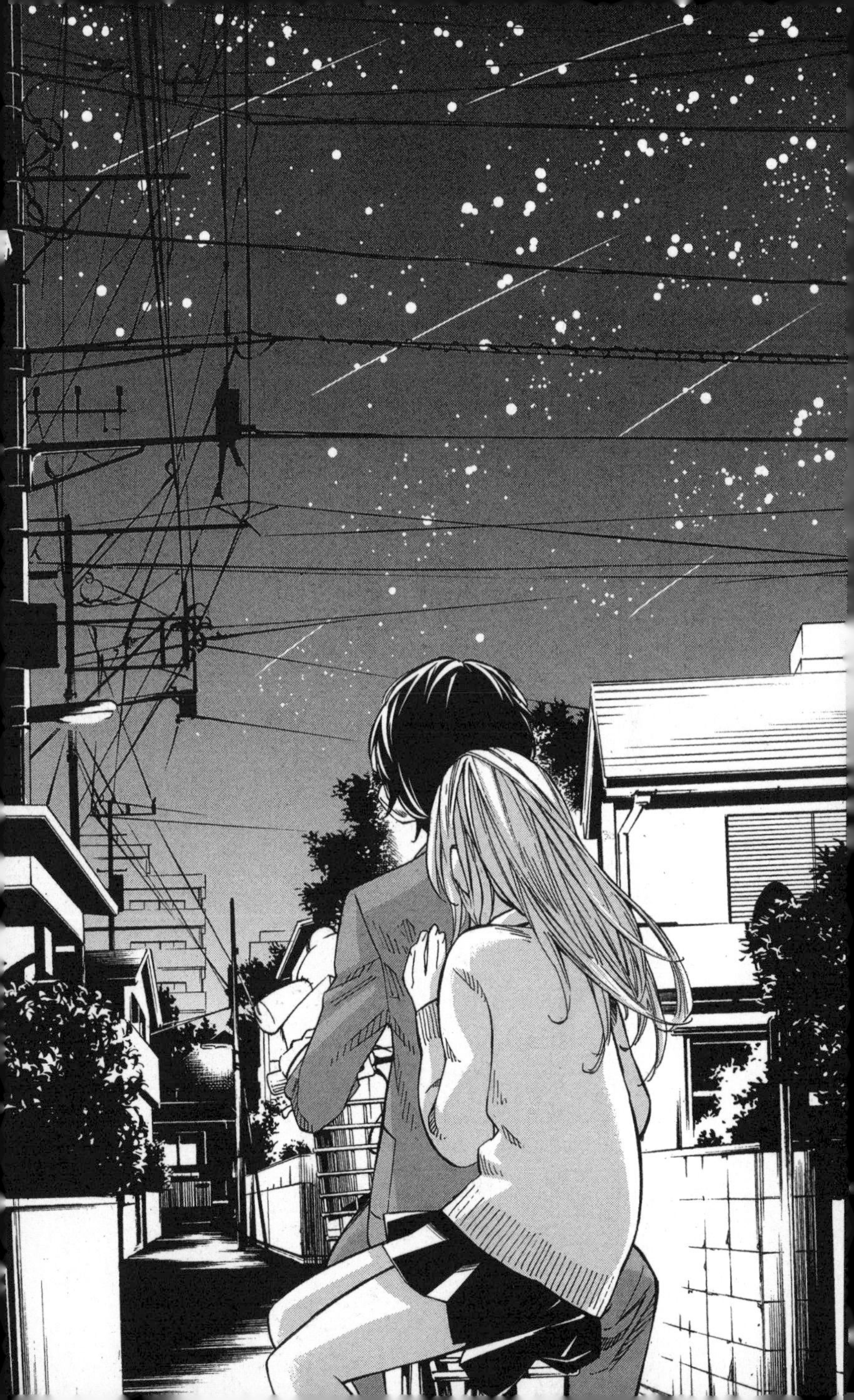

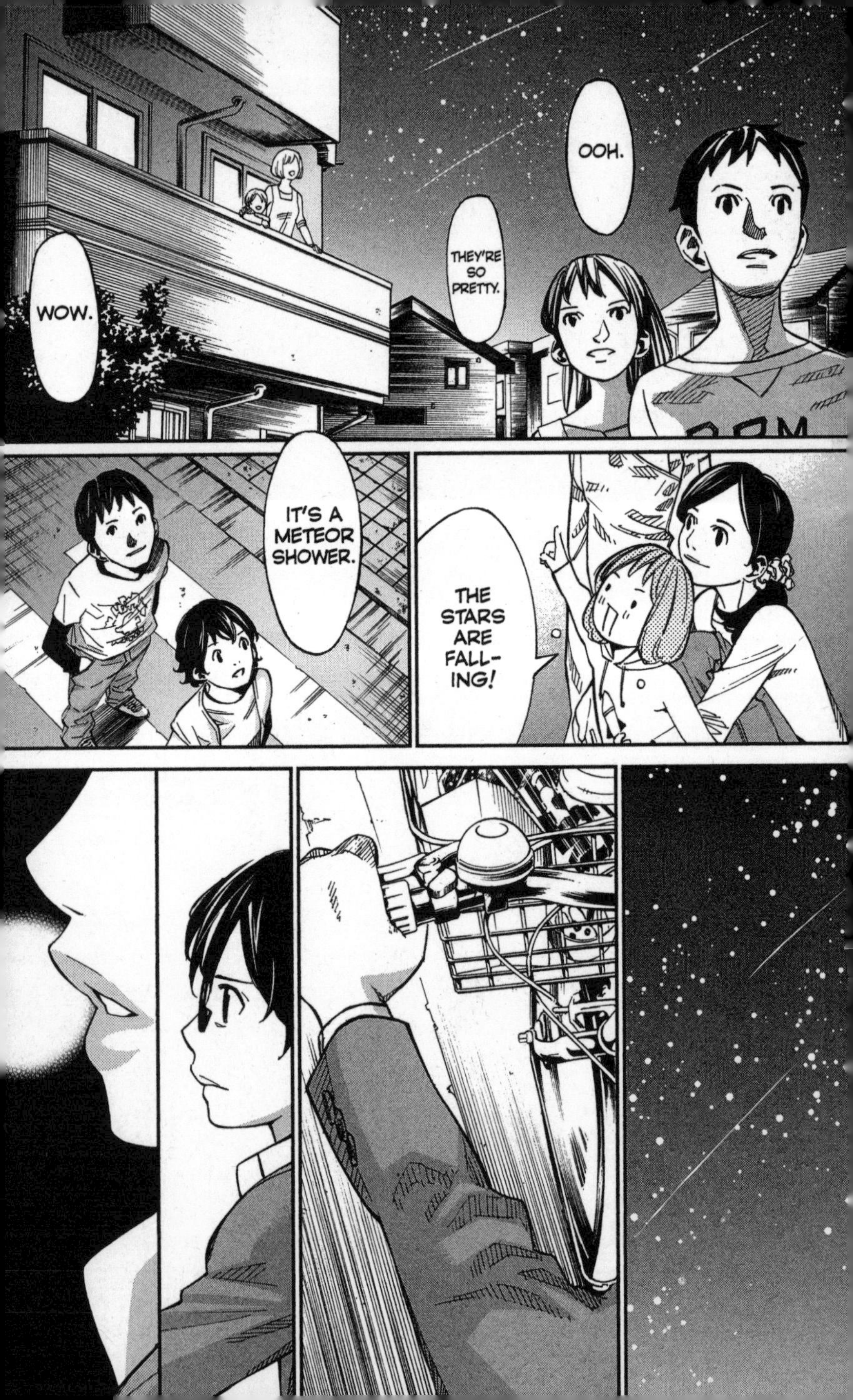
OOH.
THEY'RE SO PRETTY.
WOW.
THE STARS ARE FALL-ING!
IT'S A METEOR SHOWER.

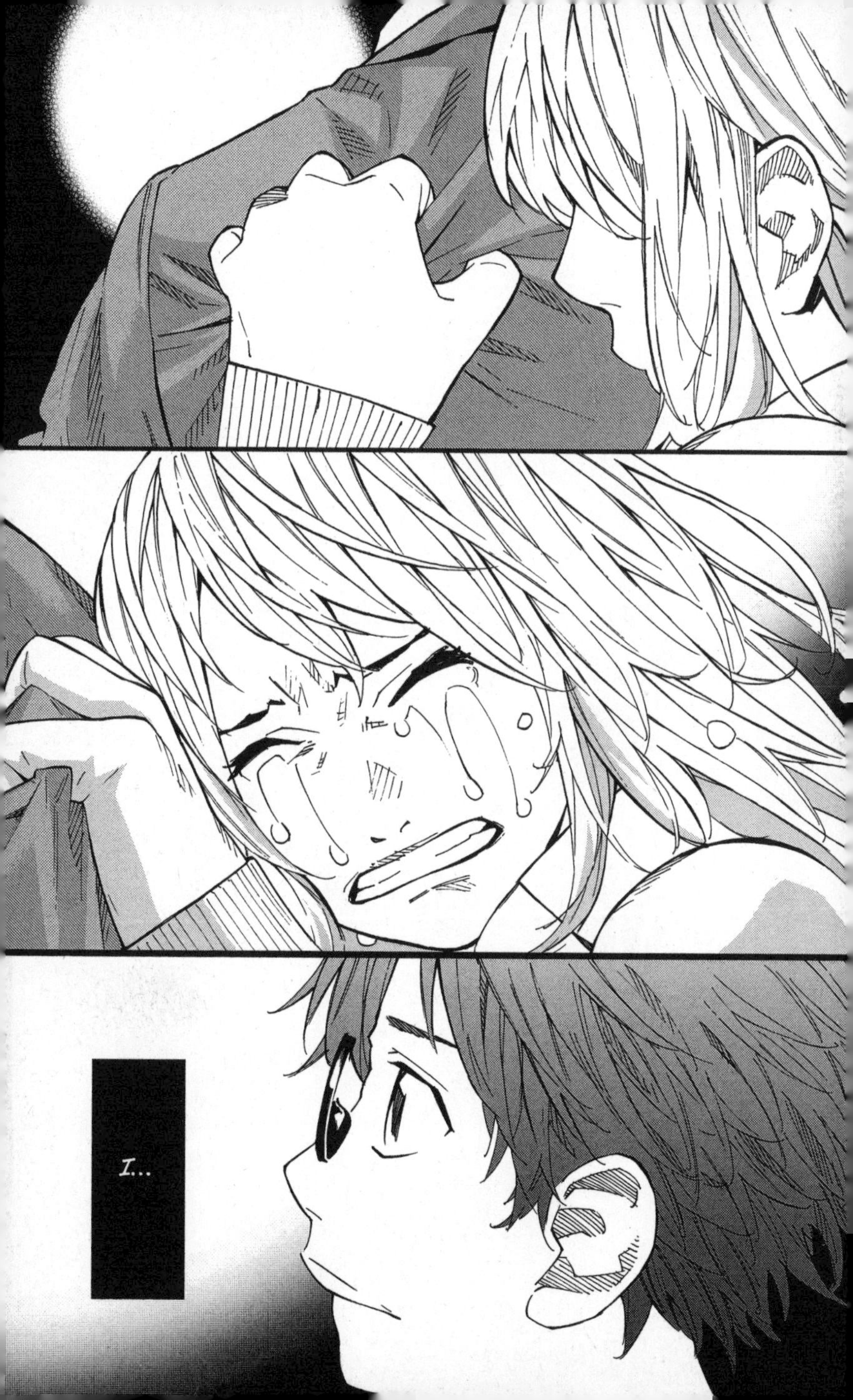
I...

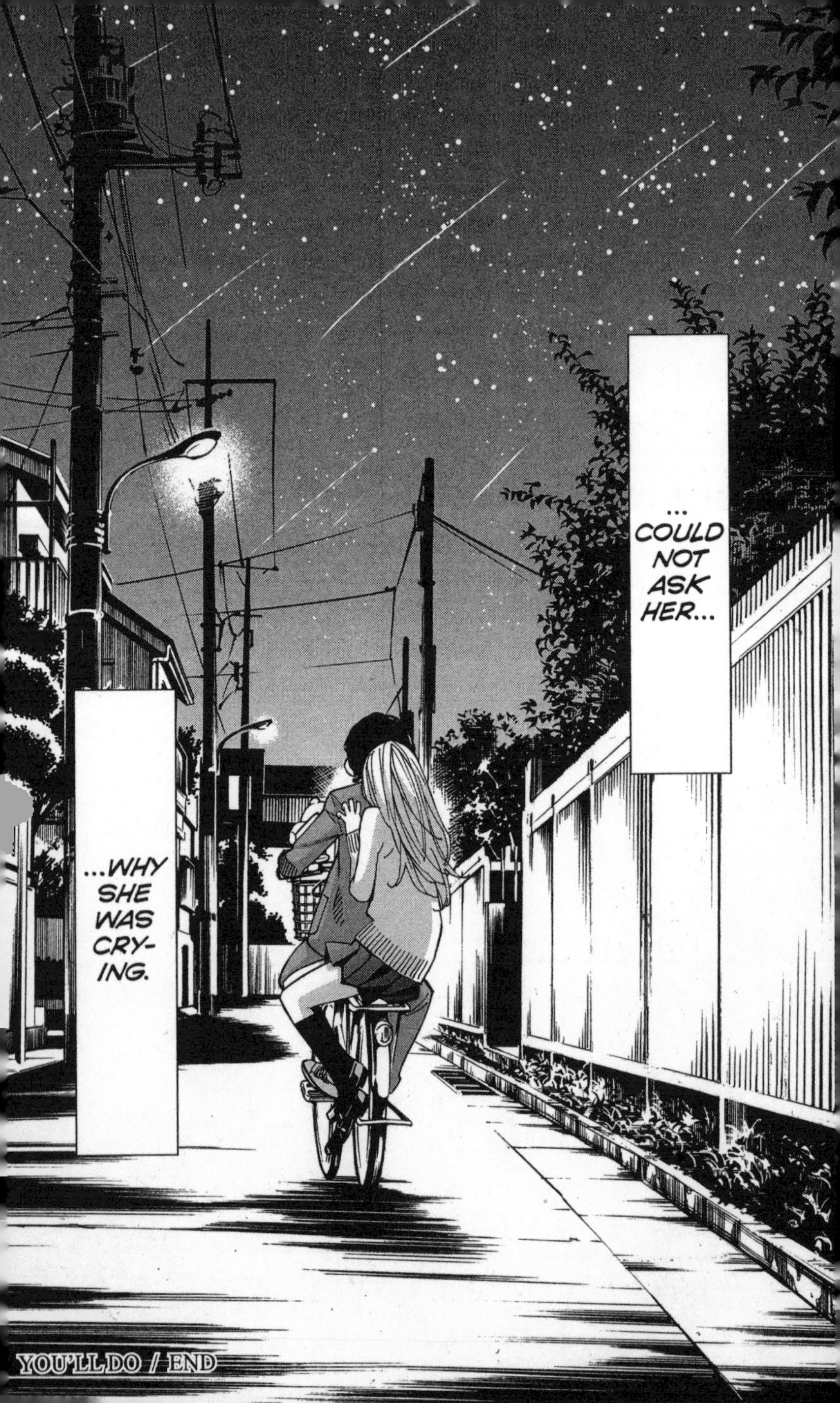
...COULD NOT ASK HER...
...WHY SHE WAS CRY-ING.
YOU'LL DO / END

Your Lie in April

I met the girl under full-bloomed cherry blossoms, and my fate has begun to change.

Your Lie in April

I met the girl under full-bloomed cherry blossoms, and my fate has begun to change.

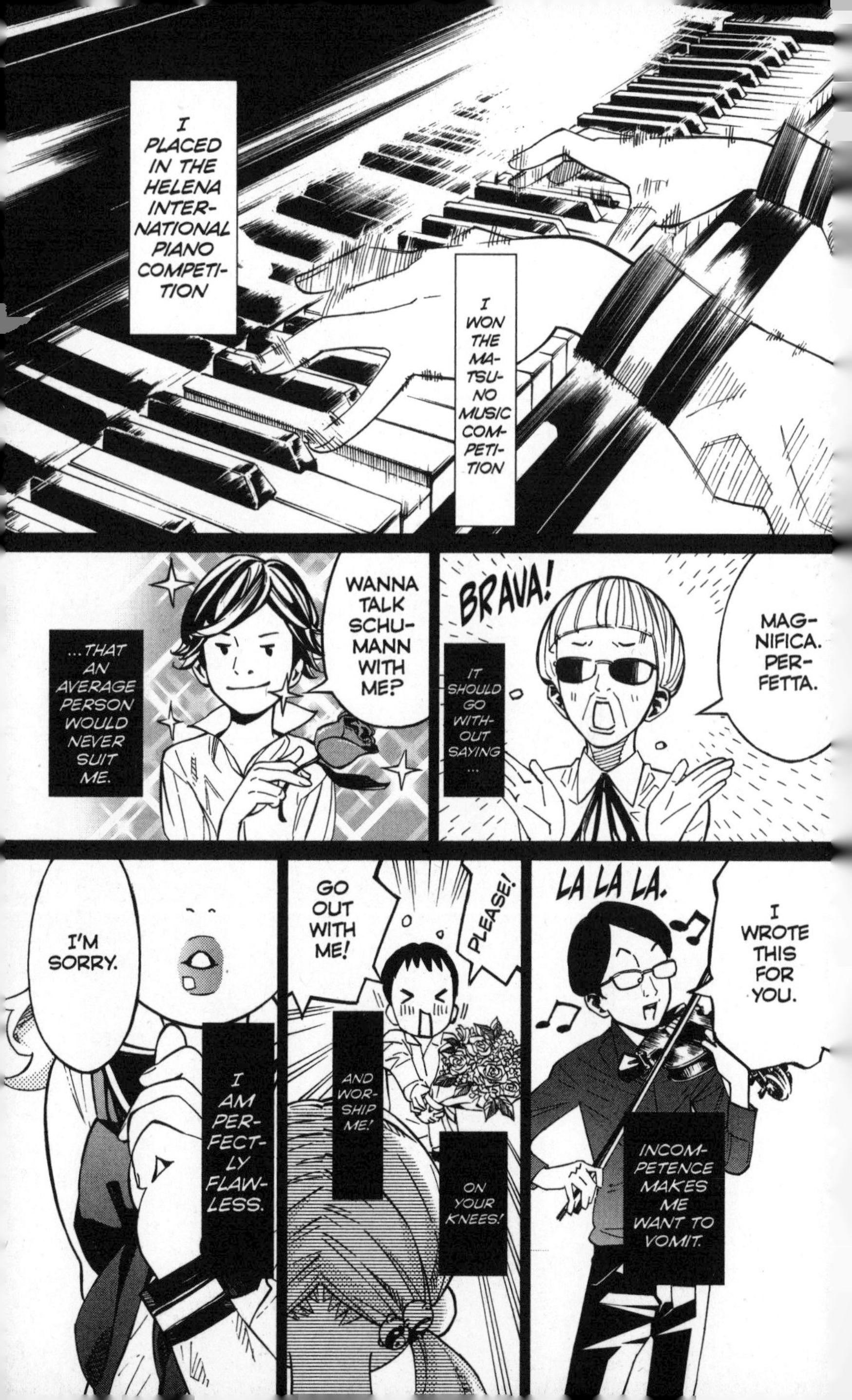
I WON THE MATSUNO MUSIC COMPETITION
I PLACED IN THE HELENA INTERNATIONAL PIANO COMPETITION
MAGNIFICA. PERFETTA.
BRAVA!
IT SHOULD GO WITHOUT SAYING...
WANNA TALK SCHUMANN WITH ME?
...THAT AN AVERAGE PERSON WOULD NEVER SUIT ME.
I WROTE THIS FOR YOU.
LA LA LA.
INCOMPETENCE MAKES ME WANT TO VOMIT.
PLEASE!
GO OUT WITH ME!
AND WORSHIP ME!
ON YOUR KNEES!
I'M SORRY.
I AM PERFECTLY FLAWLESS.

Chapter 32: Two of a Kind

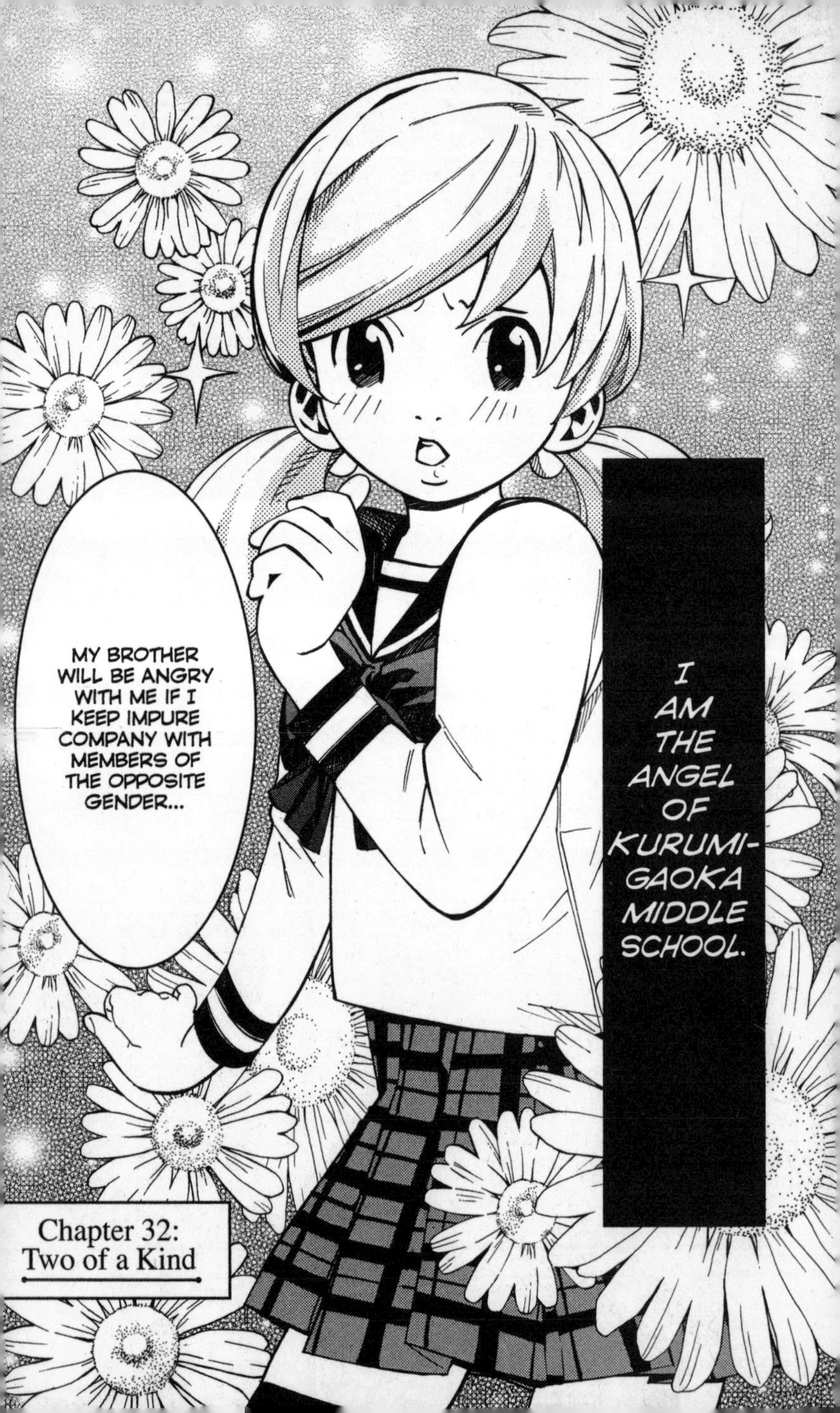
I AM THE ANGEL OF KURUMI-GAOKA MIDDLE SCHOOL.
MY BROTHER WILL BE ANGRY WITH ME IF I KEEP IMPURE COMPANY WITH MEMBERS OF THE OPPOSITE GENDER...

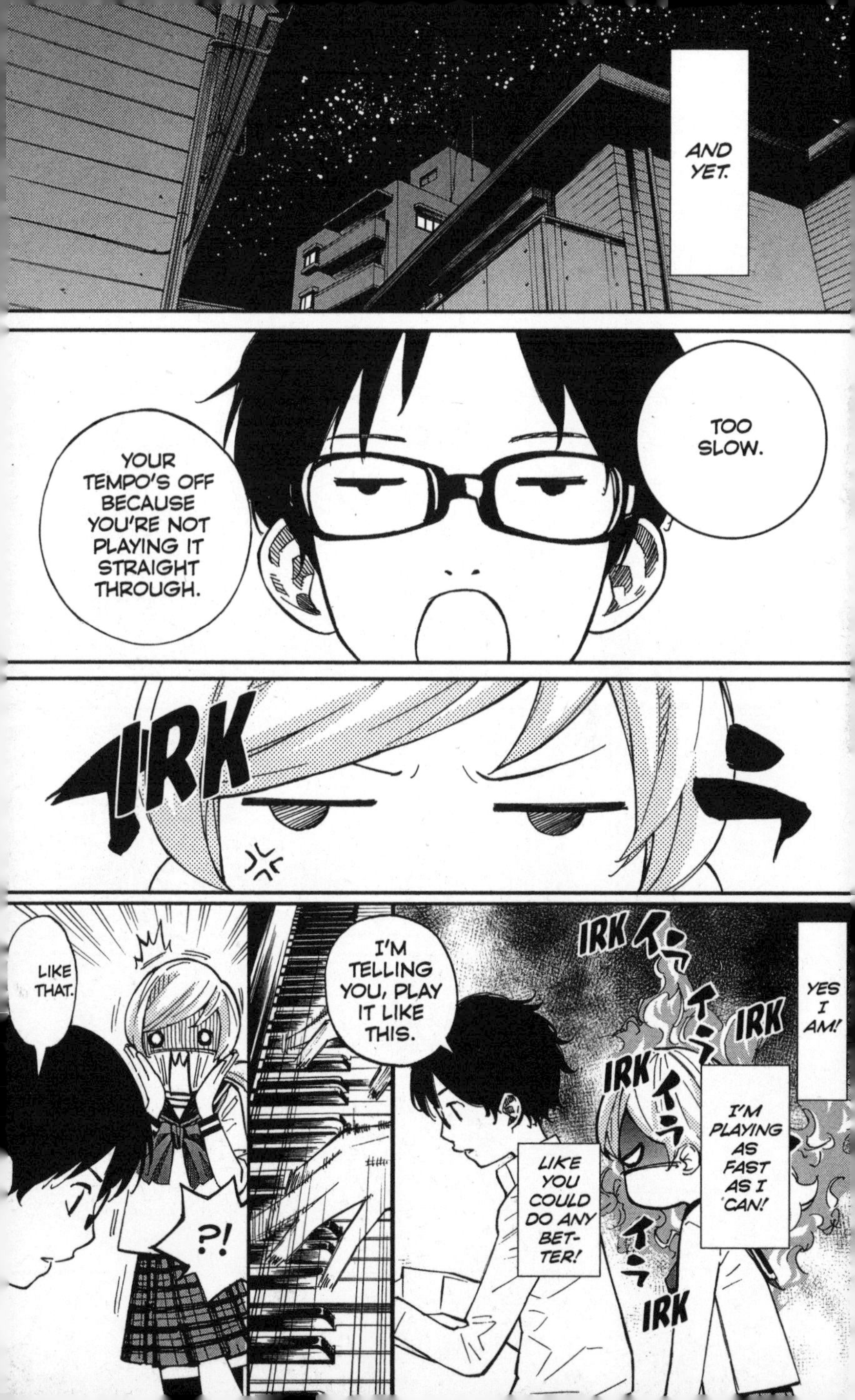

AND YET.
TOO SLOW.
YOUR TEMPO'S OFF BECAUSE YOU'RE NOT PLAYING IT STRAIGHT THROUGH.
IRK
IRK
YES I AM!
IRK
IRK
I'M PLAYING AS FAST AS I CAN!
LIKE YOU COULD DO ANY BET-TER!
IRK
I'M TELLING YOU, PLAY IT LIKE THIS.
LIKE THAT.
?!

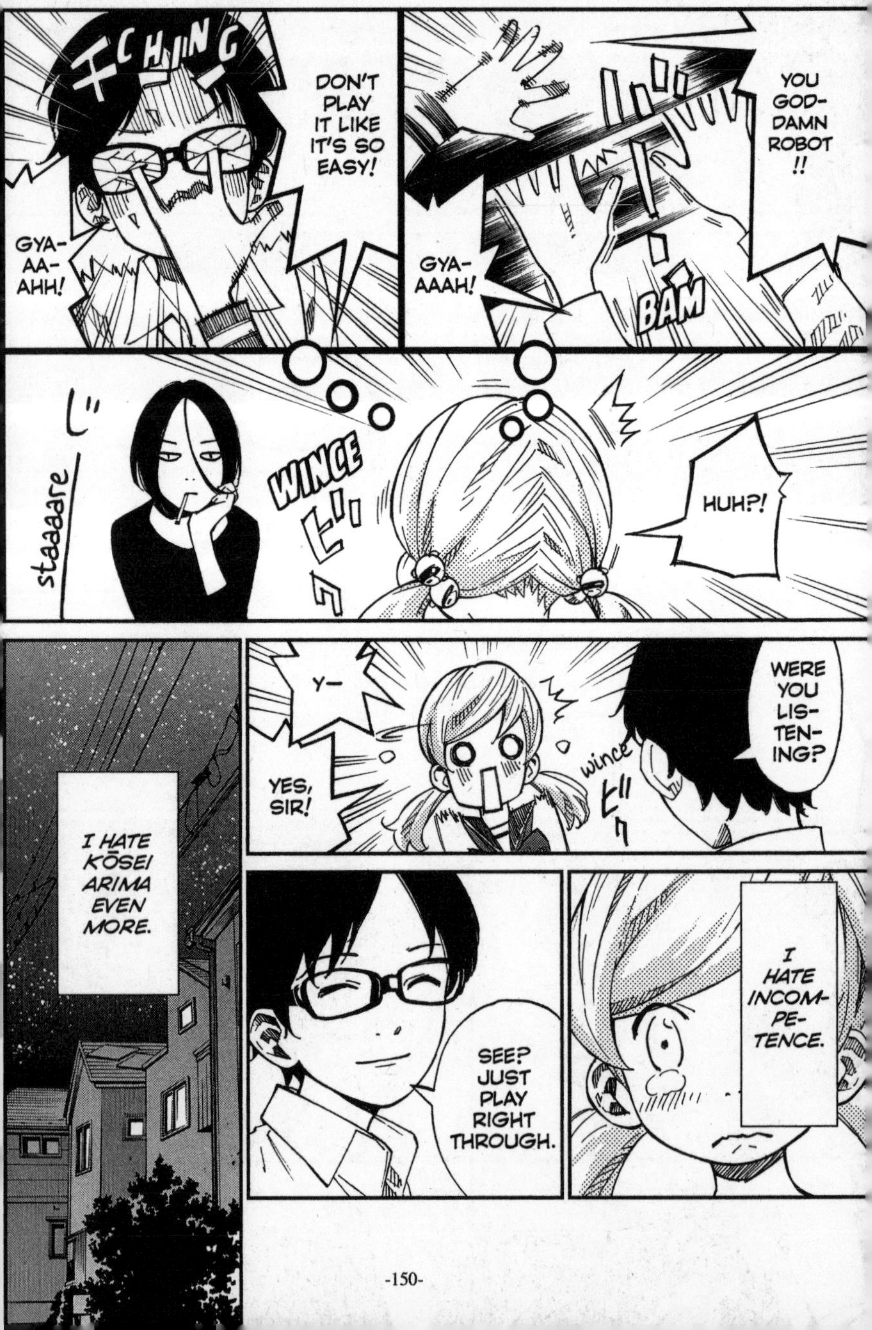
YOU GOD-DAMN ROBOT!!
GYA-AAAH!
BAM
CHING
DON'T PLAY IT LIKE IT'S SO EASY!
GYA-AA-AHH!
HUH?!
WINCE
staaaare
WERE YOU LIS-TEN-ING?
wince
Y—
YES, SIR!
I HATE INCOMPE-TENCE.
SEE? JUST PLAY RIGHT THROUGH.
I HATE KŌSEI ARIMA EVEN MORE.

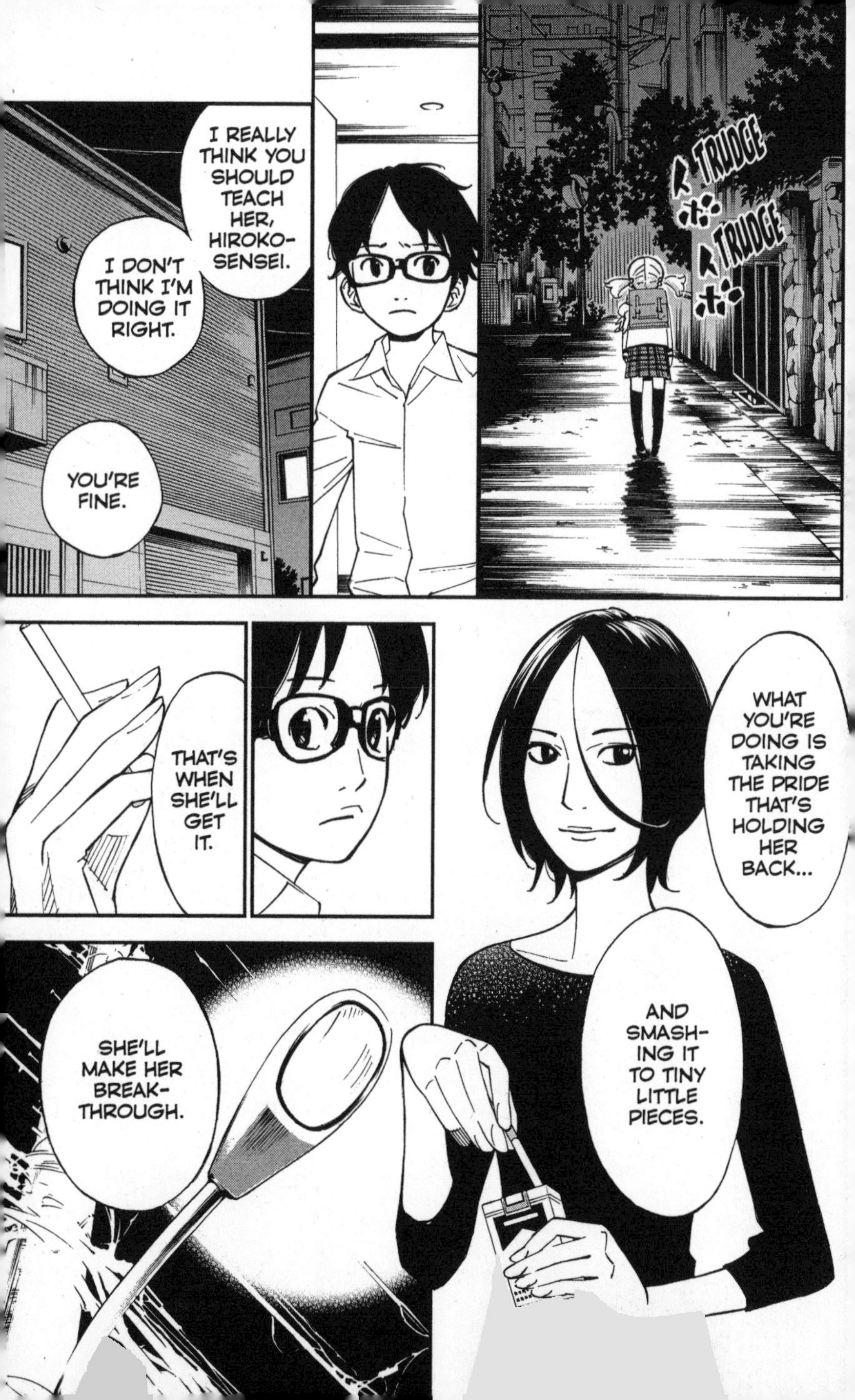
TRUDGE
TRUDGE
I REALLY THINK YOU SHOULD TEACH HER, HIROKO-SENSEI.
I DON'T THINK I'M DOING IT RIGHT.
YOU'RE FINE.
WHAT YOU'RE DOING IS TAKING THE PRIDE THAT'S HOLDING HER BACK...
AND SMASHING-ING IT TO TINY LITTLE PIECES.
THAT'S WHEN SHE'LL GET IT.
SHE'LL MAKE HER BREAK-THROUGH.

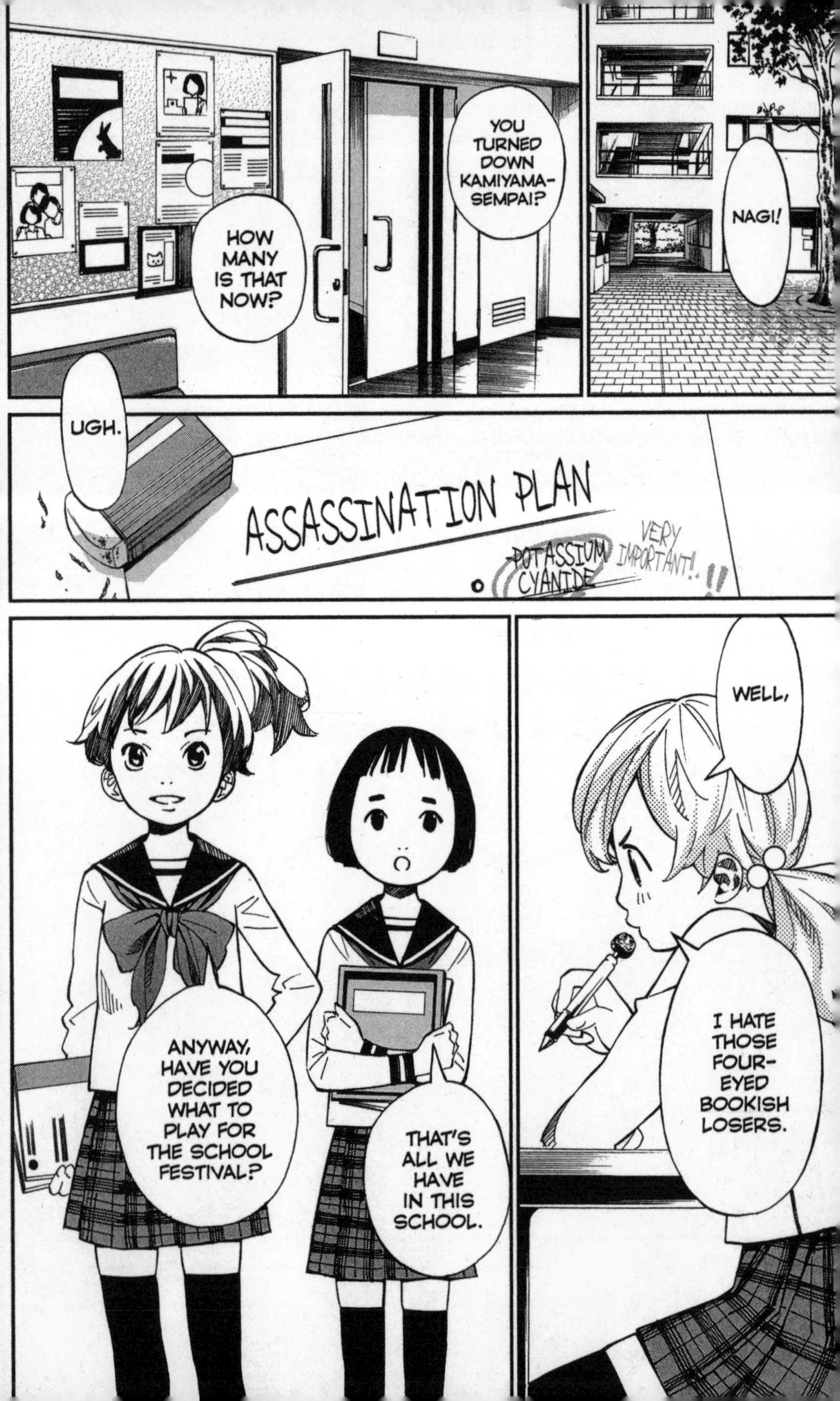
NAGI!
YOU TURNED DOWN KAMIYAMA-SEMPAI?
HOW MANY IS THAT NOW?
UGH.
ASSASSINATION PLAN
-POTASSIUM CYANIDE
VERY IMPORTANT!!
WELL,
I HATE THOSE FOUR-EYED BOOKISH LOSERS.
THAT'S ALL WE HAVE IN THIS SCHOOL.
ANYWAY, HAVE YOU DECIDED WHAT TO PLAY FOR THE SCHOOL FESTIVAL?

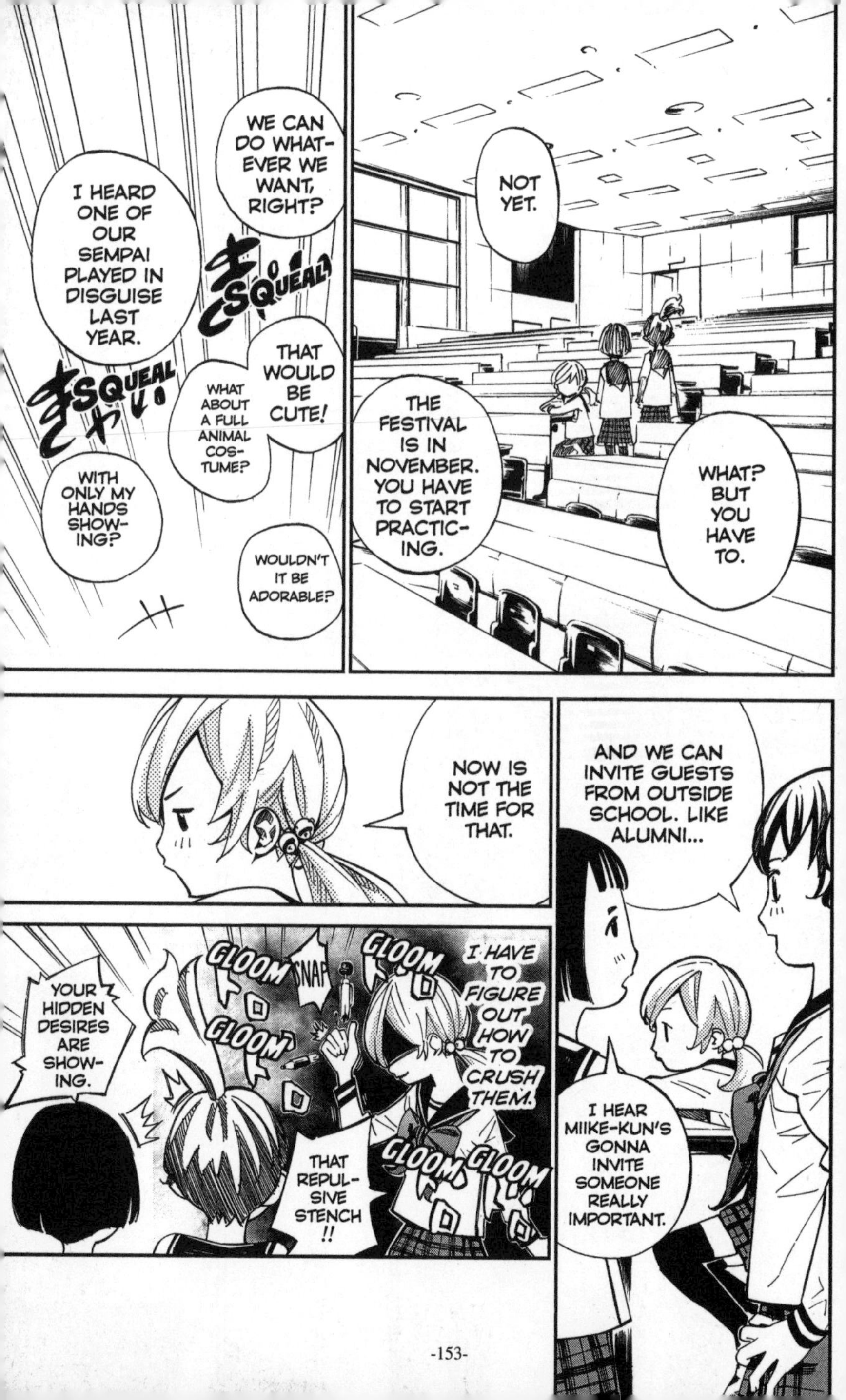
NOT YET.
WHAT? BUT YOU HAVE TO.
THE FESTIVAL IS IN NOVEMBER. YOU HAVE TO START PRACTICING.
WE CAN DO WHATEVER WE WANT, RIGHT?
I HEARD ONE OF OUR SEMPAI PLAYED IN DISGUISE LAST YEAR.
SQUEAL
THAT WOULD BE CUTE!
WHAT ABOUT A FULL ANIMAL COSTUME?
SQUEAL
WITH ONLY MY HANDS SHOWING?
WOULDN'T IT BE ADORABLE?
AND WE CAN INVITE GUESTS FROM OUTSIDE SCHOOL. LIKE ALUMNI...
I HEAR MIIKE-KUN'S GONNA INVITE SOMEONE REALLY IMPORTANT.
NOW IS NOT THE TIME FOR THAT.
I HAVE TO FIGURE OUT HOW TO CRUSH THEM.
GLOOM
SNAP
GLOOM
GLOOM
YOUR HIDDEN DESIRES ARE SHOWING.
GLOOM GLOOM
THAT REPULSIVE STENCH!!

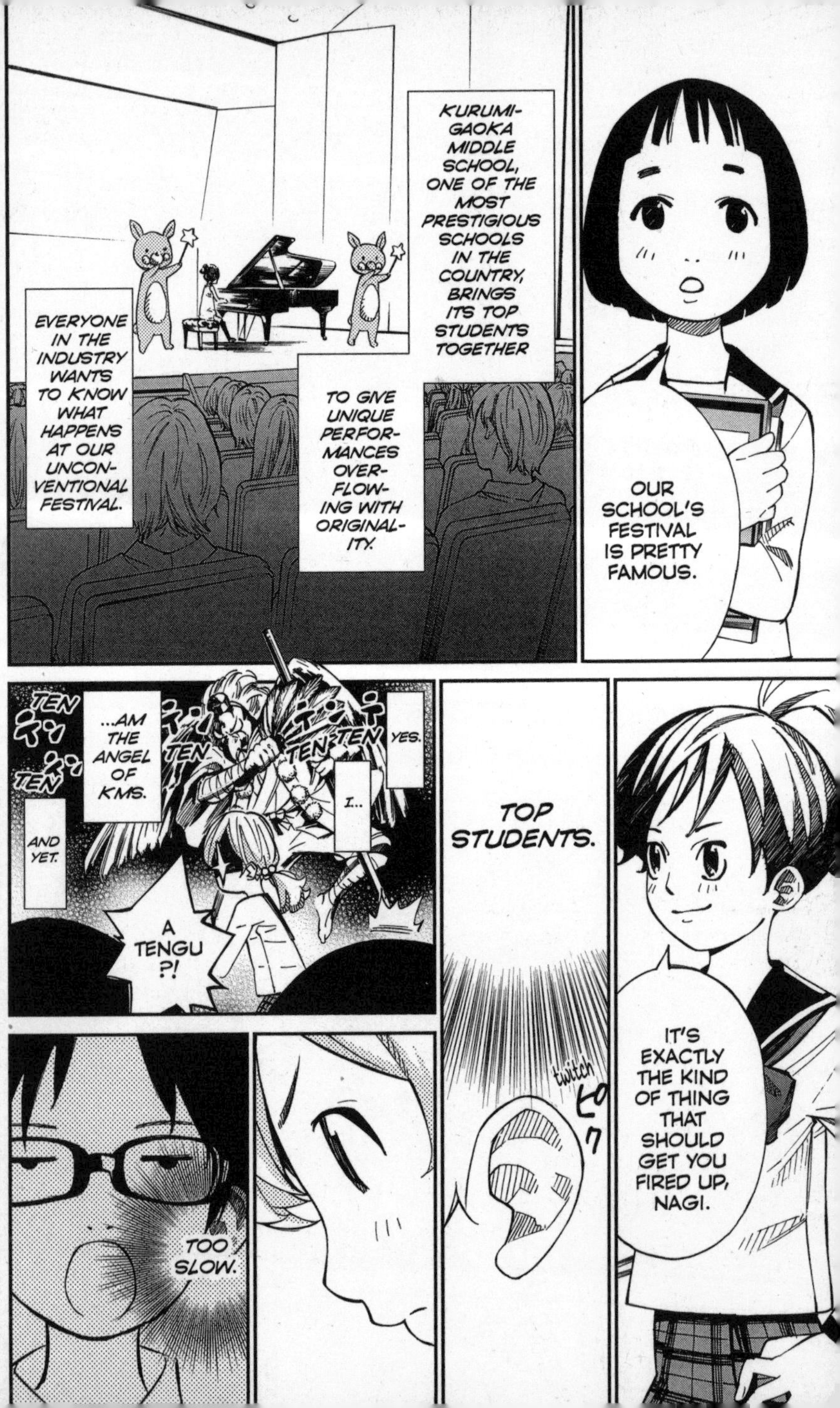
OUR SCHOOL'S FESTIVAL IS PRETTY FAMOUS.
KURUMI-GAOKA MIDDLE SCHOOL, ONE OF THE MOST PRESTIGIOUS SCHOOLS IN THE COUNTRY, BRINGS ITS TOP STUDENTS TOGETHER
TO GIVE UNIQUE PERFORMANCES OVERFLOWING WITH ORIGINALITY.
EVERYONE IN THE INDUSTRY WANTS TO KNOW WHAT HAPPENS AT OUR UNCONVENTIONAL FESTIVAL.
IT'S EXACTLY THE KIND OF THING THAT SHOULD GET YOU FIRED UP, NAGI.
TOP STUDENTS.
twitch
YES.
I...
...AM THE ANGEL OF KMS.
TEN TEN
TEN
TEN
TEN
AND YET.
A TENGU?!
TOO SLOW.

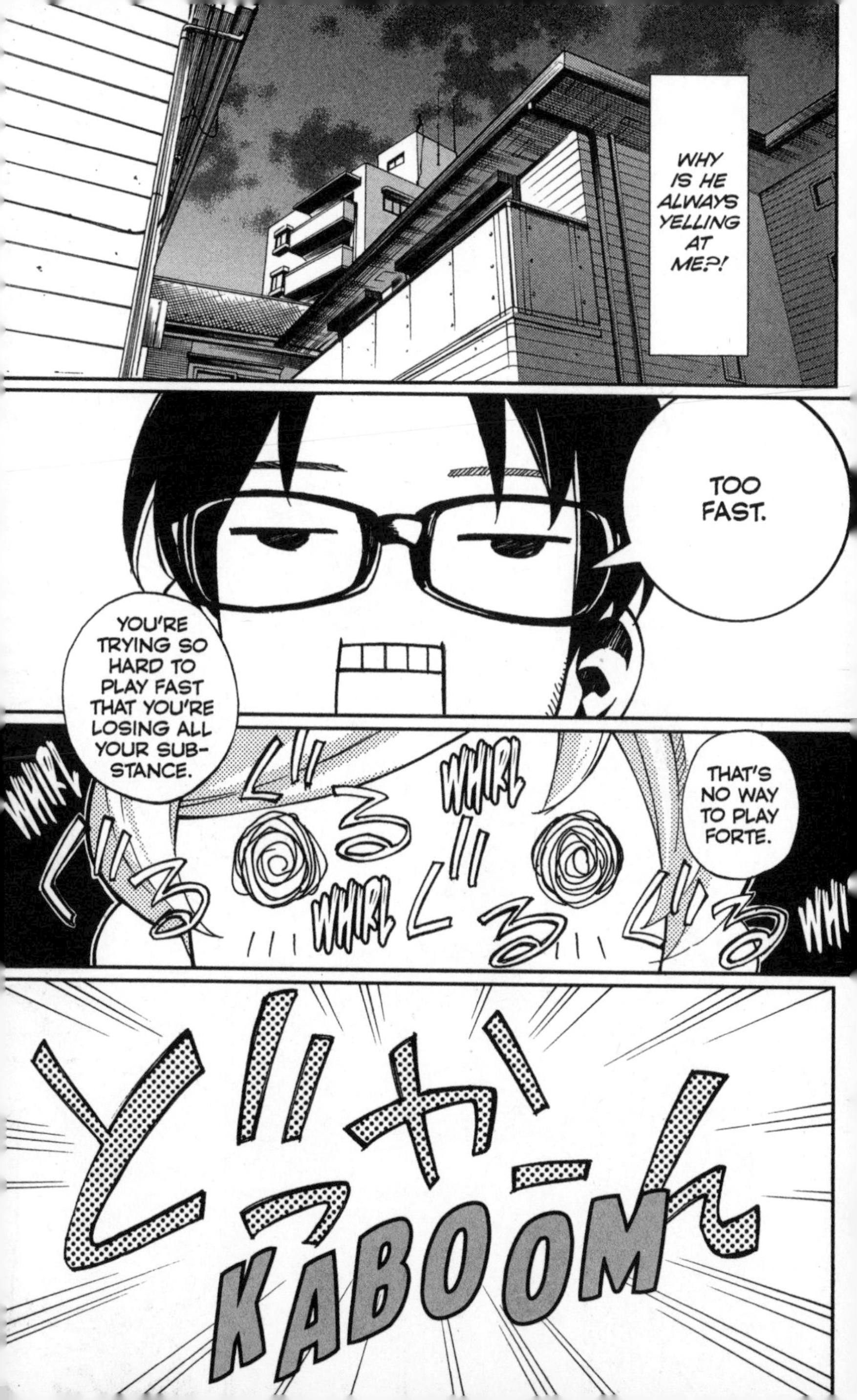
WHY IS HE ALWAYS YELLING AT ME?!
TOO FAST.
YOU'RE TRYING SO HARD TO PLAY FAST THAT YOU'RE LOSING ALL YOUR SUB-STANCE.
THAT'S NO WAY TO PLAY FORTE.
WHIRL
WHIRL
WHIRL
WHIRL
KABOOM

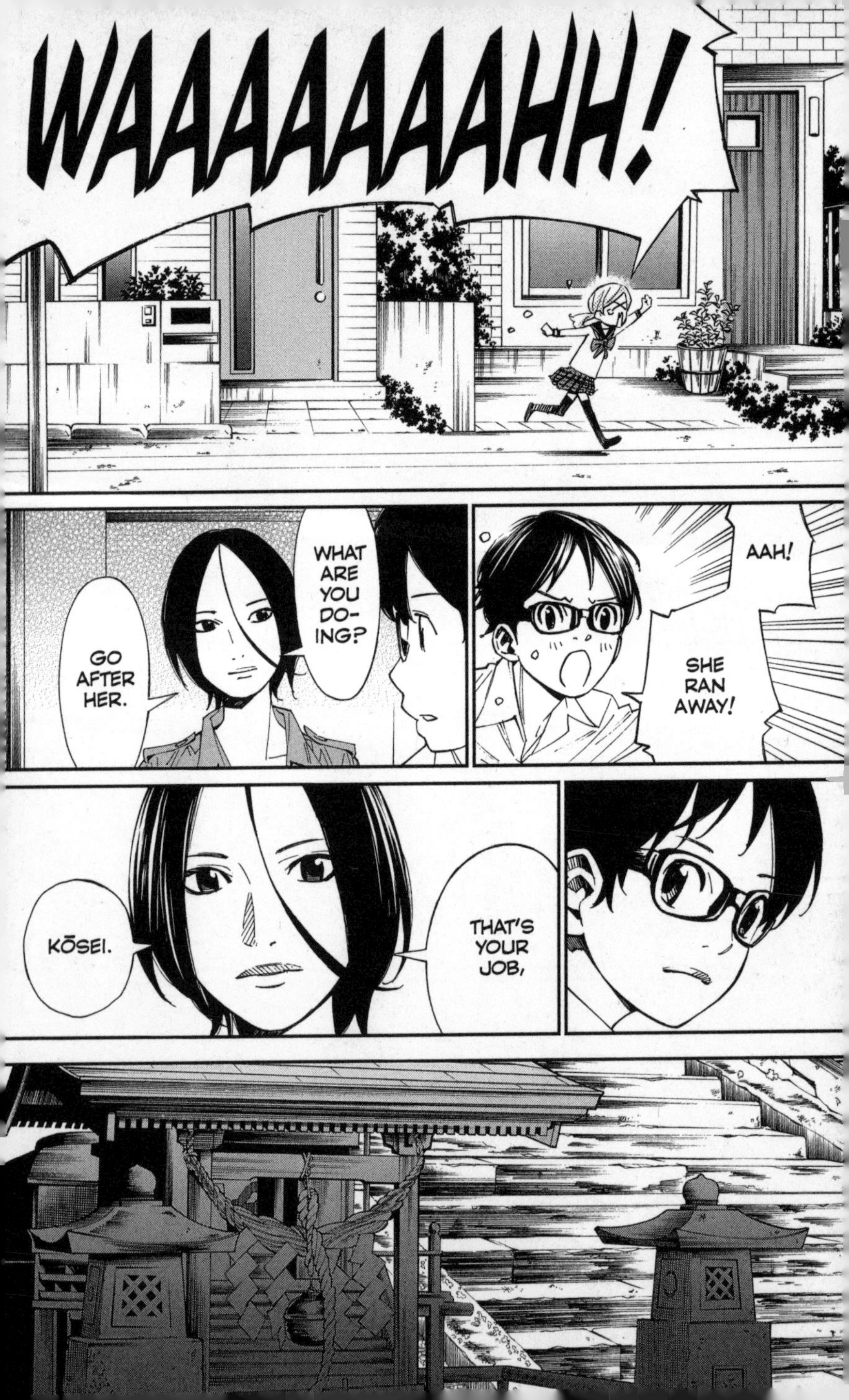
WAAAAAAAHH!
AAH!
SHE RAN AWAY!
WHAT ARE YOU DO-ING?
GO AFTER HER.
THAT'S YOUR JOB,
KŌSEI.

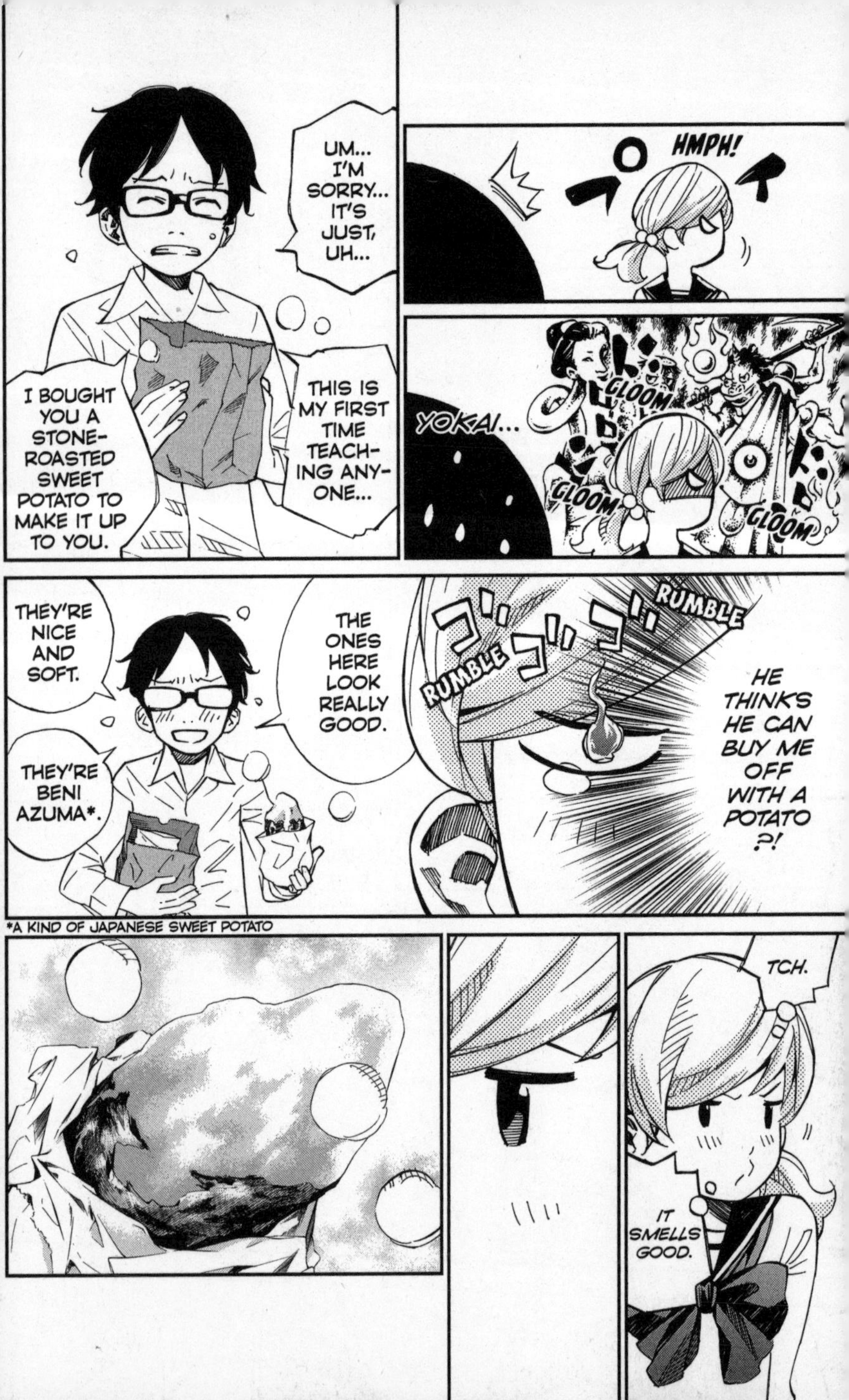
HMPH!
YOKAI...
GLOOM
GLOOM
GLOOM
UM... I'M SORRY... IT'S JUST, UH...
THIS IS MY FIRST TIME TEACHING ANYONE...
I BOUGHT YOU A STONE-ROASTED SWEET POTATO TO MAKE IT UP TO YOU.
RUMBLE
RUMBLE
HE THINKS HE CAN BUY ME OFF WITH A POTATO ?!
THE ONES HERE LOOK REALLY GOOD.
THEY'RE NICE AND SOFT.
THEY'RE BENI AZUMA*.
TCH.
IT SMELLS GOOD.

*A KIND OF JAPANESE SWEET POTATO

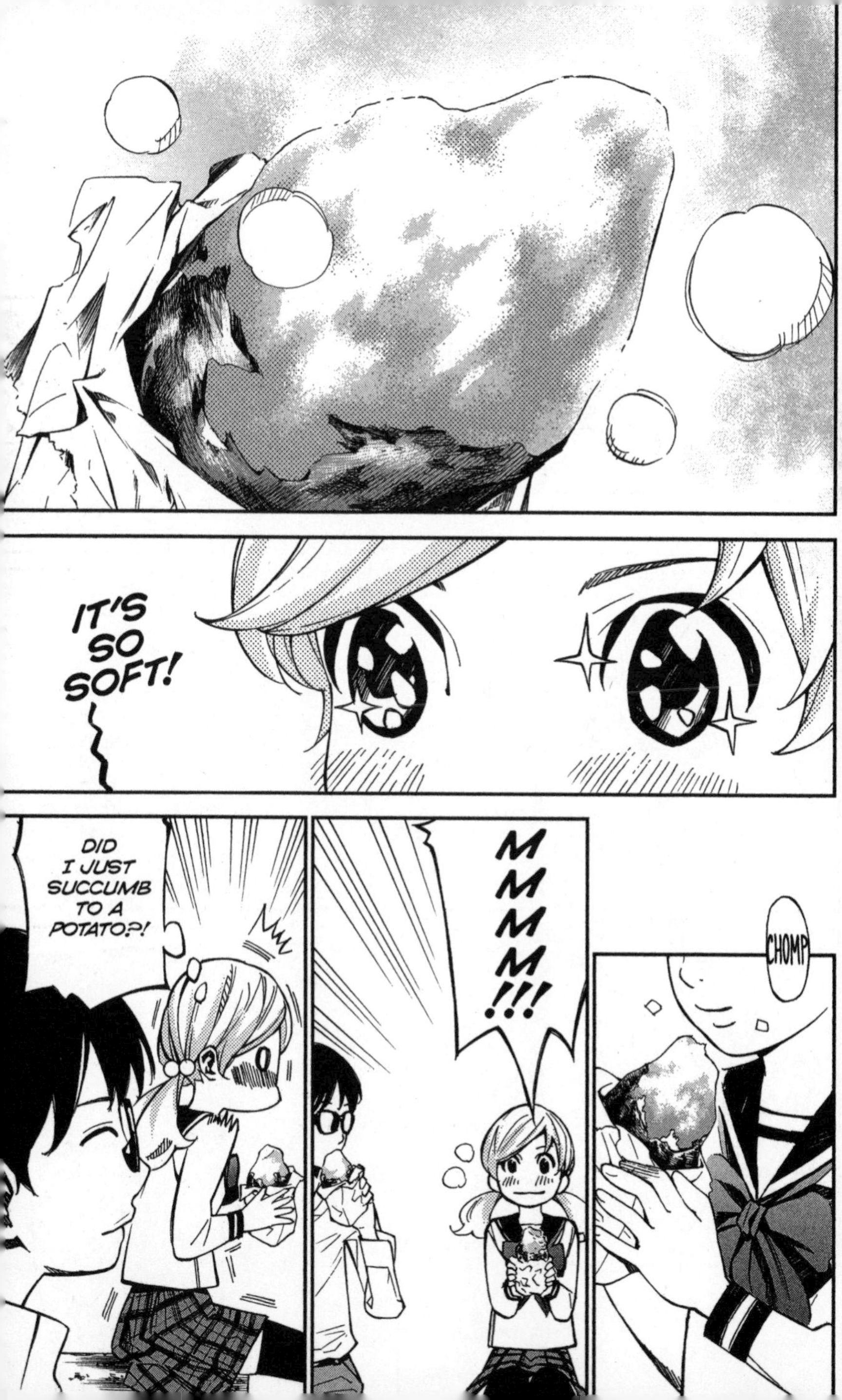
IT'S SO SOFT!
CHOMP
MMMM!!!
DID I JUST SUCCUMB TO A POTATO?!

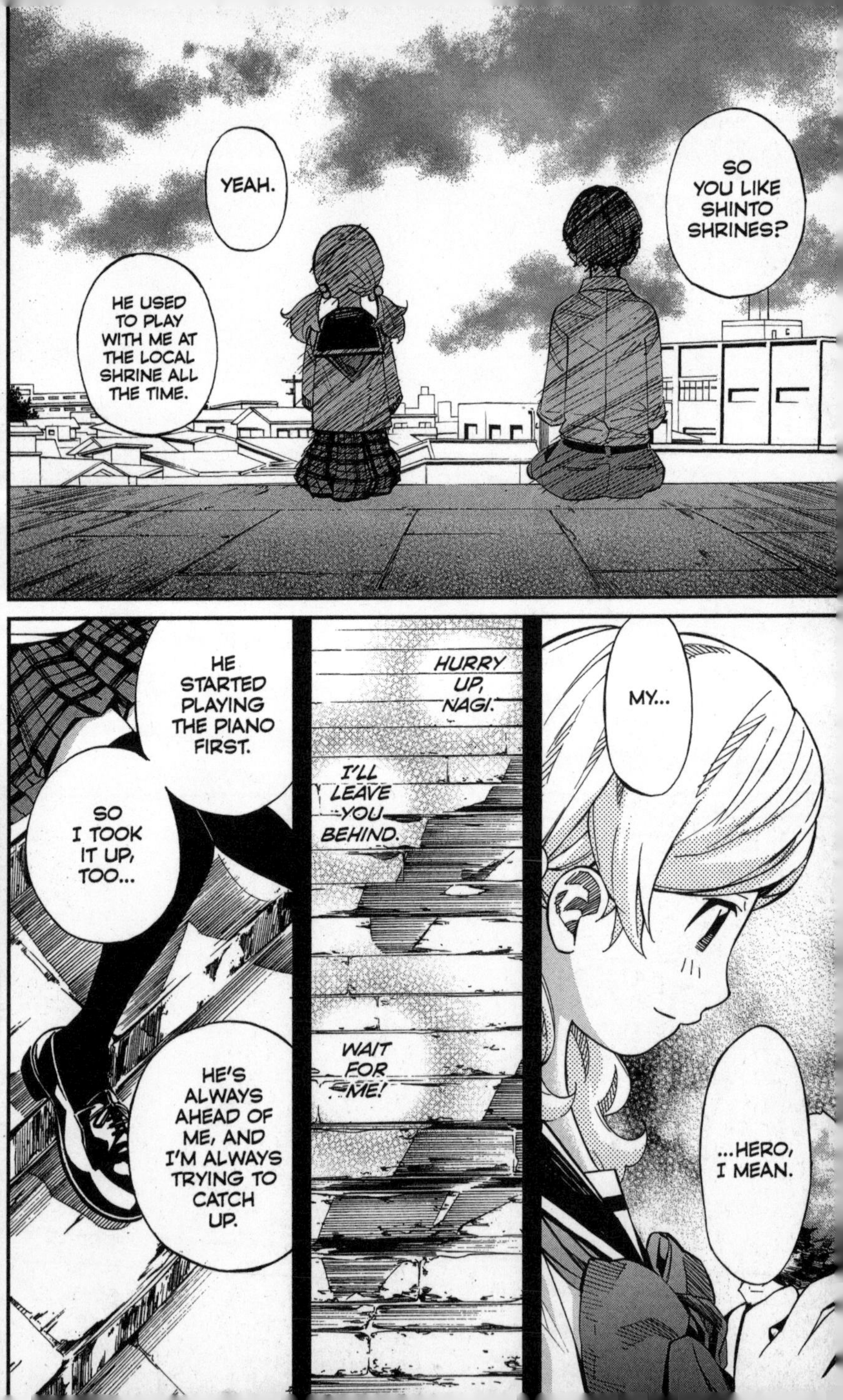
SO YOU LIKE SHINTO SHRINES?
YEAH.
HE USED TO PLAY WITH ME AT THE LOCAL SHRINE ALL THE TIME.
MY...
...HERO, I MEAN.
HURRY UP, NAGI.
I'LL LEAVE YOU BEHIND.
WAIT FOR ME!
HE STARTED PLAYING THE PIANO FIRST.
SO I TOOK IT UP, TOO...
HE'S ALWAYS AHEAD OF ME, AND I'M ALWAYS TRYING TO CATCH UP.

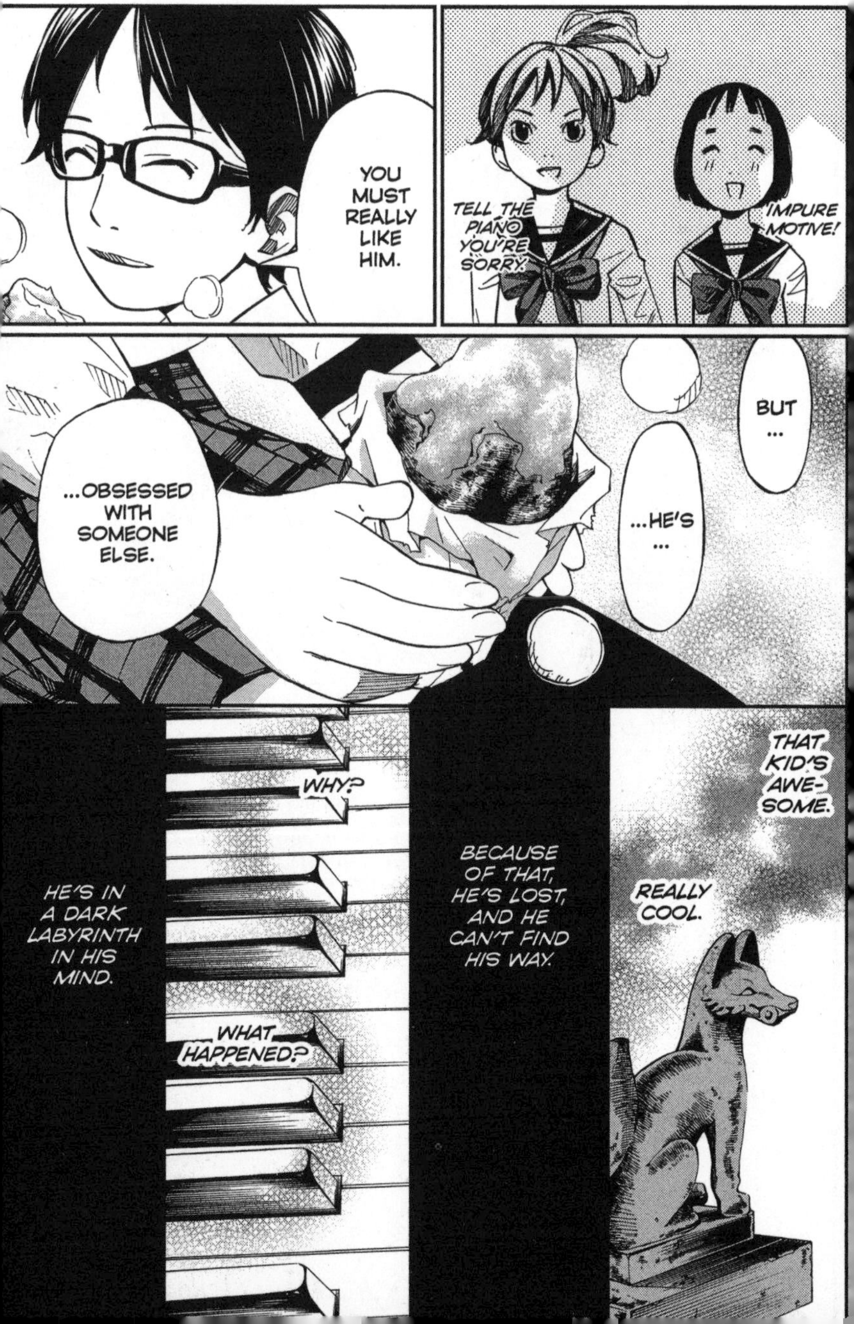
IMPURE MOTIVE!
TELL THE PIANO YOU'RE SORRY.
YOU MUST REALLY LIKE HIM.
BUT ...
...HE'S ...
...OBSESSED WITH SOMEONE ELSE.
THAT KID'S AWESOME.
REALLY COOL.
BECAUSE OF THAT, HE'S LOST, AND HE CAN'T FIND HIS WAY.
WHY?
HE'S IN A DARK LABYRINTH IN HIS MIND.
WHAT HAPPENED?

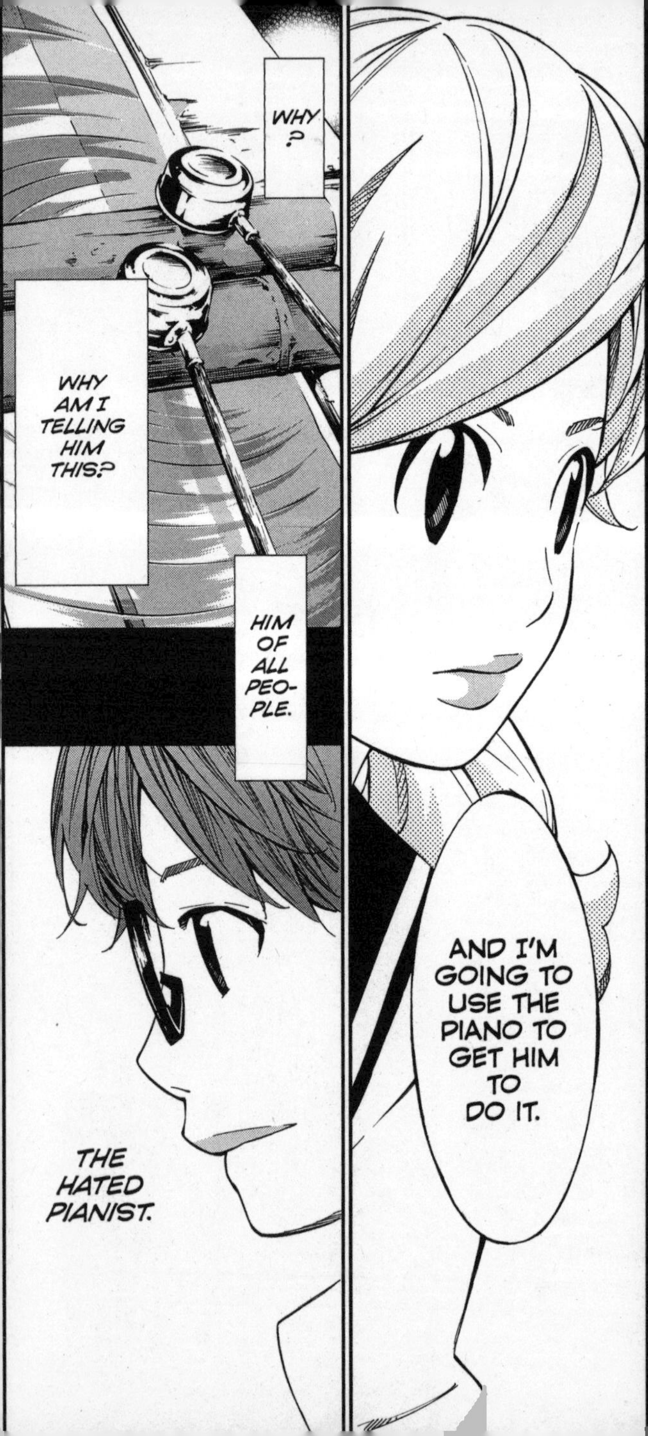
AND I'M GOING TO USE THE PIANO TO GET HIM TO DO IT.
WHY?
WHY AM I TELLING HIM THIS?
HIM OF ALL PEOPLE.
THE HATED PIANIST.

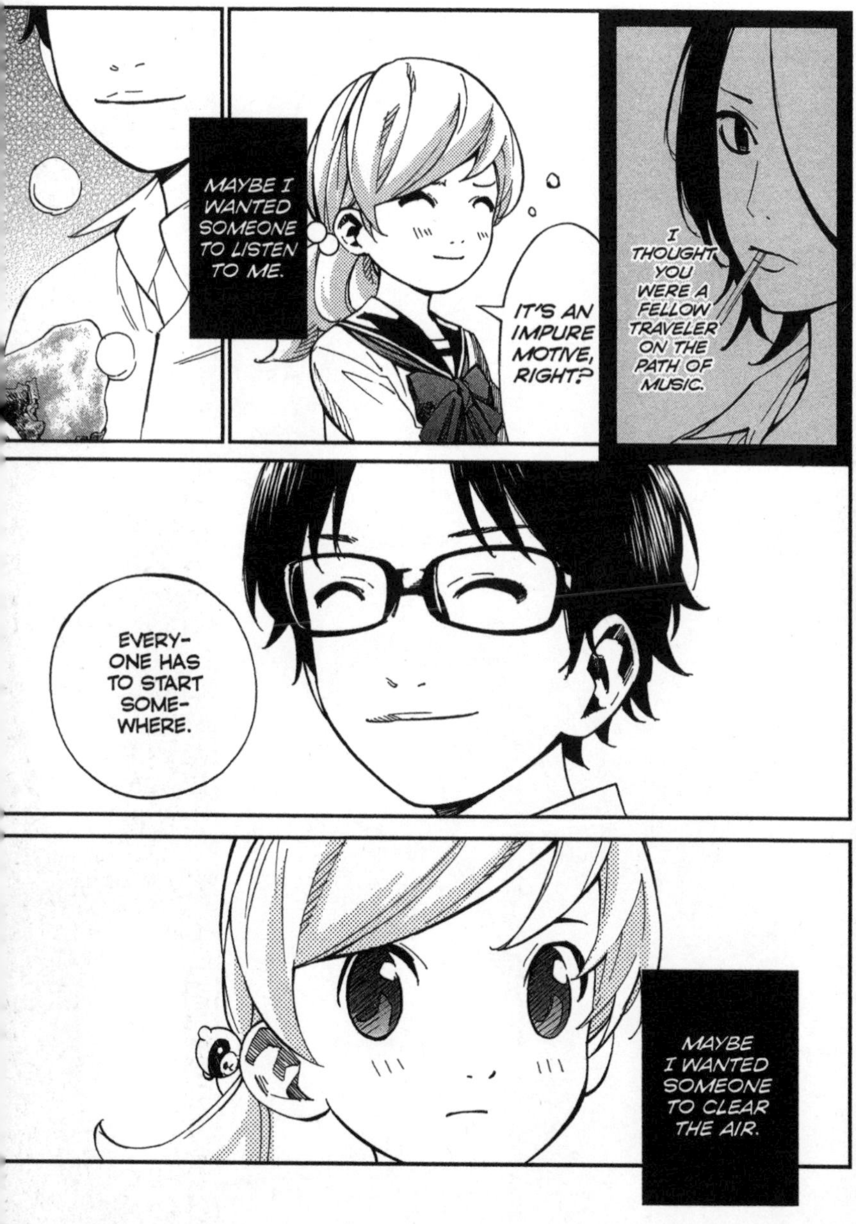
I THOUGHT YOU WERE A FELLOW TRAVELER ON THE PATH OF MUSIC.
IT'S AN IMPURE MOTIVE, RIGHT?
MAYBE I WANTED SOMEONE TO LISTEN TO ME.
EVERY-ONE HAS TO START SOME-WHERE.
MAYBE I WANTED SOMEONE TO CLEAR THE AIR.

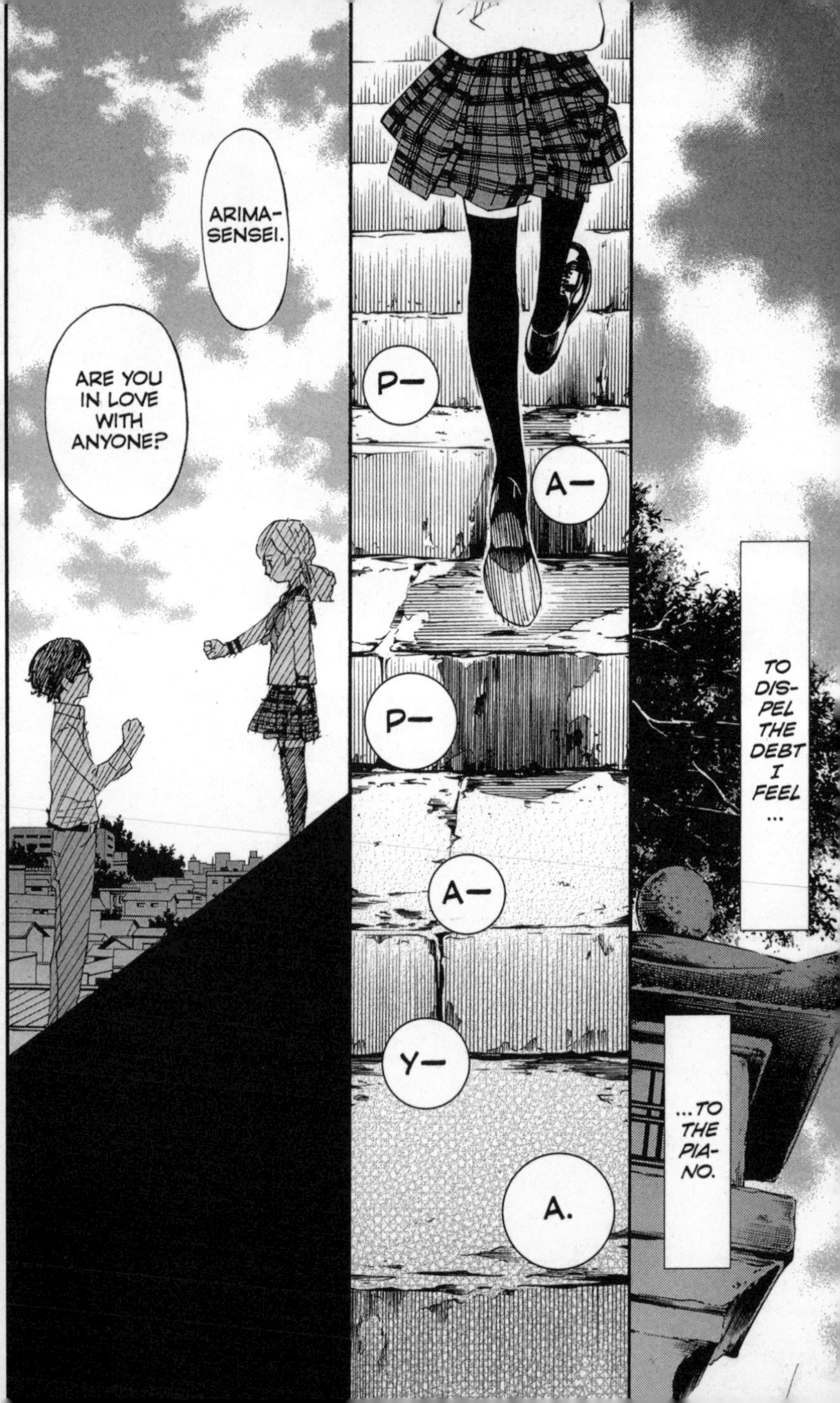
TO DIS-PEL THE DEBT I FEEL ...
...TO THE PIA-NO.
P—
A—
P—
A—
Y—
A.
ARIMA-SENSEI.
ARE YOU IN LOVE WITH ANYONE?

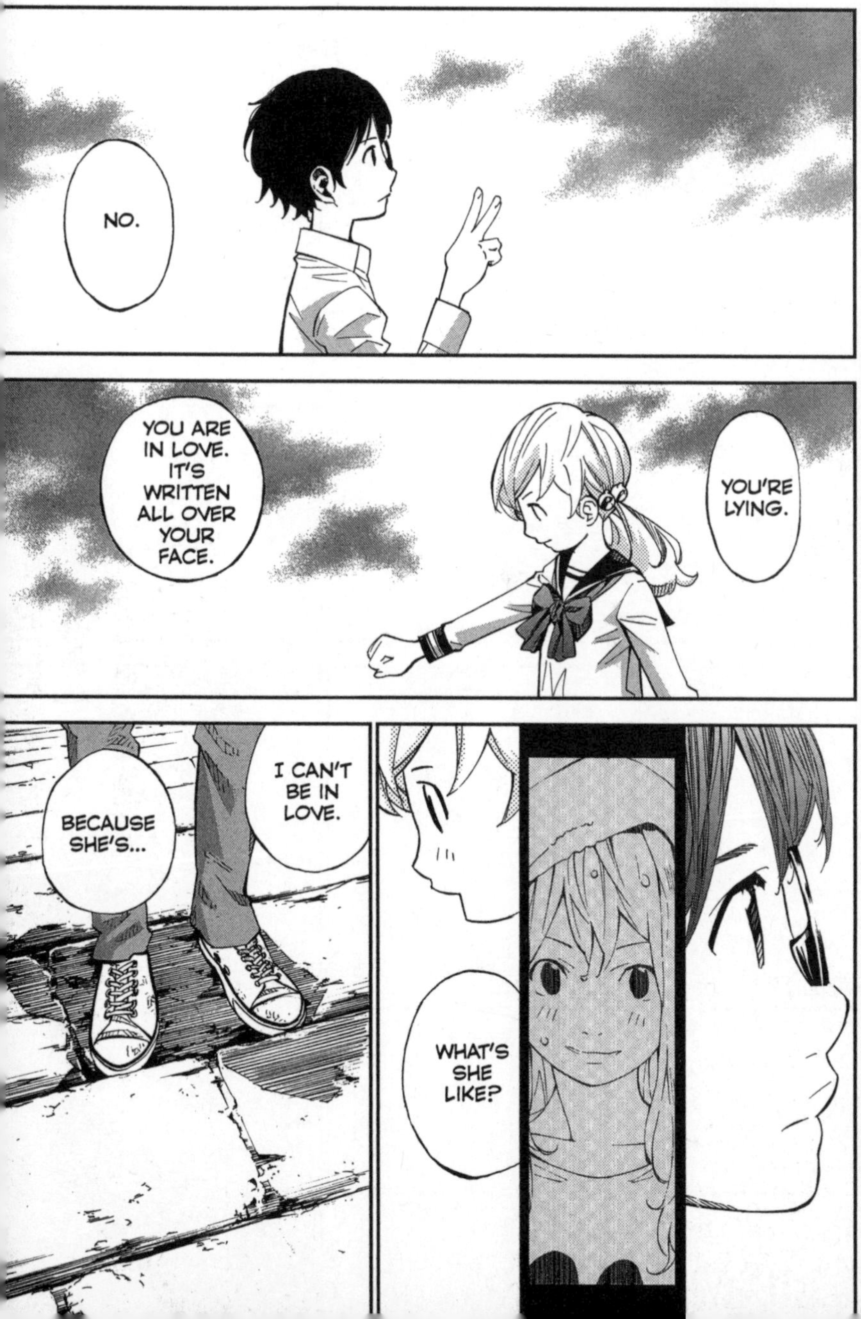
NO.
YOU'RE LYING.
YOU ARE IN LOVE. IT'S WRITTEN ALL OVER YOUR FACE.
WHAT'S SHE LIKE?
I CAN'T BE IN LOVE.
BECAUSE SHE'S...

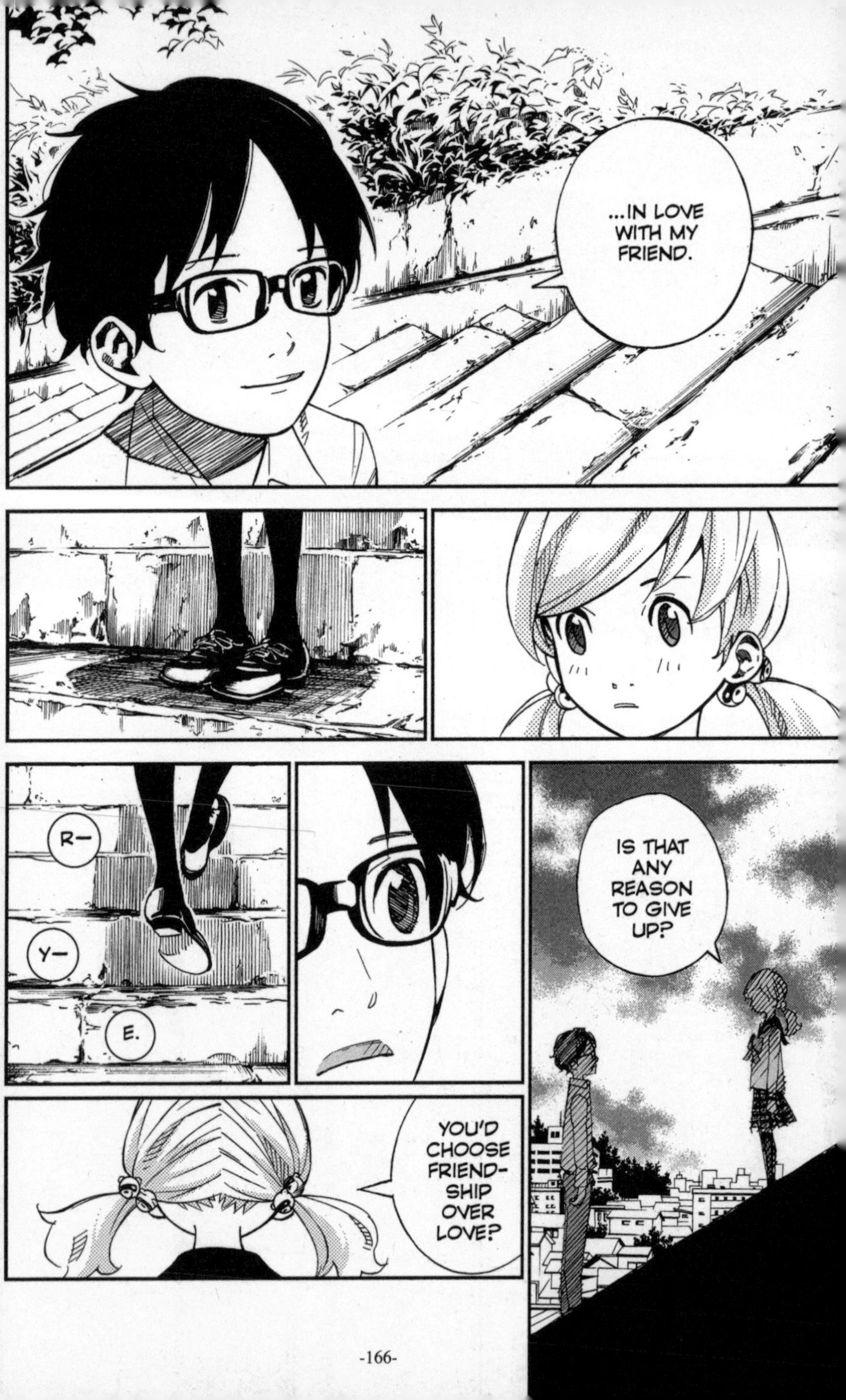
...IN LOVE WITH MY FRIEND.
IS THAT ANY REASON TO GIVE UP?
R—
Y—
E.
YOU'D CHOOSE FRIEND-SHIP OVER LOVE?

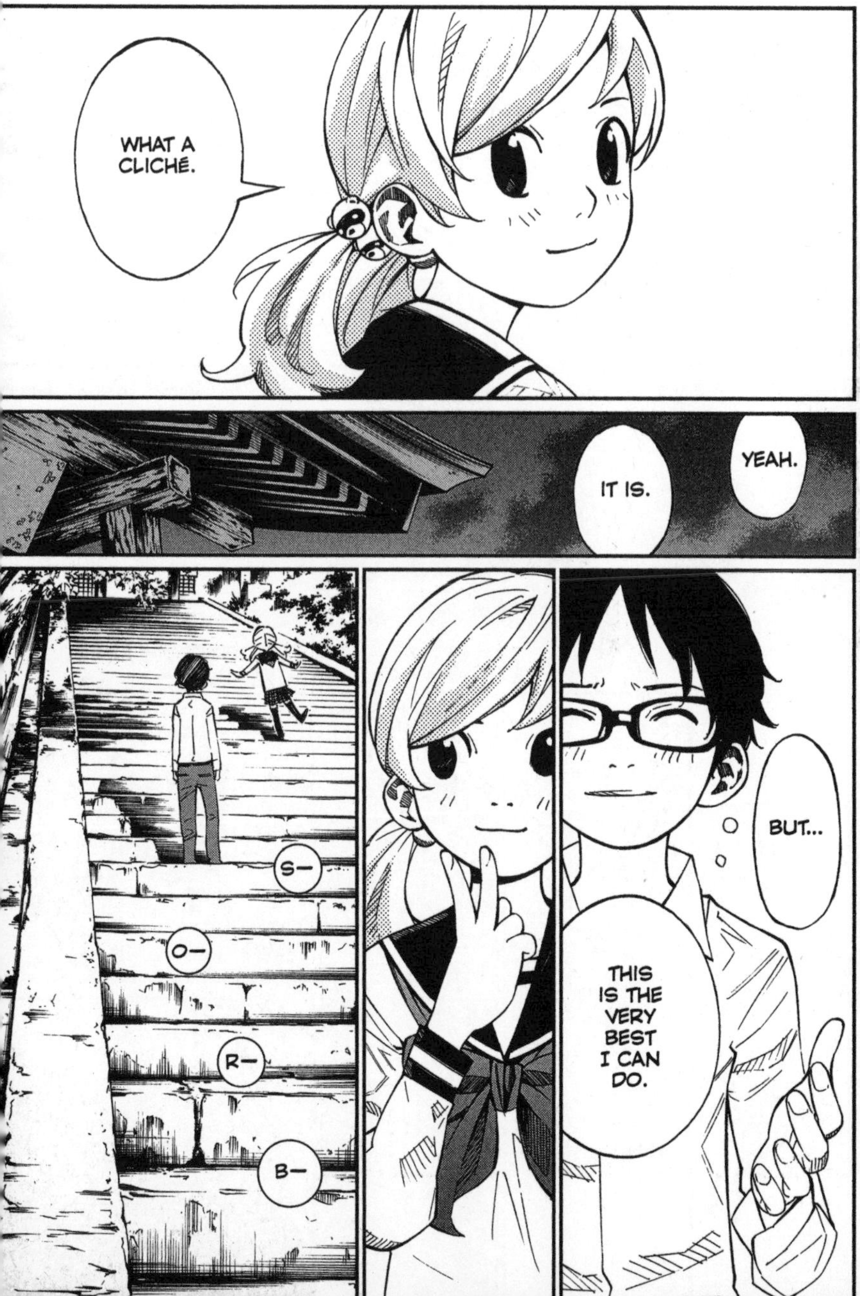
WHAT A CLICHÉ.
YEAH.
IT IS.
BUT...
THIS IS THE VERY BEST I CAN DO.
S—
O—
R—
B—

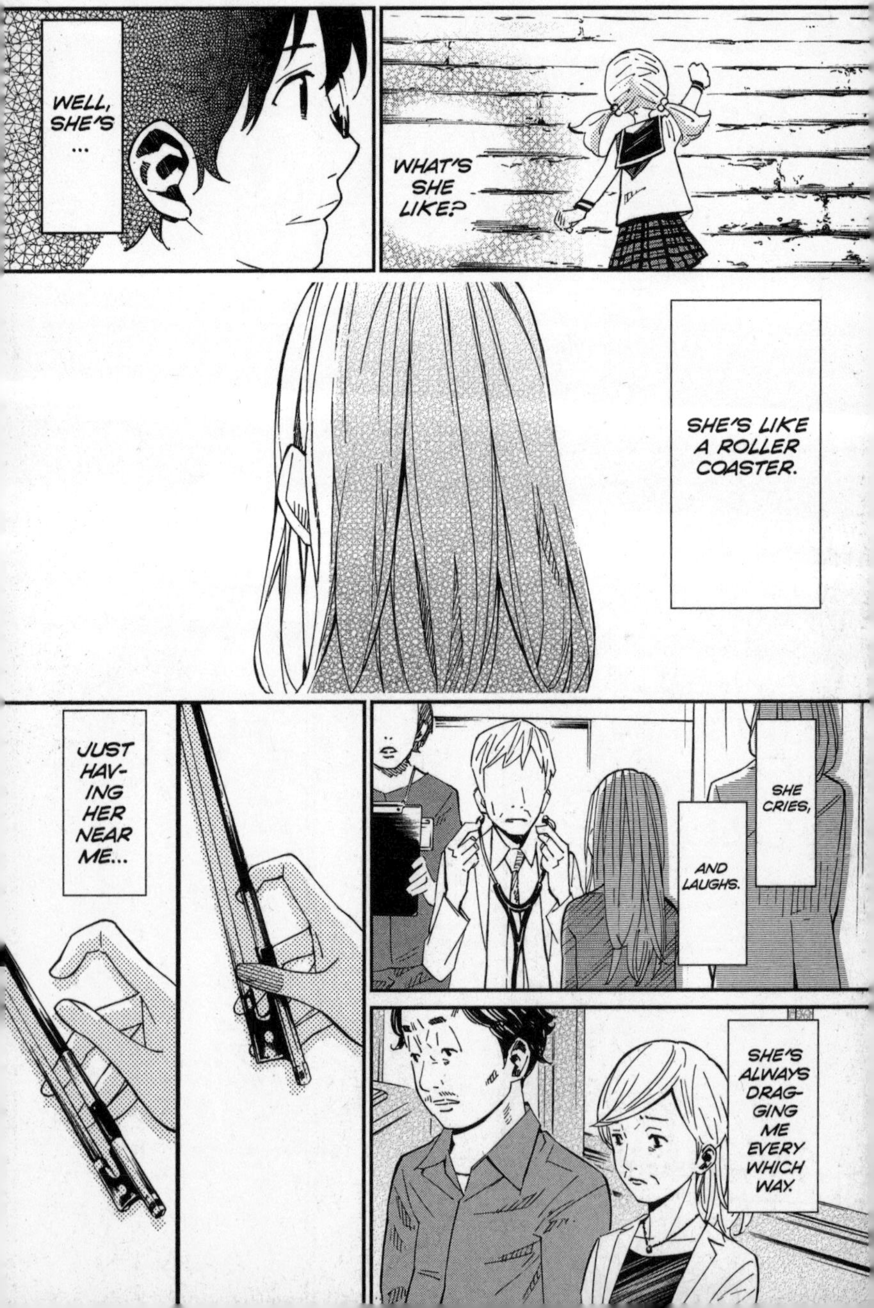
WHAT'S SHE LIKE?
WELL, SHE'S ...
SHE'S LIKE A ROLLER COASTER.
SHE CRIES,
AND LAUGHS.
SHE'S ALWAYS DRAG-GING ME EVERY WHICH WAY.
JUST HAV-ING HER NEAR ME...

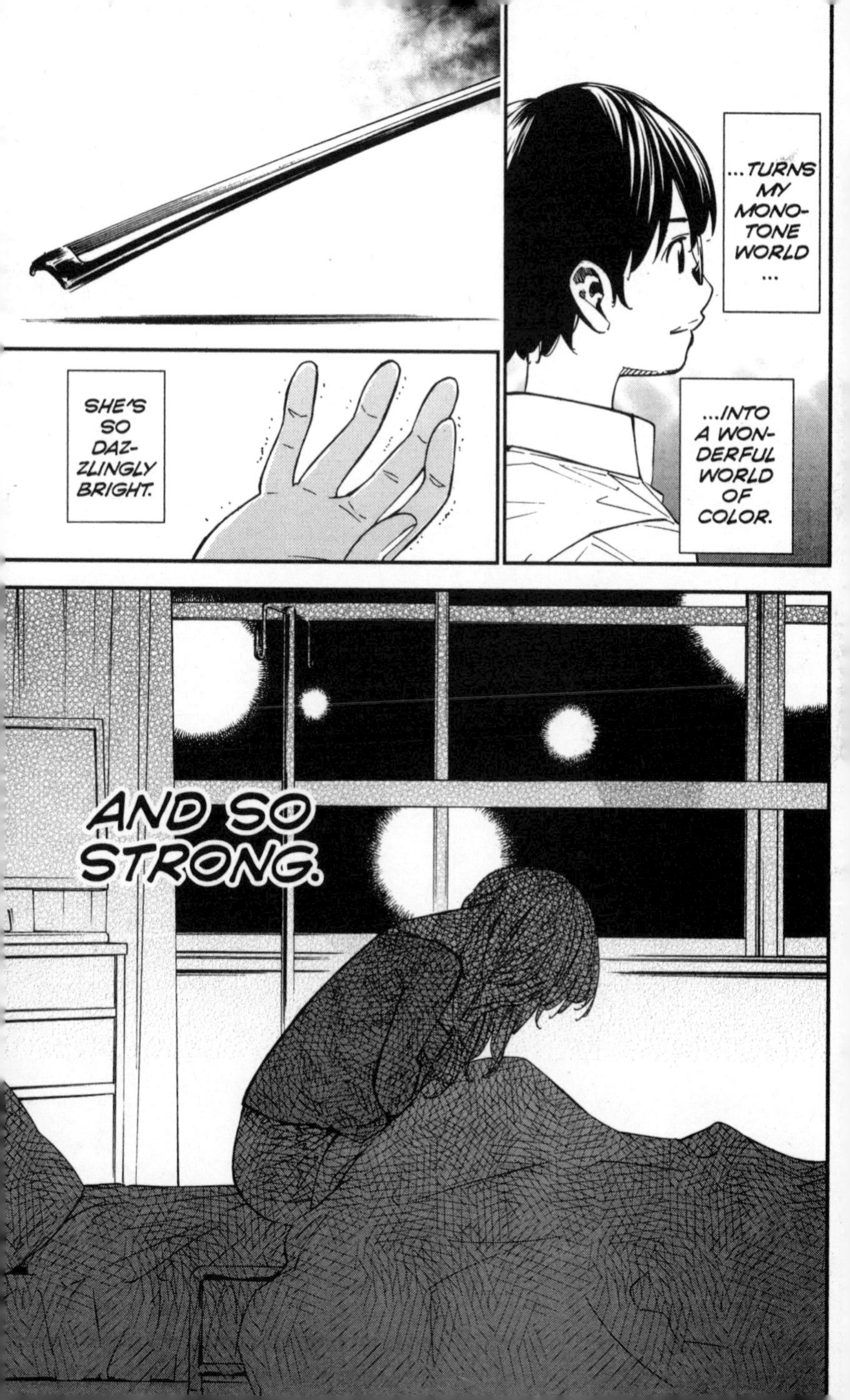
...TURNS MY MONOTONE WORLD ...
...INTO A WONDERFUL WORLD OF COLOR.
SHE'S SO DAZZLINGLY BRIGHT.
AND SO STRONG.

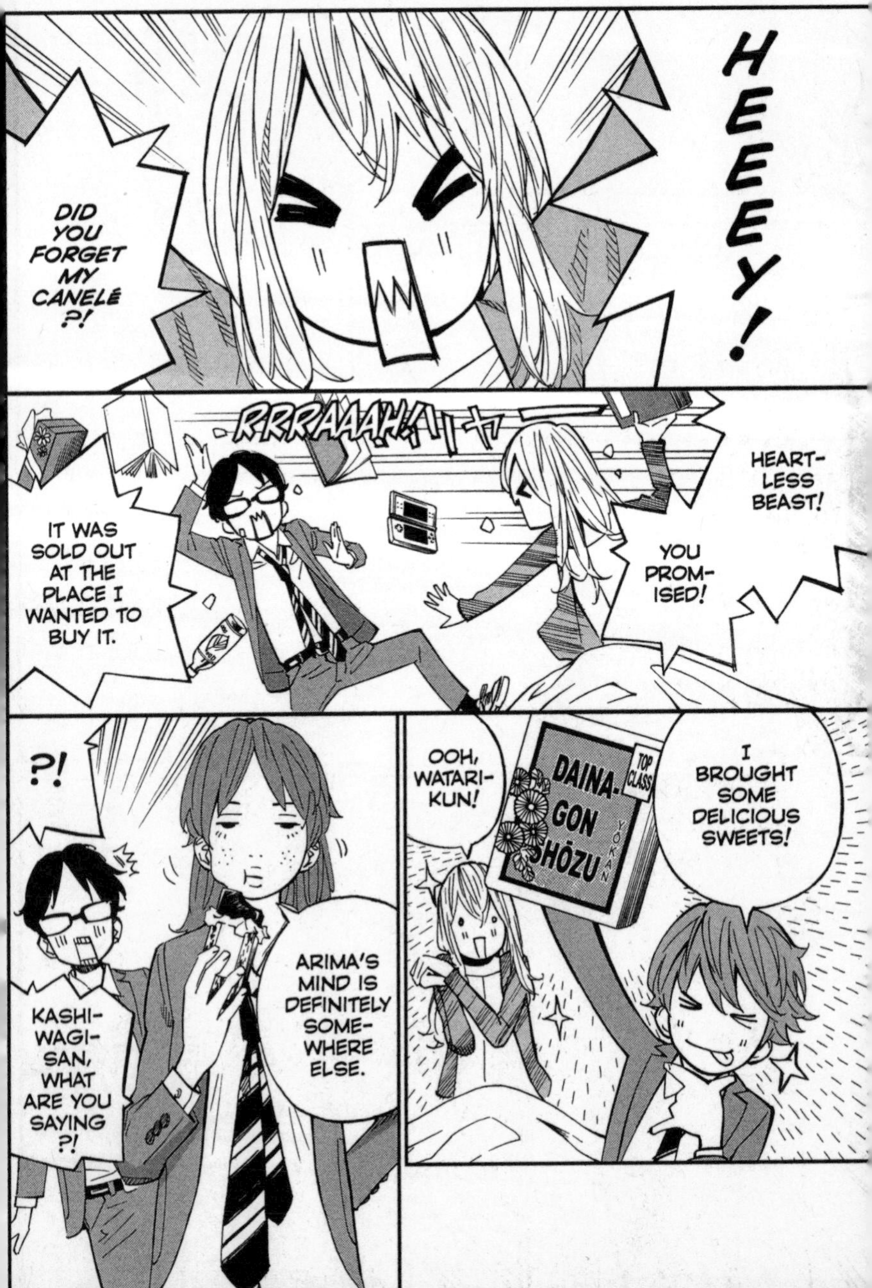
HEEEY!
DID YOU FORGET MY CANELÉ?!
HEARTLESS BEAST!
YOU PROMISED!
RRRAAAH!!
IT WAS SOLD OUT AT THE PLACE I WANTED TO BUY IT.
I BROUGHT SOME DELICIOUS SWEETS!
TOP CLASS
DAINAGON SHŌZU
YŌKAN
OOH, WATARI-KUN!
?!
ARIMA'S MIND IS DEFINITELY SOMEWHERE ELSE.
KASHIWAGI-SAN, WHAT ARE YOU SAYING?!

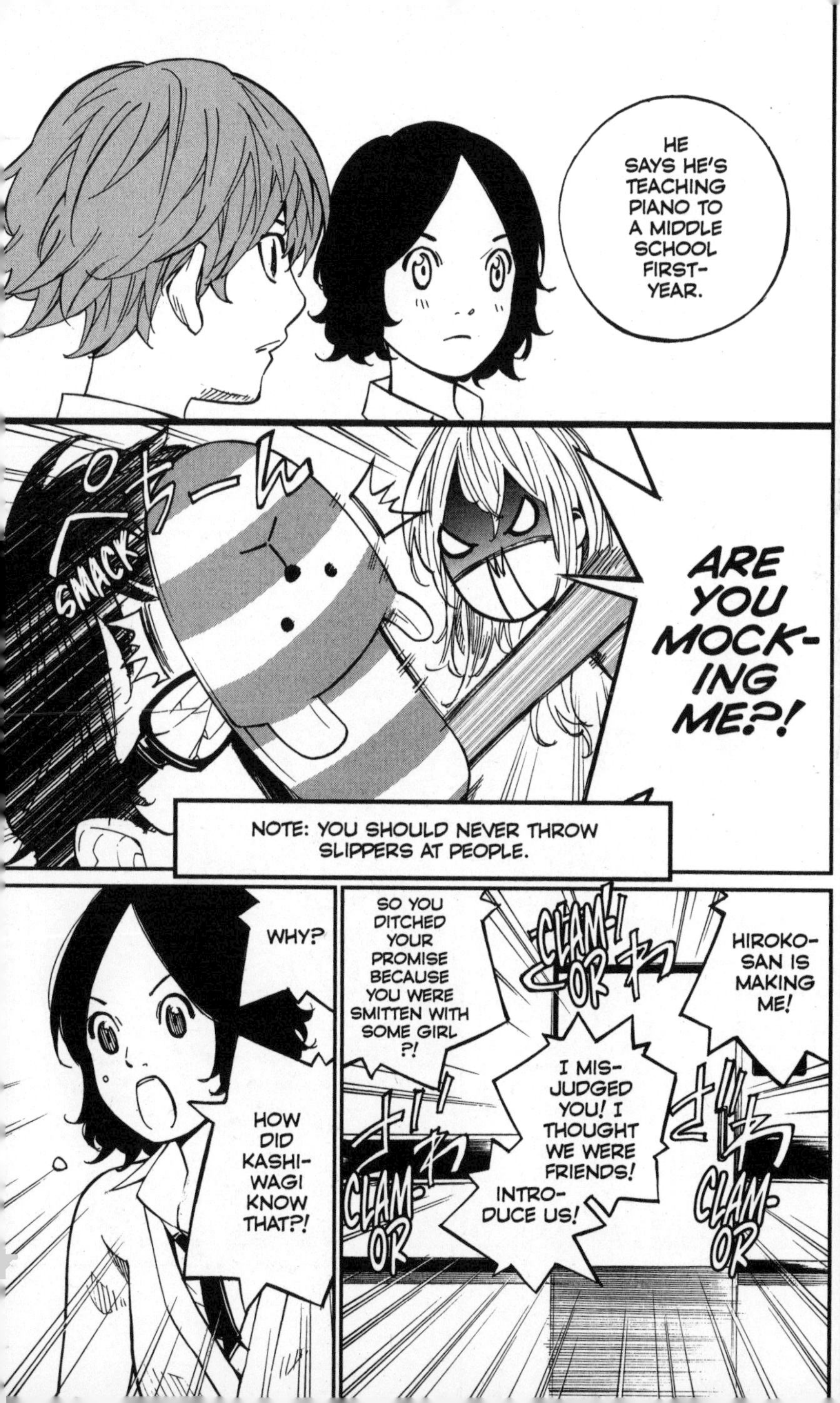
HE SAYS HE'S TEACHING PIANO TO A MIDDLE SCHOOL FIRST-YEAR.
ARE YOU MOCKING ME?!
SMACK
NOTE: YOU SHOULD NEVER THROW SLIPPERS AT PEOPLE.
HIROKO-SAN IS MAKING ME!
CLAMOR
SO YOU DITCHED YOUR PROMISE BECAUSE YOU WERE SMITTEN WITH SOME GIRL?!
I MISJUDGED YOU! I THOUGHT WE WERE FRIENDS!
CLAMOR
INTRODUCE US!
CLAMOR
WHY?
HOW DID KASHIWAGI KNOW THAT?!

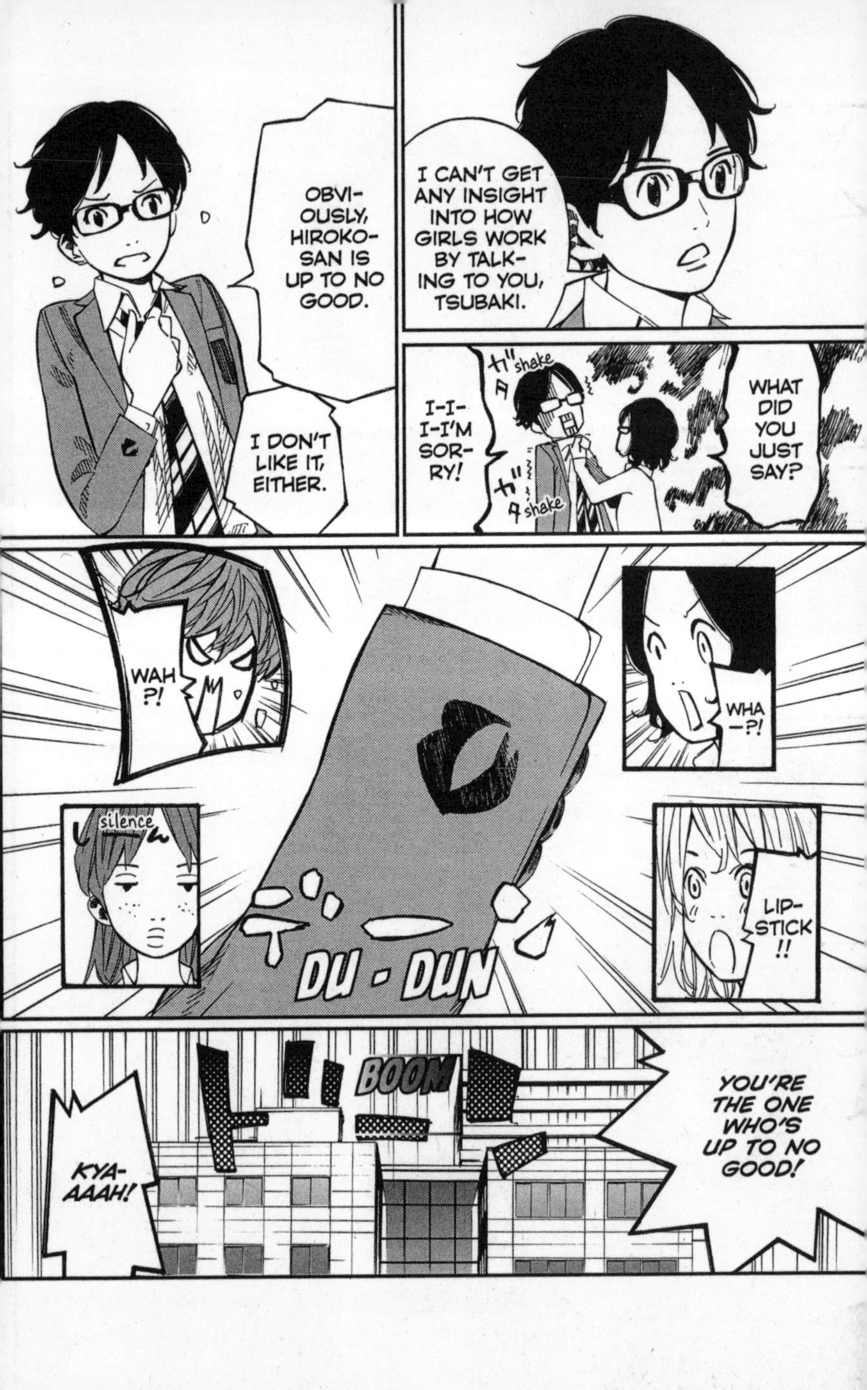
I CAN'T GET ANY INSIGHT INTO HOW GIRLS WORK BY TALK-ING TO YOU, TSUBAKI.
WHAT DID YOU JUST SAY?
shake
I-I-I-I'M SOR-RY!
shake
OBVI-OUSLY, HIROKO-SAN IS UP TO NO GOOD.
I DON'T LIKE IT, EITHER.
WHA—?!
WAH?!
LIP-STICK!!
DU-DUN
silence
YOU'RE THE ONE WHO'S UP TO NO GOOD!
BOOM
KYA-AAAH!

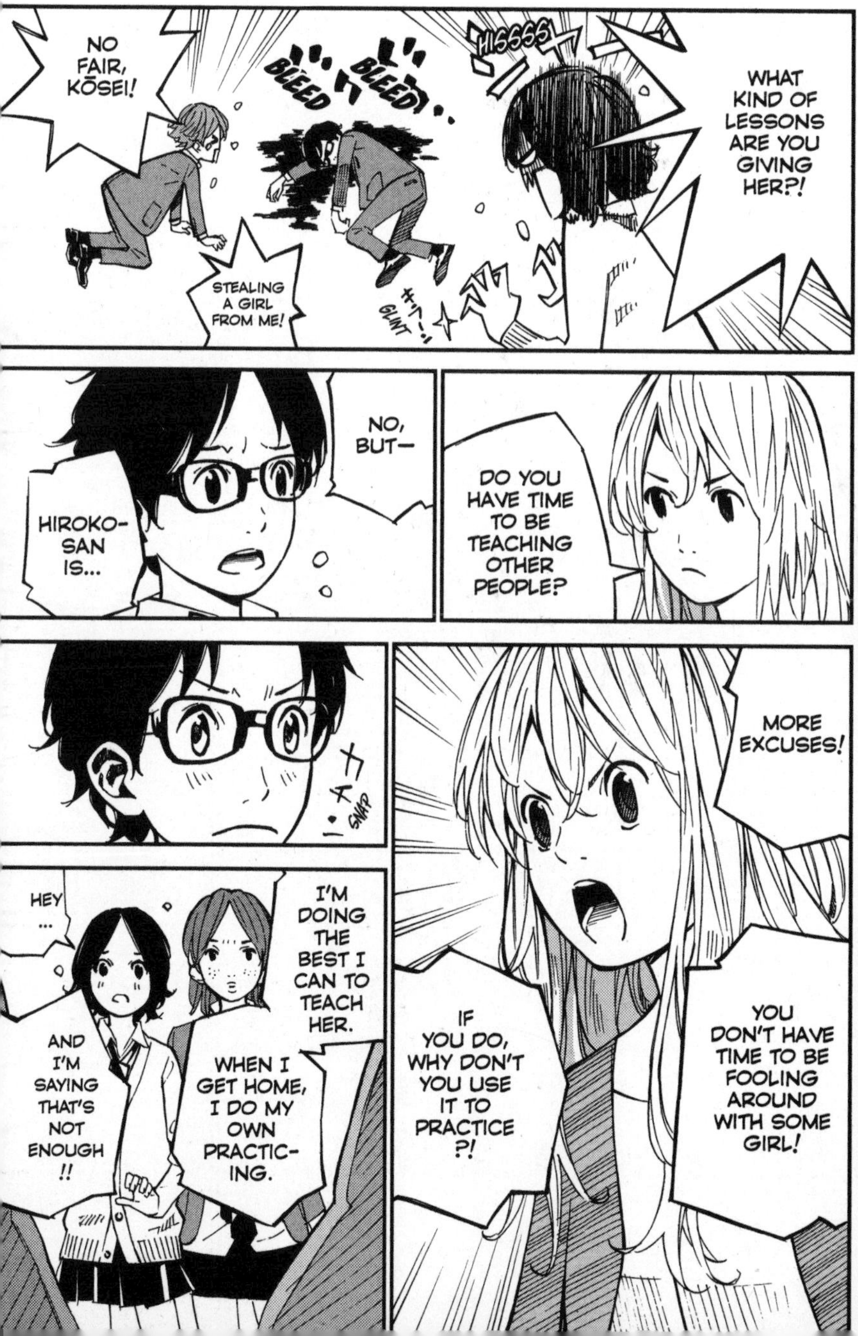
HISSSS
WHAT KIND OF LESSONS ARE YOU GIVING HER?!
BLEED
BLEED
NO FAIR, KŌSEI!
GLINT
STEALING A GIRL FROM ME!
DO YOU HAVE TIME TO BE TEACHING OTHER PEOPLE?
NO, BUT—
HIROKO-SAN IS...
MORE EXCUSES!
YOU DON'T HAVE TIME TO BE FOOLING AROUND WITH SOME GIRL!
IF YOU DO, WHY DON'T YOU USE IT TO PRACTICE?!
SNAP
I'M DOING THE BEST I CAN TO TEACH HER.
WHEN I GET HOME, I DO MY OWN PRACTICING.
HEY ...
AND I'M SAYING THAT'S NOT ENOUGH!!

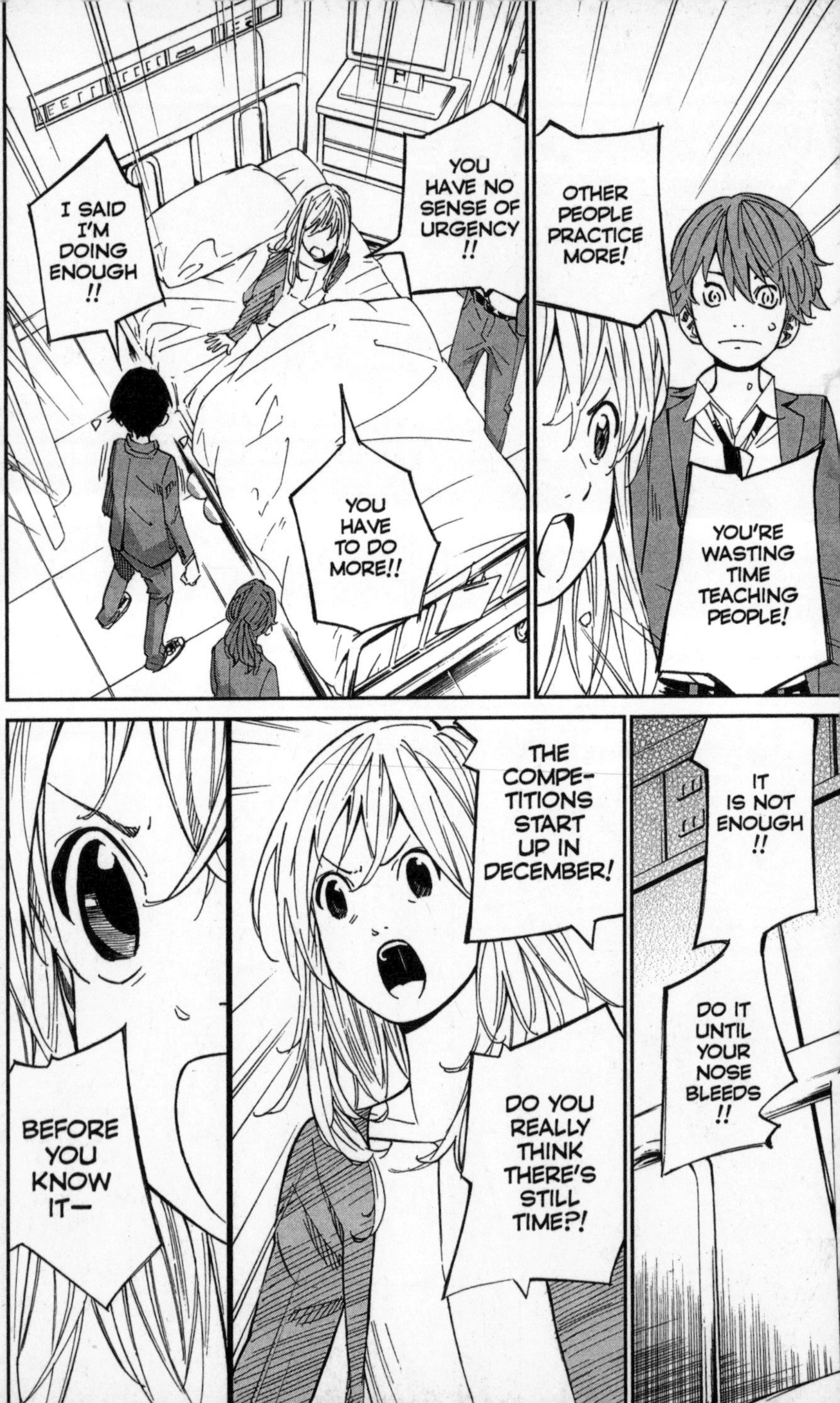
OTHER PEOPLE PRACTICE MORE!
YOU'RE WASTING TIME TEACHING PEOPLE!
YOU HAVE NO SENSE OF URGENCY!!
I SAID I'M DOING ENOUGH!!
YOU HAVE TO DO MORE!!
IT IS NOT ENOUGH!!
DO IT UNTIL YOUR NOSE BLEEDS!!
THE COMPETITIONS START UP IN DECEMBER!
DO YOU REALLY THINK THERE'S STILL TIME?!
BEFORE YOU KNOW IT—

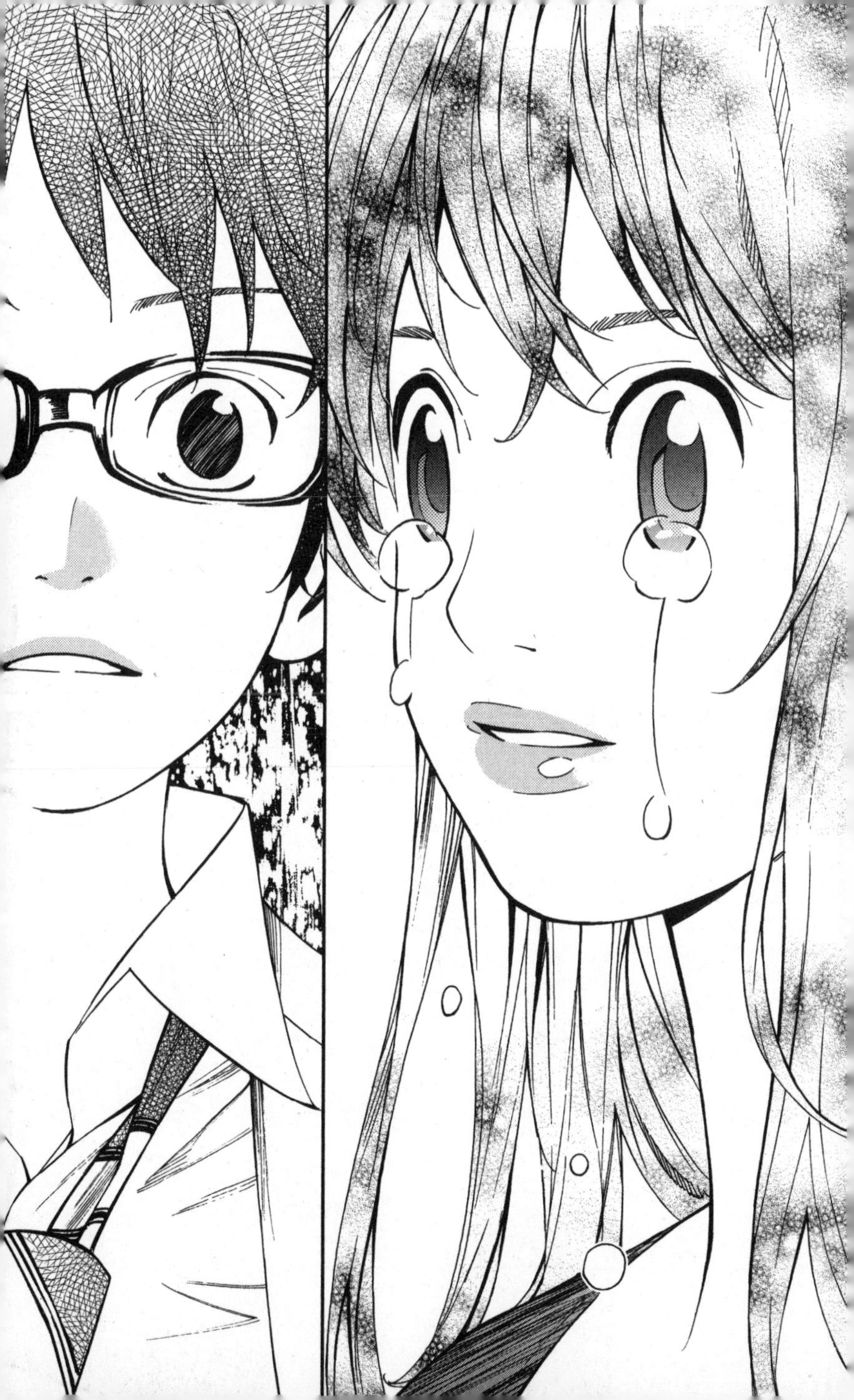

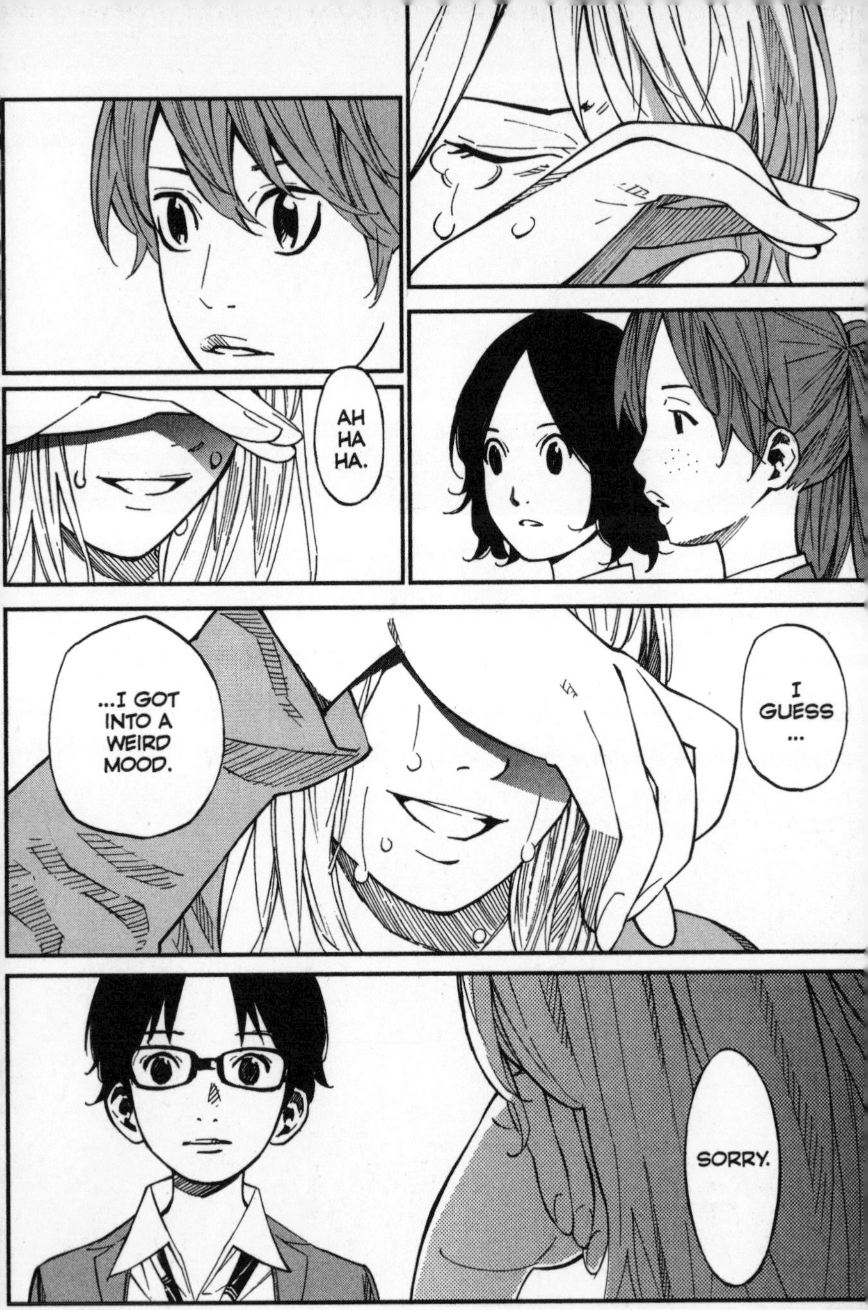
AH HA HA.
I GUESS ...
...I GOT INTO A WEIRD MOOD.
SORRY.

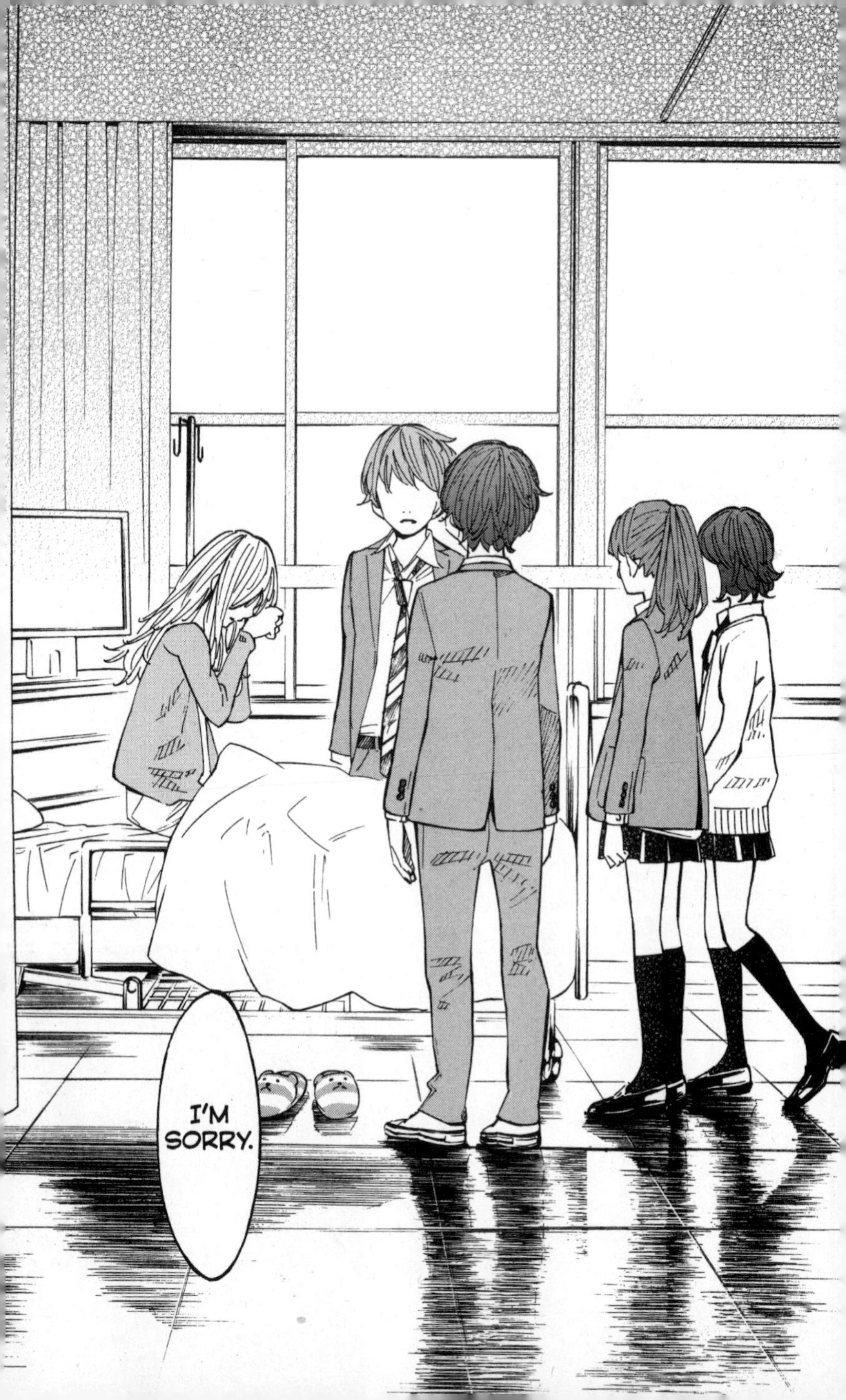
I'M SORRY.

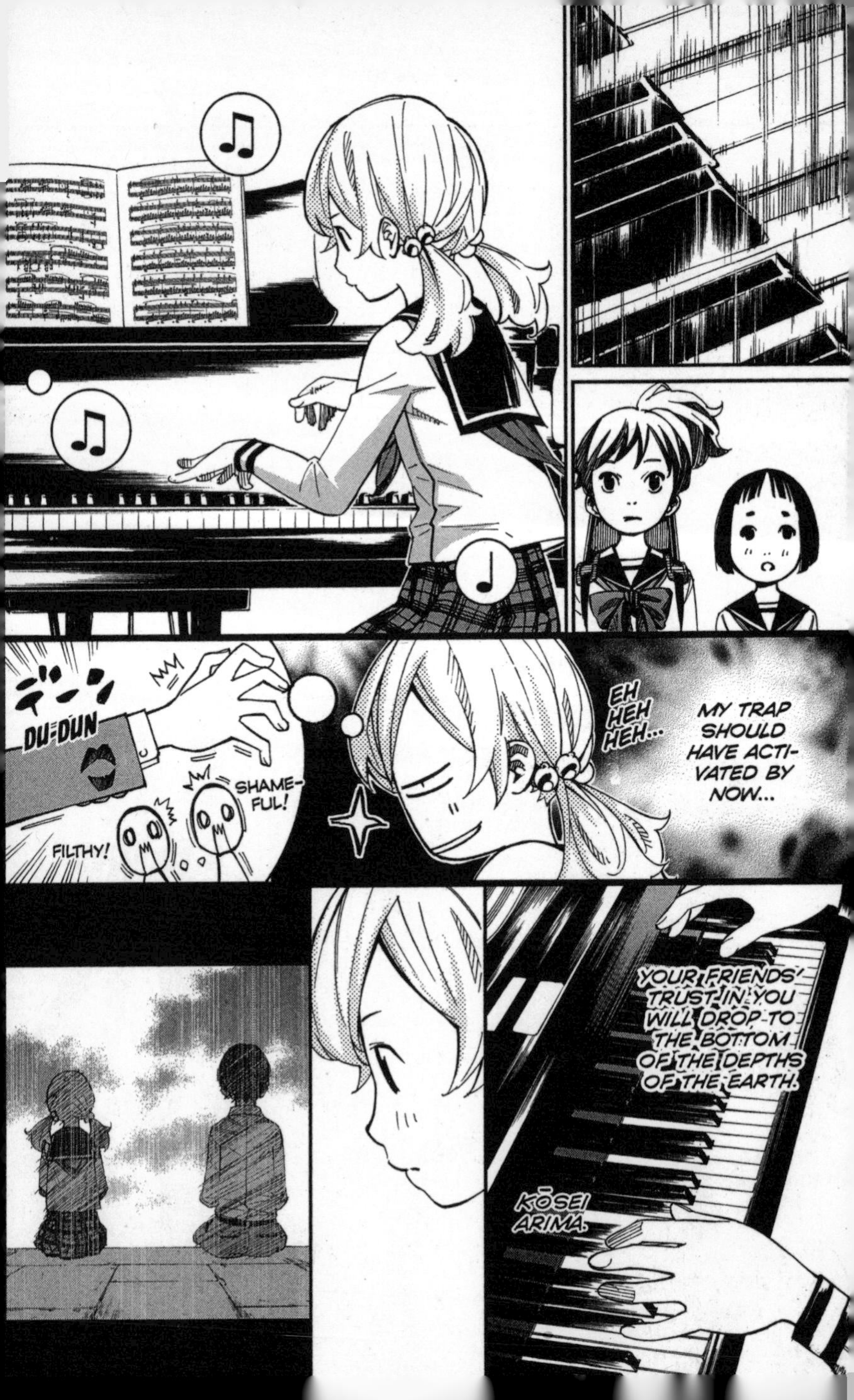
MY TRAP SHOULD HAVE ACTIVATED BY NOW...
EH HEH HEH...
デーン
DU-DUN
SHAMEFUL!
FILTHY!
YOUR FRIENDS' TRUST IN YOU WILL DROP TO THE BOTTOM OF THE DEPTHS OF THE EARTH.
KŌSEI ARIMA.

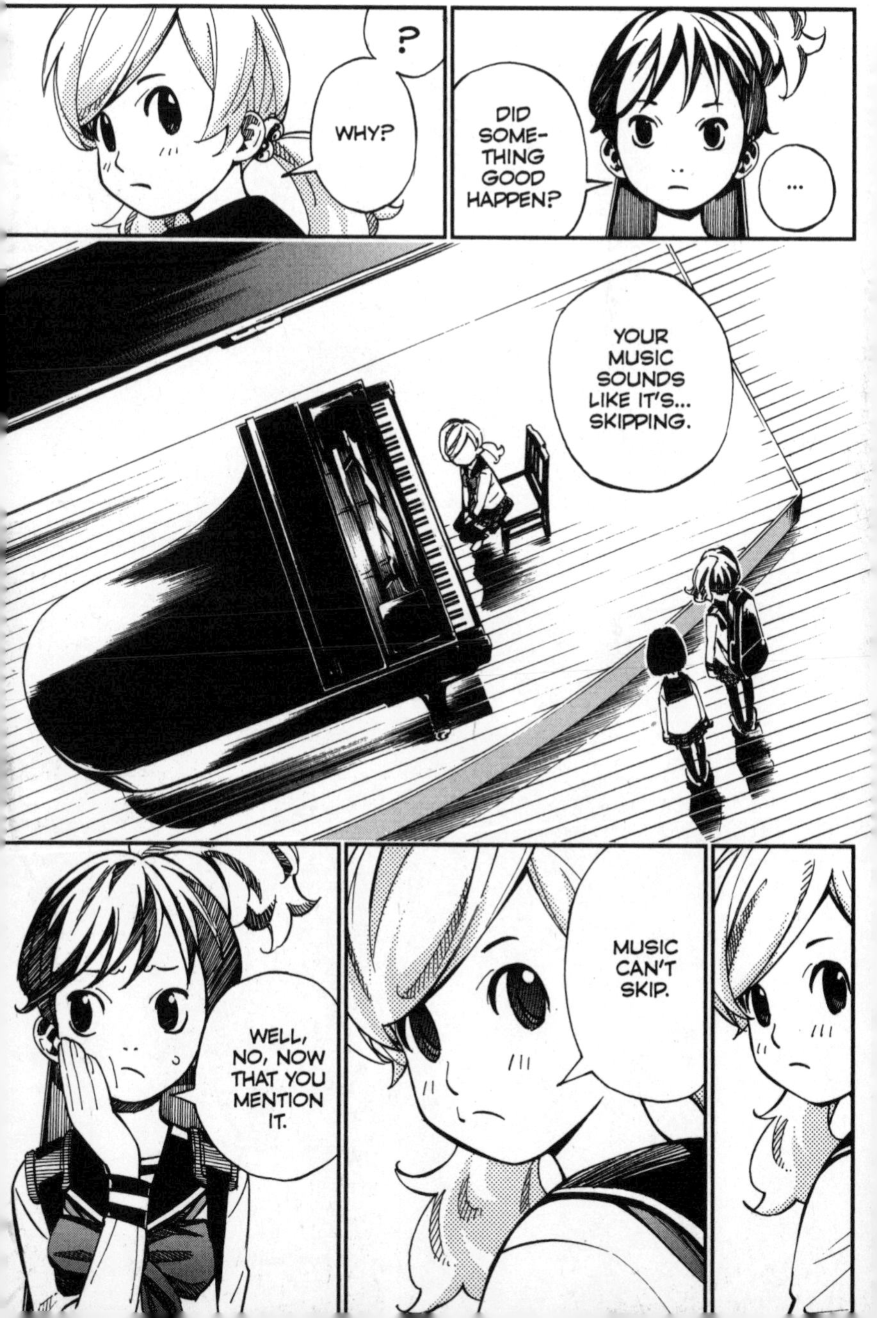
...
DID SOMETHING GOOD HAPPEN?
?
WHY?
YOUR MUSIC SOUNDS LIKE IT'S... SKIPPING.
MUSIC CAN'T SKIP.
WELL, NO, NOW THAT YOU MENTION IT.

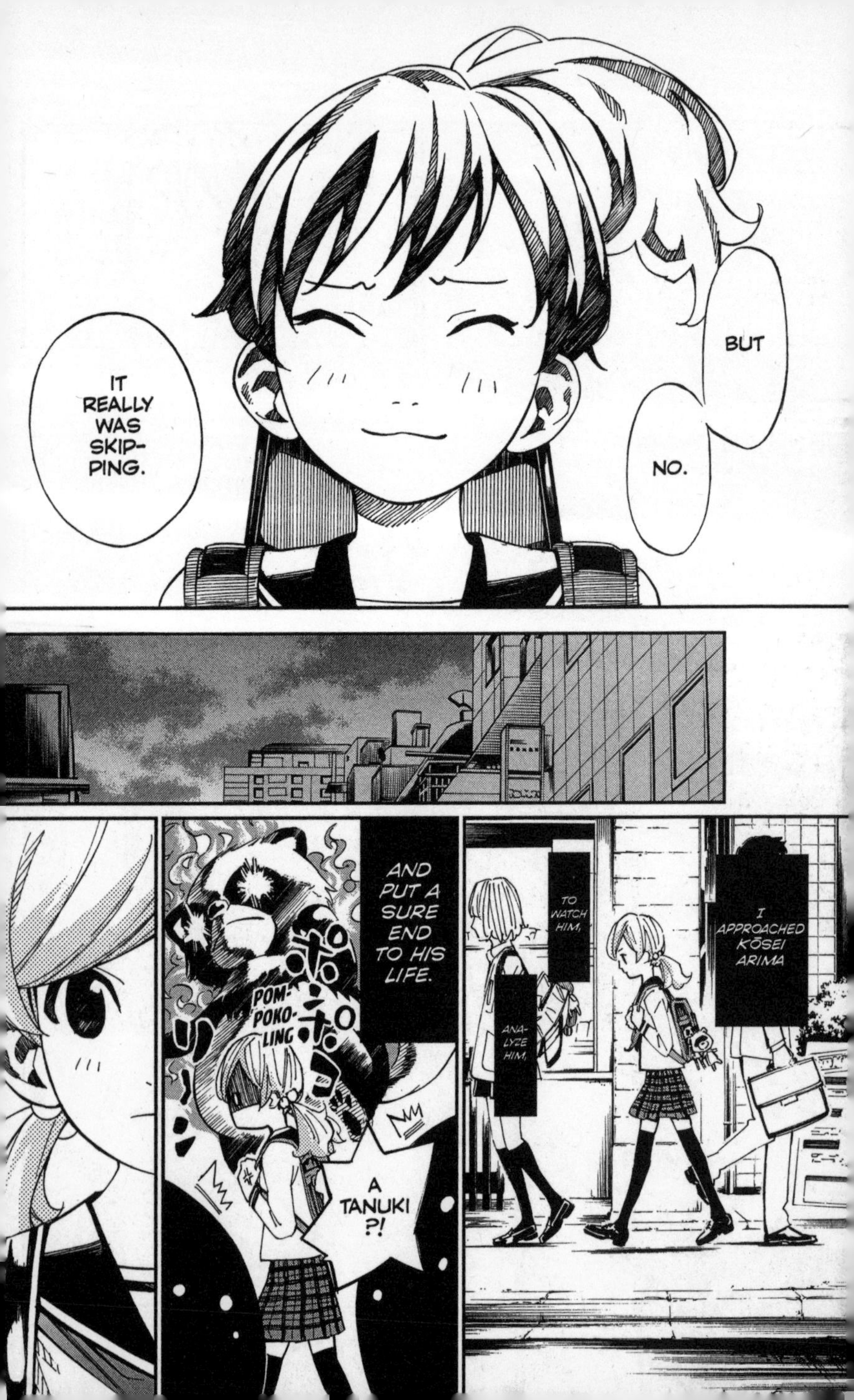
BUT NO.
IT REALLY WAS SKIP-PING.
I APPROACHED KŌSEI ARIMA
TO WATCH HIM,
ANA-LYZE HIM,
AND PUT A SURE END TO HIS LIFE.
POM-POKO-LING
A TANUKI ?!

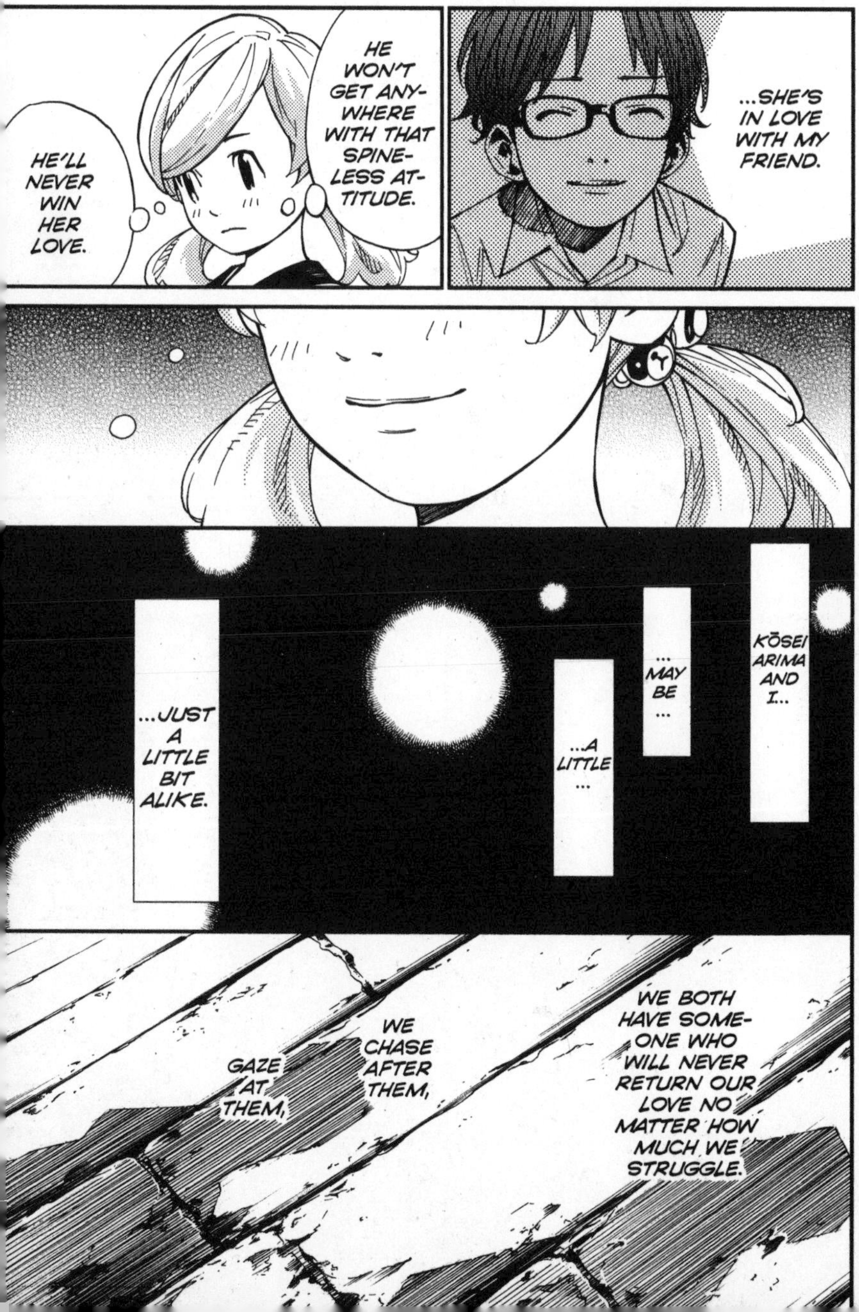
...SHE'S IN LOVE WITH MY FRIEND.
HE WON'T GET ANYWHERE WITH THAT SPINELESS ATTITUDE.
HE'LL NEVER WIN HER LOVE.
KŌSEI ARIMA AND I...
...MAYBE...
...A LITTLE...
...JUST A LITTLE BIT ALIKE.
WE BOTH HAVE SOMEONE WHO WILL NEVER RETURN OUR LOVE NO MATTER HOW MUCH WE STRUGGLE.
WE CHASE AFTER THEM,
GAZE AT THEM,

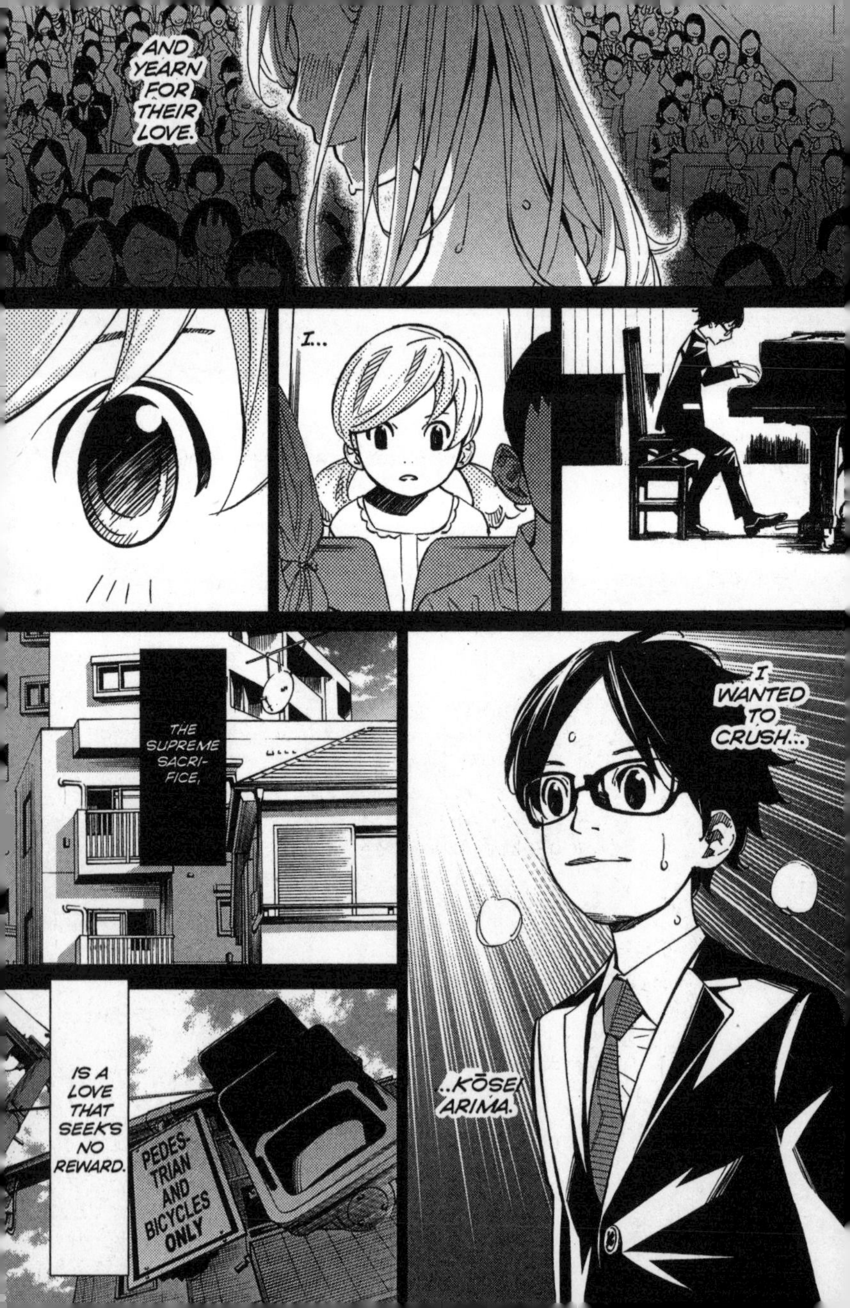
AND YEARN FOR THEIR LOVE.
I...
I WANTED TO CRUSH...
...KŌSEI ARIMA.
THE SUPREME SACRI-FICE,
IS A LOVE THAT SEEKS NO REWARD.
PEDES-TRIAN AND BICYCLES ONLY

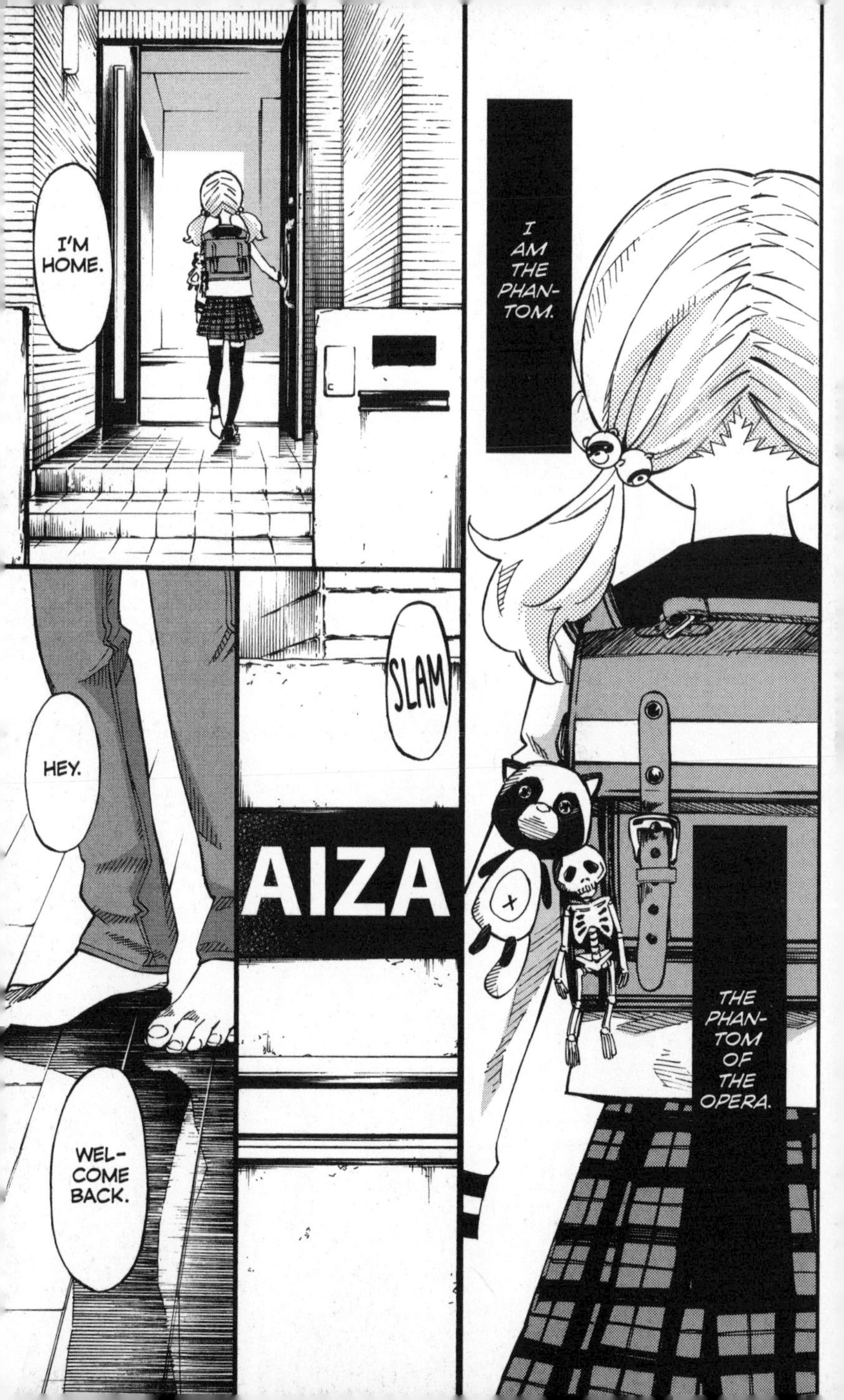
I AM THE PHANTOM.
THE PHANTOM OF THE OPERA.
I'M HOME.
SLAM
AIZA
HEY.
WELCOME BACK.

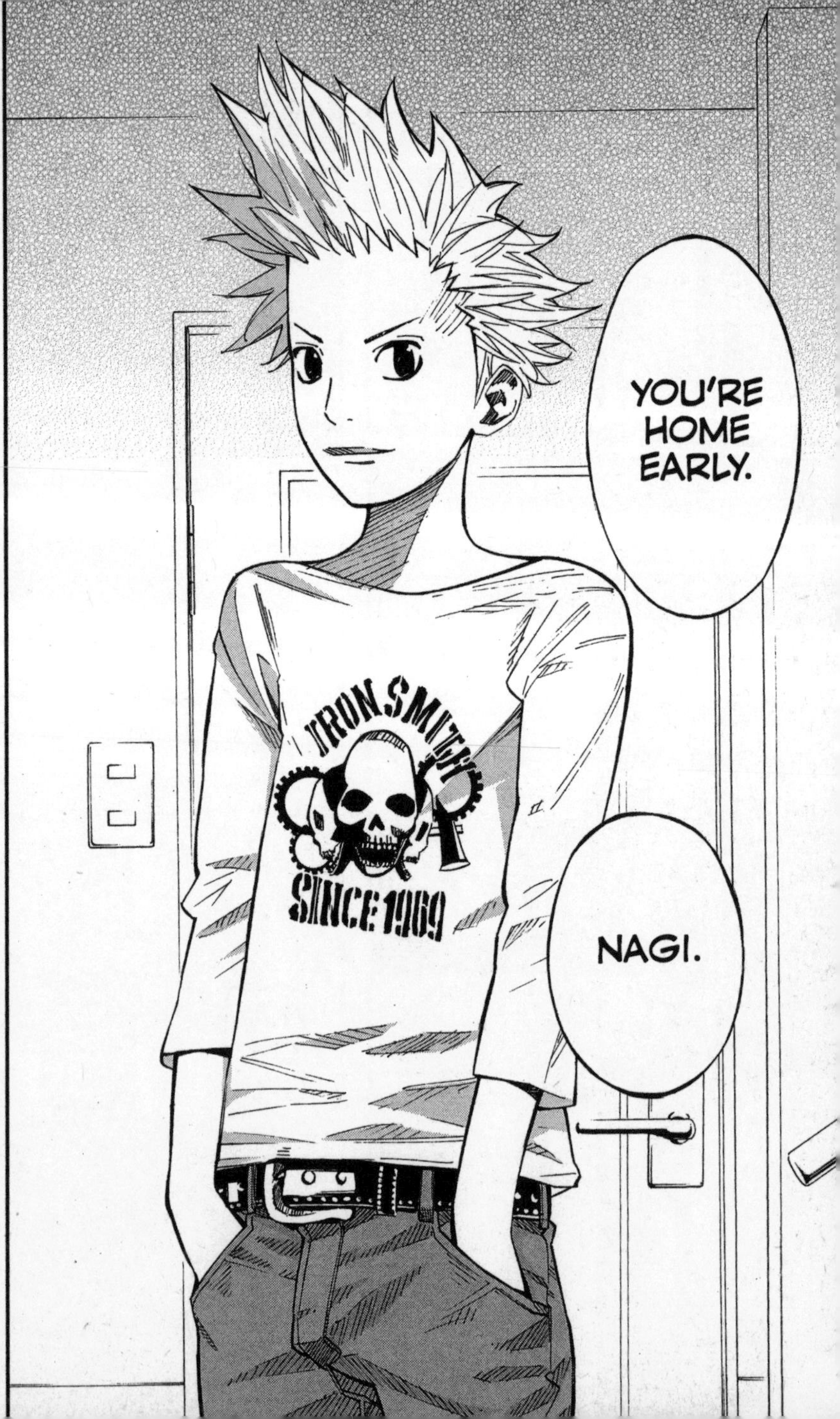
YOU'RE HOME EARLY.
NAGI.
IRON SMITH
SINCE 1969

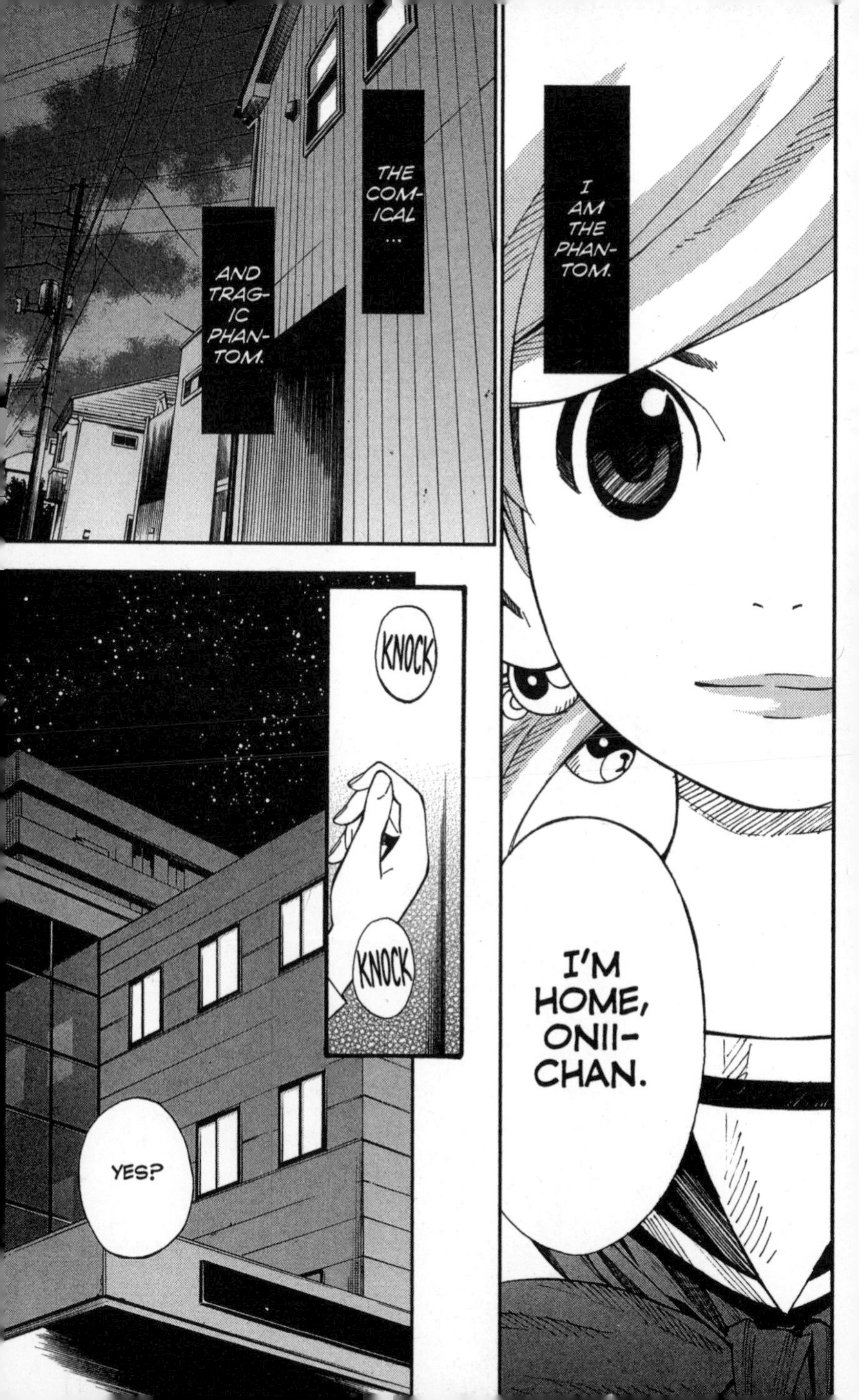
I AM THE PHANTOM.
I'M HOME, ONII-CHAN.
THE COMICAL...
AND TRAGIC PHANTOM.
KNOCK
KNOCK
YES?

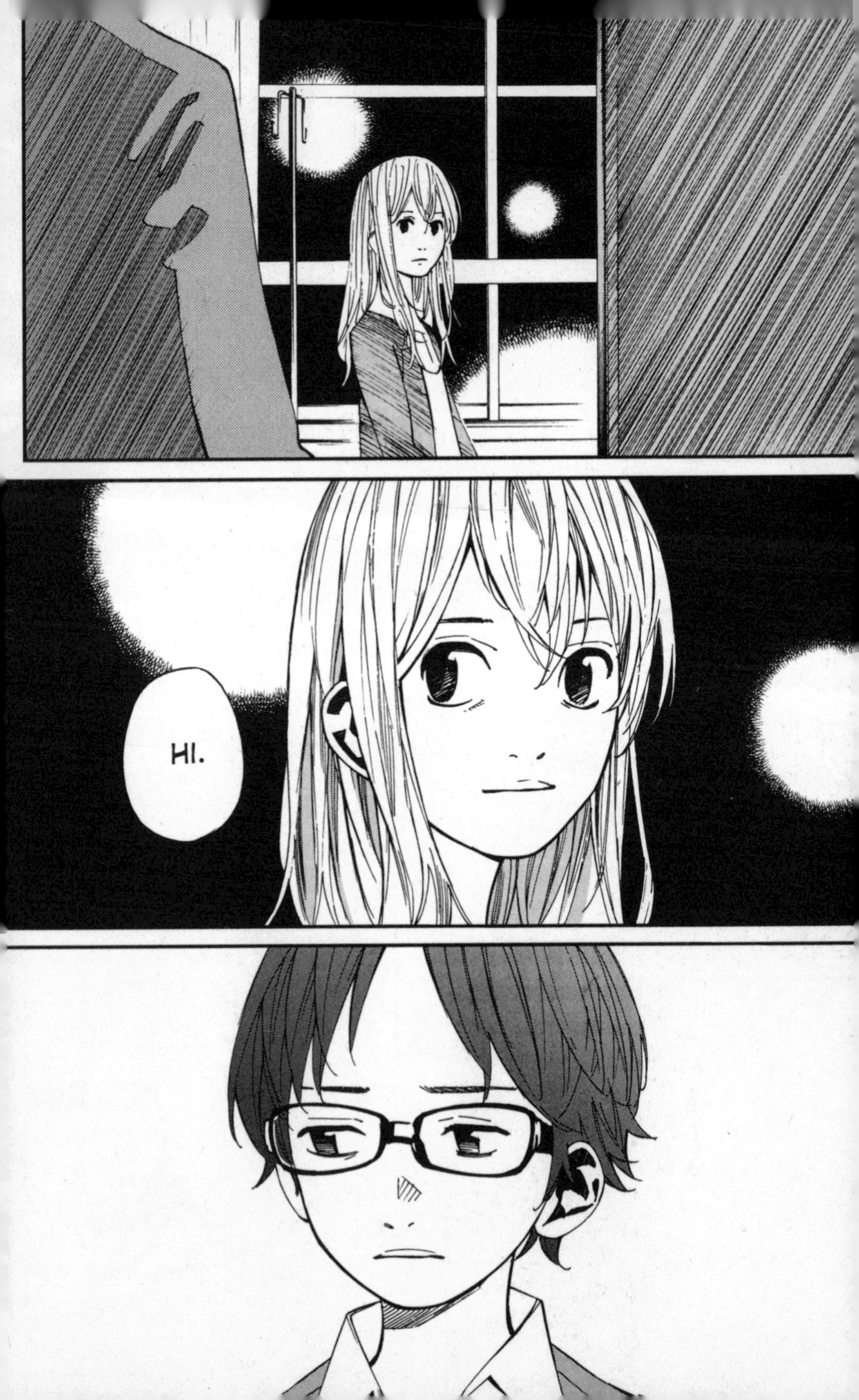
HI.

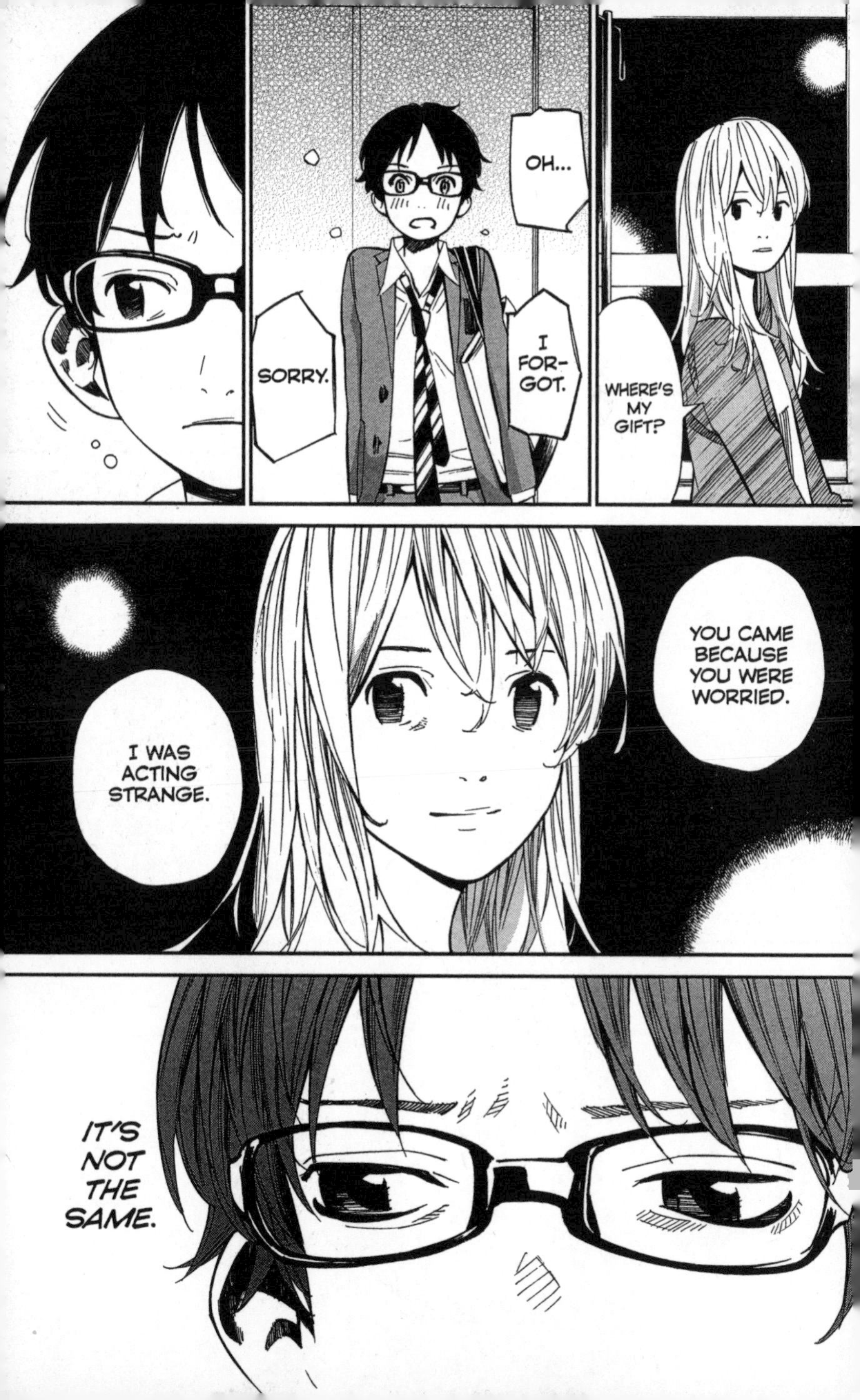
WHERE'S MY GIFT?
OH...
I FORGOT.
SORRY.
YOU CAME BECAUSE YOU WERE WORRIED.
I WAS ACTING STRANGE.
IT'S NOT THE SAME.

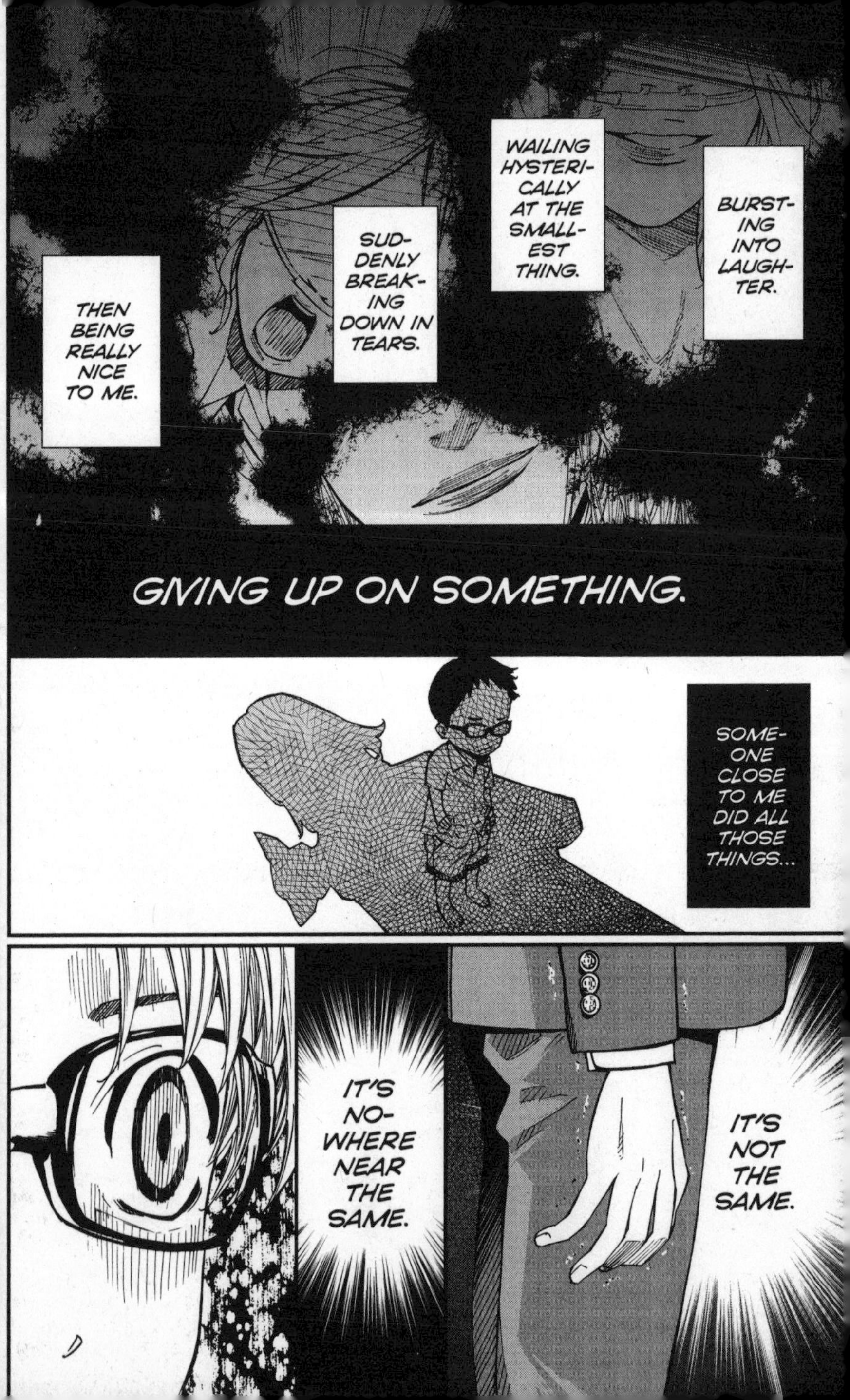
BURSTING INTO LAUGHTER.
WAILING HYSTERICALLY AT THE SMALLEST THING.
SUDDENLY BREAKING DOWN IN TEARS.
THEN BEING REALLY NICE TO ME.
GIVING UP ON SOMETHING.
SOMEONE CLOSE TO ME DID ALL THOSE THINGS...
IT'S NOT THE SAME.
IT'S NOWHERE NEAR THE SAME.

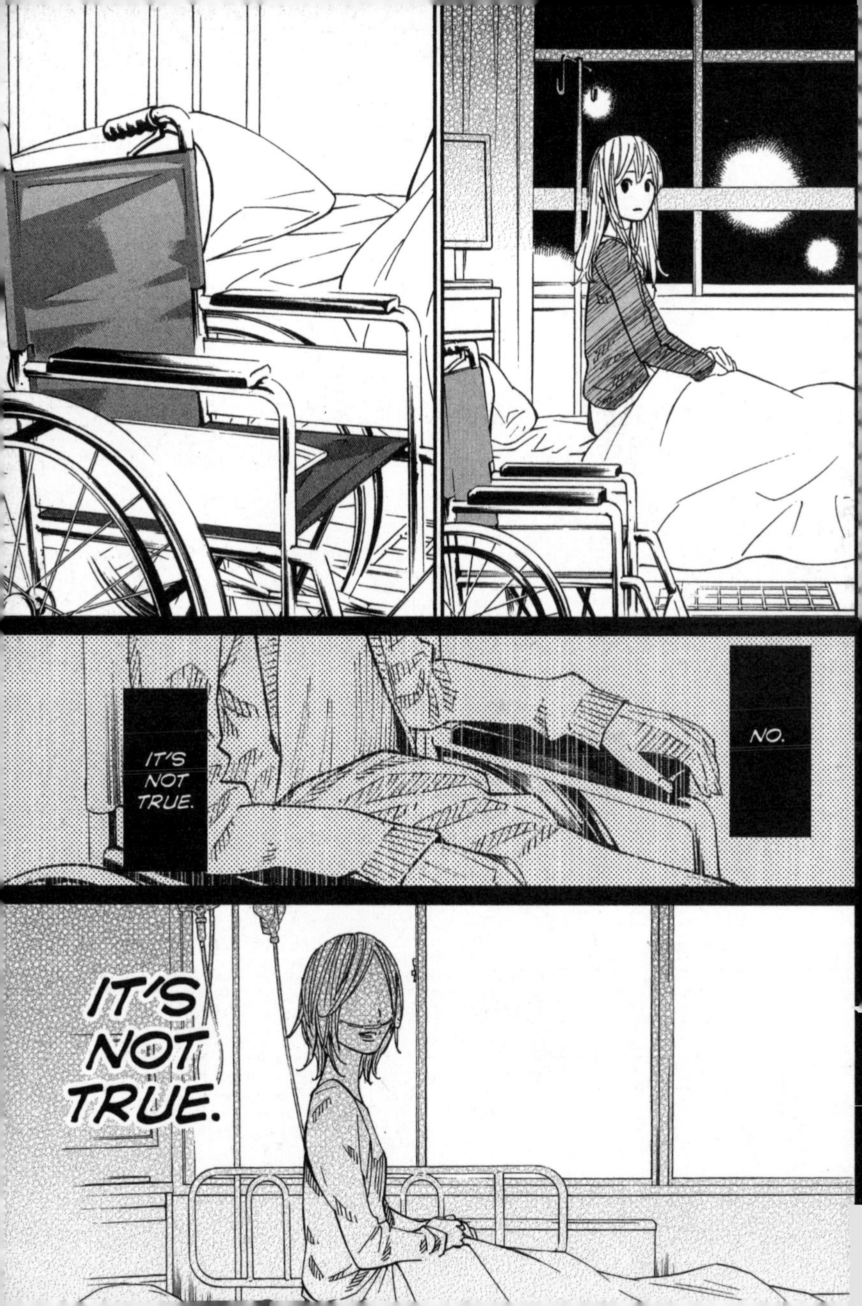
NO.
IT'S NOT TRUE.
IT'S NOT TRUE.

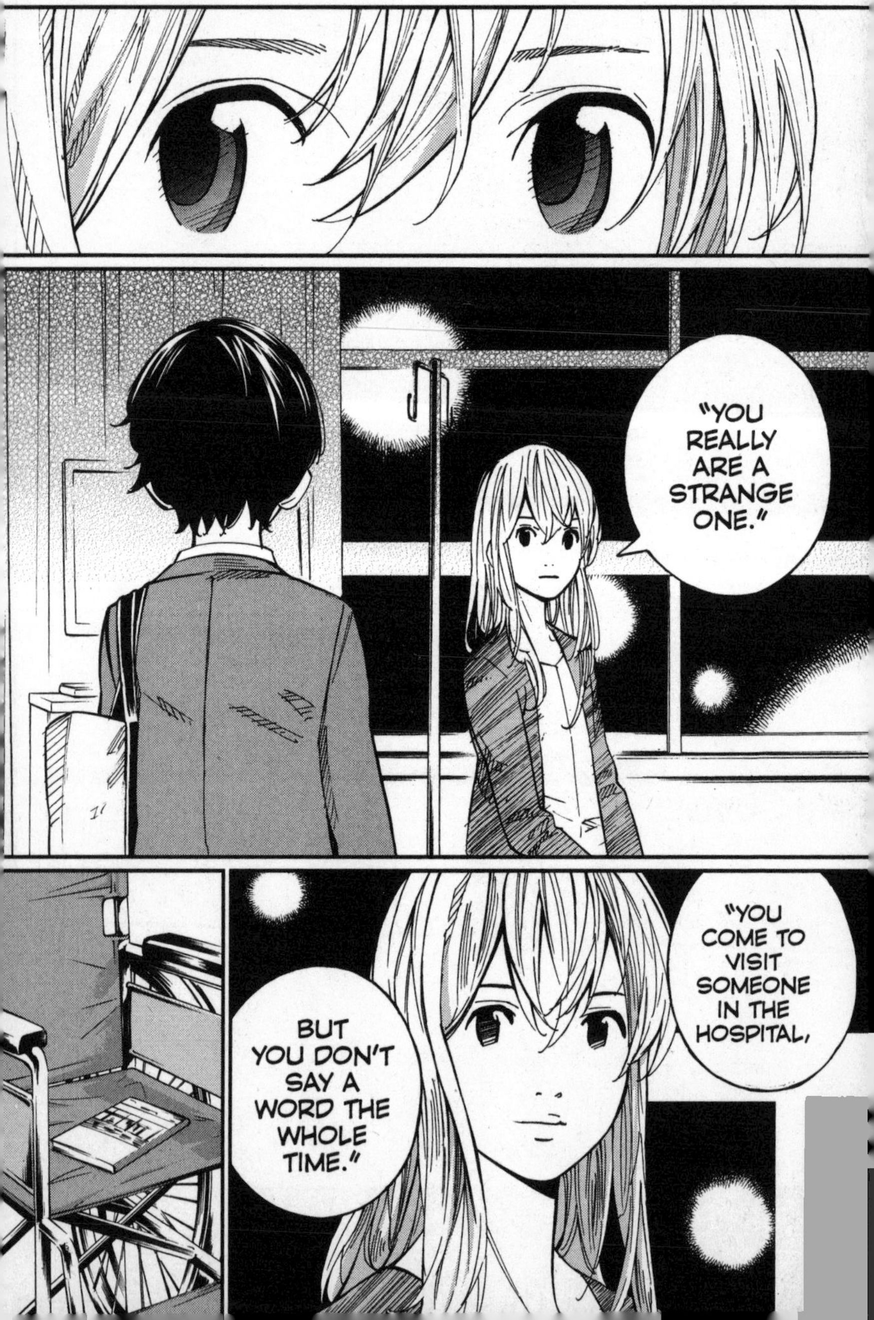
"YOU REALLY ARE A STRANGE ONE."
"YOU COME TO VISIT SOMEONE IN THE HOSPITAL,
BUT YOU DON'T SAY A WORD THE WHOLE TIME."

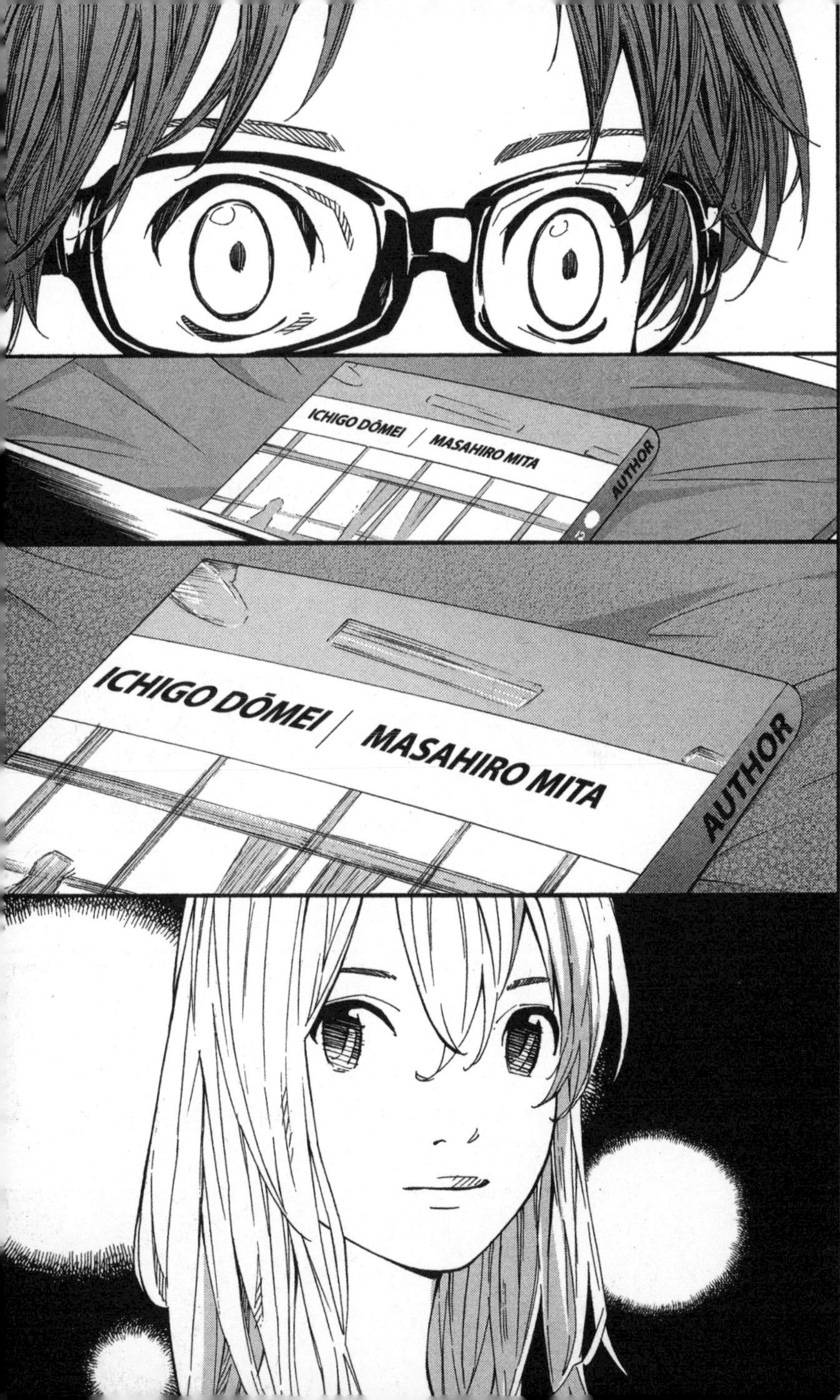
ICHIGO DŌMEI / MASAHIRO MITA
AUTHOR
ICHIGO DŌMEI / MASAHIRO MITA
AUTHOR

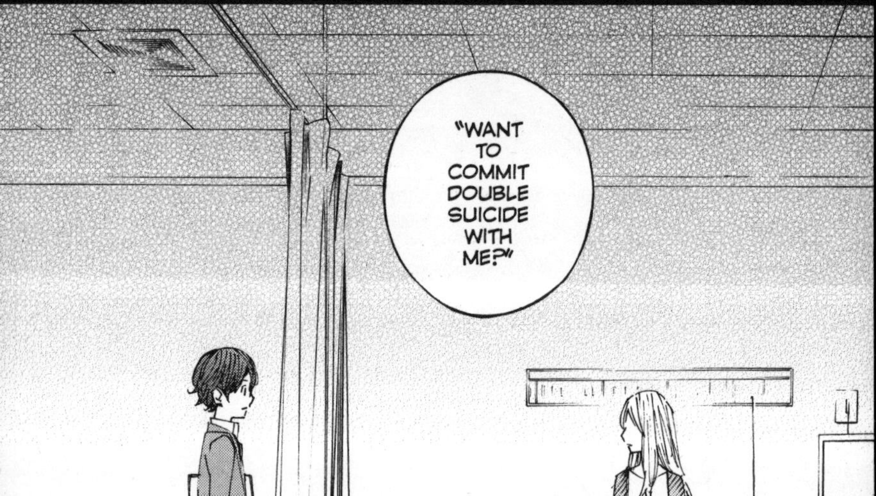
"WANT TO COMMIT DOUBLE SUICIDE WITH ME?"

'OUR LIE IN APRIL.
O BE CONTINUED

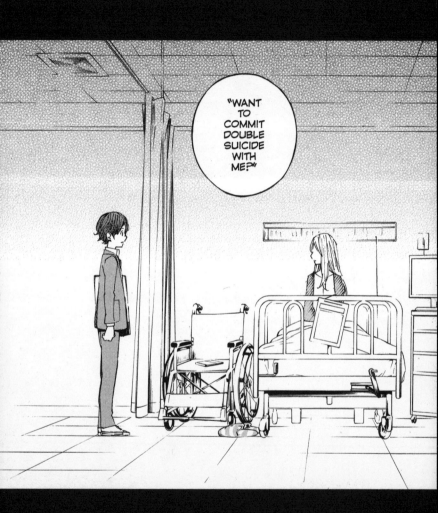

Special Thanks:

AKINORI ŌSAWA

MASANORI SUGANO

RIEKO IKEDA

KAORI YAMAZAKI

"WANT TO COMMIT DOUBLE SUICIDE WITH ME?"

KAORI'S QUESTION SHAKES KŌSEI'S HEART TO ITS CORE.

AMIDST HIS SUFFERING, WHAT PATH WILL THE BOY CHOOSE?!

THE GIRL'S QUESTION PIERCES THE BOY'S HEART.

...met the girl under full-bloomed cherry blossoms, and my fate has begun to change.

Your Lie in April

NEXT VOLUME **9** ON SALE SOON!

Naoshi Arakawa

Translation Notes

Konnyaku,
page 61

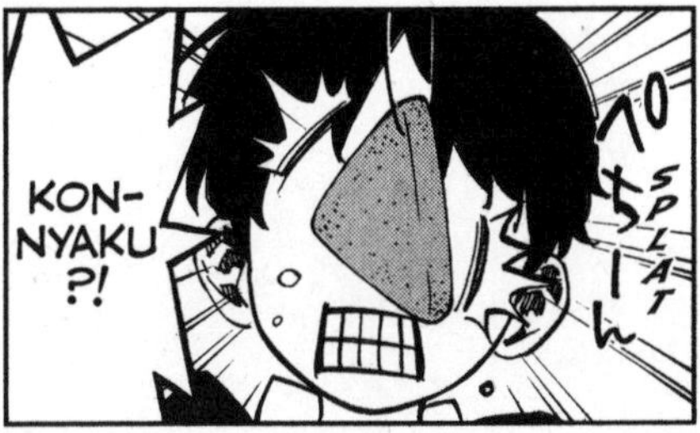
KON-NYAKU ?!
SPLAT

Konnyaku, or konjac, is a type of tuber that is used to make a gelatinous substance of the same name. In the world of manga, this jelly is often seen hung from fishing poles, used in amateur haunted houses to smack people in the back of the neck to startle them with its slimy texture.

Kōsei's pick-ups,
page 64

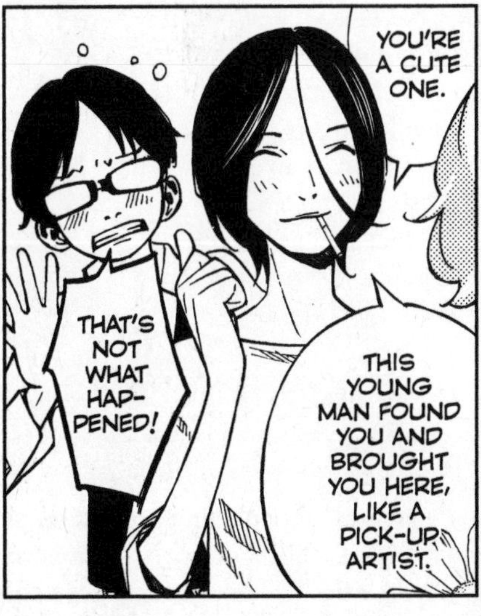
YOU'RE A CUTE ONE.
THIS YOUNG MAN FOUND YOU AND BROUGHT YOU HERE, LIKE A PICK-UP ARTIST.
THAT'S NOT WHAT HAP-PENED!

In Japanese, there's a word that means "to take home with one." This can refer to finding an animal on the street, it can refer to takeout food. Which is why Koharu keeps asking if they're talking about hamburgers or potstickers. However, it can also refer to someone that an individual found while out on the town and took home or to a hotel for a one night stand. While Kōsei did find this girl and bring her to a place he could consider his home, Hiroko is clearly just enjoying the double entendre.

Ryōta and Shiho,
page 131

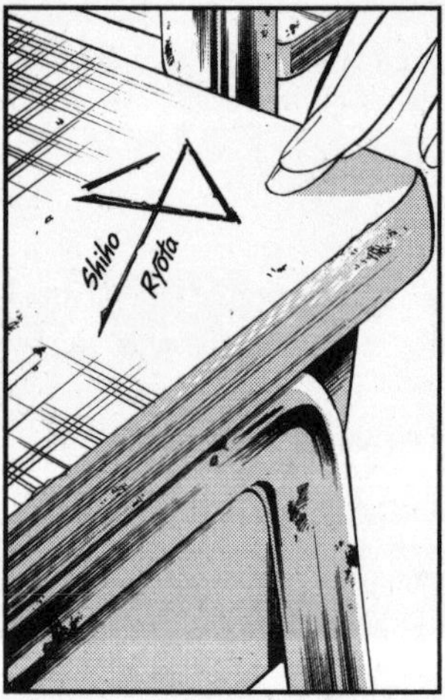
Shiho
Ryōta

The type of graffiti seen on this desk is called an *aiai-gasa*, which means "sharing an umbrella." The triangle with the vertical line through it represents an umbrella, and the names underneath represent the couple sharing it. It's a way of showing how close the two of them are, or a way of expressing a desire to become close, sort of like drawing a heart with the two names in it.

Nagi's tengu,
page 154

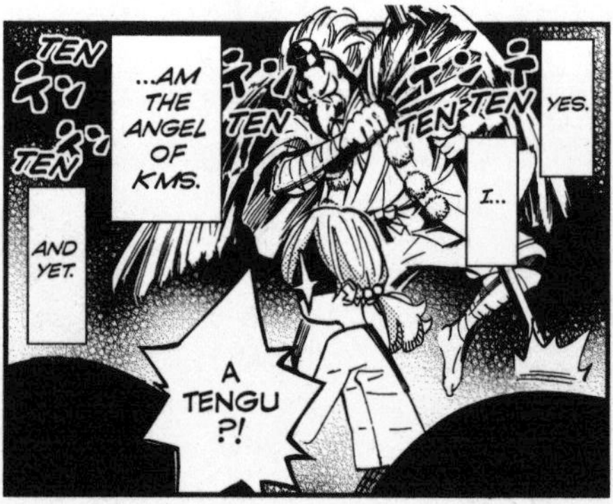
YES.
TEN TEN
TEN
I...
...AM THE ANGEL OF KMS.
TEN
TEN
AND YET.
A TENGU ?!

A tengu is a creature from Japanese folklore with a long nose, red face, and wings. It can also represent arrogance. The Japanese word for angel is *tenshi*, so it's possible that Nagi's vision of an angel was distorted by her self-importance and negative energy into something more suited to her attitude.

Rye,
page 166

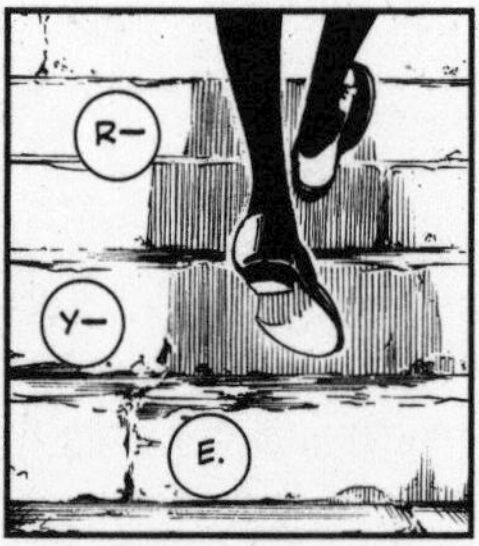
R—
Y—
E.

Nagi and Kōsei are playing a variation of rock-paper-scissors called "Glico" (pronounced *guriko* in Japanese), after the name of a candy company. It's usually played on stairs, and whoever wins a round of rock-paper-scissors is allowed to hop up a certain number of stairs. If the player wins by throwing out rock, or *gu* in Japanese, she goes up three steps, one for each syllabic character in the word Glico (*gu-ri-ko*). If she wins by throwing out paper, or *paa*, she goes up six steps, one for each character in the word pineapple (*pa-i-na-ppu-ru*), and for scissors, or *choki*, she gets another six steps for chocolate (*chi-yo-ko-re-e-to*). The translators attempted to localize the game by using English words that begin with the same letters as rock, paper, and scissors. For the curious, because Nagi didn't finish it, the scissors word was "sorbet."

Yōkan,
page 170

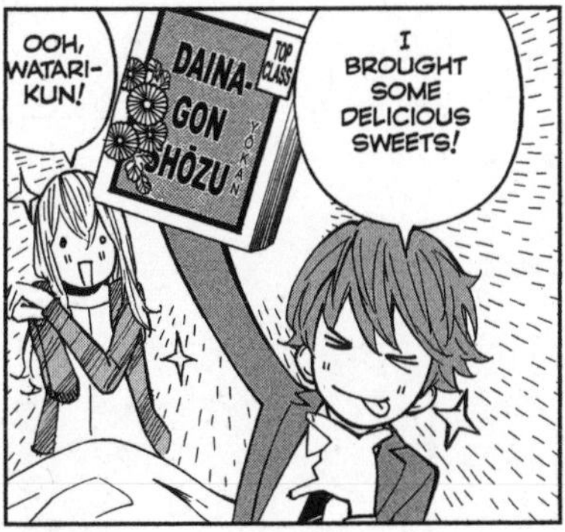
I BROUGHT SOME DELICIOUS SWEETS!
TOP CLASS
DAINA-GON SHŌZU
YŌKAN
OOH, WATARI-KUN!

Yōkan is a traditional Japanese dessert consisting of a thick jelly made from bean paste. In this case, it's made from a type of red bean called *dainagon shōzu*.

Tanuki,
page 180

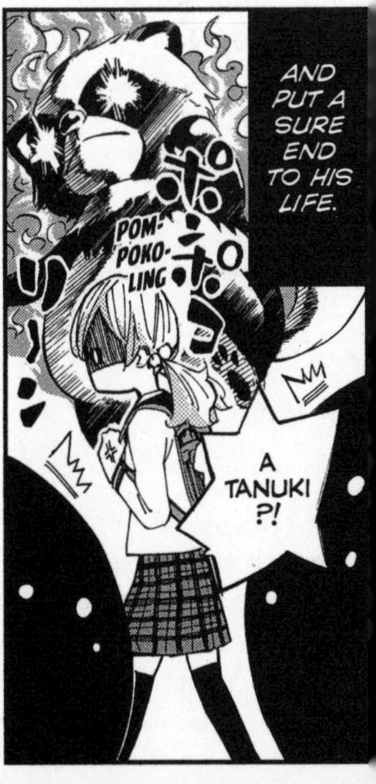
AND PUT A SURE END TO HIS LIFE.
POM-POKO-LING
A TANUKI ?!

Tanuki are raccoon-dogs native to Japan. In folklore, they're known for using their shapeshifting abilities to gain people's trust and trick them. Nagi may feel a sense of camaraderie with these creatures.

A Kodansha Comics Trade Paperback Original
Your Lie in April volume 8 copyright © 2014 Naoshi Arakawa
English translation copyright © 2016 Naoshi Arakawa

Published in the United States by Kodansha Comics, an imprint of Kodansha USA Publishing, LLC, New York.

Publication rights for this English edition arranged through Kodansha Ltd, Tokyo.

ISBN 978-1-63236-178-3

Special thanks:
Akinori Osawa, Rieko Ikeda, and Kaori Yamazaki

Printed in the United States of America.

www.kodanshacomics.com

9 8 7 6 5 4 3 2 1
Translation: Alethea and Athena Nibley
Lettering: Scott Brown
Editing: Haruko Hashimoto
Kodansha Comics edition cover design by Phil Balsman

TOMARE!
STOP

You're going the wrong way!

Manga is a completely different type of reading experience.

**To start at the beginning,
Go to the end!**

That's right! Authentic manga is read the traditional Japanese way—from right to left, exactly the opposite of how American books are read. It's easy to follow: Just go to the other end of the book and read each page—and each panel—from right side to left side, starting at the top right. Now you're experiencing manga as it was meant to be!